TIBULLUS:
A HELLENISTIC POET AT ROME

TIBULLUS:
A HELLENISTIC POET
AT ROME

FRANCIS CAIRNS

CAMBRIDGE UNIVERSITY PRESS
CAMBRIDGE
LONDON   NEW YORK   NEW ROCHELLE
MELBOURNE   SYDNEY

Published by the Press Syndicate of the University of Cambridge
The Pitt Building, Trumpington Street, Cambridge CB2 1RP
32 East 57th Street, New York, NY 10022, USA
296 Beaconsfield Parade, Middle Park, Melbourne 3206, Australia

© Cambridge University Press 1979

First published 1979

Phototypeset in V.I.P. Bembo by
Western Printing Services Ltd, Bristol
Printed in Great Britain at the
University Press, Cambridge

Library of Congress Cataloguing in Publication Data
Cairns, Francis.
Tibullus, a Hellenistic poet at Rome.
Includes index.
1. Tibullus, Albius—Criticism and interpretation.
I. Title.
PA6789.C26   874'.01   79-50231
ISBN 0 521 22413 6 hard covers
ISBN 0 521 29683 8 paperback

To David West

CONTENTS

	Preface	page ix
	Abbreviations	xi
1	The setting	1
2	Imitation as learning	36
3	Analogy as learning	64
4	Verbal learning	87
5	Exposition	111
6	Informing	144
7	Deceiving	166
8	Ordering	192
9	'The origins of Latin love-elegy'	214
	Indexes	
1	General index	231
2	Index of Latin and Greek words	244
3	Index of ancient works and passages referred to in the text	246

PREFACE

Tibullus was among the leading poets of Augustan Rome and there is growing interest in his work today. This book seeks to relate Tibullus to the Hellenistic literary tradition in which he worked and to examine aspects of his craftsmanship which derive from it. Since his poetic practice is characteristic of much Greek and Roman poetry, the book in consequence also offers students of ancient poetry analytic techniques capable of wider application. Not all the elegies of Tibullus are covered with equal thoroughness; but I have tried to give greater coverage to those not discussed in my earlier work and lacking a satisfactory modern treatment.

Greek quotations, but not Latin, are translated. Tibullus is quoted only where minutiae are in question, on the assumption that readers will have a text at hand. The line numbers and, for the most part, the punctuation of the Oxford Classical Text of J. P. Postgate (2nd ed. Oxford 1915) have been followed; with disputed readings I have made my own judgements. The text of Lenz–Galinsky (3rd ed. Leiden 1971) is of course more up to date and their apparatus is fuller. But the OCT is more likely to be available to readers of this book; and the text of Tibullus is relatively unproblematic.

There is a large secondary literature on Tibullus. The older material is admirably assembled and analysed by A. Cartault, *A propos du Corpus Tibullianum: un siècle de philologie latine classique* (Paris 1906). H. Harrauer, *A Bibliography to the Corpus Tibullianum* (Bibliography to Augustan Poetry 1, Hildesheim 1971) collects material up to 1970; and some later work is reported by R. J. Ball, 'Recent work on Tibullus (1970–1974)', *Eranos* 73 (1975) 62ff. These compilations have permitted me to dispense with a full bibliography. In citing secondary literature I have confined myself to works relevant to the points under discussion and either making real contributions or deserving notice.

Tibullus was written over the period 1971–7, with revision continuing up to mid-1978. But the text was substantially finalised by mid-1977 and regretfully I have not been able to take account of work published after that date, except superficially or in cases where it was known to me prior to publication. In the years 1974–7 chapters of *Tibullus* formed the basis of lectures given in the universities of Athens, Birmingham, Edinburgh and Lund, at Birkbeck College London, at the Freie Universität Berlin and at University College Dublin. Stimulating and helpful comments made on these occasions have materially advanced it, as have discussions with colleagues at the universities of Edinburgh and Liverpool, and with participants in the Liverpool Latin Seminar from British and foreign universities.

A number of particular debts must be acknowledged. The University of Liverpool gave a generous grant in aid of research. Mr Guy Lee, Mr C. W. Macleod and Professor R. G. M. Nisbet read a draft of *Tibullus*, saved me from many follies and made numerous useful comments and observations. Mr I. M. Le M. Du Quesnay laboured upon two successive drafts with Herculean endurance, and the book owes much to his learning and judgement. Enquiries about Hellenistic poetry were patiently answered by Professor G. Giangrande; Mr Angus Bowie checked the translations of Greek passages; the referees for Cambridge University Press made some valuable points; and my wife Sandra typed endless drafts and contributed many matters of substance. Finally, Dr F. J. Williams read proofs of the work. For the errors that remain in *Tibullus* I alone am responsible.

Francis Cairns

Liverpool
November 1978

ABBREVIATIONS

Ancient authors, periodicals and standard editions and reference works are abbreviated in accordance with normal conventions throughout. In addition, the more commonly cited works, listed below, will be abbreviated as follows:

Ball   R. J. Ball, 'The structure of Tibullus's elegies' (unpubl. Diss. Columbia 1971)

Copley   F. O. Copley, *Exclusus Amator: A Study in Latin Love Poetry* (Philological Monographs published by the American Philological Association No. 17, 1956)

Cornell, *PCPhS*
   T. J. Cornell, 'Aeneas and the twins: the development of the Roman foundation legend', *PCPhS* 201 N. S. 21 (1975) 1ff.

Cornell (thesis)
   T. J. Cornell, 'Cato's *Origines* and the non-Roman Historical tradition about Ancient Italy' (unpublished University of London Ph.D. thesis (Arts), 1972)

Fraser   P. M. Fraser, *Ptolemaic Alexandria* (3 vols. Oxford 1972)

GC   F. Cairns, *Generic Composition in Greek and Roman Poetry* (Edinburgh 1972)

Gow – Page, *HE*
   A. S. F. Gow and D. L. Page, *The Greek Anthology: Hellenistic Epigrams* (2 vols. Cambridge 1965)

Graham
   A. J. Graham, *Colony and Mother City in Ancient Greece* (Manchester 1964)

Kambylis
   A. Kambylis, *Die Dichterweihe und ihre Symbolik* (Bibliothek der Klassischen Altertumswissenschaften N. F. 2, Heidelberg 1965)

Kroll   W. Kroll, *Studien zum Verständnis der römischen Literatur* (Stuttgart 1924)

Newman
   J. K. Newman, *Augustus and the New Poetry* (Coll. Latomus 88, Brussels 1967)

Pfeiffer   R. Pfeiffer, *History of Classical Scholarship* (2 vols. Oxford 1968, 1976)

PLLS 1976
   Papers of the Liverpool Latin Seminar 1976 (Arca Classical and Medieval Texts, Papers and Monographs 2, Liverpool 1977)

PLLS 1979
   Papers of the Liverpool Latin Seminar Second Volume 1979 (Arca Classical

and Medieval Texts, Papers and Monographs 3, Liverpool 1979)
Powell   *Collectanea Alexandrina*, ed. J. U. Powell (Oxford 1925)
Puelma Piwonka
           M. Puelma Piwonka, *Lucilius und Kallimachos* (Frankfurt am Main 1949)
Schmid
           P. B. Schmid, *Studien zu griechischen Ktisissagen* (Diss. Freiburg i. d. Schweiz 1947)
Smith   *The Elegies of Albius Tibullus*, ed. K. F. Smith (New York 1913, repr. Darmstadt 1971)
Weinstock
           S. Weinstock, *Divus Julius* (Oxford 1971)
Wimmel, *DFT*
           W. Wimmel, *Der frühe Tibull* (Studia et Testimonia Antiqua 6, Munich 1968)
Wimmel, *Kallimachos*
           W. Wimmel, *Kallimachos in Rom* (*Hermes* Einzelschriften 16, Wiesbaden 1960)
Wimmel, *TDI*
           W. Wimmel, *Tibull und Delia I: Tibulls Elegie 1, 1* (*Hermes* Einzelschriften 37, Wiesbaden 1976)

1
THE SETTING

In the years from around 31 BC to 19/18 BC[1] a poet from Pedum[2] in the Latian countryside wrote and circulated at Rome two books of elegies. There are only sixteen poems in all; and the longest of them contains only one hundred and twenty-two lines. But they pose a considerable critical problem. This shows itself most clearly in the divergence of ancient and modern views of Tibullus. His contemporaries and immediate posterity considered him to be a great elegiac poet and a majority of them regarded him as the greatest Roman elegist. The evidence for this assessment is clear: from the Augustan age comes the testimony of Ovid;[3] that of Velleius Paterculus is Tiberian;[4] and the verdict of Quintilian, which is not just a personal judgement but a report of current views, derives from the latter half of the first century AD.[5] The 'Life of Tibullus', medieval in its present form but probably Suetonian in origin,[6] echoes this ancient appraisal: *hic multorum iudicio principem inter elegiographos obtinet locum.* Modern scholars have found this attitude difficult to understand: the more factual of the ancient observations seem hard to substantiate from Tibullus' poetry; and the more evaluative seem exaggerated or even misapplied. Tibullus' contemporary and fellow-elegist, Propertius, is less problematic in this respect. Whether or not his work has found favour for the same qualities in antiquity and today, there is at least a consensus about his merit.[7] This sharpens the problem of Tibullus.

The strongest modern reaction to it was that of Felix Jacoby.[8] In 1909 Jacoby denied the validity and relevance of the ancient assessment. He

[1] The exact date is disputed. For a judicious summing-up of the controversy see M. J. McGann, 'The date of Tibullus' death', *Latomus* 29 (1970) 774ff.
[2] He lived *in regione Pedana* (Hor. *Ep.* 1.4.2). A conjecture of Baehrens on the anonymous *Vita Tibulli* would make him born at nearby Gabii.
[3] Esp. *Am.* 1.15.27; 3.9; *Tr.* 2.445ff.
[4] Velleius 2.36.3.
[5] *Inst. Or.* 10.1.93 (on which see below, pp. 3ff.).
[6] Cf. G. Townend, 'Suetonius and his influence' in *Latin Biography* ed. T. A. Dorey (London 1967) p. 81.
[7] The *testimonia* on Propertius, which show the favourable ancient view of him, are collected in *The Elegies of Propertius* ed. H. E. Butler and E. A. Barber (Oxford 1933) introd. pp. ixf. For a characteristically favourable modern assessment of Propertius see M. Hubbard, *Propertius* (London 1974), and cf. also Smith introd. pp. 67f.
[8] 'Tibulls erste Elegie', *RhM* 64 (1909) 601ff.; *RhM* 65 (1910) 22ff. = *Kleine philologische Schriften* (Berlin 1961) II pp. 122ff.

declared that Tibullus, although a sympathetic personality, was a minor poet who lacked inspiration and poetic merit. Jacoby's views were unrepresentative of his generation and they were promptly criticised.[9] But the ensuing controversy showed that, however extreme, they reflected to some extent the misgivings of many scholars. Moreover the defenders of Tibullus, then and since, have not been able to make a truly cogent case for the poet. In some ways they have even enlarged the gulf between ancient and modern views instead of closing it.

Such a defence was made fairly soon after Jacoby's attack by Kirby Flower Smith in 1913. In the introduction to his commentary on Tibullus[10] Smith first poses the critical problem outlined above. He then turns to characterising the two other major elegiac poets of the Augustan age, Propertius and Ovid. In this field he is happy and eloquent. Finally, and almost reluctantly, Smith closes issue with Tibullus. In his hands Tibullus becomes a string of negatives. He is 'not a man of brilliant passages . . . there is no elaborate use of mythological lore, no deep and recondite learning, no signs of the close and fervid study of specific literary models'. His diction, style and metrical technique are simple and natural. He possesses neither 'the daring imagination' nor 'the ardent temperament' of Propertius; nor does he have 'the inexhaustible vivacity and wit, the infectious animal spirits, of Ovid' (pp. 68ff.).

Several useful positive suggestions accompany these negatives. Smith points out, for example, that Tibullus' work is not artless, but an example of art concealing art; he declares that Tibullan elegy may reflect a particular type of Greek elegiac poetry – in Smith's view, that of 'Mimnermus as modified by Philetas' (p. 69); finally he adduces the humour of several Tibullan elegies as an answer to that unhelpful critical commonplace, 'the gentle elegiac melancholy' of Tibullus (p. 70). But Smith's defence of Tibullus is inevitably unsatisfactory. His list of negatives could never make a writer the greatest of Roman elegists. Moreover in dealing with particular adverse criticism of Tibullus, such as lack of learning, or lack of the energy, ambition or ability to perfect his work, Smith does not fight hard enough for him. Instead he falls back on the common resort of Tibullan scholars who favour their poet. He makes repeated assertions of Tibullus' merits, but either leaves them unsupported or else tries to justify them with reference to critical canons reserved for Tibullus alone.

Since 1913 many valuable contributions to a more positive view of Tibullus have been made. The work of Mauriz Schuster,[11] Georg Luck,[12]

---

[9] Cf. R. Reitzenstein, 'Noch einmal Tibulls erste Elegie', *Hermes* 47 (1912) 60ff.

[10] pp. 65ff. Views similar to those of Smith are still found in M. Schanz and C. Hosius, *Geschichte der römischen Literatur* (Handbuch der Altertumswissenschaft ed. W. Otto 8,2, 4th ed. 1935) II p. 183 §281.

[11] *Tibull-Studien* (Vienna 1930, repr. Hildesheim 1968), usefully reviewed and summarised by H. T. Rowell, *AJP* 63 (1942) 230ff.

[12] *The Latin Love Elegy* (2nd ed. London 1969).

J. P. Elder,[13] J. K. Newman[14] and other scholars has advanced understanding of Tibullus' compositional methods, of his techniques of transition within single poems and of his indebtedness to his Hellenistic predecessors. But it seems fair to say that the case for Tibullus has not yet been made satisfactorily. The view is still widespread that individual elegies of Tibullus consist of loosely-connected themes and, in part due to confusion between Tibullus the man and Tibullus the poet, the old characterisation of him as an anaemic dilettante still survives in modern criticism. How much real advance has been made since 1913 is shown in the assessment of Tibullus offered by Gordon Williams in 1968.[15] Williams discusses several elegies of Tibullus and details many positive aspects of his work: his power to unify a diverse collection of themes in a single poem; his ability in transitions and structuring, and the consequent subtlety and delicacy of the movements of his ideas; the economy and precision of his language; his humour and his tendency to surprise the reader with new twists to old ideas. But there is still emphasis on negative traits (esp. pp. 499ff.): Tibullus' 'reflective, musing tone', his 'muted, gentle, humorous, melancholic' voice, his lack of drama and intensity of feeling, his small range and lack of architectonic qualities, his failure to employ 'arresting phrases' and to use language in a novel way. In this representative modern account, Tibullus is a good poet but not a great one: in comparison with Propertius and Ovid he seems dull and uninteresting.

It would clearly be wrong to demand a description of Tibullus couched totally in positive terms, or one which made no distinction between his work and that of Propertius and Ovid. It is obvious that Tibullus' poetry differs in texture from that of his fellow elegists and that he lacks certain qualities which they possess. But he himself ought to possess the qualities of the greatest Roman elegist, unless ancient critical opinion was wrong or has been misunderstood. Now there is no reason why the literary critics of antiquity should always be trusted. However the judgement of qualified contemporaries and near-contemporaries of Tibullus, native Latin speakers, fully acquainted with the literary background of elegy, must carry weight. A better understanding of their assessment of Tibullus can be achieved by close scrutiny of what they say. The most important text is from Quintilian:

> Elegia quoque Graecos provocamus, cuius mihi tersus atque elegans maxime videtur auctor Tibullus. Sunt qui Propertium malint. Ovidius utroque lascivior, sicut durior Gallus.
> (*Institutio Oratoria* 10.1.93)

---

[13] 'Tibullus: *Tersus atque Elegans*' in *Critical Essays in Roman Literature: Elegy and Lyric* ed. J. P. Sullivan (London 1962) pp. 65ff.
[14] pp. 383ff.
[15] *Tradition and Originality in Roman Poetry* (Oxford 1968) pp. 496ff.

With rough equivalents for the critical terms, the following rendering can be offered:

> In elegy too we Romans challenge the Greeks. In this field the writer who seems to me most polished and elegant is Tibullus. There are those who prefer Propertius. Ovid is more exuberant than either, just as Gallus is harsher.[16]

An objection to treating this text as evidence of a general verdict might be that Quintilian is expressing a personal opinion in putting Tibullus first. Quintilian certainly does not record his judgement as one universally accepted in his own time: he grants that 'some' prefer Propertius. But this statement implies that the majority favoured Tibullus.

It might also be felt that Quintilian's critical terms are vague and non-significant. The exact meaning of *tersus* and *elegans*, *lascivus* and *durus*, is indeed hard to determine. But they are applied by Quintilian in a precise way and they are all technical terms of literary criticism. Tibullus is said to be *tersus atque elegans maxime*; but no adjective is applied to Propertius. However, Propertius and Tibullus are compared and Quintilian prefers Tibullus. The implication is that Quintilian regards Propertius, like Tibullus, as *tersus* and *elegans*, but less so than Tibullus. Gallus is *durior* than Tibullus and Propertius, Ovid *lascivior*. Both therefore diverge from being *tersus atque elegans*: Gallus is not refined enough in his style and so is over harsh; Ovid has gone too far in the opposite direction and is too exuberant, showy and self-indulgent.[17]

The status of such terms in Roman literary criticism can be gauged fairly well from a passage in one of the younger Pliny's letters. Pliny is describing the work of a contemporary poet, Passennus Paulus, a descendant of the Augustan poet Propertius. Passennus not only wrote elegies like his ancestor Propertius but also lyrics. Pliny therefore elegantly compliments Paulus by comparing him as an elegist with Propertius before going on to compare him as a lyric poet with Horace:

> praeterea in litteris veteres aemulatur, exprimit, reddit, Propertium in primis, a quo genus ducit, vera suboles eoque simillima illi, in quo ille praecipuus. si elegos eius in manum sumpseris, leges opus tersum, molle, iucundum et plane in Properti domo scriptum.   (*Epistles* 9.22.1f.)
> Besides, in his literary work he rivals, imitates and reproduces the work of

---

[16] M. Hubbard, *Propertius* p. 2 translates the passage as follows: 'We challenge the Greeks in elegy too. Here the most polished and choice writer is, I think, Tibullus; others prefer Propertius. Ovid is less pruned than either and Gallus harsher.' She rightly stresses that Propertius and Tibullus are being praised for the same qualities.

[17] This analysis is brief because it coincides with that of Hubbard, *Propertius* pp. 1ff. who is primarily concerned with Propertius.

the classical poets. In particular he is a true descendant of his ancestor Propertius and most resembles him in the literary field in which Propertius was master. If you read Passennus' elegies you will find them polished, tender and charming, and very much a product of the family of Propertius.

Here is the same range of critical vocabulary applied again, and quite independently of Quintilian, to an elegist. The terms used by Quintilian and Pliny clearly denote recognised standard qualities of elegy; and Pliny is attributing to Passennus, and hence implicitly to Propertius, the same virtues as Quintilian explicitly finds in Tibullus and Propertius.

Quintilian's judgement then is a meaningful one in terms of ancient criticism of elegy; and his award to Tibullus of the primacy in Roman elegy is confirmed by other ancient references to him.[18] Most of these simply speak of Tibullus in general terms: but several Ovidian passages add interesting details to Quintilian's sketch. In Ovid's eyes Tibullus is *cultus* (*Amores* 1.15.28; 3.9.66) and *ingenium come* (*Tristia* 5.1.18); *cultus* and *ingenium come* lie in the same range of vocabulary as *elegans* and *mollis*. Finally Tibullus himself supplies a useful piece of information about his literary aims, when indirectly he claims to be *doctus: Pieridas, pueri, doctos et amate poetas* (1.4.61).

The qualities attributed to Tibullus by Quintilian, by Ovid and by himself are related to the literary ideals espoused by the Hellenistic Greek poets of the third century BC and later claimed by many of their Roman successors. *Doctrina* refers to the best known characteristic of Hellenistic poetry.[19] *Tersus* and *cultus* relate both to the πόνος (*labor*) which Hellenistic poets claimed as a necessary part of their poetic activity[20] and to the λεπτότης (fineness) which was the result of it.[21] Being *mollis* and *iucundus* and *ingenium come* is to some extent connected with the Hellenistic emphasis on small scale composition (*nugae*);[22] it is also linked with the 'sweetness' of the Hellenistic poet[23] and of the honey-bee, that frequent

---

[18] Esp. Velleius 2.36.3: *inter quae maxime nostri aevi eminet princeps carminum Vergilius Rabiriusque et consecutus Sallustium Livius Tibullusque et Naso, perfectissimi in forma operis sui*; *Vita Tibulli* (quoted above p. 1); Diomedes p. 484 17(K) (quoted and discussed below, p. 6.

[19] For the evidence see Kroll pp. 37ff.; chh. 8, 12, 13, 14; and see below, pp. 11ff. and nn. 47ff.

[20] Cf. Kroll pp. 38ff.; Puelma Piwonka pp. 125f.; 130; 139 n.2; Wimmel, *Kallimachos Stichwortindex* s.v. *labor, lima Mühsamkeit*; F. Cairns, 'Catullus 1', *Mnenosyne* s.IV 22 (1969) 153ff.; and see below, n. 24 and pp. 28f.

[21] Cf. Puelma Piwonka pp. 160ff.; Wimmel, *Kallimachos Stichwortindex* s.v. λεπτός; Kambylis pp. 81, 119, 141f.; and see below n. 23.

[22] On Callimachus see Fraser I pp. 625, 641f., 749, 754f., II pp. 1058f. nn. 287f.; Puelma Piwonka pp. 138ff.; Wimmel, *Kallimachos* pp. 39 n. 1, 83ff.; Pfeiffer I pp 136f.: Cairns, *Mnem.* s.IV 22 (1969) 153ff.

[23] Cf. Call. *Aet.* Fr. 1.11 (of Mimnermus), 15 (Pf.) and Pfeiffer *ad loc.*; *Epigr.* 27 (Pf.) (of Aratus, combining τὸ μελιχρότατον with λεπταί/ῥήσιες).

symbol of the Hellenistic poet.[24] It is no surprise to find Tibullus regarded in these terms by ancient critics: the other two major Roman elegiac poets whose work survives, Propertius and Ovid, implicitly acknowledge their indebtedness to Hellenistic masters and Propertius does so explicitly.[25] Tibullus makes no such acknowledgement and mentions no literary predecessor. But his indebtedness to Hellenistic poetry was just as great. This was understood by the ancient critics when they wrote of him in the terms discussed above and it is explicitly stated by the grammarian Diomedes:

> Elegia est carmen compositum hexametro versu pentametroque alternis ⟨in⟩vicem positis, ut
>> divitias alius fulvo sibi congerat auro
>> et teneat culti iugera multa soli
>
> quod genus carminis praecipue scripserunt apud Romanos Propertius et Tibullus et Gallus imitati Graecos Callimachum et Euphoriona.　　　　　　　　　　　(Diomedes p. 484.17(K))
> *Elegy is a type of poem composed alternately in hexameters and pentameters, e.g.*
>> *Let another heap up for himself wealth in yellow gold*
>> *and be master of many arable acres.*
>> [*Tibullus 1.1.1f*]
>
> *At Rome the principal writers of this type of poem were Propertius and Tibullus and Gallus, who imitated the Greek poets Callimachus and Euphorion.*

That Diomedes is correct about Tibullus' literary ancestry is confirmed both by his independently attested information about Propertius and Gallus, and by a number of known imitations of Callimachus in Tibullus.[26] In addition, Tibullus' pre-eminence in Roman elegy is implicitly supported by Diomedes' use of the first couplet of his first elegy as an example of the elegiac metre.

Since all the ancient critics lay stress on what Tibullus has in common with the other Roman elegiac poets rather than on the differences between them, and describe him in terms applicable to a follower of Greek Hellenistic poetry, it seems sensible for a modern critic to begin by trying to fit Tibullus into this background. In this way the Roman evaluation of Tibullus in terms of cultivated and polished elegance may become more comprehensible.

To see Tibullus as a 'Hellenistic' poet it is necessary to arrive at a

---

[24] Cf. Pfeiffer I p. 284; Wimmel, *Kallimachos* Stichwortindex *s.v.* Bienen. The concept is of course also related to that of *labor* (see above, n. 20).

[25] *Callimachus*: Prop. 2.1.40; 2.34.32; 3.1.1; 3.9.43; 4.1.64; *Philetas*: Prop. 2.34.31; 3.1.1.

[26] Collected by A. W. Bulloch, 'Tibullus and the Alexandrians', *PCPhS* 199 (1973) 71ff. Cf. also M. Pino, 'Echi Callimachei in Tibullo', *Maia* 24 (1972) 63ff.

description of Hellenistic poetry. This is not easy, since Hellenistic poetry involves a great range of subjects and styles. Some differences between Hellenistic poets may be reflected in the alleged 'battle of the books',[27] whether or not this had a historical reality or is based in part, like the polemical language of Callimachus, on the ancient scholiasts' misunderstandings of Pindar.[28] But the very range of Hellenistic poetry is in one sense helpful and reassuring where Tibullus is concerned. It is not necessary, in order to show that Tibullus can meaningfully be described as a Hellenistic poet, to depict him simultaneously as a Callimachus and a Lycophron. If he professes at least some of the literary principles which Hellenistic poets espouse and if his work lies somewhere within the range of subject and style found in Hellenistic poetry, then the description is applicable. It is all the more applicable since the concept of being a Hellenistic poet was paradoxically more significant for the Romans than for the Hellenistic Greeks. Roman 'Hellenistic' poets were converts to a foreign literary tradition which stood in contrast to an older Roman view of literary excellence[29] still widely held in their own day. This increased their zeal, as did their realisation that the great achievements of Greece in literature remained still to be equalled and surpassed by Roman writers. Of literary forms practised in the late Roman Republic and early Empire, elegy, along with its close relative pastoral, was the most heavily influenced by Hellenistic poetry. This means that it makes excellent literary-historical sense to aim, whatever the difficulties and whatever the risk of oversimplification, at a general characterisation of Hellenistic poetry in the study of a Roman elegist.

How is this to be done? K. J. Dover has emphasised recently how it should not be done:

> The least profitable way of attempting to characterize Hellenistic poetry as a whole is to begin with second-hand generalizations about it (or about Greek morals, politics or intellectual developments), find passages in Hellenistic poetry which bear out these

---

[27] For a summary of the evidence about literary controversies involving Callimachus, cf. Fraser I pp. 741ff. and esp. pp. 749ff.

[28] For the links between Pindar and Callimachus' vocabulary of literary criticism cf. Newman pp. 45ff. Much of the 'autobiographical' material in Pindar is now generally regarded as literary convention (cf. e.g. E. L. Bundy, *Studia Pindarica* I, II (University of California Publications in Classical Philology 18, Berkeley and Los Angeles 1962); D. C. Young, *Three Odes of Pindar* (*Mnemosyne* Suppl. 9, Leiden 1968); *Pindar Isthmian 7, Myth and Exempla* (*Mnemosyne* Suppl. 15, Leiden 1971); W. J. Slater, 'Futures in Pindar', *CQ* n.s. 19 (1969) 86ff.; 'Pindar's house', *GRBS* 12 (1971) 141ff.; 'Doubts about Pindaric interpretation', *CJ* 72 (1977) 193ff.). The Callimachean imitations of Pindaric literary polemic may also be at least in part conventional, just as many Augustan reworkings of Callimachean literary apologia material clearly involve an element of fiction.

[29] Expressed e.g. by Cicero in the *Pro Archia* (62 BC).

generalizations, and omit to ask to what extent archaic and classical poetry bear out the same generalizations.

(*Theocritus Select Poems*, ed. K. J. Dover, Introd. p. lxvii)

Dover points out (pp. lxviff.) that Hellenistic poetry has in common with archaic poetry some of the very features which are supposed to be Hellenistic – new words and senses of words, the incorporation of epic words, the use of epic material to a different point, mythological allusiveness and inventiveness, humanisation of the gods and a flippant attitude to mythology, contrived naivety. He concludes that if most of the poetry of the fourth century BC had not been lost, it might well be thought that 'Hellenistic' poetry began with the deaths of Euripides and Sophocles. It is to the fourth century that Dover dates the change from a 'primary' to a 'secondary' stage in tragedy; and he observes that Homeric exegesis of a philological type goes back in poetry to Antimachus of Colophon (*circa* 400 BC).[30]

Dover's observations are undoubtedly correct and could be pressed further. In particular his point about 'Hellenistic' poetry starting in the late fifth century could be amplified. In that period, in Aristophanes, *Frogs* 785–1481, the literary criticism and terminology later associated with Hellenistic writers and surviving most prominently in Callimachus, *Aetia* Fr. 1 (Pf.), is already found in a detailed if embryo form.[31] In the contest between 'Aeschylus' and 'Euripides' Aeschylus represents the older school and Euripides the beginnings of the new poetry. First the chorus speaks of a κρίσις . . . τέχνης (judgement of art) (785f.), cf. *Aetia* Fr.1.17f.: τέχνῃ . . . [κρίνετε] (judge by art). They also mention the process of weighing and measuring which will take place (797) and which will provide a visual basis for the last section of the poetic contest (cf. also 797ff., 958 and 1378ff., esp. 1398: καθέλξει (will outweigh) and *Aetia* Fr. 1.9: καθέλκει (outweighs) and 18: σχοίνῳ Περσίδι (measuring-tape)). In their preliminary remarks the chorus speak of Aeschylus as a 'thunderer' (814) – contrast Callimachus' rejection of thunder as a symbol for his work (*Aetia* Fr. 1.20). Aeschylus, according to the chorus, has a 'giant's breath' (825), while Callimachus speaks of the giant Enceladus in contrast to himself (*Aetia* Fr. 1.35f.). Aeschylus' words are said to be ἱπποβάμονα (horse-prancing) (821), whereas Callimachus is told by Apollo to avoid the chariot road (*Aetia* Fr. 1.25ff.).

In the actual contest Euripides criticises Aeschylus' bombast (838f., 923ff., 961, 1056f. – compare Callimachus, *Aetia* Fr. 1.19f., the refusal of a μέγα ψοφέουσαν ἀοιδήν (a mighty sounding song)). Euripides also speaks of slimming tragedy[32] (938ff. – compare *Aetia* Fr. 1.24, where Callimachus

---

[30] Cf. Pfeiffer I General Index *s.v.* Antimachus of Colophon.
[31] See Wimmel, *Kallimachos* p. 115 n. 1, where a number of the links discussed below are listed.
[32] 'Thinness' is linked with the concepts of 'smallness' and 'poverty' which are also

is told by Apollo to keep his Muse thin) and of the upper air as feeding him (892 – compare *Aetia* Fr. 1.34 where Callimachus wants to be the cicada ἐκ ... ἠέρος εἶδαρ ἔδων (eating food from the air)). Finally Euripides contrasts his own humble characters with those of Aeschylus (948ff. – cf. *Aetia* Fr. 1.3ff. where Callimachus says he is criticised because he does not write long accounts of the deeds of kings and heroes). Aeschylus had introduced the question of Euripides' low characters earlier (840ff.); and there is a third mention of the topic at lines 1038ff., where Aeschylus contrasts his own heroic characters with Euripides' loose women and again later, at 1062ff. where he criticises Euripides for portraying royalty in rags. Euripidean practice, of course, conforms to the general Hellenistic tendency to give emphasis to the representation of humble characters and to humanise gods and heroes. In Roman Hellenistic poetry this process is taken one step further: real people, in particular the poet and his mistress, take the place of the humanised gods and heroes of Greek Hellenistic poetry in analogous situations.[33]

Aeschylus also criticises Euripides' interest in incest as a theme for his plays (850, 1081). With this may be compared the considerable use of this theme in Hellenistic literature: the largest collection of such material is to be found in Parthenius' *Erotika Pathemata*, which contains summaries of a number of legends involving incest treated by earlier Hellenistic poets. Again, Aeschylus attacks Euripides' introduction of procuresses (1079). Here New Comedy, and in its train Roman Comedy and Roman Elegy, may be compared. Euripides is also criticised for teaching immorality and this criticism is linked with a statement of the didactic function of poetry (1043ff. and esp. 1053ff.). Here a didactic emphasis broader than that of Hellenistic poetry is involved although the latter is not unconcerned with that area (see below, pp. 29ff.). Finally Aeschylus takes issue with Euripides over the latter's interest in Cretan monodies (848), drinking songs, Carian flute songs, dirges and dance-music – that is, in music of highly emotional types. Again, Hellenistic literature seeks in music, as in every area, the unusual and the emotionally vivid;[34] Roman elegy is above all associated with the *tibia*, the Phrygian αὐλός, with its notorious capacity to arouse the feelings.[35]

Euripides for his part invokes novel personal gods, including 'Hyper-

> part of the Callimachean literary manifesto. Cf. above, n. 22; below, nn. 85 and 93. Aristophanes is of course primarily being humorous and Euripides almost immediately is made to say that he nourished up tragedy again (944).
>
> [33] For an example see F. Cairns, 'Propertius i.18 and Callimachus, *Acontius and Cydippe*', *CR* N.S. 20 (1969) 131ff.; and see below, pp. 111f.
>
> [34] Gow–Page, *HE* II Index to Commentary – B. English *s.v.* Music and Musicians; Catullus 63.8ff.; and see Nisbet–Hubbard on Hor. *Od.* 1.18.13.
>
> [35] Cf. for the connections between elegy and the *tibia R–E s.v. Elegie* pp. 2262f., 2270. For the capacity of the *tibia* to arouse feelings see e.g. Dioscorides 35 (GP); Lucr. 2.620; Cat. 64.264 and Kroll *ad loc.*; Hor. *Od.* 3.19.18f.; Ov. *Met.* 11.16; *Fast.* 4.341.

Intelligence' and 'Over-fastidious Criticism'[36] (891ff., cf. also 973f.). There is of course a gap between the novelty of Euripides' gods and the novelty and originality which was a desideratum for Hellenistic poets.[37] Nevertheless there is a line of descent. Similarly the idiosyncratic character of Euripides' gods is related however remotely to the notion of poetic individuality which is conveyed through various other Hellenistic programmatic concepts.[38] The critical acumen of Euripides, as it is seen in action in Aristophanes' *Frogs*, again relates to Hellenistic literary controversy.[39] Euripides goes on to speak of his metrical subtlety (958), cf. 1309ff.: metrical niceties were another Hellenistic preoccupation.[40] The banausic metaphor he employs, probably from building (cf. 799ff.), is analogous to the wood- and metal-working and weaving metaphors used by Hellenistic poets of their work.[41] Finally Euripides notes that his prologues are brief and informative (1177ff.); and brevity is one of the main aspects of Hellenistic poetry.[42] The chorus contributes the concepts of subtlety, epigrammatic quality, sharp-wittedness, learning, word-play (875ff.), urbanity, smoothness and refinement (901f.) (cf. also 1099ff.), all concepts which recur in the Hellenistic period.[43] An interesting point is that Euripides' diction is said to be 'filed' (902), a symbol which does not appear in extant Callimachus but is standard in manifesto-literature deriving from Callimachus.[44]

Dover's remarks are therefore fully justified. Nevertheless the career of Alexander the Great, as Dover admits, does stand between two distinct literary and cultural epochs. Moreover some of the generalisations Dover offers about the second can stand as valid characterisations of it, particularly his remarks about the concern of Hellenistic poetry with learned reflection on the literature, myth and cult of the past, its interest in real human life and high technical aims; and its connection with the transition from a primary to a secondary stage in literature, a transition marked by the formation of a canon of 'classical' authors within each area of writing. It does not particularly matter if some characteristics of Hellenistic poetry can also be found here and there, or even widely, in fifth century or archaic Greek writers. To begin with, what is peculiar to Hellenistic as opposed to

---

[36] These translations of ξύνεσις and μυκτῆρες ὀσφραντήριοι are derived from Stanford *ad loc.*
[37] Cf. Kroll pp. 12ff.; Ch. 7; Puelma Piwonka pp. 167ff.; Nisbet–Hubbard on Hor. *Od.* 1.26.6; 1.26.10 [*novis*]; Wimmel, *Kallimachos* p. 98; Stichwortindex *s.v. primus*-Motiv, Erstheitsidee; Kambylis pp. 155f., 159ff., 203.
[38] Notably those of novelty and originality (see above, n. 37); and 'purity' (see Nisbet–Hubbard *locc. citt.*, above, n. 37); Wimmel, *Kallimachos* pp. 222ff.
[39] Cf. Kroll Ch. 6; Puelma Piwonka pp. 127ff. Also see above, n. 27.
[40] Cf. Gow–Page, *HE* II Index to Commentary – B. English *s.v.* Metre; P. Maas, *Greek Metre* (Oxford 1962) pp. 11ff., 61ff., 79f., 85ff.
[41] Cf. Puelma Piwonka p. 161; Prop. 2.34.43 and Rothstein *ad loc.*; 3.1.5.
[42] See above, n. 22. [43] See above, nn. 21, 23, 32, 38.
[44] See above, n. 20.

earlier literature is the conscious combination and concentration of those characteristics of earlier writers which Hellenistic poets found particularly effective and admirable and therefore imitated. Secondly, with respect to Tibullus, a Roman standpoint can be adopted. For an Augustan elegist the primary models were the Hellenistic poets, whose literary practices were regarded by the Augustans as specifically Hellenistic and were imitated by them as such.

It is primarily from this Roman viewpoint then that the characteristics of Hellenistic literature will now be examined.[45] Specifically they will be linked as far as possible with Tibullus 1.1 which, like the prologues of all Hellenistic poetry-books, both Greek and Roman, is programmatic. Unlike, for example, Callimachus, *Aetia* Fr. 1f. (Pf.) Tibullus 1.1 is not an explicit literary manifesto. Like some other Hellenistic prologues it is implicitly programmatic and achieves its ends by describing the poet's 'life' which, by an equivalence standard in ancient poetry, symbolises his poetic work.[46] Not all the characteristics of Hellenistic poetry are alluded to in Tibullus 1.1. This makes the elegy all the more valuable as a literary manifesto in that it allows something of Tibullus' place within the great range of Hellenistic poetry to be understood. Although much of the Hellenistic manifesto material in Tibullus 1.1 will be paralleled from Callimachus, this is due as much to the survival of a fair amount of Callimachean manifesto poetry as to his intrinsic importance for Tibullus. It will be seen that Tibullus was influenced by several other Hellenistic poets besides Callimachus.

Any account of Hellenistic literature must begin with its most important and best known characteristic: *doctrina*. This was the key-note of Hellenistic attitudes to poetic subject-matter. The words σοφός (learned) and σοφία (learning) had already been applied to poets and poetry in certain contexts in earlier Greek poetry, particularly by Pindar.[47] Sometimes the praise of the victor may be more in question in these contexts than self-praise by the poet; and in any case the words mean no more in archaic poetry than 'good poet' and 'good poetry'. But in the Hellenistic and Roman periods σοφός and *doctus* came to mean 'learned poet' in situations where the art (τέχνη) of learned poets was being emphasised; and the term σοφός/*doctus* was sometimes used to distinguish 'Hellenistic' poetry from an older type of poetry. For Greek Hellenistic poets being 'learned' meant first being familiar with the literature of the past. Homer had an undisputed primacy here. But Hesiod,[48] Pindar, Archilochus and the early lyric

---

[45] For documentation of the non-controversial general statements about Hellenistic literature made in the remainder of this chapter the discussions of Fraser I Chh. 10, 11 and Kroll (*passim*) may be consulted.

[46] Cf. Wolf Steidle, 'Das Motiv der Lebenswahl bei Tibull und Properz', *WS* 75 (1962) 100ff. and F. Cairns, 'Propertius, 2.30 A and B', *CQ* N.S. 21 (1971) 204ff.

[47] See Newman p. 46; Nisbet–Hubbard on Hor. *Od.* 1.1.29.

[48] See Wimmel, *Kallimachos* Stichwortindex *s.v.* Hesiodfigur; Pfeiffer I pp. 177, 220;

poets in general[49] also had special places in the affections of Hellenistic poets. This interest in earlier literature was scholarly as well as literary. Studies of the authenticity of works attributed to great writers, textual criticism, the editing of texts, the classification of poetry and lexicography, all these areas of research accompanied the writing of poetry and contributed material to it.[50] The Romans inherited these interests and extended them to their own early literature.[51] Literary learning of this type is not prominent in Tibullus 1.1. There may be a reflection, direct or indirect, of Bacchylides in lines 3f.[52] and an echo of Mimnermus at the end of the elegy.[53] But there is no known Hellenistic imitation in Tibullus 1.1 to parallel the Meleagrian reminiscence with which Propertius 1.1 begins[54] and the manifestly Hellenistic programmatic material of the first elegy of Ovid's *Amores*.[55] Of course it may be present and simply unknown to us; and there are many imitations of earlier literature elsewhere in Tibullus.[56] But it seems clear that Tibullus is not so eager to draw attention to his learning in his first elegy as are Propertius and Ovid. This characteristic ties in with others noted below (p. 28) and helps to locate him within the whole field of Hellenistic literature.

The Hellenistic Greek interest in earlier literature was accompanied by a universal intellectual curiosity fed by the growing volume of information made available in part by Alexander's conquests, which opened up vast new areas to the Greeks. But even before Alexander, increased affluence

Fraser III General Index *s.v.* Hesiod; H. Reinsch-Werner, *Callimachus Hesiodicus* (Diss. Berlin 1976).

[49] See Pfeiffer I General Index *s.vv.* Archilochus, Alcaeus, Alcman, Anacreon, Bacchylides, Ibycus, Pindar, Sappho, Simonides, Stesichorus; Index of passages discussed *s.v.* Archilochus; Fraser III General Index under the same headings.

[50] See Pfeiffer I *passim*; Fraser I Part II *passim*; G. Giangrande, 'Three Alexandrian epigrams: *APl.* 167; Callimachus *Epigram* 5 (Pf.); *AP* 12,91', *PLLS 1976* pp. 253ff. and the works cited pp. 288f.

[51] Cf. for Virgil: H. D. Jocelyn, 'Ancient scholarship and Virgil's use of Republican Latin poetry', I *CQ* N.S. 14 (1964) 280ff., II *CQ* N.S. 15 (1965) 126ff.; M. Wigodsky, *Vergil and Early Latin Poetry* (Hermes Einzelschr. 24, Wiesbaden 1972). For Propertius cf. H. Tränkle, *Die Sprachkunst des Properz und die Tradition der lateinischen Dichtersprache* (Hermes Einzelschr. 15, Wiesbaden 1960) pp. 30ff. On comic influences (including Plautus and Terence) on Roman elegy, see below (Ch. 7 n. 86). For Ovid cf. A. Zingerle, *Ovidius und sein Verhältnis zu den Vorgängern und gleichzeitigen römischen Dichtern* II (Innsbruck 1871, repr. Hildesheim 1967) pp. 1ff.

[52] See Smith *ad loc.* and also Tib. 1.10.45ff., where in the epilogue to Bk 1, a poem which interacts with the book's prologue, 1.1 (see below, p. 20), Tibullus may again be indebted to the same passage of Bacchylides (*Pae*. 4.61ff. (Sn.–Mae.)). On the fact that the treatment of peace as a goddess is a Greek concept see F. Solmsen, 'Tibullus as an Augustan poet', *Hermes* 90 (1962) 298 = *Kleine Schriften* (Hildesheim 1968) II p. 327.

[53] Cf. Smith on ll. 69–74 and cf. Mimnermus Frr. 2, 5 (D).

[54] *AP* 12.101.1–4 = Prop. 1.1.1–4.

[55] Cf. Wimmel, *Kallimachos* pp. 300ff.; K. Morgan, *Ovid's Art of Imitation* (*Mnemosyne* Suppl. 47, Leiden 1977) pp. 7ff.

[56] Cf. Smith on Tibullus *passim*; A. W. Bulloch, *PCPhs* 199 (1973) 71ff.; and below, Chh 3, 4.

The setting

and leisure had stimulated scholarly interest in systematising knowledge; and the philosophical activity of the late fifth and fourth centuries produced the methodology for critical and comparative thought in many fields. While loss of real political power by the Greek cities must have reduced the attractions of an active political life for the urban intelligentsia, the wealthy kingdoms were able and willing to finance and provide facilities for scholarship. The libraries and courts of the Hellenistic kings found a parallel at Rome in the libraries and wealthy households of the late Republic and early Empire;[57] and the philosophical activity of the late Republic, in which the names of Cicero, Lucretius, Philodemus, Posidonius and Varro are the most prominent, again provided a stimulus and sub-structure for scholarly work in many non-philosophic fields. As a polymath, Varro in particular stands firmly in the Hellenistic tradition and can almost be seen as the Callimachus of his own age.

One area of learning prominent in Hellenistic poetry must be the result of political developments. It is antiquarian interest. Citizens of now powerless cities fostered their local identity through scholarship: their foundations and histories, their idiosyncratic variant legends and customs, their local festivals, rites and deities, their petty notables and heroes, all these became sources of immense pride as links between the city and its splendid past. Hellenistic poets gratefully exploited monographs on local history and antiquities, which also contributed to Hellenistic 'comparative' treatments of legend and history and lists of comparable incidents, personalities and so forth. Part of the much later Ps.-Hyginus' *Fabulae* consists of catalogues – 'the seven wonders of the world'; 'human beings later deified'; 'those who killed their daughters'; 'suicides'; 'people nursed by wild beasts'; 'the biggest islands' – which are the crude descendants of Hellenistic literary and rhetorical scholarship, and represent the lowest common denominator of knowledge handed down to succeeding generations.

The Hellenistic age was not of course the first time that Greeks had looked back to a heroic past and seen it as a period distinct from their own. Homer himself had done this;[58] and Pindar again had seen earlier mythography, including Homeric epic, as belonging to a different world from his own.[59] But the Hellenistic age seems to have felt an overwhelming sense both of the distinctness of contemporary society from the past and of its continuity with the past, and to have derived an intense and sophisticated enjoyment from its cultural heritage. Again the Augustan age reproduced

---

[57] On libraries at Rome cf. A. J. Marshall, 'Library resources and creative writing at Rome', *Phoenix* 30 (1976) 252ff. On the Augustan situation in particular see 261ff. and the works cited 261 nn. 56, 58.

[58] For a useful recent view relevant to this question cf. A. M. Snodgrass, 'An historical Homeric society?', *JHS* 94 (1974) 114ff.

[59] Cf. *Nem.* 7.20ff.; *Pae.* 7b.11ff. and see below, n. 81. Pindar's understanding of the gulf between his own work and earlier epic may be one of the many factors which made him attractive as a model to Hellenistic writers.

this sentiment. In Tibullus it is most prominent in 2.1 and 2.5 (on which see below, Chapters 5 and 3 respectively), although it surfaces elsewhere, notably in 1.1 and 1.10. In 1.1 it expresses itself for the most part in Roman religious antiquarianism. It involves simple objects of rustic reverence – the *stipes* and the old *lapis* (11f.), the *agricola deus* (14), the dedication of a *corona spicea* to Ceres (15f.), the installation of a Priapus figure (17f.), the worship of the ancestral Lares (19ff.), the rites of Pales (35f.) and the country festival of the gods (37ff.). The traditional nature of the cult features is emphasised in *vetus* (12), in 19ff. and in 39ff., in order to convey Tibullus' attachment to an idealised primitive Roman past. This sentiment, the poet's yearning for a past age, is paralleled in a late fifth-century BC poem and may be a programmatic feature of Tibullus 1.1.

> ἆ μάκαρ, ὅστις ἔην κεῖνον χρόνον ἴδρις ἀοιδῆς,
> Μουσάων θεράπων, ὅτ' ἀκήρατος ἦν ἔτι λειμών·
> νῦν δ'ὅτε πάντα δέδασται, ἔχουσι δὲ πείρατα τέχναι,
> ὕστατοι ὥστε δρόμου καταλειπόμεθ', οὐδέ πῃ ἔστι
> πάντῃ παπταίνοντα νεοζυγὲς ἅρμα πελάσσαι.
>   Choerilus Fr.1 (Kinkel))[60]
> *Ah happy the man who was skilled in song and a servant of the Muses at that time when the meadow was still unmown. But now when everything has been portioned out and the arts have already reached the limits of their achievement, we are left behind like the last runners in the race and though you look everywhere you can find nowhere to drive a new yoked chariot.*

Tibullus' religious antiquarianism has of course a dimension which its Hellenistic antecedents lacked. Tibullus is aware that Rome is the mistress of the world, not a political back-water like many of the Greek cities, the cults and institutions of which were written about by Hellenistic poets. Therefore Roman gods and festivals are of interest to the whole world, and not as mere survivals, but as the powerful gods and efficacious religious rites of the conquering nation.

History and mythology had always been standard preoccupations of Greek poetry. The Hellenistic poets continued this interest[61] and added new areas of knowledge. Geography, astronomy, medicine, winds and weather, plants, animals and stones, everything known or knowable was laid under contribution; and there was a vigorous output of didactic poetry. The philosophy of the Hellenistic period, derived from the Socratic and post-Socratic schools of the late fifth and fourth centuries, entered Hellenistic poetry.[62] Tibullus seems to have been particularly attracted to

---

[60] On the general sentiment cf. Wimmel, *Kallimachos Stichwortindex s.v.* Epigonengefühl.
[61] Cf. Kroll Chh. 8, 12, 13 and esp. 14.
[62] Cf. Wimmel, *Kallimachos Stichwortindex s.v.* peripatetische Kunstlehre; F. Jacoby, *opp. citt.* above (n. 8); Fraser III General Index *s.v.* Peripatetic influence etc.; Pfeiffer I

contemporary popular philosophy, since much of his moralising has a philosophical/rhetorical basis. Elegies 1.1, 1.3, 1.10, 2.4, and 2.6 move in the world of diatribe[63] and of philosophical controversies about whether a man's life ought to be lived in public or in private, whether staying at home or going abroad is preferable and whether certain occupations are morally superior to others. Unlike Horace[64] Tibullus does not seem to offer views attributable in detail to particular philosophical schools or to allude to technicalities. But his poetry reflects the concerns of popular philosophy and 1.1, which anticipates all the themes mentioned above, is strongly programmatic in this respect.

Another preoccupation of learned Hellenistic poets is language. Greek had a long written history and several dialects and its literature contained many archaic terms, the precise meaning of which had already been forgotten by Homer's time. All this caused the Greeks to be fascinated with the meaning of words: etymological interest is manifest even in Homer and Hesiod.[65] The fifth-century sophists were primarily involved in the arts of speech and argument; and among them Prodicus and Hippias showed considerable interest in grammar and semantics. Kindred interest is shown in Plato's *Cratylus* and the Stoics were concerned with theories of language. As a result of this expansion of technical studies, grammar, lexicography, etymology and textual criticism became staples of Hellenistic poetry, much of which is a tissue of allusive interpretation of Homer and other poets. Words are constantly found with glossographical and lexicographical explanations and in extended or unusual applications clarified by their context. There are also many dialectal experiments and etymologies.[66] In the late Roman Republic Varro's work on the Latin language helped Roman poets to experiment in a parallel way with their own mother tongue. Tibullus, like his contemporaries, is obsessed with language, as will be demonstrated in Chapter 4. Tibullus 1.1 is programmatic in this respect as in others since it contains its full share of learned linguistic points (see pp. 94, 100ff. below). A few of these in the

General Index *s.vv.* Peripatos; philosophy etc.; Puelma Piwonka Sachregister *s.v.* Philosophie etc.

[63] On this area cf. especially A. Oltramare, *Les origines de la diatribe romaine* (Lausanne 1926).

[64] Cf. E. Burck's bibliographical supplement to Kiessling–Heinze (8th ed. Berlin 1955) §8 and, most recently, on the *Epistles*, M. J. McGann, *Studies in Horace's First Book of Epistles* (Coll. *Latomus* 100, Brussels 1969) Ch. 1; and on the *Odes* Nisbet—Hubbard I *Index Rerum s.v.* philosophy; H. P. Syndikus, *Die Lyrik des Horaz* 2 vols. (Darmstadt 1972, 1973) *passim*. On the philosophical depth of a single ode (1.29) see J. R. G. Wright, 'Iccius' change of character: Horace, *Odes* I 29', *Mnemosyne* s. IV 27 (1974) 44ff. and F. Cairns, 'The philosophical content of Horace, Odes 1.29', *Liverpool Classical Monthly* 1 (1976) 71ff.

[65] Cf. M. L. West, *Hesiod Theogony* (Oxford 1966) Index I General *s.v.* etymologising; Pfeiffer I pp. 4, 12; L. P. Rank, *Etymologiseering en verwante Verschijnselen bij Homerus* (Diss. Utrecht 1951). See also below, pp. 92f.

[66] Cf. G. Giangrande, *PLLS 1976* pp. 253ff. and bibliography at pp. 288f.

16   The setting

opening lines may be pointed out here since their programmatic function is particularly prominent. 1.1 begins

> Divitias alius fulvo sibi congerat auro
> et teneat culti iugera *magna* soli (1f.)

The *iugerum* is a measure of land. Editors have therefore felt that it was absurd to speak of large *iugera*, since a *iugerum* is a *iugerum*, no more, no less. They have therefore replaced *magna* with *multa*, a reading found in the *florilegia* and in Diomedes. But *magna* is correct. *magna iugera* is, as Guy Lee has recently shown,[67] an unusual but perfectly acceptable phrase. The best of the parallels cited by him are *magnis regum cum milibus* (Valerius Flaccus, *Argonautica* 5.273) and *spatiosa iugera* (Statius, *Thebaid* 5.550). There are two possible explanations of Tibullus' usage. A line of Posidippus (Gow–Page *HE* 3105) might suggest that a Hellenistic Greek usage is involved: πύργος ὅδ' ἀπλάτων φαίνετ' ἀπὸ σταδίων 'This tower [i.e. the Pharos lighthouse] is visible from boundless miles.' Here too 'large' is used where 'numerous' would be normal. But it is more likely that Tibullus is employing here the Latin idiom whereby words denoting size are employed in place of words denoting number.[68] This is attested for *magnus* (*TLL s.v.* I III D, cf. Pliny, *Natural History* 35.72), for *magnitudo*, for *parvus* and for similar words (Leumann–Hofmann–Szantyr, *Lateinische Grammatik* II p. 206).[69] The examples of this phenomenon are for the most part late or vulgar; and this reveals Tibullus' purpose in employing the idiom. It is similar to Virgil's purpose in beginning the third *Eclogue* with *Dic mihi, Damoeta, cuium pecus? an Meliboei?* Deliberate vulgarisms are a learned feature of Hellenistic poetry, especially of bucolic.[70] Tibullus, in beginning his heavily bucolic first elegy with a couplet containing the learned vulgarism *magna iugera*, is both asserting his learning and the character and stylistic level of his work.

Verbal learning of another type, namely etymological, is also prominent

[67] '*Otium cum indignitate*: Tibullus I. 1' in *Quality and Pleasure in Latin Poetry* ed. T. Woodman and D. West (Cambridge 1974) pp. 111f. Of the parallels offered by Lee some could be interpreted in different ways, viz. *magni mensus* (Virg. *Ecl.* 4.12) and *magnae legiones* (Sall. *Cat.* 53; cf. Hor. *Sat.* 1.6.4). In an earlier discussion of the point, F. K. Ball defended *magna* (*CR* 8 (1894) 198) and K. P. Harrington upheld *multa* (*CR* 9 (1895) 108f.) The *iugera parva* of some MSS at Ov. *Am.* 3.15.12 (an epilogue!), which was debated in these notes, may deserve some consideration as a possible Ovidian *imitatio cum variatione* of *iugera magna*.
[68] For the reverse phenomenon cf. Hor. *Od.* 3.30.6: *multaque pars mei*.
[69] Cf. also E. Löfstedt, *Philologischer Kommentar zur Peregrinatio Aetheriae* (Oxford/Uppsala/Leipzig 1911) (on 5, 8); J. Svennung, *Untersuchungen zu Palladius und zur lateinischen Fach- und Volkssprache* (Arbeten Utgivna med Understöd av Vilhelm Ekmans Universitetsfond, Uppsala 44, 1935) pp. 323f.
[70] See G. Giangrande, 'Theocritus' Twelfth & Fourth Idylls: a study in Hellenistic irony', *Quad, Urbin.* 12 (1971) 95ff.; *L'Humour des Alexandrins* (Classical and Byzantine Monographs 2, Amsterdam 1975) pp. 15ff. Further on Virgil's reproduction of this Theocritean feature see *Vergil: Eclogues* ed. R. G. G Coleman (Cambridge 1977) index *s.v.* colloquialism.

The setting

and programmatic in *adsiduus* (Tibullus 1.3.3).[71] The word was often etymologised so as to mean 'rich' (cf. *divitias* etc., 1) and it also had a special association in etymological contexts with soldiers. Cf. Ps.-Placidus (*Corpus Glossariorum Latinorum* 5.7.7): *et adsidui milites [et] ab adsiduitate officii* and Paulus (Festus) p. 8 (L): *Alii eum,* [i.e. *assiduum*] *qui sumptu proprio militabat, ab asse dando vocatum aestimarunt.* Tibullus exploits these etymologies to enhance the contrast between the *adsiduus labor* of the soldier and his own hearth with its *adsiduo igne.* The etymology of the opposite concept *paupertas* (1.1.5) is implied later at 19f.:

> vos quoque, felicis quondam, nunc pauperis agri
>   custodes, fertis munera vestra, Lares.

Cf. *Pauper a paulo lare* (Varro, *De Lingua Latina* 5.92).

Another area of subject-matter important in Hellenistic poetry is the countryside. Of the Hellenistic works where the countryside is a prominent theme the pastoral idylls of Theocritus are the best known. But rustic and bucolic subjects had wider currency.[72] Their importance is in part reflected in, and in part a reflection of, the importance of Hesiod in Hellenistic poetic thought. Callimachus used the Hesiodic Theogony framework to frame his own *Aetia*; Hesiod's meeting with the Muses lies behind all Hellenistic manifesto literature;[73] Euphorion appears to have written a poem called 'Hesiod'; and in addition there is constant use of and allusion to the Hesiodic corpus in Hellenistic poetry.[74] At first sight the countryside may appear to fall completely outside the sphere of 'learning'. But in fact Hellenistic interest in the countryside does seem to have been in essence learned, that is, it reflects the intellectual curiosity of the Hellenistic poet in anything and everything outside his everyday experience. For urban Hellenistic man the countryside was no longer familiar as an everyday part of life.[75] It was another world, to be comprehended as such. The

---

[71] For etymologies in Tibullus see below, Ch. 4. For the etymologies of *adsiduus* cf. J. André, 'Les étymologies d'*Adsiduus* et la critique textuelle', *Rev. Phil.* 50 (1976) 22f., from which the evidence for what follows about the word is derived. Cf. also Tib. 2.1.51f.: *agricola adsiduo primum satiatus aratro | cantavit certo rustica verba pede*, where etymological interest is also present.

[72] In addition to the works mentioned below in the text see the discussions of P.-E. Legrand, *Étude sur Théocrite* (Bibliothèque des Écoles françaises d'Athènes et de Rome 79, Paris 1898, repr. 1968) pp. 154ff.; K. J. Dover, *Theocritus: Select Poems* (Basingstoke and London 1971) introd. pp. lxf.; Fraser II p. 880 nn. 41–4, esp. 44.

[73] Archilochus' confrontation with the Muses is also a significant part of this tradition, which is excellently documented by West on Hes. *Theog.* 22–35.

[74] See above, n. 48 and with particular reference to Tibullus: P. Grimal, 'Tibulle et Hésiode' in *Hésiode et son influence* (Entretiens sur l'Antiquité classique 7, Vandoeuvres – Genève 1960) pp. 273ff.

[75] A nostalgic and therefore distanced view of the countryside is already obvious in the late fifth century in Aristoph. *Ach.* and *Pax* (esp. in the second parabasis – 1127–90). In philosophical literature it appears in Plato's *Phaedrus* in the early fourth century. Interplay between town and country is frequent in Theocritus, cf. e.g. *Id.* 3 (and Gow's introd.); 10 and 14 (cf. F. Cairns, 'Theocritus Idyll 10', *Hermes*

same is probably true of the low urban life of Herodas' *Mimes* or of Theocritus, *Idylls* 2 and 15. Some confirmation that the countryside was part of 'learning' is provided by its conjunction in Hellenistic poetry with other indisputably learned themes – antiquarianism, and the concepts of poetic poverty, piety, smallness and simplicity which play a large part in Hellenistic manifesto poetry. A short epigram by Nicaenetus[76] combines these notions in a revealing way:

> Οὐκ ἐθέλω, Φιλόθηρε, κατὰ πτόλιν, ἀλλὰ παρ' Ἥρῃ
> δαίνυσθαι, Ζεφύρου πνεύμασι τερπόμενος.
> Ἀρκεῖ μοι λιτὴ μὲν ὑπὸ πλευροῖσι χάμευνα,
> ἐγγύθι γὰρ προμάλου δέμνιον ἐνδαπίης,
> καὶ λύγος, ἀρχαῖον Καρῶν στέφος. Ἀλλὰ φερέσθω
> οἶνος, καὶ Μουσέων ἡ χαρίεσσα λύρη,
> θυμῆρες πίνοντες ὅπως Διὸς εὐκλέα νύμφην
> μέλπωμεν, νήσου δεσπότιν ἡμετέρης.
>
>   (Fr. 6 (*Collectanea Alexandrina*, ed. J. U. Powell))
> *I don't want to dine in town, Philotheros, but by the temple of Hera where I can enjoy the breath of the West Wind. A humble pallet to support my back is enough for me for I shall have a couch of our native willow and a garland of withy, the ancient wreath of the Carians. Let wine be brought and the pleasant lyre of the Muses so that we can drink and delight ourselves and sing in praise of the famous bride of Zeus, the mistress of our island.*

Here Nicaenetus lovingly interweaves past and present, his personal life and the history of his city, and reveals his taste for the countryside, piety, smallness and simplicity. He wants to dine simply, lying on a humble couch in rural surroundings fanned by the wind and to the accompaniment of wine and song. But there is learned local religious and antiquarian interest in his chosen picnic spot – the temple of Hera in Samos, one of the most ancient in Greece, designed on an archaic pattern and inhabited by a prehistoric wooden statue of the goddess; in the material of his couch, πρόμαλος, a native Samian tree; and in his wreath of *agnus castus* with its association with the Carians, a non-Greek people culturally related to and in contact with the Greeks at an early period.[77] The combination of themes found in Nicaenetus again appears in Tibullus 1.1, where the antiquarian aspects not only have religious associations but are intimately bound up

---

98 (1970) 38ff. and *GC* pp. 145. 172f.); 6 and 11 (*GC* pp. 145f.; 194); [Theocr.] *Id.* 20.4. For town and country in Hellenistic literature in general cf. Puelma Piwonka, Sachregister *s.vv. urbanitas* etc. *rusticum* etc.

[76] His date is uncertain: 'probably second half of 3rd or beginning of 2nd BC' according to *OCD*² *s.v.* Nicaenetus; second half of third century BC (Gow–Page, *HE* II p. 417; *Kl.P. s.v.* Nikainetos); Fraser would apparently place him earlier (I p. 559 and n. 57).

[77] See Gomme on Thuc. 1.8.1; *R–E s.vv.* Karer; Karia; *Kl.P s.v.* Karer, Karia §5.

The setting

with a country life of poverty, simplicity and smallness. The same is true of the other Tibullan elegies which have a prominent bucolic content, notably 1.5, 1.10, 2.1, 2.3 and 2.5. It is not surprising that Tibullus should have made so much of these themes: for the Romans the countryside had an additional importance since in Italian cultural terms the *agricola* was the modern representative of the old Roman ideals of simplicity, poverty, attention to duty, hard work, serious involvement in the community and all domestic virtues.[78]

The themes of piety, poverty, simplicity and smallness, which are related to the theme of *rus*, need some amplification in view of their importance in Tibullus 1.1 and in other Hellenistic manifesto poetry. First, piety: early Greek poets believed themselves actually inspired by the gods;[79] and the lyric poets exploited this notion to declare themselves priests and spokesmen of the Muses[80] and so to enhance popular respect for their work. In order to strengthen their religious status they adopted a pious *persona*: Pindar, for example, made ostentatious gestures of avoiding impious or slanderous versions of myths.[81] Hellenistic poets imitated this lyric religiosity, and copied its pious attitudes and utterances.[82] They were not, or rather, they professed not to be, interested in traditional religious rites, festivals and antiquities merely as part of the Greek cultural heritage. They also claimed respectful belief in all these matters. The fact that their ostensible belief was far from the religious scepticism or agnosticism of many of their philosophically influenced contemporaries made it all the more striking.

The undisguised programmatic use of piety can be seen most clearly in Hellenistic poetry in *Aetia* Fr. 1 (Pf.). Here (lines 21ff.) Callimachus not

---

[78] Cf. F. Solmsen, *Hermes* 90 (1962) pp. 297ff. = *Kl. Schriften* II pp. 326ff. for Roman aspects of the *rus* theme in Tibullus.

[79] Cf. Kroll pp. 24ff. and see below, n. 80; also R. Harriott, *Poetry and Criticism before Plato* (London 1969) Chh. 1–4.

[80] Cf. Nisbet–Hubbard on Hor. *Od.* 1.31.2; 1.26.1.

[81] E.g. *Ol.* 1.25ff. esp. 35; 3.16; 9.35ff.; *Pyth.* 3.27ff.; *Nem.* 3.34 (cf. D. S. Robertson, *CR* 37 (1923) 6); *Nem.* 7.102ff. See also D. S. Robertson, *CR* 54 (1940) 177ff. on Pindaric 'corrections' of earlier versions of myths; E. L. Bundy, 'The "Quarrel between Kallimachos and Apollonios"' Part I 'The epilogue of Kallimachos's *Hymn to Apollo*', *CSCA* 5 (1972) 66; 71f. For a view of Pindar's 'religious commitment' which is earlier than Bundy's *Studia Pindarica* and for a useful collection of material cf. E. Thummer, *Die Religiosität Pindars* (Commentationes Aenipontanae 13, Innsbruck 1957).

[82] Cf. e.g. É. Cahen, *Callimaque et son oeuvre poétique* (Bibliothèque des Écoles françaises d'Athènes et de Rome 134, Paris 1929) pp. 342ff.; K. Kuiper, *Studia Callimachea II: De Callimachi Theologumenis* (Leiden 1898) pp. 117ff.; H. Fränkel, *Noten zu den Argonautika des Apollonios* (Munich 1968) p. 539 n. 172; D. N. Levin, *Apollonius' Argonautica Reexamined* I (*Mnemosyne* Suppl. 13, Leiden 1971) Index *s.v.* Piety etc.; K. J. McKay, *The Poet at Play: Kallimachos, The Bath of Pallas* (*Mnemosyne* Suppl. 6, Leiden 1962); *Erysichthon: A Callimachean Comedy* (*Mnemosyne* Suppl. 7, Leiden 1962); Fraser III General Index *s.v.* Callimachus of Cyrene (ii) attitude to gods etc.; claim to patronage etc. On Call. *Aet.* Fr. 75.1ff. (Pf.) see below, pp. 117f.

only claims that Apollo dictated to him in detail the nature of his poetic oeuvre; he also goes on to stress that the Muses have had an affectionate interest in him throughout his whole life (37f.). This prologue introduced a work structured as a set of questions addressed by Callimachus to the Muses and a set of answers (αἴτια) given in reply by the Muses. The pious *persona* which such claims required clearly became an integral part of the Hellenistic manifesto and Tibullus follows Hellenistic practice: throughout his work unquestioning belief in the gods and respect for their powers is shown. In 1.10, the epilogue elegy of Book I, Tibullus' relationship with the Lares is reminiscent of the *rapport* between Callimachus and the Muses in the *Aetia*.[83] Thus 1.10 helps to explain and reinforce the more indirect use of the piety theme in the prologue elegy, 1.1, where Tibullus is notably pious in his rustic activities: he prays to the gods of the countryside, including the Lares, sacrifices first-fruits to them, honours hallowed posts and stones and scrupulously keeps the recurrent sacred festivals. Tibullus' piety has of course in addition Roman dimensions: it is linked with the official Augustan attempt to revive religion; and it is specifically connected with the concept of the countryside as the last stronghold of piety, a notion also cultivated by Virgil throughout the *Georgics*.[84]

Another part of the same complex of themes is Tibullus' rejection of wealth and acceptance of '*paupertas*' as a way of life in 1.1. *Paupertas* is not 'poverty' in the modern sense but 'simple sufficiency without surplus'. Although no ancient poets claim to be rich, poverty seems to have a particularly significant connection with Hellenistic manifesto poetry.[85] Callimachus, *Iambus* 3 attacks wealth and, interestingly, its evil effects in the sphere of love (cf. also *Epigram* 32 (Pf.)).[86] In addition Leonidas of Tarentum employs the theme[87] and Theocritus, *Idyll* 16, a Hellenistic manifesto poem probably independent of Callimachus, *Aetia* Frr. 1ff.,[88] is another important example. *Idyll* 16 is supposedly an appeal to Hiero for funds. It combines programmatic allusion to Pindar, Bacchylides and Simonides with the *paupertas* theme, a combination which places Theo-

---

[83] M. Pino, *Maia* 24 (1972) 63ff. suggests links between Tib. 1.10.17–20 and other Callimachean passages. This might help to confirm and certainly does not weaken the suggestion made here.

[84] Cf. esp. *Georg.* 1.338ff.

[85] Cf. Puelma Piwonka Sachregister *s.v.* Armut der Dichter etc.; Wimmel, *Kallimachos* Stichwortindex *s.v. paupertas*; Wimmel, *TDI* Stichwortindex *s.v.* Armut etc.; G. Giangrande 'Symposiastic literature and epigram' in *L'Épigramme grecque* (Entretiens sur l'Antiquité classique 14, Vandoeuvres–Genève 1968) pp. 135ff. and see below, n. 87.

[86] This topos may be the antithesis of the frequent Hellenistic aspiration for πλοῦτος/ ὄλβος: cf. Call. *Hymn* 1.94ff. and *IG* XII 3.421 (quoted by Fraser II p. 351 n. 141). *Aet.* Fr. 1.23f. (Pf.) which is echoed in later programmatic poetry (cf. Wimmel, *Kallimachos* Stichwortindex *s.v.* Opfervergleich) may also be relevant. See below, p. 21.

[87] See Gow–Page, *HE* II pp. 307f.

[88] *Id.* 16 is almost certainly earlier. On its date see Gow, introd. to *Id.* 16; on that of the *Aetia* and its prologue cf. Fraser I pp. 719ff.

critus firmly within a Hellenistic manifesto framework.[89] There are also a number of programmatic references to *paupertas* in Propertius 2.10.23f.; 2.13.21ff., where luxurious substances are anti-Callimachean symbols;[90] and 3.23, where, in a similar manifesto, the cheapness of Propertius' wood and wax writing tablets is a Callimachean symbol in contrast to gold, which symbolises anti-Callimachean poetry.[91] Except for the occasional deliberate lapse which gains its effect from its paradoxical quality,[92] Tibullus maintains his espousal of *paupertas* throughout his work; and its prominence in 1.1 is a sign of its importance as a programmatic theme.

Simplicity and smallness as Hellenistic poetic themes are almost too well known to require illustration.[93] In Tibullus they generally accompany and complement the themes of the countryside, piety and poverty. In 1.1 Tibullus' life in the country is simple in every respect: thus it accords with Hellenistic contempt for the inflated and pompous in literature.[94] Smallness is emphasised frequently: Tibullus' farm, his flock, his harvest and his sacrifice are all declared to be small.[95] The small sacrifice is itself such a well-established Hellenistic topos as to be a programmatic element even in isolation.[96] At some point the topos was doubtless introduced as a telling variant on the θύος πάχιστον (very fat sacrificial beast) of *Aetia* Fr. 1.23 (Pf.); but it then clearly developed a life of its own.

A final important area of learned subject-matter in Hellenistic poetry and in Tibullus is love. A surprisingly large number of surviving Hellenistic poems and fragments deal with love or with erotic legends and many more treatments are known from synopses.[97] The single main source of information on this matter is the Greek writer Parthenius, a contemporary and literary associate of the Roman elegist Cornelius Gallus. He dedicated to Gallus the *Erotika Pathemata*, which still survives, a handbook of interestingly obscure legends, most of which are variants of better known ones. One of the professed motives of the collection was that Gallus might be able to use the most suitable stories in his poetry. All the legends summarised are erotic, as the title of the work shows, and in each case Parthenius notes which Hellenistic writer or writers treated the story. It is clear from these and other love-stories known to have been told by Hellenistic writers that their erotic interests were highly sophisticated. The stories

[89] On *Id.* 16 see further below, pp. 159f.
[90] Cf. L. P. Wilkinson, 'The continuity of Propertius ii.13', *CR* N.S. 16 (1966) 141ff.
[91] Cf. *GC* pp. 76ff.
[92] See below, pp. 154f.; pp. 209ff.
[93] See above, nn. 22 and 85; Puelma Piwonka pp. 116ff. and Sachregister *s.vv.* Kleindichtung etc.; *inflatum*; *tumidum*; *turgidum*; Wimmel, *Kallimachos* Stichwortindex *s.v.* Opfervergleich; Kambylis pp. 98, 144ff.
[94] See above, n. 93.
[95] *Farm*, 22; *flock*, 33; *harvest*, 43; *sacrifice*, 22.
[96] See Wimmel, *Kallimachos* p. 299; Stichwortindex *s.v.* Opfervergleich; and (specifically on Tib. 1.1) p. 271 n. 1.
[97] Cf. Powell *passim*; Gow–Page, *HE passim*; Kroll pp. 315ff. and Sachregister *s.v.* Erotik; Puelma Piwonka Sachregister *s.v.* Erotik etc.; and see below, n. 99.

were not just 'boy meets girl' or 'man meets boy' situations. Usually some barrier was interposed between the lovers. This barrier could be hostility between the lovers' families or cities, or social differences, or a powerful rival, or consanguinity, or jealousy, or the fact that one party was married or about to be married to someone else. Frustrated or stolen love was therefore the writers' main concern.

Homosexual love, already an archaic theme, again became popular with Hellenistic writers. Their attitude to it is less relaxed than that of the archaic poets. Homosexuality, as represented in archaic literature, is an upper-class phenomenon. In the Hellenistic period homosexuality has become bourgeois; and it may be for this reason that it became a subject of moralising discussion early in the fourth century.[98] Some Hellenistic poets, particularly Phanocles, seem almost to have been propagandising on behalf of pederasty,[99] possibly as a counter to growing disapproval of the social spread of homosexuality. For Hellenistic poets the fascination of homosexual love as a subject was partly that it interlocked with another ancient erotic interest – in the different reactions of men and women to the experience of falling in love.[100]

The typical Hellenistic expository manner (see below, Chapter 5) allowed writers dealing with love to concentrate on exhaustive descriptions of the psychological phenomena connected with all love-affairs both heterosexual and homosexual – the lovers' hopes, joys, fears, despairs and doubts. Emotions are more likely to be prominently described – both in love-stories and others – if they contain an element of oddity, grotesquerie and *faux naïveté*. Frequently the love-affair ended in death for the lovers. A dramatic and unreal tone pervaded many renderings of erotic legends. In

[98] The main source of this discussion is Plato (*Symposium*; *Phaedrus*; *Lysis*) although it also features in Xen. *Symp.* 4.15ff.; 8.7ff. For later poetic reflections of such discussions cf. *AP* 5.19 (Rufinus); *AP* 5.65 (Anon.); *AP* 5.116 (Marcus Argentarius); *AP* 5.208 (Meleager); *AP* 5.277 (Eratosthenes Scholasticus); *AP* 5.278 (Agathias Scholasticus); *AP* 10.68 (Agathias); *AP* 12.7 (Straton); *AP* 12.17 ((?) Asclepiades); *AP* 12.41 (Meleager); *AP* 12.86 (Meleager); *AP* 12.90 (Anon.); *AP* 12.245 (Straton). Later prose reflections include Plutarch, *Erotikos*; [Lucian], *Erotes*; Achilles Tatius 2.35ff. K. J. Dover, *Greek Popular Morality in the Time of Plato and Aristotle* (Oxford 1974) pp. 210, 213ff. gives an account of Greek homosexuality which is a valuable corrective to most assumptions made about it and which stresses the comparative lack of moral stigma upon homosexuality up to the end of the fifth century. Dover notes (pp. 205ff.) the increase of sexual inhibition through the classical period.
[99] Cf. also Alexander Aetolus Fr. 5.4f. (Powell) where the poet seems, by asserting that Mimnermus wrote homosexual love-poetry, to be claiming him as a precedent and Gow–Page, *HE* I ll. 988ff. = *AP* 12.17 ((?) Asclepiades). On homosexuality in Callimachus and the 'neoterics' cf. Puelma Piwonka pp. 248ff.; Fraser III General Index *s.v.* Callimachus of Cyrene (ii) homosexuality. On the process of transforming heterosexual legends into homosexual ones cf. R. Beyer, *Fabulae Graecae quatenus quave aetate puerorum amore commutatae sint* (Diss. Leipzig 1910).
[100] Cf. Virg. *Ecl.* 8; Hor. *Od.* 3.12; Ov. *Her.* 19.7ff.; *AP* 5.297 (Agathias); (in more general terms) Eur. *Med.* 230ff. and F. Cairns, 'Horace on other people's love affairs (*Odes* I 27; II 4; I 8; III 12)', *Quad. Urbin.* 24 (1977) 121ff. esp. 141.

addition to their love-stories, Hellenistic poets produced many erotic epigrams and some other larger scale but non-elegiac erotic poems in which the poet, in his own *persona* or in another, speaks in the first person.[101] The experiences and emotions described in these poems are not autobiographical; but they have literary reality. The poetic *persona* found in them is that of a man in love. He is not an ordinary person, in the sense of a man in the street, but a member of the leisured upper middle class of the period, educated, cultured and sensitive to the emotional stimuli of love for, and affairs with, high-class prostitutes and boys. The great emphasis placed on love by Hellenistic writers is not in itself an explanation of the existence of 'subjective' Roman elegy. But it does help to justify the claims made by Roman elegists to literary descent from Hellenistic predecessors (see below, Chapter 9).

Tibullus is clearly working within this tradition of Hellenistic erotic composition. He employs both heterosexual and homosexual material and he creates out of it complex and unusual situations. Tibullus 1.8 and 1.9 may be mentioned particularly in this context (see below, Chapter 6). In his first elegy Tibullus emphasises his status as a lover in a paradoxical way. The paradox does not lie in the combination of the erotic and rustic in itself. This is found in Hellenistic poetry, notably in Theocritus, and was probably found in Philetas also.[102] But in 1.1 Tibullus is not just a rustic but a working farmer. In the rhetorical tradition which lies behind Tibullus 1.1 the farmer is characterised specifically as a non-lover; so when Tibullus reveals that he is a lover, this is a startling piece of information for the reader.[103] Tibullus is thus underlining sharply this aspect of his personality; and he is doing so for the programmatic reason that much of his subject-matter in Book 1 is his love for Delia and for Marathus. Tibullus' lover character is the more startling, since by alluding to the *exclusus amator* topos (55f.) he suggests an urban rather than a country context, particularly after the reference to Messalla's house (54). The paradoxical context of Tibullus' programmatic declaration for love may fulfil another typical Hellenistic literary aspiration, originality.[104] Certainly Tibullus is consistently original in his combinations and modifications of the standard topoi which he inherited from the Hellenistic world.

For Hellenistic poets love was, as has been noted, an important means whereby they could indulge their interest in psychology and particularly

---

[101] Non-epigrammatic examples are: Call. *Iamb.* 3; 4; 5 (Pf.); Theocr. *Id.* 12; 29; 30.
[102] It is infrequent in epigrams, probably because of their brief compass. But cf. e.g. *AP* 9.437 (Theocritus); *AP* 12.102 (Callimachus). The erotic lyric fragment of Lycophronides, where the speaker is a goatherd, also combines the two themes (Bergk, *PLG* iii Fr. 2, p. 633). Further on the erotic-bucolic combination cf. M. C. Mittelstadt, 'Bucolic-lyric motifs and dramatic narrative in Longus' Daphnis and Chloe', *RhM* N.F. 113 (1970) 211ff., esp. 213ff.
[103] See F. Cairns, 'Horace, *Epode* 2, Tibullus I,1 and rhetorical praise of the countryside', *Mus. Phil. Lond.* 1 (1975) 79ff.
[104] See above, n. 38.

in the basic emotions of humanity. This interest more than compensated for other drier aspects of Hellenistic learning and it led to innovations in the portrayal of character. Hellenistic characterisation works by concentrating on the internal man, whereas earlier literature looked primarily to the external man. The action consequent upon an emotion was what was important to most earlier Greek writers; and the emotion itself was a necessary stimulus to and prerequisite of action. For Hellenistic writers the emotion itself is the more interesting phenomenon and the action often not as important. Theocritus, *Idyll* 13, the story of Heracles' loss of his beloved Hylas to the nymphs of a spring, exemplifies this principle well. The incidents described in the poem are few and Theocritus does not linger over their description: the landing of the *Argo* with its crew of heroes in the Propontis; the capture of Hylas by the Nymphs; the departure of the *Argo* without Heracles. The real highlights are the passages with emotional content or effect: the love of Heracles for Hylas (5–15); the depiction of the pool and the nymphs (39–45); Heracles' miserable search for Hylas (55–67).

In the Roman elegists this principle is carried even further. Many Roman elegies have no narrative basis whatsoever. They are discourses where the incidents are mental events and where the main purpose of a poem may be to depict a complex and unusual emotional condition. Tibullus is a master of this art, and his first elegy vividly represents a gamut of emotions: serene content with a way of life, pious reverence for the gods, sentimental nostalgia for an ideal past, quiet enjoyment of the pleasures of love, horror of war and finally a piquant combination of anticipation of death and eager acceptance of the pleasures of youth.

Tibullus' espousal of simplicity, poverty and love in 1.1 involves a rejection of wealth and war. Hellenistic poets do not always reject war. Hostility to it does appear in the Hellenistic stereotype of the *miles gloriosus*, but both Menander[105] and Theocritus[106] are able to represent war and soldiers in a more favourable way.[107] Tibullus' rejection of war in 1.1 is therefore not a simple programmatic element but a complex matter which will be discussed again below (pp. 33f.). In literary terms it is of course related to rejection of epic, the main theme of which is war; and in thus implicitly rejecting epic Tibullus 1.1 resembles many other Hellenistic programmatic poems from *Aetia* Fr. 1 (Pf.) on. The injunction '*vos signa tubaeque | ite procul*' (75f.) is an example of the topos which began with the ἔλλετε etc. of *Aetia* Fr. 1.17 (Pf.),[108] just as the sea voyages rejected in lines

[105] Cf. T. B. L. Webster, *Studies in Menander* (Publications of the University of Manchester 309, Classical series 7, 2nd ed. Manchester 1960) index *s.v.* soldier.
[106] Cf. *Id.* 14.55ff.; 16.73ff.; 17.86ff.
[107] See further on Hellenistic literary attitudes to war G. Giangrande, 'Das Epyllion Catulls im Lichte der hellenistischen Epik', *Ant. Class.* 41 (1972) 123ff.
[108] See Wimmel, *Kallimachos* p. 100 n. 3 and Stichwortindex *s.v.* Wegstoss-Gebärde.

49ff. are another Hellenistic symbol of epic composition.[109] Tibullus' *persona* also contributes to this trend: Tibullus, being unwarlike, is by implication unable as well as unwilling to write an epic, with its standard subject-matter of *reges et proelia*. However, Tibullus' pronouncements about war must be seen in an additional light when questions are raised about his relationship to Messalla and his verdict on the campaigns of the Augustan period (see below, pp. 33ff.).

A clue to how some of these themes, of the countryside, poetry, piety, simplicity and love, interlocked in wider terms in Hellenistic poetry, and also to Tibullus' place in the Hellenistic tradition may be given by three passages of the late Greek novel *Daphnis and Chloe* by Longus. One of the characters in this novel is an old herdsman called Philetas. Many aspects of this character, as he is presented by Longus, suggest that he is based on the Hellenistic poet Philetas,[110] who may from two other independent pieces of evidence be regarded as having written bucolic poetry.[111] If Longus' Philetas reflects the poet, then it might not be too rash to see in the descriptions and discourses of the herdsman Philetas reminiscences of the bucolic poetry of the poet Philetas.[112] The herdsman is described as garbed in rustic gear and he introduces himself with the words:

'Φιλητᾶς, ὦ παῖδες, ὁ πρεσβύτης[113] ἐγώ, ὅς πολλὰ μὲν ταῖσδε ταῖς Νύμφαις ᾖσα, πολλὰ δὲ τῷ Πανὶ ἐκείνῳ ἐσύρισα, βοῶν δὲ πολλῆς ἀγέλης ἡγησάμην μόνῃ μουσικῇ. ἥκω δὲ ὑμῖν ὅσα εἶδον μηνύσων, ὅσα ἤκουσα ἀπαγγελῶν.' (2.3)

'*I, children, am old Philetas, who have sung many a song to these nymphs and piped many a tune to Pan there; and I have led many a herd of cattle by the power of my music alone. I have come to reveal to you the things I have seen and to tell to you the things I have heard.*'

These words, which have the appearance of double significance, are fol-

[109] Wimmel, *Kallimachos* pp. 222ff.; F. Cairns, *CQ* N.S. 21 (1971) 204ff., esp. 206ff.
[110] The suggestion of a link goes back to the nineteenth century. Cf. Legrand, *Étude sur Théocrite* pp. 155ff. and the works cited by him; *R-E* s.v. Bukolik p. 1007; R. Herzog, 'Der Traum des Herondas', *Philol* 79 (1924) 413; J. Hubaux, 'Le dieu Amour chez Properce et chez Longus', *Acad. Roy. de Belgie, Bulletin de la classe des Lettres et des Sciences morales et politiques* 5 sér., 39 (1953) 263ff. The identification is also accepted by W. E. McCulloh, *Longus* (New York 1970) p. 94. But these are merely comments made in passing and there seems to be no extended analysis of the implications of identifying the two. See also below, n. 112.
[111] Theocr. *Id.* 7. 37ff. esp. 40; Antig. Caryst. *Histor. Mirab.* 19 (23) (ed. Keller). A modern attempt to identify a fragmentary Hellenistic bucolic hexameter poem as Philetan is rejected as lacking 'any positive foundation' by Fraser II p. 792 n. 21.
[112] On traces of Philetan material in Longus see also Mittelstadt, *RhM* N.F. 113 (1970) 211ff., esp. 214. However Mittelstadt believes that most of Longus' pastoral material comes from Theocritus.
[113] The self-identification of Philetas as an 'old man' is doubly interesting in view of the shared concern of Mimnermus and Tibullus about old age and K. F. Smith's description of Tibullus – see above, p. 2. See also above, p. 12 and n. 53 and below pp. 60f.

lowed by a description of Philetas' garden and his encounter there with the boy Eros. The depiction of the garden and of Love is ornate and involves many poetic commonplaces.[114] Particularly significant is the account of Eros' care and affection for Philetas which ends in the statement: καὶ χαῖρε μόνος ἀνθρώπων ἐν γνήρᾳ θεασάμενος τοῦτο τὸ παιδίον (and rejoice, since you are the only man who in his old age has seen this boy) (2.5 ad fin.). This is reminiscent of *Aetia* Fr. 1.37f. (Pf.): . . . Μοῦσαι γὰρ ὅσους ἴδον ὄθμᾳτι παῖδας | μὴ λοξῷ, πολιοὺς οὐκ ἀπέθεντο φίλους. (For those whom the Muses have looked on as children with kindly eye, these they do not cast aside in their old age since they are their friends). It is followed by an exercise of prophetic power on the part of Philetas, when he makes a prediction about the love of Daphnis and Chloe (2.6 ad fin.). The two topoi together suggest that Longus is here harking back to a Philetan poetic confrontation with the god Eros. If so, the meeting was one of those encounters between the poet and his inspiring deity, who is usually Apollo or the Muses, but is sometimes another god, which are standard in Hellenistic manifesto poetry. Another such encounter with Eros/Amor as the inspiring deity takes place in Ovid, *Amores* 1.1, an unmistakably Hellenistic, if also parodic, version of this type of literary programme.

The mixture of erotic and rustic themes in this passage is pronounced: and Philetas goes on in the next chapter to answer the questions 'What is Love?' and 'What are his powers?' Philetas describes Love as a cosmic force;[115] and then he gives an account of his own early experience of falling in love with Amaryllis. Nothing, he found, could cure this except actually making love. The erotodidactic commonplace[116] with which this chapter ends:

> Ἔρωτος γὰρ οὐδὲν φάρμακον, οὐ πινόμενον, οὐκ ἐσθιόμενον, οὐκ ἐν ᾠδαῖς λεγόμενον, ὅτι μὴ φίλημα καὶ περιβολὴ καὶ συγκατακλιθῆναι γυμνοῖς σώμασι.   (2.7 ad fin.)
>
> *There is no medicine to cure love, neither one you can drink nor one you can eat nor one you can speak as an incantation, except kissing and embracing and going to bed together naked.*

indicates something which is immediately confirmed at the beginning of the next chapter: Φιλητᾶς μὲν τοσαῦτα παιδεύσας αὐτοὺς ἀπαλλάττεται (When Philetas had given them these instructions he went off) (2.8). Philetas has been acting as *magister amoris* to the two young people.

---

[114] For a recent attempt to investigate the implication of one such commonplace cf. O. Schönberger, 'Spiegelungen eines alten Verses?', *RhM* N.F. 119 (1976) 95f. Schönberger however reconstructs an iambic trimeter, viz: ποικίλον τι χρῆμα κἀθήρατον ἦν.

[115] For this aspect of the novel see H. O. O. Chalk, 'Eros and the Lesbian pastorals of Longus', *JRS* 80 (1960) 32ff.

[116] Cf. in particular Theocr. *Id.* 11.1ff. and Gow *ad loc.* Theocritus' line may thus be an echo of Philetas.

The setting

Philetan bucolic poetry of an erotodidactic character may lie behind this.[117]

This picture of Philetas is amplified in *Daphnis and Chloe* 2.32ff., where Philetas turns up with his son Tityrus at a rustic feast, bringing garlands and grapes for Pan. Philetas boasts that in his youth he was second only to Pan in piping. Daphnis and Chloe ask him for a display of his skill. Eventually, after an interval, Philetas plays pastoral music and Dionysiac music for the wine harvest (2.35f.). At 2.34 there is a description of the Pan-pipes which suggests that Philetas introduced this topos into Hellenistic poetry.[118] In addition we were told at 2.15 that Philetas had acted as judge in a contest. This was not a bucolic song-contest, but an informal court case. However the incident may allude to the bucolic musical ἀγών (contest).

The links which bind the Longan Philetas to the *persona* of the farmer/herdsman/*magister amoris* Tibullus are too clear to need spelling out in detail. Tibullus is more *agricola* than *pastor* because the nature of the Latian countryside and the Roman ideal of the farmer involve mixed and arable farming whereas the bucolic tradition was set in a pastoral landscape, whether it was Sicily or Arcadia.

At this point it may be useful to ask two questions: what claims of Hellenistic manifesto poetry are not obviously reflected in Tibullus, and in Tibullus 1.1 in particular; and what elements found in Tibullus and prefigured in Tibullus 1.1 are not part of the Hellenistic manifesto. The first Hellenistic claim absent from Tibullus is to authority. Callimachus, for example, claimed that his work contained nothing unattested (Fr. 612 (Pf.)). Elsewhere he annotated his material with a reference to his learned source (*Aetia* Fr. 75.53ff.).[119] The earlier and later parallels for this type of claim, particularly the omnipresent *ferunt* etc.[120] of Hellenistic poetry, make it virtually certain that other Greek Hellenistic writers also asserted it. Tibullus does not assert authority for his statements in 1.1.

Callimachus also claimed an elite audience, a concept which matches the special personal status that was already a commonplace factor in the self-portrait of an early Greek poet. Callimachus took the pure path, was set apart from the majority, and spoke only to a select few.[121] Again the frequency with which such concepts recur in later poetry[122] makes it a

---

[117] Theocr. *Id.* 11 would then be imitating this Philetan type. See above, n. 116.
[118] For a list of parallels see Smith on Tib. 2.5.31–2. It is interesting that τοὺς καλάμους κηρῷ συνδήσας (Longus 2.34) is particularly close to *calamus cera iungitur* (Tib. 2.5.32) and *calamos cera coniungere* (Virg. *Ecl.* 2.32).
[119] Cf. also *Hymn* 5.56 and Wimmel, *Kallimachos* pp. 6 n. 3, 98. Call. *Hymn* 1.65 (ψευδοίμην ἀίοντος ἅ κεν πεπίθοιεν ἀκουήν) is not a counter-example. It is 'ironic' (McLennan *ad loc.*) and can be paraphrased 'If I were to compose fiction (which I do not), it would at least be convincing.'
[120] Cf. Newman p. 46.
[121] Cf. *Epp.* 7.1; 28 (Pf.); *Aet.* Fr. 1.25ff. (Pf.); *Hym.* 2.110ff. (Pf.).
[122] Cf. Kroll pp. 117ff.; Puelma Piwonka pp. 120ff.; Wimmel, *Kallimachos* Stellenindex under *locc. citt.* above, n. 121.

near-certainty that Callimachus was not the only Hellenistic poet to put forward such claims. Learned Hellenistic poetry was inevitably accessible only to a highly educated minority among contemporary readers. Mere literacy was no longer enough; and this restriction of audience could easily become a matter for boasting. The historical situation as regards the audience for poetry was of course the same at Rome, which was in many respects another Hellenistic city, and this is one reason why similar boasts are found in Roman poets. But Tibullus does not claim an elite audience.

Now it is possible that Tibullus' audience understood him to be making both these claims by implication. He is narrating what he asserts are his own personal experiences, and autopsy may be functioning here as a guarantee of truth and thus as an alternative for the naming of a learned source.[123] Again Tibullus' dedication of his book in 1.1 to Messalla, a known purist who is included in an elite literary audience by Horace (*Satires* 1.10.81ff.), may imply a claim to such an audience. But the absence of explicit claims in these areas must be significant. It ties in with other characteristics of Tibullus' work; and it may well be that Tibullan elegy, with its large bucolic/rustic element, is the spiritual descendant of an area of Hellenistic poetry in which such boasts were felt to be out of keeping with the subject-matter.

This suggestion may be confirmed by the lack of showy literary learning in the prologue elegy already noted (above, p. 12) and by the ambivalent use in Tibullus 1.1 of the concept of *labor*. This was a standard element of the Hellenistic manifesto,[124] the point being that the polished quality of Hellenistic writing could only be achieved by much toil. Tibullus doubtless subscribed to this notion, but he goes out of his way to declare his life *iners* in 1.1.5. This self-description is of course related to his erotic *persona*, and specifically it reinforces the paradoxical conjunction he makes in 1.1 of his twin roles of lover and farmer within the rhetorical context of the standard progymnasmata dealing with the countryside. The farmer was traditionally hardworking. Tibullus in 1.1 quite deliberately attributes *labor adsiduus* not to himself but to his antithesis, the soldier (3).

This, as has been explained above (p. 20), is partly in order to exploit etymologies of *adsiduus* which suggest the sense of 'rich' and which at the same time associate it with soldiering. Thus Tibullus achieves a neat antithesis between the *adsiduus labor* of 3 and the *adsiduo igne* at 6. But it is also partly to confirm the obliqueness of some of Tibullus' other claims to Hellenistic ideals. It is not that Tibullus does not seek in his poetry *elegantia*, the product of *labor*. He manifestly does so and the steady work-routine of his farmer *persona* as described in lines 7–44 may symbol-

[123] Note the oblique but strong emphasis on autopsy at Tib. 1.7.9ff. and see *GC* p. 168 and nn. 14f.
[124] See above, nn. 20 and 24.

The setting

ise a less obvious but just as effective type of πόνος as the *labor adsiduus* of the soldier. If this is so, then Tibullus may not only be contrasting the steady toil of the rustic/erotic elegist with the great labours of the epic poet; he may also be partially denying that he is writing Hellenistic poetry of a Callimachean type involving obvious *labor*, and asserting his identity as a Hellenistic poet of a more covertly bookish and more ostentatiously bucolic type.

Of the features not found in Hellenistic poetry but present in Tibullus, the first is the very scope of the erotic *persona* which he adopts. The processes of poetic scholarship in the Hellenistic and Augustan period seem to have been analogous, involving in both cases the use by poets of literary and of non-literary sources; and the appearance of libraries at opportune points in both periods is obviously an important factor. But because the Roman poets could draw on the wide range of Hellenistic literature in a way that Hellenistic poets could not, the Romans seem to have achieved in elegy a much more sophisticated and complete portrayal of the *persona* of the lover than Hellenistic literature achieved in any one form. The exact history and development of Roman elegy are still matters for dispute (see below, Chapter 9). But it is clear that Roman elegy drew on a great variety of sources, New Comedy, rhetoric, several types of hexameter poetry, epigram, iambic and lyric poetry, both archaic and Hellenistic, and perhaps also lost novels and letters, as well as Hellenistic elegy, in order to create its poetic universe. The result transcends anything which survives or can be conjectured to have existed on the Greek side. Each one of the Roman elegists, for all his brief compass, is as full and varied and subtle in incident, character and emotion, as the whole large corpus of Greek 'personal' literature, including the work of the later novelists and erotic epistolographers; and it is this richness which goes far to make Roman elegy one of the great literary achievements of Latin culture.

The second factor found in Tibullus, and also Propertius, but absent from Hellenistic literature, is a concern with public morality.[125] Ancient literature has a varied history in this respect. The Homeric epics were designed to be morally and socially educational, both in the public and in the private sphere.[126] The patterns of behaviour attributed to the Homeric characters and their results were intended to indicate to the young what was acceptable and unacceptable moral and social behaviour. In most cases the lessons were subtle and the hearer had to draw them for himself. But sometimes moral intentions expressed themselves in direct precept. In the *Iliad*, which concentrates for the most part on public morality, the exhortation which most clearly sums up Homer's moral teaching is the twice

---

[125] Kroll Ch. 4 deals with a related subject, the moral interpretation of ancient literature.
[126] The *locus classicus* on this topic is Xen. *Symp.* 3.5 cf. 4.6ff.

repeated dictum: αἰὲν ἀριστεύειν καὶ ὑπείροχον ἔμμεναι ἄλλων (always to excel and to be superior to the rest) (*Iliad* 6.208; 11.783). Such excellence was further specified in the skills Phoenix was enjoined by Peleus to teach the young Achilles: μύθων τε ῥητῆρ' ἔμεναι πρηκτῆρά τε ἔργων (to be a maker of speeches and a doer of deeds) (*Iliad* 9.443), which amount to the substance of public virtue for Homeric man – political and military distinction.

The *Odyssey* concentrated on private morality, ranging from ethics to etiquette. Telemachus' adventures were meant as a model of how an adolescent learnt to behave in the adult world of high society and to conduct himself in other people's houses. On the negative side the suitors and the Cyclops were patterns of bad social behaviour. On another level the domestic virtues, Homeric style, were demonstrated by the attitudes and conduct of Penelope and Odysseus; and there are explicit sermons like the attack on drunkenness (*Odyssey* 21.293ff.) and the diatribe on obsessive eating (*Odyssey* 7.216ff.).

The value of epic material as a means of universal moral and social instruction in the archaic period is seen again in the 'private' lyric poems. There epic myths helped to integrate the individual addressee's circumstances with an easily understood social background; and they brought out the general implications of what at first may have seemed only to be the concern of one or two individuals.[127]

When there was a conflict in the epic tradition between private interests and public morality the epic poet was in no doubt where right lay. An example of this is the Homeric Paris who upheld his own private concerns to the detriment of his city. Homer constantly opposes the two interests and leaves his audience in no doubt that Paris' choice is evil and will be the cause of his people's destruction. Similarly the arrogance of Agamemnon and the wrath of Achilles run counter to the best interests of all the Greeks and they must both be removed before the Greek army can achieve its purpose before Troy. Such literary attitudes prevailed throughout the archaic and classical periods and they were particularly stressed in fifth-century Athens, when poetry was often explicitly political.

However the Hellenistic moral emphasis is much more in the private sphere; and the private interests of individuals have little connection with the public interest. Callimachus *Aetia* Frr. 80ff. (Pf.), the story of Phrygius and Pieria, which at first sight might seem to be a counter-example, in fact underlines this point in a particularly neat and telling way. Two cities in Asia Minor, Miletus and Myous, have been at war for a long time. All efforts to end the war have failed; but the women of Myous are allowed to go under truce to a religious festival in Miletus. Phrygius, the king of Miletus, sees and falls in love with a girl of Myous called Pieria, who has

[127] Cf. J. G. Howie, 'Sappho *Fr.* 16 (LP): self-consolation and encomium', *PLLS 1976* pp. 207ff.

come to this festival. They go to bed and then Phrygius asks Pieria what she wants in return for her love. She asks for none of the luxuries she might have demanded, but only that she and her kinsfolk can come to Miletus in safety whenever they wish. The king realises that she is asking for peace between their two cities, and peace is made.

The crucial point in the story as told by Callimachus is that the public and political effects of Phrygius' and Pieria's affair are almost an afterthought; they are not an integral and essential factor in the central portion of the narrative. The poet concentrates rather on the lovers' emotional attachment and its fruition. Phrygius' political decision simply follows as a subsidiary consequence of his private affair with Pieria. In the emotional world of Callimachus individuals take precedence over state matters.

A similar view emerges from the account of Pollux in Theocritus, *Idyll* 22. He and his brother Castor come to the land of the Bebrykes and there Pollux fights and defeats Amycus, king of the Bebrykes. The fight is preceded by a dialogue between Pollux and Amycus (54ff.) which has a morally instructive function, but exclusively in the private sphere. Amycus is bullying, boorish and aggressive to Pollux. These faults are intensified in Greek eyes because Pollux is a stranger and therefore under the direct protection of Zeus. Amycus actually insults Pollux on the ground that he is a stranger; he refuses him the basic human necessity, water; finally, he challenges him to fight – and not for a prize like civilised men, but for liberty. In the dialogue between Amycus and himself, Pollux is a model of the Hellenistic social virtues. He is polite and deferential. He declares his peaceable intentions and offers to enter into terms of friendship with Amycus. Finally he expresses willingness to pay for water and wants to limit the fight between the two in a civilised way. As well as being a preparation for Pollux's well-deserved victory and self-restraint in victory, Pollux's behaviour is a pattern of decent social conduct. But apart from the general distinction between barbarian and Greek, there is no political content. Although leaders, the pair are treated in the *Idyll* as individuals and not as representatives of their peoples.

It is this interest in individuals which leads Hellenistic poets to emphasise the portrayal of ordinary people, such as the herdsmen of many Theocritean Idylls, the haymakers of *Idyll* 10, the fishermen of *Idyll* 21, Callimachus' Hecale, and the urban intelligentsia and demi-monde of the epigrammatists. It is not that these portrayals are realistic: Theocritus' pastoral Idylls do contain some genuine elements drawn from rustic life;[128] but the literary moulds in which many of the pastoral Idylls are cast have transformed and subordinated these elements in accordance with the tastes of Theocritus' sophisticated audience, so that he is able to bring urban

---

[128] Cf. L. E. Rossi, 'Mondo pastorale e poesia bucolica di maniera: l'Idillio Ottavo del Corpus Teocriteo', *Stud. Ital. di Fil. Class.* 43 (1971) 5ff.

sensibilities into rural settings.¹²⁹ The same applies to other cases of 'realistic' representation of ordinary people in Hellenistic poetry. Like comparable portrayals in Hellenistic art, they are completely romanticised. The Hellenistic age was just as concerned with 'kings and heroes' as any other. But the specifically Hellenistic factor in all these portrayals is the interest in individuals: even when kings and heroes are treated, their private lives are the main focus of interest. The theme of conflict between a man's private life and the public good seems to be avoided. Consonant with this interest in individuals was a Hellenistic view of the function of poetry which may have been shared by Callimachus. This contradicted the usual ancient attitude, and was that poetry was meant to entertain and not to instruct.¹³⁰ The didacticism of Hellenistic poetry was academic and intellectual rather than moral and political, and its interest in human behaviour was primarily in the private sphere. All this reflects the political impotence of the average Hellenistic writer both as a writer and as a man.

Rome was much more important politically than any single Hellenistic kingdom and in spite of the power of leading politicians throughout the first century BC Augustan poets did not regard themselves as politically powerless. It is clear for example that Tibullus and Propertius felt themselves to be citizens, not subjects, of a powerful city, and men who could, if they had wished, have had an active political career. Although in retrospect they can be seen to have lived in Imperial Rome, in their own day they could still believe that they were living in the Republic. The deep indifference to political life and concern only with the personal which is manifest earlier in Greek Hellenistic literature and which in the next decade reappears in Ovid is not present in Propertius and Tibullus. This is not to say that they return to an archaic and classical view of man as primarily a political animal, whose private interests, when they conflict with the public interest, are automatically wrong. Nor is poetry at Rome at all political in the sense that poetry was in fifth-century Athens. It is instead encomiastic and moral and related closely to individual patronage. But the patrons of Augustan Rome wanted poetry written by Roman citizens within a context of civic involvement, whereas all the influence of the Hellenistic models being followed by the poets and of current philosophical attitudes was pulling them in the direction of writing as passive subjects totally dependent on the ruler. It is this dichotomy which brings individual interests into direct conflict with political morality in Augustan poetry. The context is one in which it is no longer assumed, as it was in classical and older Greek literature, that the interests of the state must always take precedence.

This is a situation which provides much of the interest of Roman elegy

---

¹²⁹ E.g. *Id.* 3 with Gow *introd.*; *Id.* 6 with *GC* pp. 194f.; *Id.* 10 with Cairns, *Hermes* 98 (1970) 38ff.; *Id.* 11 and *GC* pp. 144ff.; *Id.* 14 and *GC* pp. 171ff.
¹³⁰ See Fraser I pp. 527 and n. 56, 541 and n. 171, 548 and esp. 759ff.

The setting

for modern readers, since Roman elegy can be seen, to some extent correctly, in terms of a constant assertion of the rights of the individual against the pressures of society and the state. The elegists were aware of the importance both of private life and of public morality. They looked back to both the pre-Hellenistic and the Hellenistic stances, and, accepting neither, made their own moral synthesis. It is true of course in one sense that their choice of the life of the elegiac lover puts them firmly on the Hellenistic side as individuals aspiring to live their own private lives in preference to serving the state. But their constant awareness of the two possibilities gives great ethical value to their work. To begin with, they develop an interesting approach to the personal morality of love and the love-affair, which for them becomes a substitute for and antithesis to public morality.[131] The love-poet is *segnis*, *iners*, *nequam* and a *servus amoris*, and in this sense he is from a practical and public point of view a helpless negative *exemplum*. But he is also a teacher of love and his own love-affair is exemplary and helpful to other lovers. Moreover in his love life he exhibits the virtues of fidelity and hard work and, in a paradoxical sense, he can thus claim equality with the *dux milesque bonus* (Tibullus 1.1.75). Secondly, the elegists' grasp of the nature and demands of a public ethic, its effect on the individual personality, and, most strange of all, its necessity and rightness for the citizens of the city ruling the world, is firm and instinctive – and all the more so for the many inevitable and teasing paradoxes which these insights generate.

The implications of the Roman elegists' grasp of the antithesis between public morality and private interest can be seen in Tibullus' attitudes to his patron in 1.1, attitudes which are again programmatic. 1.1. is a synkrisis, a comparison, between his own life and that of his patron, the contemporary general M. Valerius Messalla Corvinus.[132] His own 'life' is described as that of a peaceful countryman who does not wish to be a soldier, and Messalla's life is that of a soldier. In Roman elegy the *persona* of the elegist is usually that of a non-soldier. This does not of course mean that Roman elegists deny their patrons praise for military achievements. On the contrary, they exploit their own professed unsuitability for war as a guarantee that the praise given to their patrons for their military achievements is truthful.[133] In addition, the praises of peace are a constant implicit reiteration of the achievements of those generals, and notably of Augustus himself, who had established and were preserving this peace by their military victories. Augustus' own words indicate the attitude of the time: *cum per totum imperium populi Romani terra marique esset parta victoriis pax*

---

[131] On this topic, cf. Copley pp. 91ff. esp. 97ff.; G. Lee, *Tibullus: Elegies* (Cambridge 1975) introd. pp. 19ff.

[132] Cf. Cairns, *Mus. Phil. Lond.* 1 (1975) 79ff.

[133] Cf. *GC* pp. 117 (on Prop. 1.6); 185ff. (on Prop. 3.4); 197ff. (on Prop. 3.12) and F. Cairns, 'Propertius on Augustus' marriage law (II, 7)', *Grazer Beiträge* (forthcoming).

(*Res Gestae* 13). Tibullus in 1.1, a poet-farmer in his peaceful fields, knows that it is right for Messalla to practise his military skill (*te bellare decet*, 53). Peace and the farmer in Tibullus 1.1 have the same import as they have in Virgil's *Georgics*, where the poet's wish to eulogise the achievements of the *princeps* is quite explicit. Tibullus' rejection of wealth in 1.1, which is another programmatic element (see above, pp. 20f.) and is associated with his wish to give up war, is qualified in a similar way. Tibullus admits that his own family was once wealthy and he accepts that this was a good thing (19ff., 41ff.). This implies that he is not criticising the present wealth of Messalla. He is choosing to be poor and peaceful himself while admitting that wealth and soldiering are good in themselves, as are those who choose them as a way of life. The *inertia* of his own way of life may even be in part an indirect criticism of his own moral standards, while the *labor* of those who follow another path may, morally speaking, be a credit to them.

Tibullus' rejection of war as a career for himself in 1.1 must therefore be seen as primarily a literary gesture rather than a political stance. This is shown by his assertion in 1.7.9ff. that he had witnessed Messalla's military achievements. Whether this claim is historically true or not – for it too is a literary topos – it places in context Tibullus' stance in 1.1. Another modification of Tibullus' position appears in 1.10, where his decision to go, albeit unwillingly, to war is another literary device apt for the epilogue of a book of elegies. It also compliments his patron Messalla, who is taking him off to war, by complying with his wishes. The relationship of Tibullus to Messalla, that of poet/*cliens* to patron, is worth emphasising here. It not only gives the poet a socially accepted standpoint from which he can praise Messalla without seeming to be a flatterer. It is also, because of its importance in Roman society, a sign of support by the poet for Roman social and political institutions and thus implicitly for the moral values of the society in which he lived.

The portrait of Tibullus in his Hellenistic setting which has emerged so far is a complex one. Many aspects of the Hellenistic manifesto have appeared in his prologue elegy. The absence of others is equally significant, as is the presence in Tibullus of a distinctly Roman consciousness. The Tibullus revealed in his programmatic prologue is thus very far from being a Callimachean stereotype. Nevertheless he remains a Hellenistic poet with significant resemblances to Callimachus and Theocritus among major surviving Hellenistic writers, and possibly also to Philetas.

The examination of programmatic concepts in this chapter has been limited to subject-matter. This does not mean that style is not equally important for the understanding of Tibullus as a Hellenistic poet. Some of the programmatic concepts, the smallness and simplicity themes in particular, relate to *elegantia* and λεπτότης (fineness) (see above, p. 21). The verbal learning mentioned above also has much to do with stylistic aims. However this area, which is in any case more difficult to pin down than subject-matter, will receive extensive treatment in the remainder of this book. Chapters 2–4 will consider Tibullus mainly as a *doctus poeta* and Chapters 5–8, together with some sections of Chapter 4, will deal with the style that makes him a *cultus poeta*. The final chapter will offer a new view of the historico-literary development of Roman elegy and of Tibullus' place in it.

2
IMITATION AS LEARNING

In Chapter 1 an impression began to emerge of Tibullus as a learned poet but one more subtle and less obtrusive in his learning than some of his Greek predecessors. In the present chapter Tibullus' learning will be subjected to closer scrutiny. Two questions will be asked: how much of the wealth of mythographical, rhetorical, philosophical, historical, literary and other learned material found prominently in extant Hellenistic Greek poetry and claimed by Hellenistic poets as one of the chief qualities of their work is imitated by Tibullus? and what use does Tibullus make of it?

As regards the first question, great progress has been made in the past sixty or so years. No scholar could now, as Smith did, believe that Tibullus made no use of 'deep and recondite learning'.[1] Smith's commentary was a landmark in the process of establishing Tibullus as a learned poet, even if he did not fully understand his own achievement. A measure of the change of opinion since his time is the title and contents of the fifth chapter of G. Luck's *The Latin Love Elegy*:[2] 'Alexandrian themes in Tibullus'. Other scholars have contributed useful insights into single elegies;[3] and Bulloch's collection of 'Alexandrian' material in Tibullus is highly instructive.[4] Even if some of the examples he gives are not direct Tibullan reminiscences of a Hellenistic writer but simply Hellenistic topoi, the very fact that Tibullus is full of Hellenistic topoi is of the highest importance.

Not a single elegy of Tibullus could nowadays be regarded as unlearned. 1.1 and 1.10 can be seen to depend on Hellenistic philosophical and rhetorical motifs.[5] 1.2 and 1.5 draw on the komos tradition, which was prominent in the Hellenistic period and which goes back to much earlier antecedents.[6] 2.6 also belongs to the same genre, as will be shown in Chapter 7. Erudite Hellenistic homosexual interest lies behind Tibullus 1.4, 1.8 and 1.9.[7] 1.4, like 1.6, also of course draws on the learned conven-

---

[1] p. 68. See above, pp. 2f. [2] 2nd ed. London 1969.
[3] See below, p. 36 and nn. 5–10.
[4] A. W. Bulloch, 'Tibullus and the Alexandrians', *PCPhS* 199 (1973) 71ff.
[5] F. Jacoby, 'Tibulls erste Elegie', *RhM* 64 (1909) 601ff.; *RhM* 65 (1910) 22ff. = *Kleine philologische Schriften* (Berlin 1961) II pp. 122ff.; F. Cairns, 'Horace, *Epode* 2, Tibullus I,1 and rhetorical praise of the countryside', *Mus. Phil. Lond.* 1 (1975) 79ff.
[6] Cf. Copley pp. 91ff.
[7] Cf. C. M. Dawson, 'An Alexandrian prototype of Marathus?', *AJP* 67 (1946) 1ff.; F. Wilhelm, 'Zu Tibullus (I 4)' in *Satura Viadrina* (Breslau 1896) pp. 48ff.; 'Zu Tibullus I 8 und 9' *Philol.* 60 (1901) 579ff. On the subject matter see above, p. 22 and nn. 98f.

Imitation as learning 37

tions of erotodidaxis.[8] Callimachus' *Hymns* and comparable Hellenistic poems are the starting point for 1.7 and 2.1,[9] while 2.5, as will be shown in Chapter 3, draws heavily on Hellenistic and earlier *ktisis* material. 2.3, like many individual passages of Tibullus, depends on Hellenistic pastoral poetry as well as Hellenistic rhetorical commonplaces about the countryside.[10] 2.2 is an example of the epideictic genre genethliakon;[11] and the epideictic travel genres surface in 1.3,[12] which in addition uses learned Golden Age/Hades themes of great antiquity (see below, pp. 47ff.), as also in 1.10 and 2.3.[13]

Apart from these generic and thematic links with Hellenistic learning, there are, as was noted above, many known allusions to and imitations of Hellenistic topoi or specific passages of Hellenistic poetry in Tibullus. The richness of Tibullus in such learned material is also shown by the fact that it is still possible to make new suggestions and reinforce old ones in this area.

I

At the beginning of 1.4 Tibullus is addressing Priapus:

> quae tua formosos cepit sollertia? certe
>   non tibi barba nitet, non tibi culta coma est;
> nudus et hibernae producis frigora brumae,
>   nudus et aestivi tempora sicca Canis. (3ff.)

Tibullus makes two comments about Priapus: the god is scruffy-bearded and unkempt; and he is naked. The first remark is easy to understand. Tibullus is amazed at Priapus' success with boys because the god lacks the elegant appearance and personal attractiveness which the successful pederast might be expected to possess. But what is the point of mentioning Priapus' nudity? Tibullus is probably referring to Priapus' poverty. The god, because he is naked, has no pockets to keep money in and therefore he is poor. Ovid makes a similar point about Amor:[14]

> et puer est et nudus Amor, sine sordibus annos
>   et nullas vestes, ut sit apertus, habet.

---

[8] Cf. A. L. Wheeler, 'Propertius as Praeceptor Amoris', *CPh* 5 (1910) 28ff.; 'Erotic teaching in Roman elegy and the Greek sources. Part I', *CPh* 5 (1910) 440ff.; '*id*. Part II', *CPh* 6 (1911) 56ff.
[9] On 1.7 see below, pp. 41f. On 2.1 cf. P. Pöstgens, *Tibulls Ambarvalgedicht* (Kieler Arbeiten zur Klassischen Philologie 6, 1940) and below, pp. 126ff.
[10] See below, Chh. 7 and 8.
[11] See GC pp. 112f. and below, p. 204.
[12] See GC pp. 63ff.; 165; and below, pp. 45f.
[13] On 1.10 see GC pp. 45ff.; on 2.3 see below, Ch. 6.
[14] Amor is, in ancient terms, a beloved, while Priapus is a lover. But the witty point is the same.

quid puerum Veneris pretio prostare iubetis?
quo pretium condat, non habet ille sinum.
(*Amores* 1.10.15–18)

The notion that Love is poor is found in Plato, *Symposium* 203c and the concept of Love's nakedness as a sign of his poverty must go back at least to the Hellenistic period. This can be concluded from its appearance in the later epistolographer Philostratus' *Epistle* 7(44) *ad init.*:

Ὅτι πένης εἰμί, ἀτιμότερός σοι δοκῶ· καὶ μὴν καὶ αὐτὸς ὁ Ἔρως γυμνός ἐστι καὶ αἱ Χάριτες καὶ οἱ ἀστέρες.
You think less of me because I am a poor man; and yet Love himself is naked and so are the Graces and the stars.

In Tibullus this commonplace is conjoined with the well-known Hellenistic topos about poverty and lack of success in love, particularly homosexual love.[15] If this explanation is correct Tibullus is marvelling that Priapus is a successful lover of boys, when he is unprepossessing in appearance and a pauper. Allusion to a Hellenistic topos, namely that a naked divinity is inevitably poor, which the reader is expected to recognise, is the means whereby the poet implicitly makes a witty point, which of course links his own condition of 'poverty'[16] with that of his divine adviser, Priapus.

II

A Hellenistic topos which occurs at two places in Tibullus and has not been fully noted is that divine or magical power can help the lover in two ways: either by ridding him of love or by rendering his love successful.[17] In Tibullus 1.4 Priapus first advises Tibullus to shun boys (9–14); but then he goes on (15ff.) to counsel him on how to win them. Similarly at 1.2.59ff. the witch whom Tibullus consulted about his love for Delia undertook to free him from that love. He however asked that his love be returned:

non ego totus abesset amor, sed mutuus esset,
orabam, nec te posse carere velim. (1.2.63ff.)

[15] E.g. Call. *Iamb.* 3 (Pf.); *Ep.* 32 (Pf.); *AP* 12.42 (Dioscorides); *AP* 12.44 (Glaucos); *AP* 12.212 (Straton); G. Giangrande, 'Symposiastic literature and epigram' in *L'Épigramme grecque* (Entretiens sur l'Antiquité classique 14, Vandoeuvres–Genève 1968) pp. 135ff.; on the general theme of poetry versus money cf. Wheeler 'Erotic Teaching II' cited above, n. 8, 65ff. and W. Stroh, *Die römische Liebeselegie als werbende Dichtung* (Amsterdam 1971) Indices I *s.v. carmina-munera* – Topik; on love versus money cf. Smith on Tib. 1.4.61–70; *Anthologia Graeca* ed. H. Beckby (Munich 1958) Namen- und Sachverzeichnis *s.v.* Liebe: Armut u. Liebe; Geld u. Liebe.
[16] Tibullus' *paupertas* – the standard Hellenistic manifesto topos – is programmatically stated at 1.1.5. (See above, Ch. 1 n. 85.) It is thus a standing aspect of his *persona* and therefore in play in this elegy.
[17] Cf. Smith on Tib. 1.2.59–62; Pease on Virg. *Aen.* 4.479; 487 *solvere*.

It is interesting, although not necessarily significant, that this topos, in the form of a prayer by a lover, also occurs in Theocritus, *Epigram* 4,[18] of which the addressee, in the technical sense,[19] is Priapus.

III

At 1.5.38 the concept of wine turning into tears is found: *at dolor in lacrimas verterat omne merum*. Smith declares that this concept is unparalleled; and this seems to be the case. However there are indications that Tibullus is drawing on a traditional association of ideas; and the particular conceit he produces has some of the signs of deriving from a Hellenistic source or at least of having been invented on the model of one. The association of wine and tears is found in Greek literature as early as Homer: φῇ δὲ δακρυπλώειν βεβαρηότα με φρένας οἴνῳ (He says that I am afloat on tears, my mind weighed down with wine) (*Odyssey* 19.122). Cf. Ovid, *Amores* 1.8.111f.: *lacrimosaque vino | lumina*. Vines, like other trees, but more noticeably,[20] 'weep'; and finally wine is referred to as ἀμπέλου . . . δάκρυα (the tears of the vine) at *AP* 11.298.6f. (Anon.). The last source cannot be dated firmly but it is Hellenistic in spirit; and it may be the closest surviving indication of the conceptual background from which Tibullus 1.5.38 derives.

IV

That the notion of the lover going off into the country with his mistress or to be with his mistress (Tibullus 1.1; 1.5; 2.1; 2.3) is Hellenistic is amply clear from Theocritus, *Idyll* 11 (see p. 136). But it may have had wider currency in the Hellenistic period. This is suggested by its appearance in Philostratus, *Epistle* 59 (62) and in Propertius 2.19. There are detailed coincidences between the passage of Philostratus and parts of Tibullus 2.3, which may reveal a common Hellenistic source:[21]

> τί οὖν μέλλω ποιεῖν, ἐὰν ἐξελάσῃς ἐς ἀγρόν, ὡς πέρυσι, καὶ πολλῶν ἡμερῶν τὰς ἐν ἄστει διατριβὰς καταλίπῃς; ἡγοῦμαι ἀναγκαῖον σαφῶς ἀπολωλέναι μηδὲν ἔχοντα ἡδὺ μήτ' ἀκούειν μήθ' ὁρᾶν· ἐγὼ μὲν γὰρ ἕψεσθαί σοι νομίζω τὴν πόλιν ἐξιούσῃ καὶ αὐτοὺς τοὺς ἐν ἄστει θεοὺς ἑλκομένους ὑπὸ τῆς θέας. τί γὰρ ἐνταῦθα μόνοι ποιοῦσιν; εἰ δὲ κἀκεῖνοι κατὰ χώραν μενοῦσιν, ἀλλ' ἔγωγ' οὐκ ἀπολειφθήσομαι τοῦ Ἔρωτος ἐφόλκιον· εἰ δὲ καὶ σκάπτειν δέοι, λήψομαι τὴν δίκελλαν, εἴτε κλᾶν, θεραπεύσω τὰς ἀμπέλους, εἴτ' ἐπάγειν λαχάνοις ὕδωρ, ὁδοποιήσω τὸν δρόμον. τίς γὰρ οὕτω τυφλὸς ποταμός, ὡς σὴν γῆν

---

[18] As noted by Luck, *Latin Love Elegy* p. 93.
[19] On this epigram see below, p. 190; on 'substitute addresses' cf. *GC* pp. 216f.
[20] Cf. e.g. Theophr. *De Caus. Plant.* 3.13.2; *Geopon.* 3.3.9; 5.38.
[21] The passages were juxtaposed by F. Wilhelm, 'Tibulliana', *RhM* N.F. 59 (1904) 279f.

40 Imitation as learning

μὴ γεωργεῖν· ἓν ἐξόμνυμαι τῶν ἐν ἀγροῖς εἰθισμένων, ἀμέλγειν γάλα. μόνων ἡδέως τῶν σῶν μαστῶν ἅπτομαι.

What am I going to do then, if you go out into the countryside as you did last year and for many days give up staying in town? I think that I shall be truly lost without remedy, with nothing pleasant to hear or see, for I think that the city will follow you when you leave and that the gods in the city will be drawn after you by the sight of you. For what can they do here on their own? But even if they stay in their place I shan't be left behind but shall be like a small boat towed behind by love; and if I have to dig I shall take up my mattock, if I have to prune I shall care for the vines, if I have to irrigate the vegetables I shall make channels for the water. For what river is so blind as not to help in farming your land? Only one of the country tasks do I forswear, milking; for only your breasts do I touch with pleasure.

Cf. Rura meam, Cornute, tenent villaeque puellam:
    ferreus est, heu heu, quisquis in urbe manet.
ipsa Venus latos iam nunc migravit in agros,
    verbaque aratoris rustica discit Amor.
o ego, cum aspicerem dominam, quam fortiter illic
    versarem valido pingue bidente solum
agricolaeque modo curvum sectarer aratrum
    dum subigunt steriles arva serenda boves!
nec quererer quod sol graciles exureret artus,
    laederet et teneras pussula rupta manus.
                                  (Tibullus 2.3.1–10)
ducite: ad imperium dominae sulcabimus agros:
    non ego me vinclis verberibusque nego.   (2.3.79f.)

The end of the Philostratus passage confirms that the lost line or lines at Tibullus 2.3.14a dealt with the milking of cows, which was obviously a topos in this type of fantasy, and to which Philostratus alludes for humorous purposes.

v

A piece of religious erudition seems to be present at 1.6.43–6:

sic fieri iubet ipse deus, sic magna sacerdos
    est mihi divino vaticinata sono.
haec, ubi Bellonae motu est agitata, nec acrem
    flammam, non amens verbera torta timet:

The 'great priestess' is said to be a devotee of the goddess Bellona; and she is the mouthpiece of erotodidactic prophecy. The commentators explain

Imitation as learning

correctly that Bellona had acquired some of the attributes of the Cappadocian goddess Ma and that her worship was congenial to women of Delia's class. But this explanation does not highlight the erudition of Tibullus when he combines Bellona's priestess and erotic pronouncements. The temples of the Cappadocian Ma, like those of other Asiatic mother goddesses, were served by sacred prostitutes.[22] It is this fact which may make the priestess of Bellona a suitable erotic teacher[23] and explain her goddess's interest in Tibullus' love-affairs.

VI

Several minor pieces of learning in Tibullus 1.7, which deserve greater emphasis than they have received, may be treated briefly.

(a) The identification of Osiris–Dionysus is already found in Hecataeus of Abdera (see below, (b)). The identification Osiris–Nile is also early.[24] But Tibullus' combination of all three gods conforms to the Hellenistic tendency towards theological syncretism, a phenomenon as characteristic of the period[25] as the opposite trend, towards multiplication of a single deity.[26] For a Roman Hellenistic poet these features may almost have been a trade mark of his literary affiliation.[27]

(b) The identification of Osiris with Dionysus in Hecataeus of Abdera was noted above (a). Diodorus, who preserves Hecataeus, goes on to relate that Osiris, like Dionysus, went on a conquering and civilising mission to India. It is apparently not certain that Diodorus is following Hecataeus in this latter part.[28] But it is of interest that Diodorus, like Tibullus, combined these two pieces of learning. The triumphant conquests of Dionysus are of course for Tibullus a vital thematic link with the triumphs of Messalla celebrated in 1.7, although in typical Tibullan fashion (see below, pp. 43f.) they are not explicitly mentioned in the elegy. If Diodorus is not following Hecataeus throughout, the thematic overlap between his version and that of Tibullus might point to other common Hellenistic sources.[29]

---

[22] Cf. Strabo 12.3.36.   [23] Cf. *GC* pp. 173f.   [24] Cf. Fraser I p. 263 and nn.
[25] Cf. Fraser III General Index *s.v.* Syncretism etc.
[26] Cf. Xen. *Symp.* 8.9f.; Call. *Iamb.* 10.1ff. (Pf.); and esp. Cic. *DND* 3.53ff. and Pease *ad loc.*
[27] E.g. Prop. 2.28; Cat. 3.1f; 31.3 and Fordyce *ad locc.*
[28] Cf. Fraser I pp. 497f. and nn.
[29] One such source may be the *Dionysus* of Euphorion. Cf. A. Barigazzi, 'Il Dionysos di Euforione' in *Miscellanea di Studi Alessandrini in memoria di Augusto Rostagni* (Turin 1963) pp. 416ff., esp. pp. 423ff., who suggests that the triumphant Dionysus of Nonnus derives from this work. The view is accepted in *Nonnos de Panopolis: Les Dionysiaques* I ed. F. Vian (Paris 1976) introd. p. XLI. For further discussion of Euphorion's work and of possible Roman reflections of it see I. M. Le M. Du Quesnay, 'The song of Mopsus and the new Daphnis', *PVS* 16 (1977–8) (forthcoming).

(c) The thesis of (b) may find some small confirmation – although it must be remembered that the themes go naturally together – from the fact that the next section of Diodorus, also not necessarily Hecataean,[30] deals with the sources of the Nile. This is the theme of Tibullus 1.7.23f. and it was also treated by Callimachus.[31] Either Callimachus or another Hellenistic writer may therefore have been for Tibullus the source of all the learned points here noted.

These suggestions highlight three problems in this area. First, since Tibullus neither mentions nor alludes in an indubitable fashion to any Greek poet in his two programmatic elegies (1.1 and 2.1) it is difficult to know from internal evidence where to look for his specific predecessors in Hellenistic poetry. Such echoes of individual Hellenistic passages as have been hypothesised in Tibullus may be less certain than they seem. Even in the small amount of Hellenistic poetry which survives words and concepts repeat themselves more frequently than is sometimes realised. If all of it survived, this would surely be observed even more clearly. Therefore even a fairly sound-looking link between Tibullus and a Hellenistic poet may be unreliable. A good case is the often repeated statement that the epithet *Mopsopio* at Tibullus 1.7.54 is a specific reference on his part to Callimachus Fr. 709 (Pf.). But the word is not unique to Callimachus in Hellenistic poetry. It also occurs in the title of a work of Euphorion (cf. Powell pp. 28f.).[32] In addition '*contaminatio*' is a characteristic Hellenistic and post-Hellenistic literary technique.[33] This means that even if Tibullus has imitated a particular author at one point, this may not reveal his general literary affiliation.

The second problem is that even when it is fairly certain that Tibullus is ultimately indebted to learned Hellenistic material or practice, it may be hard to define exactly what he is doing. He may simply be imitating a learned Hellenistic predecessor, which would in Roman terms be 'learning'; or he may himself be inventing[34] erudite subject-matter, as Hellenistic poets did, but without reference to their works; or finally he may be doing something intermediate, namely creating new erudition but looking to written Hellenistic sources as a pattern for it. The third problem is simply that much Hellenistic poetry has been lost and much of what survives is fragmentary.

[30] Fraser I p. 499 and nn. suggests Agatharchides as possibly Diodorus' source. But of course A. could have drawn on an earlier but post-Hecataean work which also was used by Callimachus or another poetic predecessor of Tibullus.
[31] Cf. Fr. 384.31f. (Pf.).
[32] See also Call. Fr. 709 (Pf.) and Pfeiffer *ad loc.*
[33] Cf. B. Gentili, *Lo Spettacolo nel mondo antico* (Bari 1977) Ch. 1.
[34] In literary texts such 'invention' is almost impossible to prove beyond question. On inventions in Herodotus cf. D. Fehling, *Die Quellenangaben bei Herodot* (Untersuchungen zur antiken Literatur und Geschichte 9, Berlin/New York 1971) pp. 126ff.

Imitation as learning

These problems however have not prevented a great deal of useful work being done in this area and they should not impede further work. Secondary sources point to Callimachus and Euphorion as influences on Tibullus; and there is evidence also that Philetas and Phanocles influenced him (see above, pp. 25ff. and below, pp. 54ff.). In addition, although precision may be impossible in describing Tibullus' learning, its learnedness cannot be in doubt. As for the third problem, new papyrus discoveries may one day lessen it. But in the meantime, practical considerations demand that the rules of evidence in the fragmentary field of Hellenistic poetry should not be as strict as in better documented areas. Probability, not proof, is to be sought; hints and scraps must be allowed to do duty for larger texts; and allusions and reminiscences must be allowed to carry more conviction than they would at other periods of literary history.

Hellenistic learning may sometimes be employed by Roman poets simply as literary ornament, although supposed examples of this tend, when examined closely, to be more than ornamental. Some Tibullan imitations of Hellenistic learning may function on this level, although those discussed above, if fully appreciated, do add to the overall significance of their contexts. What is perhaps more important and less debatable is that Tibullus makes important structural use of erudite material, the presence of which is signalled not in an explicit and open fashion but in a self-restrained and tactful way. In this respect Tibullus' mode of presentation seems to contrast with those of Catullus and Propertius, where the introduction of learned material of structural importance is clearly marked. The rest of this chapter will deal first briefly with this phenomenon in 1.7 and then extensively with its presence in 1.3. If it can be established that Tibullus relies on learned Hellenistic conceptual links which the reader is expected to understand from tenuous hints, and if failure on the reader's part to grasp them involves failure to understand the basic meaning of the elegy, then an important part of Tibullus' individuality and merit as a poet and one of the reasons why modern scholars do not value him as he deserves will be revealed.

First, Tibullus 1.7: as I have tried to show elsewhere,[35] this poem exploits established links between the Roman triumph and the Greek dithyramb and relies on such concepts as Dionysus the *triumphator* to link the diverse material which it presents. However another hero of the past, unmentioned in the elegy, also plays a great part in binding it together and giving it contemporary significance. This is Alexander. Like Dionysus a conqueror of the East and a *triumphator*,[36] Alexander became a standard

---

[35] *GC* pp. 95ff.; 167ff.

[36] The 'triumph' of Alexander has little historical foundation but is securely established in the 'vulgate' tradition. Cf. W. W. Tarn, *Alexander the Great II: Sources and Studies* (Cambridge 1948) index *s.v.* Dionysus. Cf. esp. Curt. 9.10.24ff. (cf. 3.12.18) where the Roman view – Dionysus as inventor of the triumph and

heroic model for the eulogy and propaganda of Greek kings and Roman generals.[37] Scipio, Pompey, Caesar and Antonius all tried to assimilate their public image with that of Alexander; Augustus followed suit later. Tibullus, in describing his patron Messalla's military campaigns, moves away from Gaul to the East and mentions in succession Cydnus, Taurus and Cilicia, Syria, Tyre and the Nile. He is evoking part of the route taken by Alexander in the first half of his conquest of the Persian empire. Messalla no doubt did actually do some campaigning in the East. But the apparent implication of Tibullus 1.7, that Messalla was in all these places in a military capacity, which has caused some difficulty to historians, may be false. Tibullus may by oblique suggestion be elevating into a major triumphal campaign some much less important activity of Messalla, in order to attach to Messalla the potent image of Alexander to which his contemporaries had learned to respond. If this is so then Tibullus is discreetly using a complex of associations established in the Hellenistic period in order not only to eulogise his patron but to unify his poem. Moreover it is of great significance for the ethos of the early principate and for the understanding of Augustan literature if Tibullus, who never mentions Augustus once, could give this kind of poetic treatment to Messalla and represent him as a semi-divine Dionysus–Alexander figure. Like the quasi-deification of Messalla in Tibullus 2.1, it reveals that the attitudes of Horace, Virgil and Propertius towards Augustus are much more in keeping with the spirit of the times and with the Roman patronage system, and much less unparalleled, than they have sometimes appeared.

Tibullus 1.3 may now be considered at greater length in the same terms. The first piece of learning in Tibullus 1.3 which enhances the understanding of the poem emerges when a fairly naive question is asked: Why is Tibullus in 'Phaeacia' when he falls mortally ill? On one level the answer could be that Tibullus did, as a historical fact, actually travel to and fall ill on Corcyra, which was sometimes identified in antiquity with the Phaeacia of the *Odyssey*. But there is no guarantee that Tibullus' journey to and illness on Corcyra is not a piece of poetic fantasy like Propertius' journey and shipwreck in 1.17. The name Phaeacia for Corcyra certainly calls attention to Tibullus' similarities and dissimilarities to Odysseus,

Alexander as following his lead – is explicitly stated. On Alexander and Dionysus see also Fraser I pp. 202f., 205, 211; Vian, *Nonnos de Panopolis*, introd. p. XLI n. 2.

[37] F. Pfister, 'Alexander der Grosse: Die Geschichte seines Ruhmes im Lichte seiner Beinamen', *Historia* 13 (1964) 37ff.; A. Heuss, 'Alexander der Grosse und die politische Ideologie des Altertums', *Antike und Abendland* 4 (1954) 65ff. (bibliography on pp. 103f.). See also M. Gelzer, *Pompeius* (2nd ed. Munich 1959) pp. 54, 78, 92f., 97, 99, 124ff.; Weinstock p. 188; D. Michel, *Alexander als Vorbild für Pompeius, Caesar und Marcus Antonius: Archäologische Untersuchungen* (Coll. *Latomus* 94, Brussels 1967); P. P. Spranger, 'Der Grosse: Untersuchungen zum Entstehung des historischen Beinamens in der Antike', *Saeculum* 9 (1958) 22ff. I am indebted to Prof. F. W. Walbank for these references.

Imitation as learning

which play a significant role in the elegy.[38] But there is an additional explanation. It involves the learned tradition whereby Phaeacia lay, in terms of mythical geography, near Elysium. This tradition appears to have sprung from the account of the voyage of Rhadamanthus in Homer, *Odyssey* 7.321ff.[39] Homer says nothing about Phaeacia being near Elysium, but the Homeric scholia have the following:

... πρὸς ... τοὺς ζητοῦντας πῶς φησιν ὡς χειμῶνος ὄντος 'Αρήτην ἀλεαίνεσθαι παρὰ τῷ πυρί. εὔκρατος γὰρ ὁ ἀὴρ καὶ οἱ καρποὶ διαμένουσιν, καὶ γειτνιῶσιν 'Ηλυσίῳ πεδίῳ μένοντες, ὅθεν καὶ τὸν 'Ραδάμανθυν διεκόμισαν. (Schol. ad Homer, *Odyssey* 7.153τ)
... *in answer to those who enquire how it is that the poet says Arete is warming herself by the fire, as though it were winter. For the weather is always good there and the crops grow throughout the year and their place of residence is near to the Elysian plain, which is why they provided transport for Rhadamanthus too.*
φαίνονται γοῦν οἱ Φαίακες πλησίον τῶν Μακάρων νήσων κατοικοῦντες. (Schol. EHPQV ad Homer, *Odyssey* 7.324)
It is clear that the Phaeacians live near the Islands of the Blessed.

Cf.   ἵν' ὀλβιόδωρος· πρὸς τῷ πυρίνῳ κύκλῳ καὶ τῇ ζώνῃ τοῦ πυρὸς ἑτέραν [γὰρ] ἐμύθευσαν εἶναι γῆν ἐν ᾗ πλεῖστα καὶ θαυμαστὰ φύοναι. ἐν ταύτῃ γὰρ καὶ τὸ 'Ηλύσιον πεδίον καὶ τὴν Φαιάκων γῆν ἐμύθευσαν εἶναι.
(Schol. ad Euripides, *Hippolytus* 750)
'Where with blessed gifts': there is a legend that close to the fiery circle and the belt of fire there is another land in which many marvellous things grow. In this land is found according to the legend the Elysian plain and the country of the Phaeacians.

These texts assure the Hellenistic currency of the tradition. Hence when Tibullus begins 1.3 by relating that he is lying mortally ill at Phaeacia and ends his fantasies about his own death by proclaiming that Venus will lead him to Elysium, it may well be that he is alluding to this learned view of the geographical proximity of the two places and exploiting it to suggest that this adds to the likelihood of his prophecy about his fate after death being correct. Tibullus may have taken this piece of learning from a Hellenistic predecessor. A lament for the dead poet Philicus of Corcyra (third century BC) portrays him as a man who had enjoyed the happy life and sociable temperament of his ancestor Alcinous the Phaeacian[40] and who is now on his way to the Isles of the Blessed.

This piece of Tibullan learning directs attention towards a piece of generic ingenuity in Tibullus 1.3. It is an inverse epibaterion. Often in this

---

[38] For this element see H. Eisenberger, 'Der innere Zusammenhang der Motive in Tibulls Gedicht I 3', *Hermes* 88 (1960) 188ff.; Wimmel, *DFT* pp. 179f.
[39] Cf. *R-E* s. vv. 'Ραδάμανθυς; Phaiaken (esp. pp. 1527f.; 1530).
[40] Cf. Fraser I pp. 608f. and nn.

46 *Imitation as learning*

variant of the genre the speaker attacks the place to which he has come.[41] But Tibullus did not want to attack Phaeacia, partly because this would have created too strong a contrast between himself and Odysseus and so damaged the effect of his self portrayal as an *alter Odysseus*;[42] and partly because Phaeacia was useful to him in mythological terms in suggesting proximity to Elysium. Therefore in accordance with attested generic practice,[43] he employed a substitute motif. He makes an attack upon the contemporary Iron Age which, because it involves travel and war, has brought him to Phaeacia (49f.): and in contrast he praises the Golden Age when such journeys were not made (35ff.).

The second piece of learning important in understanding Tibullus 1.3 is highlighted by the thematic structure of the elegy. This is a debated subject; but of the recent attempts to analyse it, that of R. Hanslik,[44] which offers a ring-structure, the arrangement which Tibullus always seems to have used (see below, Chapter 8) and which ancient poets mostly employ, appears preferable. However this point need not be pressed. It is enough for present purposes if the passage in which Tibullus imagines his own death (51–6) – a notion first adumbrated in lines 4ff. – can be regarded as the hub of the poem. It contains a mention of Tibullus' patron Messalla – who is the dedicatee of the elegy and the book – and of their relationship. It also contains Tibullus' imaginary epitaph, which conjoins the themes of death and of association with Messalla which run throughout the elegy:

HIC IACET INMITI CONSVMPTVS MORTE TIBVLLVS
MESSALLAM TERRA DVM SEQVITVRQVE MARI (55f.)

Thus its contents make it the centre-piece of the elegy and once it is recognised as such, then other structural aspects become clear. It is preceded by lines 35–50. Here Tibullus describes the Golden Age of the past, when war and death were unknown, and contrasts it with the Iron Age of the present, when his own death on a military expedition is in prospect. It is followed by lines 57–82, where Tibullus describes Elysium and Hades. The juxtaposition of these two passages shows that Tibullus intends to balance the Golden Age/Iron Age description with the Elysium/Hades section. This in turn suggests that the reader is intended to search for links between the two passages, particularly in the sphere of mythology, in which both are rich.

Before these are explored, a recently propounded view of one part of the

---

[41] Cf. *GC* pp. 60ff.   [42] See above, n. 38.
[43] The phenomenon is of course integral to originality in the case of topoi: cf. *GC* Ch. 4 and esp. pp. 123f. For other examples cf. *GC passim*. Similar features are discussed by T. Krischer, *Formale Konventionen der homerischen Epik* (Zetemata 56, Munich 1971) pp. 24ff. ('Ersatzmotif') esp. p. 35; cf. also I. M. Le M. Du Quesnay, 'Vergil's Fourth *Eclogue*', *PLLS 1976* p. 57 and see below, Ch. 3 n. 4.
[44] 'Tibulls Elegie 1 3' in *Forschungen zur römischen Literatur* ed. W. Wimmel (Wiesbaden 1970) I, pp. 138ff., with schema on p. 145.

mythological content of 1.3, which if correct would weaken the link about to be proposed, must be countered.[45] This is that in 1.3 Tibullus is identifying Venus, who appears in line 58, with Isis, who featured earlier in the poem at lines 23ff. The perfectly valid connections between Isis and Elysium in antiquity are used as arguments to support this view. However, this association has its difficulties. To begin with, from her first appearance in the elegy, Isis is firmly linked by Tibullus with Delia and not with himself. She is *tua . . . Isis* (23); and although Tibullus himself later (27f.) prays to her for help, he once again dissociates himself from her in 29ff., when he makes it clear that not he, but Delia, will pay to Isis the vows he makes. His own expressions of gratitude for his recovery will be made to his Roman Penates and Lar (33f.). Tibullus, having paid passing tribute to Delia's goddess, is making a striking return to a Roman context precisely in order to show that the Isis theme has been abandoned: Isis is not a suitable goddess for a Roman citizen to have much to do with.[46] The passage continues with Saturn (35) and the introduction of this god further stresses that Tibullus is a Roman. Saturn was intimately connected with Latium; and he was said to have hidden there after his expulsion from heaven, a fact which gave Latium its name.[47] The Isis theme is thus clearly abandoned; and the rest of the poem is thoroughly Graeco-Roman in its mythological content. Hence, when Venus appears in close association with Tibullus in line 57 as his guide through the underworld, it is hard to believe that she is intended as the Egyptian goddess Isis in a different guise. Finally, and this is directly relevant to the present discussion, the identification of Isis with Venus would not help to unify the two passages which are structurally intended as balancing sections, since the Isis material occurs before the beginning of the Golden/Iron Age passage.

The link to be suggested between the two passages lying on either side of lines 51–6 does not involve a combination of Graeco-Roman and Egyptian mythology but a connection within the Graeco-Roman field. The Golden Age was, as Tibullus explicitly states, the time when Saturn ruled (35f.). The Roman Saturn is the Greek Kronos; and the connection between the Golden Age and Elysium is that in Greek mythology Kronos, as well as being the king of the Golden Age, was the ruler of Elysium. A fair amount of evidence points to the conclusion that the association between Kronos and Elysium is old; and indeed it has been argued that the Kronos–Golden Age–Elysium link goes all the way back to Indo-European mythology and that later it was connected with Orphism–Pythagoreanism.[48] This might suggest that Tibullus derived his knowledge of the association from the general stock of religious and mythologi-

[45] Wimmel, *DFT* pp. 187ff.; 204ff.
[46] For an account of official Roman actions to control and discourage the cult of Isis cf. R-E *s.v.* pp. 2103f. esp. the Augustan measures.
[47] Cf. Ov. *Fast.* 1.238 and Bömer *ad loc.*
[48] Cf. H. C. Baldry, 'Who invented the Golden Age?', *CQ* N.S. 2 (1952) 83ff.

cal material current in his day. But given the bias of Augustan poetry and the literary aspiration both of Greek and Roman Hellenistic poets to be and to be thought learned, a literary origin for the association seems more likely.

This view is supported by the surviving literary traces of the Kronos–Elysium link. They occur in precisely those archaic authors whom the Hellenistic poets most admired and imitated; and their presence in these authors makes it easy to hypothesise that Tibullus knew the relevant archaic texts or, more likely, that a Hellenistic passage, or passages, known to Tibullus, reproduced the same concepts. The first certain allusion to an association between Kronos and Elysium is found in Pindar:

> ὅσοι δ' ἐτόλμασαν ἐστρίς
> ἑκατέρωθι μείναντες ἀπὸ πάμπαν ἀδίκων ἔχειν
> ψυχάν, ἔτειλαν Διὸς ὁδὸν παρὰ Κρό-   70
>   νου τύρσιν· ἔνθα μακάρων
> νᾶσον ὠκεανίδες
> αὖραι περιπνέοισιν· ἄνθεμα δὲ χρυσοῦ φλέγει,
> τὰ μὲν χερσόθεν ἀπ' ἀγλαῶν δενδρέων,
>   ὕδωρ δ ἄλλα φέρβει,
> ὅρμοισι τῶν χέρας ἀναπλέκοντι καὶ στεφάνους
> βουλαῖς ἐν ὀρθαῖσι 'Ραδαμάνθυος,   75
> ὃν πατὴρ ἔχει μέγας ἑτοῖμον αὐτῷ πάρεδρον,
> πόσις ὁ πάντων 'Ρέας
>   ὑπέρτατον ἐχοίσας θρόνον.   (Olympian 2.68ff.)

Those who have three times on each side been able to restrain their spirit totally from injustice go along the path of Zeus alongside the tower of Cronos. There the breezes of Ocean blow about the Island of the Blessed. Golden flowers blaze forth, some from noble trees upon the land, others nourished by the water. They weave bracelets for their arms and crowns from them under the upright decrees of Rhadamanthus, whom the great father, the husband of Rhea throned high above all, has sitting ready beside him.

The Isles of the Blessed and Elysium are more or less synonymous.[49] Here the Islands of the Blessed, which are a place of reward for those who have lived three just lives on earth, are said to contain the 'tower of Kronos' (70), and Kronos is in a position of authority there (76f.). The scholion (A) on this passage comments on παρὰ Κρόνου in the words παρὰ τοῦ Κρόνου βασιλείαν (to the kingdom of Kronos). Earlier in *Olympian* 2 Pindar called the earth, which he was contrasting with the Isles of the Blessed, 'the realm of Zeus' (58). It seems therefore that the scholiast is correct in regarding Pindar's references to Kronos' tower and authority as

[49] Cf. D. Wachsmuth, *ΠΟΜΠΙΜΟΣ Ο ΔΑΙΜΩΝ: Untersuchung zu den antiken Sakralhandlungen bei Seereisen* (Diss. Berlin 1967) p. 210.

Imitation as learning

designating his kingship of the Isles of the Blessed. In this case, Pindar's account in *Olympian* 2 of the earth as the kingdom of Zeus and the Isles of the Blessed as the kingdom of Kronos is closely parallel to Tibullus' contrast between the Iron Age, the period when Jupiter is master, and the Golden Age, when Saturn ruled. The Pindar account contains further small details which coincide with those found in Tibullus. The dead in Elysium in Pindar do not plough the earth or sail the seas as merchants, two aspects of the Golden Age stressed by Tibullus (*Olympian* 2.63ff., cf. Tibullus 1.3.35ff.); moreover the dead in Pindar's Isles of the Blessed are contrasted with those in Hades (*Olympian* 2.67, cf. Tibullus 1.3.67ff.). The full Pindar passage is as follows:

> ἴσαις δὲ νύκτεσσιν αἰεί,
> ἴσαις δ' ἀμέραις ἅλιον ἔχοντες, ἀπονέστερον
> ἐσλοὶ δέκονται βίοτον, οὐ χθόνα τα-
> ράσσοντες ἐν χερὸς ἀκμᾷ
> οὐδὲ πόντιον ὕδωρ
> κενεὰν παρὰ δίαιταν, ἀλλὰ παρὰ μὲν τιμίοις   65
> θεῶν οἵτινες ἔχαιρον εὐορκίαις
> ἄδακρυν νέμονται
> αἰῶνα, τοὶ δ' ἀπροσόρατον ὀκχέοντι πόνον.   (*Olympian* 2.61–9)[50]
> *With equal nights always and equal sunny days these noble spirits have a life without toil. They do not disturb the earth with the strength of their hands, nor the sea water seeking an empty livelihood. But those who have rejoiced in keeping their oaths have allotted to them a life without tears amid the privileges of the gods; but the others experience punishment too terrible to look at.*

It is of particular interest that this material is found in Pindar. It was Pindar who provided Callimachus with much of his technical vocabulary of literary criticism and polemic;[51] and this gives Pindar a special importance in all poetry following even tenuously along Callimachean lines.

The second literary reference to Kronos in association with Elysium refers quite unequivocally to Kronos as the king of the Isles of the Blessed and occurs in Hesiod. But it is regarded by modern editors as a later interpolation. The context is

> τοῖς δὲ δίχ' ἀνθρώπων βίοτον καὶ ἤθε' ὀπάσσας
> Ζεὺς Κρονίδης κατένασσε πατὴρ ἐν πείρασι γαίης,   168
> καὶ τοὶ μὲν ναίουσιν ἀκηδέα θυμὸν ἔχοντες   170
> ἐν μακάρων νήσοισι παρ' Ὠκεανὸν βαθυδίνην·
> ὄλβιοι ἥρωες, τοῖσιν μελιηδέα καρπόν
> τρὶς ἔτεος θάλλοντα φέρει ζείδωρος ἄρουρα.
> {τηλοῦ ἀπ' ἀθανάτων· τοῖσιν Κρόνος ἐμβασιλεύει.   173a

[50] Cf. also Pind. *Thren.* 7 (Sn.–Mae.).   [51] See above, Ch. 1 p. 7 and n. 28.

....(.) γάρ μ]ιν ἔλυσε πατ[ὴρ ἀνδρῶ]ν τε θε[ῶν τε·   b
νῦν δ' ἤδη] μετὰ τοῖς τιμὴ[ν ἔ]χει ὡς ἐ[πιεικές.   c
Ζεὺς δ' αὖτ' ἄ]λλο γένος θῆκ[εν μερόπων ἀνθρώπων,   d
τῶν οἳ νῦ]ν γεγάασιν ἐπὶ [}   e

(Hesiod, *Works and Days* 167ff.)[52]

To them Zeus son of Kronos has given a way of life and a residence far apart from mankind; and he placed them at the ends of the earth. And they live with hearts free of care in the Islands of the Blessed, beside Ocean with its deep eddies, happy heroes for whom thrice in a year the grain-giving earth brings forth flourishing honey-sweet crops. {far away from the gods. Kronos is their king, for the father of men and gods released him and now he has continual honour along with them as is fitting. And Zeus created another race of articulate men, the race which now lives on the ⟨earth, the nourisher of many⟩.}

The dubious lines had certainly entered some texts of Hesiod by the second century AD.[53] But when they did so is not known. If it was in or before the Hellenistic period, then they also could be part of the literary tradition which influenced Tibullus. Hesiod was another pre-eminent hero of the Alexandrians.[54] Callimachus paid him the supreme compliment of choosing to represent himself as an *alter Hesiodus* in his *Aetia*.[55] If the passage rejected by modern editors was thought in the Hellenistic era to be genuinely Hesiodic, or even if its authenticity was then debated, it could easily have influenced Hellenistic poetry and so have contributed further to the literary background of Tibullus 1.3.

Tibullus therefore seems to expect his readers to link the Golden Age and Elysium by recollecting the role of Saturn in both contexts. The significance of the link for the elegy is that Elysium is the recompense which Tibullus deserves for enduring the suffering and death of a world deprived of its Golden Age. Horace employs a similar concept in *Epode* 16 when he speaks of sailing to the Isles of the Blessed:

> Iuppiter illa piae secrevit litora genti,
>   ut inquinavit aere tempus aureum;
> aere, dehinc ferro duravit saecula, quorum
>   piis secunda vate me datur fuga.   (63ff.)

The use of the notion by Horace also suggests a common poetic source, Hellenistic or earlier. Its recognition by the reader of Tibullus 1.3 adds a new dimension to his understanding of the elegy. As with the Alexander material in 1.7, tactful allusion is the means whereby Tibullus makes his point.

A third piece of learning in Tibullus 1.3 with importance for the mean-

[52] In the text of M. L. West (1978).
[53] On this question see now M. L. West *ad loc.*
[54] See above, Ch. 1 n. 48.   [55] Fr. 2 (Pf.).

Imitation as learning

ing of the elegy is signalled by Venus' presence in Elysium as guide to the souls in place of Mercury, who usually fulfils this role. This is the concept of an Elysium for lovers alone. Tibullan scholarship has recognised the presence of this concept but Smith vigorously denied it.[56] It must be asserted with equal vigour that in lines 57–66 Tibullus does indeed describe a special Elysium reserved for lovers. This hardly seems far-fetched: after all, Tibullus' hell is a hell for sinners against love and for no others:

> illic sit, quicumque meos violavit amores,
>   optavit lentas et mihi militias   (1.3.81f.)

There is of course a problem in Tibullus' hell, namely the appearance in it of Tantalus, but this is dealt with below (pp. 54ff.)

It is to parallel and balance this special hell for sinners against love that Tibullus creates before it a heaven especially for lovers. Venus appears in Mercury's role as guide of souls (58) as an introductory signal of this specialisation. No parallel is known for the representation of Venus in this role, but Tibullus may have found it in a Hellenistic poet. The oldest conception of the Isles of the Blessed was of a place where great warriors practised their martial and agonistic exercises after death. But the idea that lovers were present in the Isles of the Blessed may go back to an early period. The germs of the concept may even be found in Homer: the Nekuia contains an account of the beautiful heroines of Hades (*Odyssey* 11.225ff.), some of whom were lovers (227). This may have suggested to a later writer the idea of describing some of these heroines along with their hero lovers in Elysium. This description could have given rise eventually to Tibullus' concept of an Elysium reserved for lovers alone.

Virgil in the *Aeneid* shows that the concept of a lovers' Elysium was not alien to Augustan thought. He does not remove lovers from the Underworld and place them in the Isles of the Blessed. But he does reserve part of the Underworld for lovers; and significantly this part is only for those who have died of love, which is exactly the situation found in Tibullus. The lines in which Tibullus and Virgil make this point are similar:

> illic est cuicumque rapax Mors venit amanti
>   (Tibullus 1.3.65)
> hic quos durus Amor crudeli tabe peredit
>   (Virgil, *Aeneid* 6.442)

The similarity, taken in combination with the material collected below, suggests that both Virgil and Tibullus imitated a Hellenistic source or sources,[57] and did so in full consciousness. In particular the *variatio* be-

---

[56] On Tib. 1.3.59–64.
[57] *Aen.* 6.441: *Lugentes Campi: sic illos nomine dicunt* supports the idea that Virgil, there

tween *illic* and *hic*, between the ideas of sudden death in Tibullus and lingering death in Virgil and between the emphasis on 'Death coming to a lover' in Tibullus and 'those whom Love kills' in Virgil reveals the rich Hellenistic background of the concepts. It is unlikely because of the complexity of the *variatio* that either Tibullus or Virgil is simply imitating the other. Both Roman poets are presenting their versions of an earlier topos which has already become diversified in the work of their predecessors.

Tibullus' Elysium for lovers may derive in its entirety from a Hellenistic original or it may be a compound of imitation and originality. Whatever else it is, it is a self-consistent and fully rounded concept unparalleled in surviving earlier literature. Elements differentiating it from other accounts of Elysium and of lovers' after-life are: the lovers are in Elysium, not in part of the Underworld, as they are in Virgil, *Aeneid* 6; Tibullus' Elysium seems to contain no one except lovers; and finally Tibullus has adapted his Elysian scenery to be consistent in all respects with its exclusively erotic nature. His Elysian scenery is of course in all its particulars found in other descriptions of Elysium. The singing, dancing, birds, fragrant plants, roses, general love-making and myrtle wreaths can all be paralleled from non-specific descriptions of the Islands of the Blessed.[58] But they have also been selected by Tibullus from a much larger repertoire of Elysian material and combined in order to create a unique concept.

The only slight clue to the literary background is a post-Tibullan text which gives a hint of the Elysium descriptions on which Tibullus may have drawn. Lucian's *Verae Historiae* contains an account of the Isles of the Blessed. Here there are, among others, lovers; and love-making takes place there. This is a state of affairs which contrasts sharply with the normal ancient belief that love-making was impossible after death.[59] Lucian's Elysium has points of coincidence both with the Tibullan and the Virgilian versions which appear to indicate a common source or sources, probably Hellenistic. Both in Virgil and in Lucian, lovers after death wander in the woods:

> errabat silva in magna   (*Aeneid* 6.451; cf. 473f.)

> καὶ μόνοι ἐξανιστάμενοι ἐπλανῶντο περὶ τὴν ὕλην.
> (*Verae Historiae* 2.25)

at any rate, had a Hellenistic source since this is a typical Hellenistic citation formula. Cf. Newman p. 46.

[58] On Elysium and related themes cf. *R-E* s.v. Elysion; U. Bianchi, *Studi e Materiali di Storia delle Religione* 39 (1963) pp. 143ff.; J. Kroll, *Elysium* (Arbeitsgemeinschaft für Forschung des Landes Nordrhein-Westfalen, Geisteswissenschaften 2, Cologne 1953) pp. 7ff.; B. Gatz, *Weltalter, goldene Zeit und sinnvervandte Vorstellungen* (Spudasmata 16, Hildesheim 1967).

[59] Cf. Nisbet–Hubbard on Hor. *Od.* 1.4.18. Add also Anacreon Fr. 36 (Gent.) as expounded by G. Giangrande, 'Symposiastic literature and epigram', pp. 109ff.

Imitation as learning

And getting up they wandered alone through the wood.

Tibullus 1.3.63f. is a typically refined Tibullan version of a theme which recurs in Lucian. Cf.

> ac iuvenum series teneris inmixta puellis
>   ludit, et adsidue proelia miscet Amor

and

> περὶ δὲ συνουσίας καὶ ἀφροδισίων οὕτω φρονοῦσιν· μίσγονται μὲν ἀναφανδὸν πάντων ὁρώντων καὶ γυναιξὶ καὶ ἄρρεσι, καὶ οὐδαμῶς τοῦτο αὐτοῖς αἰσχρὸν δοκεῖ· μόνος δὲ Σωκράτης διώμνυτο ἦ μὴν καθαρῶς πλησιάζειν τοῖς νέοις· καὶ μέντοι πάντες αὐτοῦ ἐπιορκεῖν κατεγίνωσκον· πολλάκις γοῦν ὁ μὲν ʽΥάκινθος ἢ ὁ Νάρκισσος ὡμολόγουν, ἐκεῖνος δὲ ἠρνεῖτο. αἱ δὲ γυναῖκές εἰσι πᾶσι κοιναὶ καὶ οὐδεὶς φθονεῖ τῷ πλησίον, ἀλλ᾽ εἰσὶ περὶ τοῦτο μάλιστα Πλατωνικώτατοι· καὶ οἱ παῖδες δὲ παρέχουσι τοῖς βουλομένοις οὐδὲν ἀντιλέγοντες. (*Verae Historiae* 2.19)
>
> Concerning intercourse and lovemaking this is their view. They make love in public with everyone looking on, both with women and with men, and they think that this is in no way shameful. Only Socrates swore that he associated in a chaste fashion with young men. But they all think that he is a perjurer. At any rate Hyacinth or Narcissus often used to say he was, but he denied it. They hold their wives in common and no one grudges his neighbour, and they are very Platonic about this matter. Boys too offer themselves to those who wish it and refuse nothing.

Although it is impossible to be certain about such a tenuous matter, it is probable that Tibullus constructed his erotic Elysium on the basis of Hellenistic texts in which lovers were present in Elysium and were able to make love. It may however have been Tibullus who first created the concept of an Elysium set aside exclusively for lovers and suited to them in every detail of its landscape. Propertius clearly understood and imitated with variation Tibullus' erotic Elysium:

> ecce coronato pars altera rapta phaselo,
>   mulcet ubi Elysias aura beata rosas,
> qua numerosa fides, quaque aera rotunda Cybelles
>   mitratisque sonant Lydia plectra choris.
> Andromedeque et Hypermestre sine fraude maritae
>   narrant historiae pectora nota suae:
> haec sua maternis queritur livere catenis
>   bracchia nec meritas frigida saxa manus;
> narrat Hypermestre magnum ausas esse sorores,
>   in scelus hoc animum non valuisse suum.
>
>   (4.7.59ff.)

Propertius compounds his compliment to Tibullus by employing typical Hellenistic alteration of the order of material borrowed by him from Tibullus and compression of part of it. Whereas Tibullus described first the erotic heaven and second the hell for sinners against love, both at similar length, in Propertius the hell for offenders against love comes first in abbreviated form and the heaven for lovers second. If the erotic Elysium may, in part at least, be Tibullus' own creation, the same may be conjectured with greater confidence about the hell for sinners against love. No earlier erotic hell is known. But even here it is possible that some Hellenistic writer, Antimachus or a successor mourning for his dead beloved, first created the notion of a hell only for sinners against love and a heaven reserved for lovers; and Propertius may have had such a passage in mind as well as Tibullus when he wrote 4.7 (see also below, pp. 58ff.).

Again the understanding of the elegy is enhanced by this piece of learning. Tibullus is creating a vision of the universe in which the lover with his yearnings after the Golden Age, his own Elysium for lovers, and his hell for enemies of love, replaces the heroic martial ideal with which Elysium was connected in the early Greek period. Tibullus is implicitly arguing that his vision has internal logical strength: the Golden Age, a time of peace and so a time ideal for lovers, is equated with Elysium, which cannot then contain the great warriors of the Iron Age but must be reserved for lovers, who alone preserve the values of the lost Golden Age.

The last piece of *doctrina* to be suggested in Tibullus 1.3 is important in three ways. First, it solves a long-standing problem in the elegy, that of Tantalus' appearance among the great sinners in Hades. Secondly, it shows Tibullus' typical way of introducing learning, namely quiet insinuation rather than open display of erudition. Thirdly it shows Tibullus as an intelligent and self-consistent poet. The problem about Tantalus is this: Tibullus, in summing up his description of hell, implies clearly that it is only for sinners against love (81f.); and when he lists the mythological persons in this hell, he states explicitly that the first and last of them were punished for crimes against love. The lines are:

> illic Iunonem temptare Ixionis ausi
>   versantur celeri noxia membra rota,
> porrectusque novem Tityos per iugera terrae
>   adsiduas atro viscere pascit aves.
> Tantalus est illic, et circum stagna, sed acrem
>   iam iam poturi deserit unda sitim,
> et Danai proles, Veneris quod numina laesit,
>   in cava Lethaeas dolia portat aquas.   (1.3.73–80)

Because Ixion in 73f. and the Danaids in 79f. are said to be such sinners, similar crimes are implied to have caused the damnation of Tityos and Tantalus. In Tityos' case it is easy to recall such a crime, Tityos' attempted rape of Leto.⁶⁰ But Tantalus' case is different. There are four well-known variant myths about the sin of Tantalus. The sin is either revealing the secrets of the gods, or serving up his son Pelops as a meal for the gods, or stealing nectar and ambrosia from the table of the gods and giving it to his young companions, or receiving a golden dog stolen from Zeus.⁶¹ None of these crimes has anything to do with love; and Tibullus at first sight seems to have failed in intellectual rigour.

It is certainly true that ancient poets, when they construct a paradeigmatic group and find difficulty in extracting from the mythological corpus at their command the appropriate number of suitable myths, sometimes cheat a little: they place the least convincing and least satisfactory paradeigma within the two more convincing parallels and bend the circumstances of all the myths to make the odd one out seem less odd.⁶² But this only happens when a poet is hard pressed to assemble the three myths which Hellenistic practice preferred. Here Tibullus mentions four myths; he could easily have dispensed with one if he had wished to do so, as indeed he omits Sisyphus, another standard mythological character in underworld scenes, presumably because no erotic offence was available in the myths about him.⁶³ The presence of the fourth and anomalous Tantalus myth here is therefore a characteristically Hellenistic challenge to his readers to divine his intentions.

Tibullus is being both learned and inventive in his inclusion of Tantalus within this group. The other members of the mythical group and their specific offences are selected and described in a way which gives clues to which offence of Tantalus Tibullus has in mind. The first two sinners, Ixion and Tityos, both attacked goddesses, one Juno and the other Leto. Both offended Jupiter by their actions, because Juno was his wife and Leto his mistress. The Danaids are said by Tibullus to have offended Venus, the love-goddess herself, who had appeared as psychopomp at the beginning of Tibullus' description of the Elysium for lovers alone, and whose reappearance at this point rounds off the whole heaven/hell section. Venus also appears here in order to confirm beyond any doubt that all the mythological characters in hell are offenders against love. Jupiter may be offended indirectly here too. Venus is his daughter; and it may be that as Zeus Xenios, the protector of guests and strangers, he was outraged by the cowardly murder of their Egyptian husbands by their wives the Danaids at the inspiration of their Argive host Danaus. All this suggests that like these criminals, Tantalus has committed a sin of an erotic type which has given offence to a god and which involved Jupiter somehow as an injured party.

⁶⁰ Cf. *R-E s.v.* Tityos pp. 1595ff.
⁶¹ For these myths see *R-E s.v.* Tantalos.
⁶² See F. Cairns, 'Two unidentified *komoi* of Propertius: I 3 and II 29', *Emerita* 45 (1977) 351ff.
⁶³ There are erotic elements in the Sisyphus legend – cf. e.g. Hyginus (ed. Rose) 60; 201 – but his crimes were not erotic.

There is a little-known myth about Tantalus which fits these requirements.[64] The story is that Tantalus carried off and raped Ganymede, who was later the beloved of Zeus. Some of the texts are collected as follows under Phanocles Fr. 4 by Powell.

> Orosius, *Hist.* 1.12 'Nec mihi nunc enumerare opus est Tantali et Pelopis facta turpia, fabulas turpiores; quorum Tantalus, rex Frygiorum, Ganymedem Trois Dardaniorum regis filium cum flagitiosissime rapuisset, maiore conserti certaminis foeditate detinuit, sicut Fanocles poeta confirmat, qui maximum bellum excitatum ob hoc fuisse commemorat; sive quia hunc ipsum Tantalum, utpote adseculam deorum, videri vult raptum puerum ad libidinem Iovis familiari lenocinio praeparasse, qui ipsum quoque filium Pelopem epulis eius non dubitaret impendere.' Cf. Euseb. *Chron.* (Helm, I, p. 51.17) ob raptum Ganymedis Troi patri Ganymedis et Tantalo bellum exortum est, ut scribit Fanocles poeta: cf. Syncellum 305.11 Bonn, Γανυμήδην ὁ Τάνταλος ἁρπάσας υἱὸν τοῦ Τρωὸς ὑπ' αὐτοῦ κατεπολεμεῖτο Τρωός, ὡς ἱστορεῖ Δίδυμος ἐν Ἱστορίᾳ Ξένῃ, καὶ Φανοκλῆς (Tantalus carried off Ganymede the son of Tros and Tros made war against him as Didymus recounts in his Foreign History, and Phanocles).

Others are:

> ὡς δὲ παρ' ἑτέροις εὕρομεν, Ἴλῳ τῷ Φρυγὶ καὶ Ταντάλῳ τῷ Λυδῷ πόλεμον ἐκεῖ γενέσθαι λέγουσιν, οἱ μὲν περὶ ὁδῶν, οἱ δὲ περὶ τῆς Γανυμήδους ἁρπαγῆς/ (Herodianus 1.11.2)
> As we find in other sources, they say that war arose there between Ilus the Phrygian and Tantalus the Lydian. Some say that it concerned roads and others that it concerned the rape of Ganymede.
> ὁπότε διὰ τὴν ἁρπαγὴν Γανυμήδους ἐμάχοντο Τάνταλος ὁ ἐραστὴς Γανυμήδους καὶ Ἶλος ὁ ἀδελφός·
> (Tzetzes Schol. ad Lycophron 355)
> ... when Tantalus the lover of Ganymede and Ilus his brother were at war because of the rape of Ganymede.
> ἀνηρείψαντο θεοί] Μνασέας μέν φησιν ὑπὸ Ταντάλου ἡρπάσθαι καὶ ἐν κυνηγεσίῳ πεσόντα ταφῆναι (bT) ἐν τῷ Μυσίῳ Ὀλύμπῳ κατὰ τὸ ἱερὸν τοῦ Ὀλυμπίου Διός, Δωσιάδης δὲ ἡρπάσθαι ὑπὸ Μίνω· (T)
> (Schol. Homer, *Iliad* 20.234)
> *The gods carried off]* Mnaseas says that he (Ganymede) was carried off by Tantalus and that when he was killed while hunting he was buried on

---

[64] Since this chapter was first drafted G. Lee, *Tibullus: Elegies* (Cambridge 1975) p. 106 n. 77 has independently adumbrated the solution offered below, viz 'Tantalus raped Ganymede, Jupiter's favourite (Orosius I. 12.4: citing Phanocles' version of the story, a Hellenistic poet).'

the Mysian Olympus by the temple of Olympian Zeus; Dosiades says that he was carried off by Minos.

Here Tantalus commits an erotic offence, which also involves Zeus as a secondary victim and which is carried out in the divine arena. It is interesting that the ultimate source of the myth is Phanocles, that inventive Hellenistic poet who created and assembled in his Ἔρωτες ἢ Καλοί (*Love-Stories or Beautiful Boys*) a whole gamut of homosexual legends involving the gods and heroes. Phanocles is known from independent evidence to have influenced Roman elegists;[65] and it is no surprise to meet a new case of his influence here.

There is however still one gap in the argument. No known source relates that Tantalus was placed in hell because of the rape of Ganymede. This however is Tibullus' clear implication. His intellectual challenge to his readers was therefore first to take the annotations to Ixion and the Danaids, the first and last of the myths, and apply them to the case of Tityos. Having done so, and realised that Tityos was in exactly the same criminal category as Ixion and the Danaids, the reader was expected to go further and recollect Tantalus' erotic crime against Ganymede, which was of a similar type to the other three. Now the reader could take the final step and understand that Ixion, Tityos and Tantalus all made attempts on objects of Jupiter's affection and that Tibullus is placing Tantalus in Hades along with the other two because of this erotic offence. As will be seen, communication of this kind between poet and audience is paralleled often in many areas of Tibullus' art.

In this novel piece of mythography Tibullus, or a Hellenistic predecessor, is demonstrating Hellenistic originality. He is 'realising' that this might be the 'real' reason why Tantalus was placed in the underworld. This process is of great antiquity: all ancient poets were involved at one level or another in refining the crude and often inconclusive myths of the pre-Homeric period and making them a useful moral and logical base for poetic instruction and ornament. Homeric creation and recreation of myth is beginning to be understood.[66] Pindar's activities in this field have been known for a long time and are now much better known.[67] The treatment of Tantalus in Tibullus 1.3 is a conspicuous Hellenistic/Roman example.

Of the learned material so far discussed in connection with Tibullus 1.3

---

[65] Cr. *R-E s.v.* Phanokles.
[66] Cf. M. M. Willcock, 'Mythological paradeigma in the *Iliad*', *CQ* N.S. 14 (1964) 141ff.; 'Ad hoc invention in the *Iliad*', *HSCPH* 81 (1977) 41ff.; B. K. Braswell, 'Mythological innovation in the Iliad', *CQ* N.S. 21 (1971) 16ff.
[67] Cf. E. L. Bundy, *Studia Pindarica* I, II (University of California Publications in Classical Philology 18, Berkeley and Los Angeles 1962); D. C. Young, *Three Odes of Pindar (Mnemosyne* Suppl. 9, Leiden 1968); *Pindar Isthmian 7, Myth and Exempla (Mnemosyne* Suppl. 15, Leiden 1971); A. Köhnken, *Die Funktion des Mythos bei Pindar* (Untersuchungen zur antiken Literatur und Geschichte 12, Berlin/New York 1971).

the geographical proximity of Phaeacia to Elysium appears to be of Hellenistic origin, the Golden Age/Elysium link is archaic Greek if not older, and the Tantalus myth and the specific Elysium for lovers are probably Hellenistic. But the other part of the last concept is archaic: it appears that Tibullus' description of his hell for sinners against love ultimately goes back to sources such as Alcman's *Partheneion*. The initial passage of this poem unfolds a similar scene:

        ] Πωλυδεύκης·
  οὐκ ἐγώ]ν Λύκαισον ἐν καμοῦσιν ἀλέγω
   'Ενα]ρσφόρον τε καὶ Σέβρον ποδώκη
    ]ν τε τὸν βιατὰν
    ]. τε τὸν κορυστὰν   5
  Εὐτείχη] τε Γάνακτά τ' 'Αρήιον
    ]ά τ' ἔξοχον ἡμισίων·
    ]ν τὸν ἀγρόταν
    ] μέγαν Εὔρυτόν τε
    ]πώρω κλόνον   10
    ]. τε τὼς ἀρίστως
    ] παρήσομες
    ]αρ Αἶσα παντῶν
    ] γεραιτάτοι
  ἀπ]έδιλος ἀλκὰ   15
μή τις ἀνθ]ρώπων ἐς ὠρανὸν ποτήσθω·
 μηδὲ πη]ρήτω γαμῆν τὰν 'Αφροδίταν
   F]άν[α]σσαν ἤ τιν'
    ] ἤ παίδα Πόρκω
  Χά]ριτες δὲ Διὸς δ[ό]μον   20
    ]σιν ἐρογλεφάροι·
    ]τάτοι
    ]τα δαίμων
    ]ι φίλοις
    ]ωκε δῶρα   25
    ]γαρέον
    ]ώλεσ' ἤβα
    ]ρονον
    ].ταίας
    ]έβα· τῶν δ' ἄλλος ἰῶι   30
    ]μαρμάρωι μυλάκρωι
    ].εν 'Αΐδας
    ]αυτοι
    ]πον· ἄλαστα δὲ
Γέργα πάσον κακὰ μησαμένοι·   35
ἔστι τις σιῶν τίσις·   (Alcman, Fr. 1 (PMG))

Imitation as learning

> *Polydeuces*
> *among the dead I (?)do not number(?) Lukaisos*
> *Enarsphoros and swift footed Sebros*
> *and the violent*
> *and the armed warrior*
> *and Euteiches and lord Areios*
> *and greatest of the demigods*
> *the savage*
> *and great Eurytos*
> *battle*
> *the best*
> *we shall pass by*
> *Fate of all*
> *the most distinguished*
> *unshod strength*
> *let no man fly up to heaven nor let him seek to marry Aphrodite*
> *queen or one*
> *or a daughter of Porkos*
> *The Graces the house of Zeus*
> *with eyes of love*
> *. . .*
> *fortune*
> *friends*
> *gifts*
> *. . .*
> *youth destroyed*
> *. . .*
> *. . .*
> *went. And one of them with an arrow*
> *with a marble millstone*
> *Hades*
> *. . .*
> *and they suffered terrible*
> *punishments having planned evil deeds:*
> *the vengeance of the gods exists.*

At lines 16ff. the poet warns human beings against aspiring to the love of goddesses, exactly the folly which in Tibullus ruined Tityos and Ixion. Lines 34f. of the Partheneion sum up what precedes. They do so in such a way as to suggest that the fragmentary lines 22–34 spoke of mythical persons who, perhaps among other crimes, attempted to ravish goddesses and paid the penalty for it. In line 32 Hades is mentioned. It could be maintained that this means nothing more than that these criminals were killed for their crimes. But lines 34f. suggest that Hades is a place of further punishment for them, as enemies of the gods normally continue to be tormented after death.[68]

But the story does not end here: the group of concepts found in Alcman reappeared in the Hellenistic period, as is seen from one surviving example of these themes in Rhianus Fr. 1.10ff. (Powell). Here a man endowed by the gods with wealth and power forgets his mortal status and aspires to divine rights. In particular:

> ἐπιλήθεται οὕνεκα γαῖαν
> ποσσὶν ἐπιστείβει θνητοὶ δέ οἴ εἰσι τοκῆες,
> ἀλλ᾽ ὑεροπλίῃ καὶ ἁμαρτωλῆσι νοόιο
> ἶσα Διὶ βρομέει, κεφαλὴν δ᾽ ὑπέραυχον ἀνίσχει,
> καίπερ ἐὼν ὀλίγος, μνᾶται δ᾽ εὔπηχυν Ἀθήνην,
> ἠέ τιν᾽ ἀτραπιτὸν τεκμαίρεται Οὐλυμπόνδε,
> ὥς κε μετ᾽ ἀθανάτοισιν ἀρίθμιος εἰλαπινάζῃ. (10–16)
>
> *He forgets that he walks on the earth with his feet and that his parents are mortal; but in his arrogance and in his wrongheadedness he thunders as loud as Zeus, he holds his head up in overweaning pride, although he is only a little man, and he wants to marry strong-armed Athena or conjectures about a road to Olympus, so that he can be numbered among the immortals and dine with them.*

The next lines describe the advent of Ate to punish the sinner, but the fragment ends before his specific punishment is revealed. But the train of thought, and especially line 14, suggest the possibility that a Hellenistic poet, not necessarily Rhianus, might have handled the theme and may have been in part or in whole Tibullus' direct predecessor.

This is not the only Tibullan example where both a Hellenistic and an archaic antecedent can be found. Luck calls attention[69] to the relationship between Tibullus 1.4.75ff.:

> pareat ille suae; vos me celebrate magistrum
>   quos male habet multa callidus arte puer.
> gloria cuique sua est: me, qui spernuntur, amantes
>   consultent: cunctis ianua nostra patet.
> tempus erit, cum me Veneris praecepta ferentem
>   deducat iuvenum sedula turba senem.

and Callimachus, *Aetia* Fr. 41 (Pf.):

> γηράσκει δ᾽ ὁ γέρων κεῖνος ἐλαφρότερον,
> κοῦροι τὸν φιλέουσιν, ἐὸν δέ μιν οἷα γονῆα
> χειρὸς ἐπ᾽ οἰκείην ἄχρις ἄγουσι θύρην
> *That old man grows old with greater ease whom the young men love and*

---

[68] Cf. *R-E* s.v. Tartaros 1.   [69] *Latin Love Elegy* p. 98.

whom they escort by the hand to his own door as though he were their father.

He comments 'Anacreon could have described himself in these terms, and the gaiety and exuberance of these lines [i.e. Tibullus 1.4.79f.] does, indeed, recall the mood of archaic Greek lyrics. It seems however that they are modelled after some lines of Callimachus [i.e. *Aetia* Fr. 41 (Pf.)].'

This suggestion can be taken a little further. No example of Anacreon saying exactly the same as Callimachus and Tibullus survives. But there is a fragment where Anacreon seems to be saying something analogous:

> ἡ δὲ τοῦ Τηίου σοφιστοῦ τέχνη τοῦ αὐτοῦ ἤθους καὶ τρόπου. καὶ γὰρ πάντων ἐρᾶι τῶν καλῶν καὶ ἐπαινεῖ πάντας. μεστὰ δὲ αὐτοῦ τὰ ἄισματα τῆς Σμέρδιος κόμης καὶ τῶν Κλεοβούλου ὀφθαλμῶν καὶ τῆς Βαθύλλου ὥρας. ἀλλὰ καὶ τούτοις τὴν σωφροσύνην ὁρᾶις·
>
> (a)   ἔραμαι ⟨δέ⟩ τοι συνηβᾶν,
> φησίν,
>   χαρίεν γὰρ †ἔχεις ἦθος.†
> καὶ αὖθις
> (b)   καλὸν εἶναι τῶι Ἔρωτι τὰ δίκαιά φησιν.
> ἤδη δέ που καὶ τὴν τέχνην ἀπεκαλύψατο·
> (c)   ἐμὲ γὰρ †λόγων εἴνεκα παῖδες ἂν φιλέοιεν·
>   χαρίεντα μὲν γὰρ ἄιδω, χαρίεντα δ' οἶδα λέξαι.
>
> (Anacreon Fr. 402 (PMG))

The art of the clever Teian poet is of the same type and character. For he is in love with all beautiful boys and praises them all. His poems are full of the hair of Smerdis and the eyes of Kleoboulos and the beauty of Bathyllos in its prime. But you can see his restraint in these lines too: (a) 'I love to sport with you' he says 'for you have charming ways' and again (b) 'love likes just dealing' he says. And I think that he shows his art too in the following (c) 'for boys would perhaps love me for my words since my songs are full of charm and I know how to utter charming words'.

The step from Anacreon's claim that boys will(?) love him for his poetry, that is, while Anacreon is still an active lover, to the Callimachean concept of the old poet enjoying the respect of boys after he has ceased to be active as a lover, is not a large one; and of course there is no need to think that this is the only passage where Anacreon discussed similar topics.

Again, the passage quoted above from Rhianus ends with a description of the activity of Ate which has some resemblance to Tibullus 1.9.3f.:

> a miser, et si quis primo periuria celat,
>   sera tamen tacitis Poena venit pedibus.

Ultimately this passage looks back to Homeric descriptions of Ate, in particular to *Iliad* 19.91ff.[70] But it may well be that Tibullus derives his concept of *Ate–Poena* and her activities not directly from Homer but through a Hellenistic reworking of the theme. This could be a portion of Euphorion's *Chiliades* or Callimachus' *Ibis* or some other Hellenistic poem of the genre arai. It is probably not Rhianus Fr. 1.17ff. (Powell). But this text discussed Ate, derives at one remove or another from the Homeric *loci* and is therefore worth quoting as an unnoted parallel to the Tibullan passage:

'Η δ' Ἄτη ἁπαλοῖσι μετατρωχῶσα πόδεσσιν
ἄκρης ἐν κεφαλῆσιν ἀνώϊστος καὶ ἄφαντος
ἄλλοτε μὲν γραίῃσι νεωτέρη, ἄλλοτε·δ' αὖτε
ὁπλοτέρῃσι γρηῦς ἐφίσταται ἀμπλακίῃσιν,
Ζηνὶ θεῶν κρείοντι Δίκη τ' ἐπίηρα φέρουσα.
Ate running after on soft feet, unexpected and unseen on the tops of mens' heads, sometimes comes as a fresh crime upon old, at other times as an old addition to fresh crimes, rendering service to Zeus, lord of the gods, and to Justice.

This last topic is of course complicated by the presence of similar concepts in Greek tragedy and elsewhere, in particular such cases as *Fr. Trag. Graec. Adesp.* 564N: ὀπισθόπους δίκη (Justice who follows behind); *AP* 12.229.2 (Straton): ὑστερόπουν . . . Νέμεσιν (Nemesis coming with later step); and especially Euripides Fr. 979(N): ἡ Δίκη . . . | . . . | . . . σῖγα καὶ βραδεῖ ποδὶ | στείχουσα μάρψει τοὺς κακούς, ὅταν τύχῃ (Justice, quietly and with slow foot walking, will seize the wicked when the time is ripe). But the very existence in these three cases of both archaic and Hellenistic versions of a similar topos which then reappears in Tibullus raises interesting questions about the traditions of ancient poetry.

There are two possibilities in such cases, which could no doubt be multiplied many times if more archaic and Hellenistic poetry survived. The first is simply that a process of relay transmission is involved: a concept first appears in early Greek poetry and then is imitated by a Hellenistic writer or writers; the Roman poet then goes to his Hellenistic predecessor for the topos. Given the literary claims made by Augustan poets it is likely that this often happened; and in such cases the existence of an early Greek parallel passage would only be a question of literary history.

On the other hand it is most unlikely that Augustan poets and their audiences did not read early Greek poets. Apart from direct references in them to early Greek poets, and such facts as Virgil's use of Pindar in the proem to *Georgics* 3, the *Odes* of Horace with their frequent and complex imitation of the *novem lyrici* presume a fairly wide knowledge of early Greek poetry among their readership. Similarly the use of 'analogising'

[70] Cf. also Hom. *Il.* 9.502ff.

techniques by Horace in such *Odes* as 3.11 where he has created a Roman analogue of an early Greek lyric ode[71] and by Tibullus himself, as will be demonstrated in Chapter 3, argues for a deep Roman understanding of Greek poetry which must have included understanding of the archaic models used by Hellenistic poets.

Attention has recently been called to two cases where a Roman poet imitates not a single predecessor but simultaneously the antecedent of that predecessor also.[72] Virgil and Persius not only copy their direct model but also pay their readers and their model the compliment of recognising the model's use of a yet earlier model by combining imitation of the two in their poem; and in the second case, the first-century AD scholiast explicitly states what is happening. There is no reason why Tibullus, in using a Hellenistic predecessor, may not have 'looked through' him to his model and combined the two in his own work. This view would help to explain some of the apparent allusions in Tibullus to archaic Greek poetry;[73] and although it cannot, because of the fragmentary nature of the evidence, be carried further in relation to the three cases discussed above, it may be useful to keep it in mind in future research in this area.

[71] Cf. F. Cairns, '*Splendide Mendax*: Horace *Odes* III.11', *Greece and Rome* 2nd ser. 22 (1975) 129ff.
[72] Du Quesnay, *PLLS 1976* p. 94 n. 213 and p. 99: Addendum to n. 213.
[73] It may e.g. account for the reminiscences of Bacchylides and Mimnermus in Tib. 1.1. See above, Ch. 1 p. 12 and nn. 52f.

3
ANALOGY AS LEARNING

Another aspect of 'learning' in Roman poetry is the creation in Latin and in Roman terms of analogues of Greek institutions, literary genres, linguistic mannerisms and so forth. This practice has been thought of in the past as 'Hellenising', that is, as Roman genuflection to Greek culture. It is perhaps more accurately seen as 'Romanising', as an affirmation of the Roman ability to absorb and surpass every Greek achievement.

The creation of such Roman analogues is more than a species of imitation. It is a continuation of an important intellectual activity initiated in the Hellenistic period. The writers of the third century BC analysed, evaluated and resynthesised the cultural heritage of early Greece in terms acceptable and comprehensible to post-classical Greece. The Roman poets of the late Republic and early Empire performed the same service for their own contemporaries. The only difference between the two groups of writers, besides language, lies in the raw material they used. For the Hellenistic Greeks, this was mainly archaic Greek literature. For the Romans the main source of raw material was the Hellenistic period itself.

A minor example of learned analogy in Tibullus can be found in 1.3.29–32. Here Tibullus depicts Delia as paying to Isis Tibullus' vows to that goddess for his safety:

> ut mea votivas persolvens Delia voces
>   ante sacras lino tecta fores sedeat
> bisque die resoluta comas tibi dicere laudes
>   insignis turba debeat in Pharia.

The epithet *Pharia* contains an interesting piece of erudition. The shrine and cult of Isis Pharia at Alexandria have recently been dated by P. M. Fraser:[1] 'There is no evidence that this cult existed before the Roman period (the earliest reference to it occurs in Ovid), and since cults of Isis proliferated from the later Ptolemaic period onwards it is quite likely that the shrine and cult may be of that date.'[2] Now Tibullus 1.3 probably dates from around 30 BC,[3] and the adjective *Pharia* clearly refers to the cult of Isis Pharia; so when commentators on Tibullus state that it simply stands for 'Egyptian' or 'Alexandrian' they are missing Tibullus' learned point. He is

---

[1] Fraser I pp. 20f. and nn. 125–8.
[2] Fraser I p. 21. The Ovidian references are: *Am.* 2.13.7f.; *Met.* 9.773f.
[3] See André introd. to Tib. 1.3.

mentioning the new, that is, late Ptolemaic, cult of Isis Pharia, just as Callimachus in typical Hellenistic fashion celebrated the new cult of Arsinoe Aphrodite in *Epigram* 5 (Pf.). In thus analogising Tibullus demonstrates his adherence to the learned Hellenistic practice which provides the pattern for his analogue.

On a much larger scale, 2.5 will serve as a clear example of the creation by Tibullus of a Latin and Roman analogue of a Greek literary theme. This is a debated elegy, but much of the debate can be evaded by approaching it from a fresh viewpoint. This will reveal the thematic unity of the elegy and thus indirectly contribute to a solution of some difficulties traditionally found in it. The elegy will be treated in three sections: first its genre, structure and content will be sketched briefly; second the subject of its central portion, in which the 'learning' under discussion lies, will be discussed at greater length; and thirdly, a short view of its literary and political implications will be offered.

Tibullus 2.5 is marked by address to Phoebus/Apollo at the most important points in it, the beginning (1;17), the middle (65) and the end (106;121).[4] In each case the *laudandus* Messalinus appears along with Apollo in the three most important positions in the poem. At the beginning Messalinus is represented as entering the temple of Palatine Apollo (1f.). In the middle he is not explicitly mentioned; but during the sacrifice which he is making (cf. lines 1–6) the good omen of the crackling laurel will be manifest (81f.). At the end he is the *triumphator* of the future, wearing a laurel wreath (115ff.).

The elegy starts with a mixture of prayer and summons: the god is asked to be propitious and is summoned to attend the induction of Messalinus as *XVvir*. Further prayer (3f.) is followed by repeated summons (5ff.). The elegy thus announces itself as a kletic/euktic hymn. The euktic element manifests itself once more at the beginning (17f.), in the middle also (79–82) and finally and most pronouncedly at the end (105–22). Prayer to a god and summons of a god go together easily, since the whole point of summons is to procure the presence of a god who will listen to his suppliant's pleas. Sappho Fr. 1 (LP) may be compared for exactly the same combination of kletic and euktic elements. In fact the correct designation of such hymns is probably simply kletic, since a casual precept of Menander Rhetor assumes that prayer will often play a prominent part in hymns so entitled:

γίνωσκε δὲ τόδε τὸ θεώρημα οὐκ ἄχρηστον, ὅτι εἰ μὲν εὐχὴ ἐπακολουθεῖ ἐπικλήσει, ἔτι ἐλάττων ἡ διατριβὴ καὶ τοῖς ποιηταῖς καὶ τοῖς συγγραφεῦσιν· εἰ δὲ αὐτὸ τοῦτο εἴη ψιλὴ κλῆσις, πλείων

---

[4] In addition Apollo is long-haired at the beginning (8) and end (121) of the poem and the Sibyl in the middle (66), the last being another 'substitute motif'. (See above, Ch. 2 p. 46 and n. 43 and below, p. 82.)

ἐστί, καὶ ζητῶν ἂν εὕροις παρὰ τοῖς ποιηταῖς τὴν συνήθειαν ταύτην πεφυλαγμένην.   (*Rhetores Graeci* (ed. Spengler) 3.335.31–336.4)
Here is a useful rule: if prayer accompanies summons both poets and prose-writers spend less time on the summons. But if you have only got summons and nothing else, it is fuller, and if you look in the poets you can see that this is a generally observed practice.

The central portion of Tibullus 2.5 contains a narrative of past events (19ff.), a prophecy (39ff.) and an account first of portents fulfilled in the past and then of a happy future (67ff.). All these passages are integral parts of the hymn. Lines 19–66 relate how Apollo inspired the Sibyl with prophetic insight. This enabled her to predict correctly the foundation and future glory of Rome. The passage thus amplifies lines 15f.:

> te duce Romanos numquam frustrata Sibylla
>   abdita quae senis fata canit pedibus.

It is therefore part of the description of the god's past achievements, which is a hymnic commonplace.[5] The function of such descriptions is both to flatter the god and to demonstrate that the prayers being made are reasonable ones which the god has the power to fulfil. Here Tibullus asks Apollo to inspire Messalinus to interpret with prophetic veracity the Sibylline books (17f.). Both the preceding couplet (15f.) and the passage which follows (19–66) describe the god's past achievements in the same field. Lines 67–104 also contain a prayer – for the peace and prosperity of Rome (79–82). It too is flanked by descriptions of Apollo's achievements. First Tibullus describes more of the god's past actions through his Sibylline mouthpieces, climaxing in the statement that all bad omens have been fulfilled – *haec fuerant olim* (79).[6] Then lines 83–104 declare that omens of peace delivered through Apollo's agency will signal the future prosperity and happiness of Rome.

There is therefore symmetry in the two major passages which make up the centre of the poem. Each consists of:

	15–66	67–104
A[1]		
Brief description of the god's power	15f. (in the past)	67–79 (in the past)
B		
Prayer	17f.	79–82

---

[5] Cf. K. Buchholz, *De Horatio Hymnographo* (Diss, Königsberg 1912) pp. 15ff.; E. Norden, *Agnostos Theos* (Leipzig/Berlin 1913) pp. 149ff.; H. Kleinknecht, *Die Gebetsparodie in der Antike* (Tübinger Beiträge zur Altertumswissenschaft 28, Stuttgart 1937, repr. Hildesheim 1967) Namen- und Sachregister *s.v.* Aretalogie.

[6] *fuerant* is the reading of all MSS except two late ones and there is no good reason to alter it.

A²
Longer description
of the god's power   19–66 (in the past)   83–104 (in the future)

Like the past achievements of Apollo, his future achievements are an integral part of the hymn.[7] They are a response to prayers made within the elegy and so can be considered as a 'reaction' within the genre kletikon. 'Reaction' can occur in any genre when its aim is fulfilled, and a reaction to a prayer in the form of fulfilment of that prayer can be paralleled. It is found in Horace, *Odes* 3.11, a euktic hymn;[8] and in the anathematikon, a genre with euktic links, future fulfilment of a prayer is predicted in Horace, *Odes* 3.23, while fulfilment of a prayer is actually recorded in *AP* 6.243 (Diodorus).[9]

Lines 101ff. introduce a personal note: Tibullus mentions his own activities as lover and love-poet. Such personal references by the author are found at the end of at least two other Augustan poems celebrating the praises of a great man, Horace, *Odes* 3.14 and Propertius 3.4. In both the personal note is erotic and in both the occasion of praise is a triumph of Augustus. It is therefore of interest that here Tibullus' thoughts on his own love are immediately followed by his prediction of a triumph for Messalinus (115ff.). The combination of a public festival and of love-making by the private participants in it is traditional,[10] and Tibullus uses it skilfully as a transitional passage in 2.5. It is the means whereby he moves back to praise of his addressee through a fantasy in which the young Messalinus wins a triumph and Tibullus, with Apollo's help, sings his praises. This final vignette is intended to recall two earlier passages in such a way that the three provide yet another thematic bond to unite the elegy. These are the initial mention of Apollo's own praise of victorious Jupiter in lines 9f., in which the laurel is worn not by the *triumphator*, as at the end of the elegy (117), but by the singer; and a central passage dealing with the victories won by Aeneas (45ff.), like Messalinus a favourite of Apollo and the Sibyl. Through all these passages runs the theme of victory; the first and last are particularly close because the *triumphator* was during his triumph the

---

[7] On a non-generic level fantasising about the future is both a Hellenistic trait (cf. Theocr. *Id.* 3.25ff.; 7.63ff.; 11.42ff.; Prop. 3.4) and part of Tibullus' literary persona (cf. Tib. 1.5.19ff., and below, pp. 179f.).

[8] See F. Cairns, '*Splendide Mendax*: Horace *Odes* III.11', *Greece and Rome* 2nd ser. 22 (1975) 129ff.

[9] Cf. F. Cairns, 'Horace *Odes* III,13 and III,23', *Ant. Class.* 46 (1977) 523ff. For a similar reaction see *GC* pp. 148ff. (on Prop. 1.8, a propemptikon) and, even more relevantly, for the opposite reaction see *GC* pp. 152ff. (on Ov. *Am.* 1.13, a kletikon).

[10] Cf. Hor. *Od.* 3.14.17ff. and *GC* pp. 179ff.; Prop. 3.4.15ff. and *GC* pp. 185ff. The concept appears to be standard in New Comedy: cf. e.g. Menand, *Epitrep.* 451ff.; *Samia* 39ff.; Plaut. *Aul.* 28ff.; 794f.; *Cist.* 89ff.; Cic. *De. Leg.* 2.14.35f.; cf. also E. Rohde, *Der Griechische Roman und seine Vorläufer* (4th ed. Darmstadt 1960) pp. 155f.; Gow on Theocr. *Id* 2.66.

incarnation of Jupiter. This was why he wore the royal *toga picta* and had his body smeared with *minium*, a colour usually reserved for the statues of the gods.[11]

Within this generic and structural framework Tibullus has achieved a remarkable feat of 'learning'. He has composed a '*Ῥώμης Κτίσις*, a 'Foundation of Rome',[12] a Roman and Latin analogue of those Greek foundation poems which arose from and enhanced the local patriotism of Greek cities. There were of course earlier versions of the foundation of Rome, some in Greek by Greeks.[13] In addition the early Roman annalists, Fabius Pictor and Cincius Alimentus, writing in Greek, dealt with the theme in the third century BC.[14] On the Latin side in verse Ennius described the fall of Troy and Aeneas' flight in the first book of his *Annales* and Naevius dealt with Roman history from Aeneas down to the Punic wars; and in prose Cato discussed early Rome, although he may not have modelled his *Origines* on Greek *ktiseis*.[15] After Cato other Roman historians reworked this material, some of them writing in Latin.[16] Tibullus in 2.5 and Virgil in the *Aeneid* brought to the subject all the sophisticated techniques of Hellenistic poetry. It is impossible to say which, if either, has priority. Most scholars assume that much of the material of Tibullus 2.5 derives from the *Aeneid*, which Tibullus is supposed to have known extensively before its publication. But such arguments as have been advanced to support this view do not appear convincing,[17] and it does not seem to explain anything in Tibullus 2.5. For this reason almost no account will be taken of the *Aeneid* in the discussion of 2.5 which follows. In this way some misunderstandings of the elegy can be avoided and its independent poetic qualities better appreciated.

Foundations of cities were a popular subject in all periods of Greek poetry.[18] Homer began the trend with his account of the foundation of

[11] H. S. Versnel, *Triumphus* (Leiden 1970) pp. 56ff.
[12] The analysis of the foundation material given in this chapter proceeds in a fashion reminiscent of generic analysis, although the elegy is a euktic/kletic hymn. I reserve for a later work the technical problems involved here.
[13] Cf. Dion. Hal. *Ant. Rom.* 1.6.1; Cornell, *PCPhS* 3ff.; 6f.; 10; 13f.; 16ff. In addition Callimachus seems to have treated some Roman themes (e.g. Frr. 106f.(Pf.)) but not necessarily the foundation of Rome.
[14] Cf. H. Peter, *Historicorum Romanorum Reliquiae* (2nd ed. 1914, repr. Stuttgart 1967) I pp. 5ff. (Pictor); 40ff. (Cincius Alimentus). On the date and identity of Fabius Pictor and the language of his *Annales* see most recently N. Horsfall, *Liverpool Classical Monthly* 1 (1976) 18 and E. Badian *ibid.* 97f.
[15] This is the conclusion of Cornell (thesis) Ch. 5.
[16] Cf. Peter, *Historicorum Romanorum Reliquiae* pp. 98ff.
[17] Cf. most recently W. Gerressen, *Tibulls Elegie 2,5 und Vergils Aeneis* (Diss. Köln 1970). But M. J. McGann's ('The date of Tibullus' death', *Latomus* 29 (1970) 778) statement (referring to V. Buchheit, 'Tibull II 5 und die Aeneis', *Philol.* 109 (1965) 104ff.): 'It seems necessary to conclude that Buchheit has brought forward no evidence to prove that in II,5 Tibullus drew on the *Aeneid* in its published form', is also true of G.'s work. Some knowledge of the *Aeneid* on T.'s part through recitations cannot be ruled out; but there is no evidence of this in Tib. 2.5.
[18] Cf. Schmid; Graham; Cornell (thesis); *PCPhS passim*; F. Jacoby, *Atthis: The Local*

Rhodes.[19] The archaic period continued it: Mimnermus wrote about the foundation of Colophon/Smyrna,[20] Kallinus about the foundation of Hamaxitos in the Troad,[21] Semonides of Amorgos about the foundation of Samos.[22] There were doubtless others. The fifth century saw verse foundations by Xenophanes (Colophon and Elea),[23] Panyassis (the cities of Ionia),[24] prose foundations by Hippys of Rhegium,[25] Hellanicus of Lesbos[26] and Charon of Lampsacus[27] and the seemingly influential work of Ion of Chios on the foundation of Chios.[28] Fifth-century interest in foundations was popular as well as literary: they were a favourite theme of stories among the Spartans.[29]

The fourth and subsequent centuries saw even further expansion of literary interest in foundation legends: and they were associated with two other important subjects of literature in that period, *paradoxa* and *aetia*.[30] Thus they embraced all those curious religious rites and antiquarian oddities of which Hellenistic poets were so fond. The titles of five poetic *ktiseis* of Apollonius of Rhodes are known.[31] Two portions of a verse 'Foundation of Lesbos' survive;[32] and there are testimonia to a number of other poetic *ktiseis*.[33] Finally – and perhaps most significantly – Callimachus treated the foundation legends of the Sicilian cities in the second book of his *Aetia*. A fair amount of the 'Foundation of Zancle' survives from this book– *Aetia* 2 Fr. 43.58ff. (Pf.); and from its aetiological and etymological interests we can conjecture the character of some of the lost Hellenistic examples. In the Hellenistic period, in addition to the poetic

Chronicles of Ancient Athens (Oxford 1949) pp. 363ff. (n. 62) and Index *s.v. ktiseis*. On the *ktiseis* mentioned in this paragraph cf. most recently Cornell (thesis) pp. 140ff.

[19] *Il.* 2.653ff. Cf. also *Od.* 6.3ff., an account of the foundation of the mythical Phaeacia.
[20] (Mimnermus) Fr. 12 (D); Strabo 14.13f.; Schmid pp. 13ff.
[21] Strabo 13.1.48; Schmid pp. 8ff.
[22] Schmid pp. 16ff.
[23] Jacoby, *Fr. Gr. Hist.* 450. The authenticity of this work is doubted by Cornell (thesis) pp. 373f.
[24] Cf. Schmid 36ff.; and most recently V. J. Matthews, *Panyassis of Halicarnassus: Text and Commentary* (Mnemosyne Suppl. 33, Leiden 1974) index *s.v.* Ionia, Ionian migration; works on.
[25] Jacoby, *Fr. Gr. Hist.* 554. On the problems of Hippys and his date see Cornell (thesis) pp. 374f.; 393ff.
[26] Jacoby, *Fr. Gr. Hist.* 4 Frr. 66–71. See Cornell (thesis) pp. 376ff.
[27] Jacoby, *Fr. Gr. Hist.* 262. See Cornell (thesis) pp. 378f.
[28] Jacoby, *Fr. Gr. Hist.* 392. In prose according to Cornell (thesis) pp. 142ff.; see also pp. 375f.; but Fraser II Ch. 11 n. 420 feels that the question of whether it was a verse or a prose work is still open. Most recently in favour of verse G. Cerri, 'La *ktisis* di Ione di Chio: prosa o versi?' *Quad. Urbin.* 26 (1977) 127ff.
[29] Cf. Plat. *Hipp. Mai.* 285d.
[30] Cf. Fraser I pp. 774ff.; Cornell (thesis) pp. 145ff., 379ff.
[31] Cf. Powell pp. 5ff.: Apollonius Rhodius Frr. 4–11. Cf. Fraser I pp. 513f., 632; Cornell (thesis) pp. 381ff.
[32] Powell pp. 7f.; the authorship is uncertain: cf. Fraser II p. 895 n. 131.
[33] Cf. Fraser III General Index *s.v.* Foundation-literature.

70 *Analogy as learning*

ktiseis, numerous prose accounts of foundations were written. There was also a minor industry of fabricating for historical and cultural purposes oracular and other documentary material relevant to foundations.[34]

Enough *ktisis* literature has survived, albeit mainly in fragments or testimonia, to allow typical ktistic themes to be recognised in Tibullus 2.5.[35] These will now be identified and discussed. The order in which these topics will be treated is roughly the logical order of events in a foundation, not the order in which they occur in Tibullus. Like all Hellenistic poets, Tibullus diverges from the obvious order. In thinking about foundations, it is particularly important to remember that a 'foundation' can include much more than an account of how and why the city was established. It can also cover both the period prior to the foundation and the period after it. In both cases there is no limit to the possible temporal extension of the account.[36] The principal ktistic features of Tibullus 2.5 are:

(i) Apollo κτίστης (founder)
(ii) The Oikist (the human founder)
(iii) The Foundation Oracle
(iv) The Continuity of Worship
(v) The Prehistory and Foundation Festival (first version)
(vi) The Post-foundation History
(vii) The Foundation Festival (second version)
(viii) The Gods of Rome

(i) APOLLO

The prominence of the god in Tibullus 2.5 reflects his central role in actual foundations and in accounts of them. This role cannot be overstated: Apollo's oracle at Delphi was the principal source of divine instigation and encouragement of colonisation in ancient Greece.[37] As the inspirer and authoriser, and also sometimes active joint builder of colonies, Apollo is himself *ktistes*.[38] The god's role in foundations is best summed up by a passage from Callimachus' Hymn to Apollo:

> Φοίβῳ δ'ἑσπόμενοι πόλιας διεμετρήσαντο
> ἄνθρωποι· Φοῖβος γὰρ ἀεὶ πολίεσσι φιληδεῖ
> κτιζομένῃσ', αὐτὸς δὲ θεμείλια Φοῖβος ὑφαίνει.   (*Hymn* 2.55f.)
> *Under Phoebus' leadership men have measured out cities. For Phoebus always takes pleasure in the foundation of cities and Phoebus himself weaves their foundations.*

[34] *Ibid.* and Schmid *passim*.
[35] Schmid's several partial schemes of *ktisis* material (esp. pp. 5f., 48f., 167ff.) and Cornell's two chapters on *ktiseis* (thesis Chh. 5, 11) permit an analytic table of *ktisis* topics to be dispensed with here.
[36] Cf. Schmid pp. 4ff., 43f., 48f.   [37] Schmid pp. 154ff.
[38] Cf. Graham index *s.v.* Apollo; Schmid pp. 154ff. and see below, p. 73 on Thurii.

Analogy as learning

Tibullus emphasises Apollo's accoutrements – lyre, laurel wreath, long musician's robe and long hair (2ff., 121) – partly because he hopes for Apollo's help in his poetry and in his love-life (3f.; 105ff.; 113f.) and so is invoking him as citharode. But the emphasis also relates to Apollo's place in foundations. It was as the inspirer of prophetic hexameters that Apollo stimulated and sanctioned new colonies; so his poetic guise is to the fore in ktistic contexts. A later dedication by the city of Apollonia stresses this attribute of Apollo with the single word 'long-haired' in the context of his 'foundation' of that city:

> μνάματ' 'Απολλωνίας ἀνακείμεθα, τὰν ἐνὶ πόντῳ
> Ἰωνίῳ Φοῖβος ᾦκισ' ἀκερσεκόμας.
> (Anon. (*ap*. Pausanias 5.22.3) 1f)[39]
>
> *We are the dedications of Apollonia which long haired Phoebus founded in the Ionian sea.*

According to Tibullus therefore, Apollo is giving the same kind of divine blessing and sanction to the foundation of Troy's colony that he later gave to so many famous Greek colonies. Moreover Apollo is also linked with colonisation as νόμιος – the pastoral god;[40] and the bucolic emphasis of much of the latter part of Tibullus 2.5 owes something to this link. Finally it may be remembered that Apollo was regarded as the founder of Troy itself (cf. e.g. *Georgics* 3.36: *Troiae Cynthius auctor*).[41]

(ii) THE FOUNDER

In any foundation legend the founder (οἰκιστής) plays a prominent part. In antiquity, as now, the founder of Rome was generally reckoned to be the eponymous Romulus. But in this elegy Tibullus seemed to be adopting another view, accepted also by some other writers, both Greek and Roman:[42] Aeneas occupies such a prominent place in Tibullus 2.5 that it is hard to regard anyone else as founder. Moreover Tibullus constantly stresses the continuity between Troy and Rome. *nec fore credebat Romam* (21) establishes at the beginning of the account that Troy's successor will be Rome. The passage from *Troica . . . sacra* (40) to *Troia* (61) emphasises the transmission of the gods from mother-city Troy to colony Rome (see below (viii)). The couplet *Troia quidem tunc* [i.e. when Rome exists] *se mirabitur et sibi dicet* | *vos bene tam longa consuluisse via* (61f.) in particular reveals that Aeneas' task will not be complete until Rome is founded. In all

---

[39] See Schmid p. 166
[40] Cf. W. Wimmel, 'Tibull II 5 und das elegische Rombild', *Gedenkschrift für G. Rohde* ed. G. Radke (Aparchai: Untersuchungen zur klass. Philologie und Geschichte des Altertums 4, Tübingen 1961) pp. 254f. and n. 5.
[41] Cf. Hor. *Od.* 3.3.65f.
[42] Including Hellanicus, Damastes and, perhaps significantly, Sallust, *Cat.* 6.1f. Cf. Cornell, *PCPhS* 13, 17f., 22.

these ways Tibullus is claiming Rome as Troy's colony and Aeneas as the founder.

The reasons for Tibullus' acceptance of the view that Aeneas is the founder are varied. Firstly, the same motives which led him to use an antedating account of the foundation oracle (see below) also lead him to place the founder early in the sequence of foundation. Secondly, the now all-powerful Julian family had elevated Aeneas to this role; and since Messalla was a supporter of Augustus, Tibullus would have found it difficult not to assent to the view that Aeneas was the founder. Finally, Romulus was a figure who presented difficulties in the Augustan context. Apart from his odd upbringing, his questionable foster mothers, she-wolf and prostitute, his banditry, his chicanery in obtaining the status of founder, his sponsoring of the rape of the Sabine women and his fratricide,[43] he had been, on one account, murdered by senators.[44] It has been suggested that these difficulties led Augustus to abandon an aspiration to be renamed Romulus.[45] It may be that similar considerations helped to persuade Tibullus to select the comparatively untainted[46] Aeneas as a more admirable founder. There are parallels within the ktistic tradition for the *eponymos* not being founder. One such hero was Chios in Ion of Chios' account of the foundation of Chios.[47] Another was Kroton, the eponymous hero of that city.[48] In both these cases however, the *eponymos* was earlier in history than the eventual physical founder of the city.

There may be one historical part-parallel to Aeneas, although an *eponymos* is not involved: Lamis led the expedition which eventually founded Megara Hyblaea after it had attempted to settle at other places.[49] Lamis himself died at Thapsus before his people moved on to Megara Hyblaea. It is not known whether Lamis was regarded as the founder of Megara Hyblaea; but the fact that his name is preserved in connection with the foundation of Megara Hyblaea is a reasonable argument for this. Tibullus is certainly unusual in making his eponymous non-founder later in time than the real founder, but of course the legendary framework within which he was writing left him little room for manoeuvre on this point.

The ktistic tradition was helpful to Tibullus on a related point. He could more easily accept the view that Aeneas was the founder of Rome because Greek foundations could be multiple as well as single: in some cases the first place of settlement might not be the final place; and the foundation

---

[43] Most recently on this subject see Cornell, *PCPhS* 8.
[44] Cf. *R-E s.v.* Romulus p. 1098.
[45] Cf. R. Syme, *The Roman Revolution* (Oxford 1939) pp. 313f.
[46] Cf. G. K. Galinsky, *Aeneas, Sicily and Rome* (Princeton Monographs in Art and Archaeology 40, Princeton 1969) pp. 46ff.
[47] Cf. Schmid pp. 43ff.   [48] *Id.* pp. 122ff.
[49] Cf. *R-E s.v.* Megara (in Sizilien) pp. 206ff.

was not regarded as complete until the final destination was reached. This can be seen in the case of Colophon, which had Smyrna as an intermediate point of settlement, and in the case mentioned above, Megara Hyblaea with its earlier abortive places of settlement. It can also be seen in the long Hellenistic inscription purporting to record the history of the foundation of Magnesia on the Maeander.[50] An eighty-year stay in Crete was intercalated between the abandonment by the Magnesians of their original home in Thessaly and their final settlement at Magnesia; but the whole process, including the Cretan interlude, was regarded as the 'foundation of Magnesia'. Tibullus narrates the chain of foundations which led to that of Rome in lines 40ff.: Aeneas settled in Lavinium, his son Ascanius established Alba Longa, and finally Romulus built Rome. By means of these links Tibullus unifies the *ktisis* and assigns Romulus his part in it (23f., 51ff.); and Romulus' city is the end of the chain.

Although Aeneas is the founder of Rome in Tibullus 2.5, Romulus' subordinate importance is recognised when he is assigned one founder's task, that of setting up the walls (24f.).[51] Remus, the brother and rival of Romulus, is mentioned after him (25). Their dispute resembles that of the founders of Zancle.[52] In the case of Rome however the dispute was settled to the clear advantage of Romulus instead of being left unsettled, as at Zancle. A third and historical account of strife between colonists about what city they should regard as mother-city and whom they should honour as founder survives. This concerns Thurii.[53]

(iii) THE FOUNDATION ORACLE

The normal pattern in foundations is that the Delphic Pythia gives oracular sanction; but in Tibullus 2.5 a Sibyl authorises the foundation of Rome. Both are of course Apollo's mouthpieces. But Tibullus' Sibyl is an *ad hoc* functionary in the field of colonisation, and she has more personality and a semi-independent status as a prophetess in her own right. Even more unorthodox kinds of foundation oracle are known. In Pindar, *Pythian* 4[54] Medea gives one of the foundation oracles of Cyrene; and there is a chain of human prophetic/inspirational delegation in one of the historically documented attempts of the Spartan king Dorieus to found a colony in the West. He was advised by a seer, Antichares of Eleon, who had in turn employed as his source of inspiration the 'Oracles of Laios'.[55]

The concept of the Sibyl as the mouthpiece of the foundation oracle of

---

[50] Cf. Schmid pp. 94ff.
[51] Cf. Call. *Aet.* fr. 43.60ff. (Pf.) and Pfeiffer *ad loc.*
[52] Cf. Call. *Aet.* Fr. 43.72ff. (Pf.) and Pfeiffer *ad loc.*
[53] Diod. Sic. 12.35.1ff. The end of the dispute – an approach to Delphi and Apollo's declaration that he (the god) was founder of Thurii – is significant. See above (i) Apollo.
[54] For further discussion of this poem, see below, pp. 114f.   [55] Hdt. 5.43.

Rome is pre-Tibullan.[56] Tibullus accepted this tradition and indeed chose to treat the whole theme of the foundation of Rome in the first place because 2.5 was written to celebrate the induction of Messalinus, the son of his patron Messalla, as a *XVvir sacris faciundis*. The *XVviri*, among their other duties, had charge of the Sibylline books. The most impressive recorded feat of any Sibyl was the giving of the foundation oracle of Rome; so Tibullus decided to write about the city's foundation. The act of delegation from Apollo to the Sibyl to Messalinus helped Tibullus in his eulogy of Messalinus: the words of Apollo were conveyed through the Sibyl; and her written prophecies are now being entrusted to the keeping and interpretation of Messalinus. Messalinus and the Sibyl are thus deliberately represented as parallel in function: just as she interpreted Apollo, so she is now to be interpreted by Messalinus.

The dating of the foundation oracle of Rome is a question of interest. Ancient sources give various dates for the foundation of Rome, mostly in the eighth century BC but ranging from 814 BC (Timaeus) to 728 BC (Cincius Alimentus).[57] The Trojan War was dated about 400 years earlier. Tibullus found in his sources and incorporated in his account a foundation oracle for Rome given about 400 years before its actual foundation. This early dating of the foundation oracle may be an attempt to make Rome seem indisputably older than the first Greek cities of Sicily and Italian Cumae. These were also eighth-century foundations and in at least one version the earliest of them was dated to the first half of the eighth century.[58] In antiquity the older a foundation the more hallowed it was, and the firmer a moral claim it gave that city to its territory. The Tibullan account of how the foundation oracle of Rome was given three or four hundred years before the historical foundations of the Greek cities of Sicily and Italy suggests that Rome had clear priority, since a *ktisis* began in the ancient view not with the settlement of the city but with the divine sanction for colonisation.[59] Antedatings of the foundation of Rome had already been made by various Greek writers – Agathyllus, 'Cephalon of Gergis' and the source(s) of Plutarch, *Romulus* 2[60] – for motives which may have been either 'scholarly' or to flatter Roman pretensions.

A parallel for this early dating of a foundation oracle can be seen in Pindar's even more audacious invention in his fourth *Pythian*. In this epinikion Pindar relates the foundation of Cyrene, a colony of Thera, which was itself originally settled from Sparta. From a historical point of view the foundation of Cyrene is the best documented of all foundations of

[56] Cf. Smith on Tib. 2.5.19.
[57] A. Momigliano, 'An interim report on the origins of Rome', *JRS* 53 (1963) 96f.; J. Pinsent, *Military Tribunes and Plebeian Consuls: The Fasti from 44V to 342V* (*Historia* Einzelschr. 24, Wiesbaden 1975) pp. 1ff.; Cornell, *PCPhS* 4,24.
[58] Cf. A. W. Gomme, A. Andrewes and K. J. Dover, *A Historical Commentary on Thucydides* IV (Oxford 1970) p. 206. On these colonies in general, pp. 198ff.
[59] Cf. Schmid *passim*. [60] See Cornell, *PCPhS* 16 n. 5, 17 nn. 4, 6.

Analogy as learning

ancient colonies. There is a full account of it by Herodotus[61] and a surviving inscription purporting to contain the text of the Foundation Decree for Cyrene as passed in Thera.[62] In these 'orthodox' accounts the foundation of Cyrene was authorised and indeed was ordered by contemporary oracles from Delphi around 630 BC.

But in *Pythian* 4 Pindar was not content to cite only Apollo's oracle to Battus as authorisation for the foundation; he goes on to claim that Battus' fulfilment of Delphic Apollo's oracular injunctions simultaneously fulfilled a much older prophecy, made seventeen generations before by Medea (13ff.). Medea was on board the *Argo* when it arrived at Thera after the theft of the Golden Fleece. There Medea prophesied the future settlement of Cyrene by Therans of Spartan descent. Medea's prophecy ends with a prediction of Apollo's oracle to Battus (53ff.) which allows Pindar to return to historical fact. Pindar's Medea episode records the Spartan origin of Thera in an elegant and entertaining way. But it also antedates the prophetic authorisation of the foundation of Cyrene and therefore makes it more hallowed and venerable. In addition it creates an intentional and apt synchronism between the first sea-voyage of the *Argo* and its crew of heroes on the one hand and the announcement of the Therans' future voyage of colonisation to Cyrene on the other.

Another aspect of the Tibullan foundation oracle deserves attention. This is the question of where it was given. Scholars have been divided on this matter; and some, assuming Virgilian influence, have claimed that the Sibyl is confronting Aeneas at Cumae. But there is no mention of Cumae in Tibullus; and had the *Aeneid* been lost, no modern scholar would have dreamed of claiming that the Tibullan Sibyl met Aeneas there. The crucial lines are

> haec dedit Aeneae sortes, postquam ille parentem
>   dicitur et raptos sustinuisse Lares
> nec fore credebat Romam, cum maestus ab alto
>   Ilion ardentes respiceretque deos.   (19–22)

The metrical pattern of dactyls and spondees in these two couplets is identical. In both couplets a temporal clause (*postquam, cum*) begins at the fourth foot caesura and ends with the pentameter. It is better to assume that *nec* joins *dedit* and *credebat* rather than take it as joining *dicitur* and *credebat*. The latter view involves a change of tense in two clauses dependent on *postquam*, something usually avoided by classical authors;[63] it also produces the inelegance of a subordinate clause within a subordinate clause

---

[61] 4.150–9. Cf. Schol. on Pind. *Pyth.* 4.10a.; Diod. Sic. 8.29.
[62] The stone was cut at a much later date: but the text or at least its substance may well be authentic. Cf. Graham p. 27; Ch. 4; appendix 2. Even if it is not so, it provides more information about the version of the foundation of Cyrene accepted as historical in the Hellenistic period.
[63] Cf. Kühner–Stegman II 2 p. 357.

76 *Analogy as learning*

and necessitates a shift in the sense of *postquam*, which would have a purely temporal meaning for *dicitur . . . sustinuisse* but a causal sense with *credebat*.[64] On the better view, that *nec* joins *dedit* and *credebat*, the text means 'The Sibyl prophesied to Aeneas after he had seized and carried away his father, as they tell, and the Lares; and he did not believe that there would be a Rome when he looked back from the sea (or 'from the height') at Troy and its gods in flames.' Thus it is quite clear that the prophecy was given after the fall of Troy but at a time when Aeneas was still within sight of his native city.[65] The consequence must be that Tibullus' Sibyl is a local Sibyl of the Troad region. The meeting of Aeneas and Sibyl on the Troad was not invented by Tibullus but already existed in the Hellenistic period.[66]

Tibullus' motives for choosing this version of how the foundation oracle was given are significant. One has to do with the destruction of the original Sibylline books in 83 BC.[67] These were believed to have been sold by the Cumaean Sibyl to Tarquinius Priscus. Their destruction meant that they had to be replaced by a new collection of oracles made from various cities where Sibyls had resided: and it was this new collection which Messalinus was going to interpret. Not mentioning Cumae therefore helped Tibullus to eulogise Messalinus. Tibullus is enhancing the new collection of Sibylline oracles by making an Asiatic Sibyl come and prophesy to Aeneas at Troy. Erythrae, where such a Sibyl had resided, was the first place to which the commission charged with replacing the lost Sibylline oracles came in its search for replacements. This alone would suggest that Tibullus' Asiatic Sibyl is the Sibyl of Erythrae; and this suspicion is confirmed – and the commission's behaviour explained – by another pre-Tibullan legend that the Sibyl of Erythrae actually became the Sibyl of Cumae when she emigrated from her native land and came to Italy.[68]

Tibullus' list of Sibyls in lines 67ff. contains yet more evidence that he is advancing such a view. The lines are (without the modern emendations in line 68):

> quicquid Amalthea, quicquid Marpesia dixit,
> Herophile Phoebo grata[69] quod admonuit,

[64] *Id.* II 2 p. 359.   [65] So Smith *ad loc.*
[66] Cf. E. Maass, 'Tibullische Sagen' *Hermes* 18 (1883) 323ff.; *R-E s.v.* Sibyllen.
[67] On this event and its consequences cf. Dion. Hal. *Ant. Rom.* 4.62.6; Tac. *Ann.* 6.12; Lact. *Div.* 1.6.14.
[68] Cf. Smith on Tib. 2.5.15; 19.
[69] The words *Phyto Graia* or *Phoeto Graia* which modern editors print in l.68 are emendations. The MSS read *Phoebo grata*. Lenz–Galinsky, citing Rzach *R-E s.v.* Sibyllen 2082, reject the decision of Rossbach (Leipzig 1859) to retain the MSS reading. But A. Kurfess, 'Die Sibyllen bei Tibull', *Würzburger Jahrbücher für die Altertumswissenschaft* 3 (1948) 402ff. (esp. 405) argues well for keeping *Phoebo grata* and simply placing a comma after *dixit*. There was so much confusion in antiquity about Sibyl names that the mere fact that the Marpessian Sibyl sometimes bears the name Herophile is not enough to force us to conjoin Marpesia (67) and

> quasque Aniena sacras Tiburs per flumina sortes
>   portarit sicco pertuleritque sinu   (67–70)

Tibullus listed the Sibyls thus in order to give primacy of place to Amalthea, who is the Sibyl of Cumae, and to suggest that she is identical with the Erythraean Sibyl. He found two difficulties in the traditional material about Sibyls: the confusion of Sibyl names and the fact that the village of Marpessos sometimes bore the qualification ἐρυθρά (red) – which caused conflation between the Marpessian and Erythraean Sibyls. In order to show his intentions Tibullus differentiated four Sibyls:

(1) Amalthea, the Sibyl of Erythrae–Cumae, given first position in the list, although her residence is omitted;
(2) a Marpessian Sibyl, unnamed (unless Tibullus is suggesting that Marpesia is her name, which is a less likely alternative);
(3) Herophile, given no place of abode, but described as *Phoebo grata* (dear to Phoebus), perhaps as a learned oblique comment on the odd fact that her name actually means 'dear to Hera'. The name Heracles, 'glory of Hera', for Hera's enemy might be compared.
(4) the Sibyl of Tibur, also unnamed.

Thus (1) and (3) are named but not given a place of abode, (2) and (4) are given a place of abode but not named. Tibullus has separated out the conflicting traditions to his own satisfaction. This list is Tibullus' learned answer to a learned question: who were the Sibyls and where did they live? But Tibullus has two additional intentions: first to make Amalthea, with her double residence, the principal Sibyl and the authoress of the prophecy to Aeneas and of the original Sibylline books; and second to dignify the new collection of oracles of different Sibyls by establishing the Sibyls as virtually a *collegium* with Amalthea at their head.

Another Tibullan device to enhance the status of the *sortes Sibyllinae*, both new and old, is found at line 19. There, immediately after speaking in lines 17f. of the *sacrae chartae vatis*, i.e. the Sibylline books, Tibullus says *haec dedit Aeneae sortes*. Tibullus is using his identification of the Erythraean Sibyl with the Cumaean Sibyl to conflate the foundation oracle and the Sibylline books. *dedit sortes* as an isolated phrase could mean either 'uttered prophecies' or 'gave prophetic writings'. Of course in context here it means the former; but it also conjures up the selling of the Sibylline books by the Sibyl to Tarquinius Priscus.

A second motive for Tibullus' choice of the Troad as the place where the foundation oracle of Rome was delivered is that this location of the prophecy makes the foundation of Rome seem more like the typical founda-

---

Herophile (68). For another view see B. Cardauns, 'Zu den Sibyllen bei Tibull 2 5', *Hermes* 89 (1961) 375ff.

tion of a Greek colony. The authorisation for a foundation was normally given while the colonists were still living in their mother city. In the case of Rome a full analogue for this event cannot be invented because the Trojans decided to move to another land only after their original city was destroyed. But Tibullus achieves the next best thing: he makes Aeneas receive the oracle about the new Troy while he can still see the old Troy in the process of destruction.[70]

Some details of the foundation oracle are characteristic. These are:
(a) The address to the founder (Aeneas) by the oracle-giver in a manner both honorific and appropriate (39ff.).[71] This is exactly how founders are usually addressed or spoken of in foundation oracles.[72]
(b) The very precise information given to Aeneas about the location of his colony (41ff.).[73]
(c) The declaration that a god (in this case Jupiter) assigns the Trojans land in Italy (41f.).[74] The agricultural bias of the colony, stressed not in the Sibyl's speech but in the two flanking passages, is also a ktistic commonplace.[75]
(d) The posthumous worship which Aeneas will receive as an oikist-hero (43f.).[76]
(e) The prophecy of the victorious wars which Aeneas will wage in Italy (45ff.).[77]
(f) The prediction of the future greatness of the colony (55ff.).[78]

(iv) CONTINUITY OF WORSHIP

The same four lines (19–22) which juxtapose Rome and Troy also contrast *raptos Lares*, the gods which Aeneas saved and brought to Rome, and *ardentes deos*, the gods' statues or temples of Troy which perished with Troy. The rescue of the Lares of Aeneas and the consequent unbroken ties of the Julian family with Troy give that *gens* the distinction of having achieved the continuity of worship which was a cardinal feature of the relationship between mother-city and colony in Greece.[79] The *ardentes deos* of Troy create a pathos similar to that aroused by Aeneas' vision of his city in destruction, and they highlight the preservation of the continuity of worship between Troy and Rome by emphasising how close it came to being broken. Another aspect of this continuity is again Apollo, founder of old Troy and inspirer of the foundation oracle of the new Troy.

---

[70] Cf. Virg. *Aen.* 2.776ff., where V. similarly makes the ghost of Creusa prophesy to Aeneas about his future realm in Italy immediately after the fall of Troy.
[71] *impiger* and *volitantis* are in 'tension' with each other. This draws attention to Aeneas' 'god-like' qualities. On such 'verbal tensions' see below, Ch. 4, pp. 99f.
[72] Cf. Schmid pp. 109; 117. [73] *Id.* pp. 95f.; 117; 158f.
[74] *Id.* pp. 95; 108ff.; 169. [75] *Id.* pp. 168f. [76] Cf. Graham pp. 29f.
[77] Cf. Schmid pp. 8; 95; 109; and esp. 174ff. [78] *Id.* p. 109.
[79] Cf. Graham index *s.v.* religion; cf. Weinstock pp. 5ff.

(v) THE PREHISTORY AND FOUNDATION FESTIVAL (first account)

There is often a close connection in foundation legends between the actual foundation and the ἀρχαιολογία – the 'prehistory' – of the place settled. The 'prehistory' could include major mythical elements: this can be seen clearly from the end of Callimachus' *Acontius and Cydippe* – *Aetia* Fr. 75.54ff. (Pf.) – which is a summary of the prose-historian Xenomedes' account of the *ktisis* and *archaeologia* of Ceos. Another *ktisis* which contained such mythical prehistory is Ion of Chios' account of his native island.[80] The ancient history of Rome, as Tibullus tells it, is not so much a mythical history like those of Ceos and Chios as a bucolic fantasy with antiquarian and etymological preoccupations. But it contains a reflection of at least one ktistic topos of a more down-to-earth type. A *ktisis* can describe the building of walls and laying out of the city.[81] This concept is referred to in Tibullus 2.5.23f.; and it may also lie behind the other topographical elements of Tibullus' description of pre-Roman Rome (25ff.; 55f.).[82]

The antiquarian side of Tibullus' 'pre-Rome' may be considered first. Its two principal deities are Pan (27) and Pales (28). Pales presents no difficulty: she was, and was regarded by Tibullus as, a genuine ancient Roman goddess of herds. But Pan is somewhat anomalous. He is a Greek god: and in fact, as opposed to legend, he was naturalised at Rome much later than the foundation period. The process involved identifying Pan with a group of Roman rustic deities themselves often mutually identified – Silvanus, Faunus and Inuus.[83] These facts were known to Tibullus' readers, and the words *silvestri . . . deo* in line 30 may be an allusion to the first of these identifications, although the reference itself is unmistakably to Pan and his syrinx. Tibullus has thrust the anomaly of Pan upon his readers to awaken their interest in the learned theorising by implication which follows.

The picture of a bucolic pre-Rome worshipping two agricultural deities, one male, one female, reminded Tibullus' readers of controversies about the identity of the god or gods who were worshipped at the festival of the Parilia.[84] In addition to the common notion that there was a single female Pales, another theory was current in antiquity: that two Pales, one male and one female, were worshipped at the Parilia. Tibullus is putting forward one solution to this problem by reminding the reader that the pre-Roman settlers of the site of Rome were Greeks under Evander the

---

[80] Schmid pp. 43f.
[81] See above, n. 51.
[82] It is even more noticeable in Propertius' reworking of this Tibullan passage (4.1.1ff.). Cf. also the topographical material in Virg. *Aen.* 8, esp. ll. 310ff.
[83] On these deities as a group see Wissowa, *Religion und Kultus der Römer* pp. 208ff.; individually, the *R-E* articles on Silvanus; Faunus; Inuus.
[84] Cf. Latte, *Römische Religionsgeschichte* pp. 59f. esp. p. 60 n. 1; 88.

Arcadian.⁸⁵ He is suggesting that the male counterpart to Pales must have been the Arcadians' god of herds Pan, and that the problem of the two Pales can be solved in this way. The strength of this view would lie in the frequency with which Pan's Latin equivalents were associated with herds and flocks,⁸⁶ and, it would seem, in the occasional association of one of them in this role with Pales.⁸⁷

The pre-foundation Rome which Tibullus describes is linked with his other learned preoccupations within the poem. W. Wimmel has explained the connections between Pan and Apollo and the pastoral associations which Apollo had as founder, particularly of Cyrene.⁸⁸ In addition Tibullus, in stressing Pan, is alluding to Evander and his Greeks, with whom Pan is strongly associated. He does so for the same reason which led him to antedate Rome's foundation – to claim for Rome greater antiquity than the Greek cities of Magna Graecia and Sicily. Evander was a pre-Trojan War Greek settler in Italy: thus Rome's Greek antecedents are more venerable than those of other Italian cities with post-Trojan War Greek links;⁸⁹ in addition he was, unlike some other post-Trojan War Greek settlers in Italy, friendly to the Trojans/Romans, having himself been driven out of Arcadia by other Greeks.

Etymologies are a standard feature of foundations.⁹⁰ The reasoning behind this interest is not so much that the explanations of local nomenclature constitute part of the city's mythical history and therefore deserve inclusion. It is rather that, in the way of ancient logic, the derivations of local names are historical evidence to support the accounts given of the city's past.⁹¹ One etymological aspect of the pre-Rome passage in Tibullus 2.5 has been discussed most usefully by W. Wimmel.⁹² This is the bond between *Pales, Pan, Palatium, pastor, diva Palatua, Parilia, de partu Iliae*. The range of Tibullus' etymological interest is even wider: Evander's *Pallanteum* is probably a part of the complex; and perhaps too the *vaccae* in line 25 may implicitly reject a derivation of *Palatium* from *balare*⁹³ on the grounds

---

⁸⁵ Cf. Dion. Hal. *Ant. Rom.* 1.11.1ff.; 7.70ff. and H. Hill, 'Dionysius of Halicarnassus and the origins of Rome', *JRS* 51 (1961) 88ff.

⁸⁶ See above, n. 83.

⁸⁷ E.g. Arnobius, *Adv. Nat.* 3.23: *armentorum et pecorum gregibus Pales praesunt Inuusque custodes*. The solution of the two Pales problem accepted by Tibullus clearly had some success in a wider field. On a parallel track Livy (1.5) associates the Lupercalia with Evander's introduction of worship of the Lycean Pan whom Livy identifies with Inuus.

⁸⁸ 'Tibull II 5 und das elegische Rombild', pp. 254f. and n. 5.

⁸⁹ A list of the Greek associations of Italian cities – of various dates – occurs at Solinus 2.5ff.

⁹⁰ Cf. Cornell (thesis) p. 155 n. 21.

⁹¹ Cf. e.g. Pind. *Ol.* 6.30; 47; 55; Ion of Chios (Jacoby, *Fr. Gr. Hist.* 392 F1); Demosthenes of Bithynia (Jacoby, *Fr. Gr. Hist.* 699 F16); Menecrates of Elea (Müller, *FHG* II p. 342 Fr. 2); Dionysius of Chalcis (Müller, *FHG* IV p. 393 Frr. 1; 12).

⁹² 'Tibull II 5 und das elegische Rombild', pp. 247f.; 258. For the frequency of this interest in Tibullus see below, Ch. 4.

⁹³ Cf. Paul. (Fest.) p. 245 (L).

that this was the sound made by sheep, whereas the Palatine hill was grazing for cattle.[94] Similarly the adjective *vagi* attached to *pastoris* (29) may be a hint at another known etymology of *Palatium* – from the sheep wandering (*palare*) about there.[95] Finally, whatever else Tibullus thinks about the etymology of Palatium he is aware of the connection both in etymology and in real life between *Parilia* and *parere*[96] (to bear). The plentifulness of milk (27) together with the cheese and the lamb (38) anticipate plenty and fecundity, stressed in the later and more extended description of the same feast of the Parilia (83ff.).

A second known[97] etymological complex appears in lines 33–7. Here the Velabrum is under discussion. When Propertius later mentioned the Velabrum, a marshy region of Rome which by the Augustan age had been drained, he wrote

> qua Velabra suo stagnabant flumine quoque
> nauta per urbanas velificabat aquas   (4.9.5f.)

In this way he implied that the name Velabrum derived from *velum* (sail). He may also have been hinting at an etymology from the Greek (F)έλος (marsh) by the allusive use of *stagnabant*.[98] Tibullus on the other hand prefers the Varronian etymology: *Velabrum a vehendo* (*De Lingua Latina* 5.44). He makes this clear in three ways: by the use of *vecta* in line 36; by specifically making the point that boats were rowed (*pulsa . . . aqua* 34) and not sailed through the Velabrum; and finally by specifying that the boats were small (*exiguus . . . linter* 34) which implies that they were too small to need or be able to carry sails. In this way Tibullus learnedly denies the 'sail' etymology adopted later by Propertius, and affirms *vehor* as the source of *Velabrum*. The difference between Propertius' bold and open approach to this problem and Tibullus' allusive subtlety is instructive.

The focus of Tibullus' pre-Rome passage is his first description of the Parilia, the festival of the birthday of Rome.[99] Other cities too held a foundation festival on the anniversary of their establishment, for example, Zancle[100] and other Sicilian cities.[101] A description of this celebration seems to be a ktistic commonplace. Callimachus' 'Foundation of Zancle' contained one; and in the 'Foundation of Chios'[102] Ion apparently substituted an account of the Pan-Ionian festival for the anniversary celebration of Chios, presumably to stress that, following the expulsion of non-

---

[94] Cf. Prop. 4.1.4 and Fedeli *ad loc.*; Varro, *LL* 5.164.
[95] Cf. Paul. (Fest.) p. 245 (L).   [96] Cf. Paul. (Fest.) p. 248 (L) (*pro partu pecoris*).
[97] Cf. D. O. Ross Jr, *Backgrounds to Augustan Poetry: Gallus, Elegy and Rome* (Cambridge 1975) p. 156.
[98] On such Greek-Latin derivations involving the digamma cf. Dion. Hal. *Ant. Rom.* 1.20.2f. (esp. on *Velia*).
[99] On the Parilia see Ovid, *Fast.* 4.721ff. and Bömer *ad loc.*
[100] Cf. Call. *Aet.* Fr. 43.78ff. (Pf.) and Pfeiffer *ad loc.*; Schmid pp. 58ff.
[101] Cf. Call. *Aet.* Fr. 43.54f. (Pf.) and Pfeiffer *ad loc.*; Schmid pp. 56f.
[102] Cf. Schmid p. 44.

Greeks from the island, Chios was now a pure-blooded Ionian city. Accounts of festivals may also have occurred at other points in literary *ktiseis*. In Plato's *Republic* the Delphic oracle is to be asked to supply his city among other things with festivals.[103] The standard nature of the foundation-festival in *ktiseis* explains the emphasis given to the Parilia in Tibullus 2.5.

The first account of the Parilia ends on an erotic note. The *festa dies* on which the girl goes to the shepherd is the Parilia itself: love-making is a particularly appropriate accompaniment of birthdays.[104] Tibullus may be relying on this fact to facilitate his introduction of erotic material here and later in the poem in his second account of the Parilia (101ff.). The proximity of the Parilia (21 April) to the Vinalia, a festival of Venus (23 April),[105] may be another relevant factor here; and the description of the *fistula* (29–32) which immediately precedes the passage about the Velabrum may be yet another link between the erotic material and the rest of the poem, since the reed for the Pan-pipes consisted of Pan's beloved Syrinx. The appearance of the Parilia, the birthday festival of Rome, as part of a description of pre-foundation Rome is yet another way in which Tibullus constantly suggests the early origin and eternity of Rome. He is creating a continuity between pre-Rome and Rome and so almost implying that Rome always existed.

(vi) THE POST-FOUNDATION HISTORY

Tibullus is very selective in what he says about the post-foundation history of Rome. For example, it is striking that he says nothing about the omens which in other accounts accompanied the establishment of Rome, even though oracular authorisations of colonies often mentioned the signs or omens which would indicate where the city should be founded or give some other important information; and even though omens often arose spontaneously at foundations, and were described in *ktiseis*.[106] Tibullus may be avoiding the subject because some of the foundation omens were associated with Romulus, whom he does not wish to be mistaken for the founder. But there is a more important reason. He wants to avoid confusion between omens and the *prodigia* and subsequent events which are described in lines 67ff. These *prodigia* are on one level a substitute motif[107]

---

[103] *Rep.* 427Bf., cf. *Laws* 738Bff.

[104] Cf. F. Cairns, 'Propertius 3,10 and Roman birthdays', *Hermes* 99 (1971) 153f. A. W. J. Holleman, 'Larentia, Hercules and Mater Matuta (Tib. II 5)', *Ant. Class.* 45 (1976) 197ff. advances stimulating suggestions about a cult origin for the passage but thinks that Tibullus 'did not understand the old tradition behind his own words' (197, cf. 203).

[105] Cf. Ov. *Fast.* 4.863ff. and Bömer *ad loc.* Note esp. 863f.: *dicta Pales nobis; idem Vinalia dicam; | una tamen media est inter utramque diem.*

[106] Cf. Schmid pp. 61f., 101, 150ff., 160f.

[107] See above Ch. 2 p. 46 and n. 43 and Ch. 3 p. 65 and n. 4.

Analogy as learning

for the missing omens. But they have another purpose. They have long been correctly identified with those prodigies which followed the murder of Julius Caesar and portended the Civil Wars.[108] Tibullus' declaration that all the prophecies of such prodigies found in the Sibylline books have already been fulfilled, that is, that all these prodigies have happened in the past, therefore implies that in the future there will be no civil wars but only peace and prosperity within the Roman state. External wars will no doubt take place, including the war in which Messalinus will win his triumph (115ff.); but internally the terrible Civil Wars will never recur. To reinforce this implication Tibullus prays to Apollo in line 79f. to prevent the reappearance of prodigies. He then introduces the one set of omens proper which does occur in the elegy, albeit not in connection with the foundation: he prays to Apollo to give good omens. The context of these omens is another commonplace one. Tibullus is asking in particular for good omens for the Parilia, the birthday feast of Rome, just as good omens are requested and bad omens are ruled out in the private birthday celebrations of individuals.[109]

The second Parilia description will bring Tibullus' sketch of post-foundation history up to date: the blessedness of the present age is being contrasted with the prodigies and wars of the past.

(vii) FOUNDATION FESTIVAL (second account)

The second description of the Parilia does not represent a past celebration of that festival in Rome; it is as Tibullus imagines it will take place in the countryside in his own time (*coloni*, 83). The contemporary rustic shepherd (87) will hold his own Parilia there, as the inhabitants of the rustic pre-Rome once did in the countryside which became the site of Rome. Tibullus is seeking after symmetry by juxtaposing these two parallel descriptions of the same event; and he exploits the possibilities which this repetition opens up in order to suggest his meaning more strongly.[110] The repeated Parilia description unites past and present, pre- and post-foundation Rome, and so stresses the theme of the eternity of Rome. The concept was associated with several Roman religious institutions and is found linked with the Sibylline books.[111] The repeated Parilia description also adopts a characteristic theme of Augustan poetry in suggesting that the Italian countryside is the place where pristine Roman piety can still be found.[112] This implies another central theme of Augustan poetry, that the whole of Italy, not just Rome, is heir to the great traditions of Rome's past.[113] Finally the double Parilia is intended to round off the course of

[108] Cf. e.g. Smith on Tib. 2.5.71ff.   [109] Cf. Cairns, *Hermes* 99 (1971) 149ff.
[110] For such techniques see below, Ch. 8.
[111] Cf. *R-E s.v.* Quindecimviri pp. 1127f.
[112] Cf. e.g. Virg. *Georg.* (*passim*); Hor. *Epod.* 2; *Od.* 1.17; 3.23 etc.; Prop. 2.19.
[113] Preeminently in Virg. *Aen.* (*passim*).

Roman history in such a way as to make the present seem better than the past. It is through the wars of Aeneas that ancient Rome was founded, just as Messalinus and others like him will guarantee the present Golden Age of peace; and it, unlike the earlier Age, will be permanent. The greater length, detail and enthusiasm of the second Parilia description is intended to show that the present holds greater joys than the past.

(viii) THE GODS OF ROME

In any *ktisis* the chief gods of the city play a part. For Augustan Rome the chief gods were Venus and Mars, the ancestors of the Julian *gens*, and Apollo, the personal god of Augustus. Jupiter stood above this triad. Tibullus' task was to represent their role in the foundation in a way consonant with Greek practice.

Tibullus briefly guarantees the conventional continuity of worship between mother-city and colony by stating in lines 20–2 that the Lares of Aeneas survived the fall of Troy[114] while its other gods perished. Apollo[115] is portrayed first as the prophet and founder of Rome, as of Troy, who inspired its foundation oracle and will oversee its new *saeculum*; and second as *pastor*. Mars figures as the husband of Ilia and father of Romulus (51ff.). The Romans are therefore a warlike people: indeed long before the birth of Romulus, Aeneas, the founder, had fought victorious wars (45ff.), and Messalinus will win more victories in the future (115ff.). Jupiter, as supervisor of all the events described, grants the land of Rome to Aeneas (41). Only Venus was not present to any great extent in the foundation legends. Tibullus in part uses Venus' son Amor to remedy this state of affairs. Amor is the brother of Aeneas (39); he is responsible, by implication, for the conception of Romulus (51ff.); and he plays a large part in the two Parilia descriptions. He is represented also in the *persona* of Tibullus the lover (105ff.). Venus' other son Aeneas is of course the founder himself. Again if the Vinalia of 23 April facilitates the introduction of erotic material into the Parilia descriptions, this would be another manifestation of Venus' importance. The two sides of Tibullus' character, his poetic inspiration by Apollo and his erotic interests, help to influence his pictures of the idealised pre-Rome and the idealised Rome of the present. Rome is portrayed as a place of peace which is achieved through the help of Mars, and under the just patronage of Apollo and Venus.

Significant in this context is the rejection by Tibullus of the hankering after a Saturnian Golden Age found in 1.3. There the rule of Saturn (1.3.35ff.) symbolised peace and freedom from the warfare and dangers of the present Age of Iron which Jupiter ruled. Here, perhaps in conscious

---

[114] See above, p. 78.
[115] For Apollo (also an ancestral god) cf. Weinstock pp. 12ff.; for Mars, Venus and the *gens Iulia* see Weinstock index I *s.vv.* Mars; Venus.

Hellenistic self-imitation with variation, Tibullus inverts this order of values. In 2.5 Saturn represents disorder[116] and Apollo is asked to sing as he once sang a paean in honour of Jupiter's victory over Saturn (9f.). This represents a change of view and an acceptance of the present as an age of peace and reason.[117]

A few further suggestions about the contemporary themes in Tibullus' representation of early Rome may be appended. Tibullus 2.5 belongs to the years preceding the Saecular Games of 17 BC. For a considerable time beforehand the project is known to have been a matter of public interest, particularly just before 23 BC when Augustus may have hoped to hold the Games.[118] The *Aeneid* contains much material which reflects such an interest;[119] and elsewhere I have advanced the view that Horace, *Odes* 1.2 also shows the regime's intent to celebrate the end of a *saeculum*.[120] Tibullus 2.5 may well have a similar Saecular interest; and this may be one reason why *prodigia*, which were integral to the Saecular traditions and heralded the coming of a new *saeculum*, are so prominent in it. This may also explain why Diana, who features largely in the Saecular celebrations and is the co-addressee with Apollo of Horace's *Carmen Saeculare*, is mentioned at the end of the elegy (122) in which her brother Phoebus is invoked throughout.

Messalinus' role as *XVvir* is another relevant feature. The *XVviri* were the college in charge of holding the Saecular Games. Again, the equation of bucolic pre-Rome with the Parilia of the near future is the equation of a past age of ideal happiness with the *aureum saeculum* which, so Augustan propaganda claimed, the god of the Saecular Games, Apollo, would bring once the old *saeculum* was over. The *felix et sacer annus* of line 82 is unlikely to be anything other than the *aureum saeculum* soon to be inaugurated. This is why the omen of the crackling laurel which will herald a *felix et sacer annus* does not necessarily indicate that Messalinus' entry to the temple takes place at the beginning of the calendar year. If any date for this event is suggested in the elegy, it may be, as R. Merkelbach has proposed,[121] the Parilia.

In Tibullus 2.5 Messalinus is the focus of attention; and his inauguration as *XVvir* is the dividing line between the disasters and wars of the past and the golden future. Thus Messalinus is a symbolic youth out of the same mould as the *puer* of the fourth *Eclogue* – another Saecular poem – and the Augustus/Mercury of Horace, *Odes* 1.2, if that ode is yet another.[122]

[116] See Smith on Tib. 2.5.5; 9f. Tib. 2.5.9f. may be influenced by and indeed allude to Callimachus' frequent implied identification of Ptolemy with Zeus: one such passage describes Philadelphus as victor over the 'lateborn' Titans i.e. the Gauls (*Hymn* 4.171ff.); cf. McLennan on Call. *Hymn* 1.3.
[117] Cf. e.g. Pind. *Pyth.* 1.1ff.; 5.65ff.
[118] Cf. Weinstock p. 196; F. Cairns, 'Horace, Odes 1.2', *Eranos* 69 (1971) 84ff.
[119] Cf. R. Merkelbach, 'Aeneas in Cumae', *Mus. Helvet.* 18 (1961) 90ff.
[120] Cairns, *Eranos* 69 (1971) 84ff.
[121] *Mus. Helvet.* 18 (1961) pp. 85f.
[122] See Cairns, *Eranos* 69 (1971) 84ff.

Different figures are treated as the pivot of the *saecula* in these three poems; but the poems themselves are very similar in spirit. It might be tempting in view of the Saecular interest in Tibullus 2.5 and of other evidence of strong Saecular concern around 23 BC to try and date the elegy rather earlier than it is usually dated. Messalinus' birth date is not certain but it lies between 43 BC and 36 BC. As a member of one of the noblest and most influential families he could easily, like Asinius Gallus, have held his consulship considerably before the legal age of 42. A birth date of 39 BC or earlier would allow him to have become a *XVvir* by 23 BC. But this seems to be special pleading and unnecessary since saecular interest was widespread throughout the first century BC[123] and must have revived around 20–19 BC. The solution of the Parthian problem in particular, which had held up Julius Caesar's proposed saecular celebration, must have made the Saecular Games seem imminent.[124] The orthodox date of 20/19 for the elegy therefore seems more attractive.

The implications of Tibullus' juxtaposition of bucolic/erotic material on one hand and martial material on the other are an interesting topic. However interpretations which make such passages of Augustan poetry into anti-imperial and anti-war political tracts are unimpressive. The Romans were realists. They knew perfectly well that the *pax Romana* had been won and was being maintained by war. The description of Messalinus as a future *triumphator* (115ff.) would be clear enough proof that Tibullus is not presenting an anti-war case, even if Jupiter himself were not presented as *victor* (9f.). Mars in Tibullus 2.5 has fulfilled a useful role in the past; and it should be remembered that Apollo's praise of Jupiter's martial activities is Tibullus' encomiastic analogy to his own praise of Messalinus.

As a learned Latin analogue of a Hellenistic *ktisis* Tibullus 2.5 is an elegy of great poetic and intellectual achievement. Its rich and colourful learning repays close investigation and guarantees Tibullus' professional status and skill.

[123] Cf. Weinstock pp. 191ff.   [124] *Id.* p. 196.

4
VERBAL LEARNING

As a Roman elegiac poet Tibullus might be expected to try to reproduce in Latin the linguistic features of his Hellenistic literary forebears. But at first sight Tibullus appears to differ strikingly from them in the field of vocabulary. This is inevitably a subjective conclusion. No meaningful statistics about vocabulary or about the frequency with which Tibullus repeats words are easily available.[1] None are available at all for the Hellenistic poets. Similarly it is not easy to say how often Tibullus uses an 'abnormal' word as opposed to a normal word. In any case it would not be useful to compare Tibullus with Hellenistic poetry in such crude terms because many fragments of Hellenistic poetry are preserved just because they contain an unusual word or form.

Nevertheless it can be said that some readers of Tibullus leave him with the impression that his vocabulary is small, repetitive and commonplace, that unusual words and compounds are rare in his work and that his syntax is regular. A few might go even further and complain that many Tibullan lines contain at least one word, usually an adjective or participle, which seems to contribute little or nothing to the meaning of the line. Such a view could affect a critical assessment of Tibullus: he might appear to suffer from poverty both of vocabulary and thought; and he might even be thought an amateur versifier using 'fillers' to complete his lines.

No such impression could be formed of Hellenistic poetry. Even a casual eye finds it full of unusual words, varied in the use of dialectal forms and invigorated by frequent new formations and uses of old words in new senses. Hellenistic scholarly interest in the text of Homer, Hesiod and other early Greek poetry led to rich semantic experimentation by Hellenistic poets around variants upon standard readings in the texts of archaic poetry; and it allowed them to allude to exegetical controversies related to difficult passages in these texts. In their syntactical formations too Hellenistic poets were fond of the uncommon, the variegated and the eye-catching. They introduced metrical refinements[2] and show a greater liking

---

[1] Extensive statistics on Tibullus are offered by S. Govaerts, *Le Corpus Tibullianum Index verborum et Relevés statistiques: Essai de Méthodologie statistique* (Université de Liège, Faculté de Philosophie et Lettres: Travaux publiés par le laboratoire d'analyse statistique des langues anciennes sous la direction du Professeur Louis Delatte 5, La Haye 1966). I have not discovered any practical use for them.

[2] Cf. P. Maas, *Greek Metre* (Oxford 1962) pp. 11ff., 61ff., 79f., 85ff.

than earlier poets for lines of certain types, particularly four- or five-word lines containing two nouns and two adjectives.[3]

When Greek and Latin poetry is being compared, allowance must always be made for the difference between the languages themselves. Latin has a far smaller corpus than Greek of individual lexical items, and shows far less capacity to vary syntactically its expression of the same underlying concepts.[4] Moreover in Latin poetry verbal allusion in the form of 'translation' of Greek takes the place of much of the scholarly approach to earlier poets on a verbal level by Greek Hellenistic poets. One of the few places where this can be observed in detail is Virgil's *Aeneid*. It has been shown that where Virgil imitates Homer he takes account of the kind of ancient criticisms and observations which survive in the Homeric scholia.[5] By such 'translation' Latin poets preserve the Hellenistic tendency to interpretation. But since they are working in a different language they do not attempt the verbal variation which the Greeks employed for the same purpose. Roman poets also exploit the greater polysemy of Latin lexemes as a substitute for the larger vocabulary of Greek.

For these reasons none of the Roman elegists can really be compared with their Hellenistic predecessors in richness and variety of language and syntax. But Propertius makes a consistent and successful attempt to convey an impression of Hellenistic verbal variegation and syntactical virtuosity; and Ovid, although far less concerned to compete in these areas than Propertius, is not as restricted as Tibullus. There is then a real problem with Tibullus; and because it is such a pressing problem some brief preliminary considerations may be set down which indicate that censure of Tibullus is unlikely to be the correct solution.

The first is that, like the other two surviving Roman elegists, but to a greater degree, Tibullus deliberately restricts his vocabulary in certain areas. Of course the Roman poets did not have the possibility of calling on a variety of literary dialects. But they did have both archaic and vulgar levels of Latin to call upon; and their literary use had been sanctioned by Ennius, the tragedians, Plautus and Lucilius. Catullus[6] and to a small extent Virgil in his *Eclogues*[7] look to these registers. But Tibullus seems for the most part to avoid them. He may here be in reaction to Gallus, whose 'harshness' possibly consisted in imitation of Euphorion's elaborate style.[8]

---

[3] Naturally Homer also has such lines (e.g. *Il.* 11.372; 13.19). On a further subtlety in Hellenistic practice see McLennan on Call. *Hymn* 1.3.

[4] For ancient complaints about and defences of Latin as a language in comparison with Greek cf. e.g. Lucr. *DRN* 1.136ff. with Munro and Ernout–Robin *ad loc.*

[5] Cf. Robin R. Schlunk, *The Homeric Scholia and the Aeneid* (Michigan 1974).

[6] On the language of Catullus see D. O. Ross Jr, *Style and Tradition in Catullus* (Harvard 1969).

[7] See R. G. G. Coleman (ed.), *Vergil: Eclogues* (Cambridge 1977) index *s.vv.* archaism; colloquialism.

[8] Cf. H. Tränkle, *Die Sprachkunst des Properz und die Tradition der lateinischen Dichtersprache* (*Hermes* Einzelschr. 15, pp. 22ff.; D. O. Ross Jr, *Backgrounds to Augustan*

Verbal learning 89

If so this is part of the quality of being *tersus et elegans* which Quintilian praised in Tibullus. On a small scale, linguistic self-denial can also be seen in Tibullus in the area of erotic language. Like most Hellenistic erotic epigrammatists, erotic epistolographers and novelists, and the other Roman elegists, he refers to sex very specifically, but does not use coarse words referring to sexual matters or go into gross sexual details.[9] This avoidance of coarse language involves using words of general or otherwise non-erotic significance in an allusive but specific erotic sense. Examples are *facere, venire, nox, ira, promittere, felix*.[10] This type of voluntary vocabulary restriction inevitably reduces the variety of words in Tibullus; and since the allusive though specific substitutes are common words, it gives an even more pedestrian appearance to his text. But far from showing Tibullan verbal incompetence, it proves that, like the other writers in the field, he was careful and selfconscious in his choice of words.

A second consideration is that Tibullus makes constant use of the *figurae rationis et orationis* of ancient rhetoric.[11] It is most unlikely that a poet so concerned with these would neglect other verbal matters. Thirdly it is unlikely from a metrical point of view that Tibullus used 'fillers'. By the time he was writing, the elegiac couplet no longer presented great technical difficulties to Roman poets. In every other aspect of his metrics Tibullus conforms to normal Augustan practice; and he was clearly to some extent a leader in metrical developments in Roman elegy: it was he who restricted the pentameter ending to disyllables, and the other two Roman elegists followed his practice. It therefore makes no historical sense to claim that, as far as adjectives and participles are concerned, Tibullus was still at the stage of hunting for 'fillers'. This view is confirmed by the fact that he is thoroughly Hellenistic in his liking for four- and five-word lines and a balance of nouns and adjectives within a line. The latter device is important in the naturalisation of the hexameter and pentameter at Rome, and poets employing it must have been particularly aware of the need to avoid unnecessary and non-significant adjectives and participles.

There ought then to be a plausible defence of Tibullus. The one offered

---

Poetry: Gallus, Elegy and Rome (Cambridge 1975) *Index rerum notabilium s.v.* Euphorion; Parthenius, *Erot. Path. praef.* (on τὸ περιττόν).

[9] The best known example of this practice is the 'erotic aposiopesis': e.g. *AP* 5.4.6 (Philodemus); *AP* 5.128.3f. (Marcus Argentarius); *AP* 5.139.6 (Meleager); *AP* 5.252.5f. (Paulus Silentiarius); *AP* 12.94.4 (Meleager); Ov. *Am.* 1.5.25; Aristaen. *Ep.* 1.16.33f. (Mazal). Occasionally a writer in these fields, e.g. Dioscorides (cf. Fraser I pp. 564; 596ff.) and Ovid in *AA* (esp. 3.769ff.) does go into obscene details but without coarse language. On general Greek attitudes to such matters cf. K. J. Dover, *Greek Popular Morality in the Time of Plato and Aristotle* (Oxford 1974) pp. 33, 206ff. For ancient distinctions of decency in language cf. e.g. Arist. *Eth. Nic.* 1128a17ff.; Cic. *Ad Fam.* 9.22; Suet. *Vesp.* 22; Varr. *LL* 6.80.

[10] For this area of vocabulary cf. R. Pichon, *De Sermone Amatorio apud Latinos Elegiarum Scriptores* (Diss. Paris 1902).

[11] Cf. H. Harrauer, *Die Komposition der Elegien des 1. Buches bei Tibull* (Diss. Vienna 1969, I Teil).

will involve a passing look at his syntax, but its main concern will be verbal. It will seek to show that there are no empty words in Tibullus, but only words whose significance has not been understood, and that like every other Greek and Roman Hellenistic poet, he shows a constant interest in the meaning and use of words which gives his diction an allusive texture of the highest intellectual calibre. The best way of approaching this aspect of Roman poetry and Tibullus' contribution to it is to consider an important area of ancient learning, 'Etymology'. Ancient 'etymology' began, but only began, with an interest in the derivations of words. From a modern point of view, it was not an exact or scholarly investigation; and since antiquity had no proper conception of comparative philology, the derivations suggested for words range from the sensible to the ridiculous without discrimination. It is this most of all which has led modern scholars to neglect and despise ancient 'etymology'. Varro's link between *canis* (dog) and *canere* (sing) appears laughable;[12] but in antiquity such speculations were for the most part serious and the intellectual status of etymology was high.

The Greeks and Romans did recognise that some names were imposed by convention; but they thought that many names were related to the nature of the things they named. Consequently they regarded conclusions about names and their derivations as conclusions about things; so etymology was considered to be a scientific and philosophic as well as a linguistic study. Another reason why etymology assumed such importance in ancient poetry, beginning with Homer and reaching its high point in the Hellenistic poets and their Roman successors, is that it was related to semantics. All this is not to say that when an ancient poet alluded to the etymology of a word he necessarily thought that he was making a contribution to science, philosophy, linguistics or semantics. But, as has been noted in the discussion of Tibullus 2.5 above (pp. 80f.), etymology could be used by the poets as the basis for serious speculation; and in general terms it was the status of etymology in antiquity as a science which allowed poets to employ it freely as part of their intellectual sub-structure.

There is a fair amount of Greek theoretical discussion and practical use of etymology.[13] But the earliest major Latin text on 'etymology', the

[12] *LL* 7.32.
[13] Cf. R. Schröter, *Studien zur varronischen Etymologie I* (Akad. der Wissenschaften und der Literatur: Abhandl. der Geistes- und Sozialwissenschaftlichen Klasse 1959 12, Wiesbaden 1959) pp. 773ff. = (5ff.) esp. pp. (25ff.) and the works cited pp. (6); (118f.). H. Steinthal, *Geschichte der Sprachwissenschaft bei den Griechen und Römern mit besonderer Rücksicht auf die Logik* (Berlin I 1890, II 1891) I pp. 319ff.; J André, 'Ovide helléniste et linguiste', *Rev. Phil.* 49 (1975) pp. 191ff.; H. Dahlmann, *Varro und die hellenistische Sprachtheorie* (Problemata 5, 2nd ed. Berlin/Zürich 1964); *R-E s.v.* Etymologika; *Kl.P. s.v.* Etymologie; K. Barwick, *Probleme der stoischen Sprachlehre und Rhetorik* (Abhandlungen der Sächsischen Akademie der Wissenschaften zu Leipzig Philol.-hist. Klasse 49,3, Berlin 1957); L. P. Rank, *Etymologiseering en verwante Verschijnselen bij Homerus* (Diss. Utrecht 1951) pp. 10ff.; H. Van Looy, 'Figura etymologica et Étymologie dans l'oeuvre de Soph-

first-century BC *De Lingua Latina* Books 5–9 of M. Terentius Varro, is the best and most succinct account of the field for our purposes, particularly since Tibullus probably knew Varro's near-contemporary work, which first brought Greek etymological theory to bear on the Latin language in a systematic way. Books 5–9 of the *De Lingua Latina* begin with their own prologue in which Varro summarises their subject:

> Cum unius cuiusque verbi naturae sint duae, a qua re et in qua re vocabulum sit impositum (itaque a qua re sit pertinacia cum requiritur, ostenditur esse a pertendendo; in qua re sit impositum dicitur cum demonstratur, in quo non debet pertendi et pertendit, pertinaciam esse, quod in quo oporteat manere, si in eo perstet, perseverantia sit), priorem illam partem, ubi cur et unde sint verba scrutantur, Graeci vocant ἐτυμολογίαν; illam alteram περὶ σημαινομένων. De quibus duabus rebus in his libris promiscue dicam, sed exilius de posteriore. (*De Lingua Latina* 5.2)
> *Inasmuch as each and every word has two innate features, from what thing and to what thing the name is applied (therefore, when the question is raised from what thing* pertinacia *'obstinacy' is, it is shown to be from* pertendere *'to persist': to what thing it is applied is told when it is explained that it is* pertinacia *'obstinacy' in a matter in which there ought not to be persistence but there is, because it is* perseverantia *'steadfastness' if a person persists in that in which he ought to hold firm), that former part, where they examine why and whence words are, the Greeks call Etymology, that other part they call Semantics. Of these two matters I shall speak in the following books, not keeping them apart, but giving less attention to the second.*[14]

The close connection between 'etymology' and 'semantics' found in Varro is expressed even more clearly in the second major surviving Latin text on etymology, Isidore of Seville's *Etymologiae*, written in the early seventh century AD but conforming to the traditions of ancient etymology. Isidore explains how, if the derivation of a word is known, its meaning can more easily be understood:

> Etymologia est origo vocabulorum, cum vis verbi vel nominis per interpretationem colligitur. Hanc Aristoteles σύμβολον Cicero adnotationem nominavit, quia nomina et verba rerum nota facit exemplo posito; utputa 'flumen', quia fluendo crevit, a fluendo dictum. Cuius cognitio saepe usum necessarium habet in

ocle', *Mus. Phil. Lond.* 1 (1975) 109ff. (with bibliography 109 n. 2). Many of these works also contain much useful material on Roman etymological theory. Cf. also on ancient word theory Norden on *Aen.* 6.204ff.; O. Keller, *Lateinische Volksetymologie und Verwandtes* (Leipzig 1891, repr. Hildesheim/New York 1974). On etymologies especially in Virgil cf. J. S. T. Hannsen, 'Virgilian Notes', *Symb. Osl.* 26 (1948) 113ff. with bibliography 113f.

[14] The translation is that of the Loeb Classical Library text of R. G. Kent.

Verbal learning

> interpretatione sua. Nam dum videris unde ortum est nomen, citius vim eius intellegis. Omnis enim rei inspectio etymologia cognita planior est.   (*Etymologiae* 1.29)
> Etymology is the derivation of words, when the significance of a verb or noun is arrived at by a process of interpretation. Aristotle called this σύμβολον, Cicero adnotatio, *because it explains nouns and verbs by setting down a model*, *e.g.* flumen *because it has grown by 'flowing' is derived from 'flow'. Knowing this is often a necessary part of explaining the word. For if you see the derivation of a word, you understand its meaning more quickly. For it is easier to investigate anything if you know the 'etymology' of the word for it.*

This etymology/semantics framework will now be applied to Tibullus' use of words so as to achieve an ancient viewpoint. The ancient distinctions between etymology and semantics and between different aspects of semantics are of course to a great extent artificial, and they will not be invoked in detail here. However a stand will be taken on one point. Some Tibullan uses of etymology and semantics might appear to be nothing more than assonance or verbal association. These latter phenomena were recognised in antiquity: indeed they were taught as part of the rhetorical curriculum.[15] It must also be admitted that a seeker after etymologies in Tibullus may sometimes go too far. However, if Tibullus is simply engaged in word-play, it is extraordinary that ancient etymological evidence can so often be produced to back up a similarity between words. The approach through etymology and semantics is much more plausible, and it goes without saying that its heuristic value is incomparably greater. Once 'word-play' has been noted there is nothing more to say about it. The etymology/semantics view reveals the poet's mind at work.

Etymology can be approached initially through Isidore's example *flumen a fluendo*. This pattern of etymological presentation is standard: a *nomen rei*, in this case *flumen* (river), is made *notum* by the information that is derived from the word or process of 'flowing' (*a fluendo dictum*). The evidence is given in the phrase *quia fluendo crevit*. In poetry this pattern is sometimes followed: the evidence is stated clearly and the etymology is communicated through a direct statement of derivation, e.g.

> τὴν δὲ τότ' ἐν μεγάροισι πατὴρ καὶ πότνια μήτηρ
> Ἀλκυόνην καλέεσκον ἐπώνυμον, οὕνεκ' ἄρ αὐτῆς

[15] Cf. e.g. L. Spengel, *Rhetores Graeci* (Leipzig 1856) III index *s.vv.* παρήχησις; παρονομασία; Auct. ad Her. 4.29ff. (on *adnominatio*); J. C. T. Ernesti, *Lexicon Technologiae Graecorum Rhetoricae* (Leipzig 1795) *s.vv.*; *Lexicon Technologiae Latinorum Rhetoricae* (Leipzig 1797, repr. Hildesheim 1962) *s.v.* annominatio. Cf. Rank, *Etymologiseering* pp. 28ff.; H. Holst, *Die Wortspiele in Ciceros Reden (Symb. Osl.* Suppl. 1, Oslo 1925); E. Wölfflin, 'Das Wortspiel im Lateinischen', *Sitzungsberichte der kgl. bayr. Akademie der Wissenschaften Philos.-philol. u. hist. Classe Jahrgang 1887* (Munich 1888) II 187ff.; D. Fehling, *Die Wiederholungsfiguren und ihr Gebrauch bei den Griechen vor Gorgias* (Berlin 1969) Sachregister *s.v.* Etymologie.

μήτηρ ἀλκυόνος πολυπενθέος οἶτον ἔχουσα
κλαῖεν ὅ μιν ἑκάεργος ἀνήρπασε Φοῖβος Ἀπόλλων
(Homer, Iliad 9.561–4)
Then her father and lady mother gave her the name Alkyone in their halls because on her account her mother had the fate of the halcyon with its many griefs and wept that Phoebus Apollo who works from afar carried her off.
Κύκλωπες δ'ὄνομ' ἦσαν ἐπώνυμον, οὕνεκ'ἄρα σφέων
κυκλοτερὴς ὀφθαλμὸς ἔεις ἐνέκειτο μετώπῳ·
(Hesiod, Theogony 144f.)
The Cyclopes were so called because a single cyclic eye lay in the midst of their forehead.

But most poets, including Homer and Hesiod, usually employ a subtler mode of conveying etymological information. They simply record the evidence by placing in close proximity two or more words which they wish to relate etymologically. Then they leave the reader to draw his own conclusions. E.g.

ὡς δ' ὅτε Πανδαρέου κούρη, χλωρηῖς ἀηδών,
καλὸν ἀείδῃσιν ἔαρος νέον ἱσταμένοιο (Homer, Odyssey 19.518f.)
As when the daughter of Pandareos, the nightingale of the green woods, sings sweetly at the beginning of spring.
ἔνθα δὲ ναιετάει στυγερὴ θεὸς ἀθανάτοισι,
δεινὴ Στύξ, ... (Hesiod, Theogony 775f.)
There lives that goddess who is hateful to the immortals, dreadful Styx.

Tibullus' etymological method is this second, subtler one. Of course by his time poets had become accustomed to handling not just the derivations of proper names, as Homer and Hesiod do, but those of common nouns, adjectives and verbs as well. Some easily detectable Tibullan etymologies of common nouns – although commentators rarely notice such matters – are:

(1)   tune putas illam pro te disponere crines
      aut tenues *denso* pectere *dente* comas?   (1.9.67f.)

Cf. for the same combing connection in the context of weaving:

   densum a *dentibus* pectinis quibus feritur
                                              (Varro, De Lingua Latina 5.113)
   Close-woven cloth is so called from the teeth of the sley with which it is beaten.

(2)   agricolaeque modo curvum sectarer *aratrum*
      dum subigunt steriles *arva* serenda boves   (2.3.7f.)

Cf.   *arvus* (i.e. 'arable') et *arationes* ab *arando*
                                              (Varro, De Lingua Latina 5.39)

94   Verbal learning

(3)   teneorque catenis   (2.4.3)

Cf.   catenae ... quod *capiendo contineant* ...
                                          (Isidore, *Etymologiae* 5.27.9)
and   catenatum, quod *capiendo teneat*   (Isidore, *Etymologiae* 20.13.5).

Sometimes the etymology turns out to be more complex. E.g.

> *fictilia* antiquus primum sibi *fecit* agrestis
>   pocula, de *facili composuit*que *luto*   (1.1.39f.)

Cf.   *Fictilia* dicta quod *fiant* et *fingantur ex terra. Fingere* enim est *facere, formare* et *plasmare*, unde et *figuli* dicuntur
                                          (Isidore, *Etymologiae* 20.4.2)

Isidore is aware of the derivations of *fictilia* from *fingo* and from *facio*. Tibullus gives priority to the derivation from *facio* in *fecit* (39). He speaks of the clay (*de ... luto* (40), cf. Isidore's *ex terra*) as *facili* (40). *Facilis* is of course derived from *facio* as was understood in antiquity (Varro, *De Lingua Latina* 10.17) and this is a supplementary or alternative derivation. Either the *fictilia* are so called because they are 'made' and/or because the clay they are made from is 'makeable'. Finally Tibullus may be hinting indirectly at the derivation from *fingo* in the gloss *composuitque* (40) (cf. Isidore's *formare et plasmare*?).

Sometimes the reader needs greater perspicacity to realise that Tibullus is etymologising, e.g.

(1)   ... det munera canus amator
        et foveat *molli frigida* membra sinu   (1.8.29f.)

Cf.   *rigidum* et praeter modum *frigidum* significat et durum
                                          (Paulus (Festus) p. 347(L))

and Lucretius *De Rerum Natura* 3.891f.: aut in melle situm suffocari atque *rigere* | *frigore*.

Thus *molli*, by suggesting its opposite, hints at an etymology *rigidus–frigidus*.

(2)   nec saevo sis casta *metu*, sed *mente* fideli   (1.6.75)

Cf.   Hinc etiam *metus* a *mente* quodam modo *mota*
                                          (Varro, *De Lingua Latina* 6.45, cf. 6.48)

(3)   nec *Spes* destituat sed frugum semper acervos
            praebeat et pleno pinguia musta lacu.
        nam veneror, seu stipes habet desertus in agris
            seu vetus in trivio florida serta lapis:
        et quodcumque mihi pomum novus educat annus,
            libatum agricolae ponitur ante deo.
        flava Ceres, tibi sit nostro du rure corona
            spicea, quae templi pendeat ante fores   (1.1.9–16, cf. 2.6.21f.)

Here the whole verse paragraph is held together by the connection between *spes* and *spica* found in:

> e spe spicae   (Varro, *De Lingua Latina* 5.37)

and

> spica autem, quam rustici, ut acceperunt antiquitus, vocant *specam*, e *spe* videtur nominata; eam enim quod *sperant* fore, serunt.
> (Varro, *De Re Rustica* 1.48.2)

(4)
> vota cadunt: utinam strepitantibus advolet alis
>   flavaque coniugio *vincula* portet *Amor*,
> *vincula* quae maneant semper dum tarda senectus
>   inducat rugas inficiatque comas.   (2.2.17–20)
> servitium sed triste datur, teneorque catenis,
>   et numquam misero *vincla* remittit *Amor*   (2.4.3f.)

In these passages *Amor* suggests *Venus*, which in turn is connected etymologically with *vincire*. Cf.

> ... et horum vinctionis vis Venus. Hinc comicus: 'Huic victrix Venus, videsne haec?' Non quia vincere velit *Venus*, sed *vincire* etc.
> (Varro, *De Lingua Latina* 5.61f.)

Some of these cases involve the rules of derivation given by Varro at *De Lingua Latina* 5.6. Varro explains that, in the course of time, words can change by the loss or addition of letters, by the transposition or change of letters, by the lengthening or shortening of syllables and by the accretion or falling off of syllables.[16] *frigidus/rigidus, metus/mens/motus, spes/spica* and *Venus/vincire* are all explicable in these terms. Varro's transformation rules show how an ancient reader could have followed Tibullus' etymologising without necessarily knowing that a professional etymologist had made a specific link between two words. Poetic etymologising is thus revealed as a process demanding active involvement of the reader. The reader was not intended to recognise poetic etymologies by reference to a text-book of etymology. He was supposed instead to be engaged while reading in constant speculation about and discovery of etymological and other verbal complexes omnipresent in the text.

Consequently the analysis of Tibullan etymologies need not be confined to instances where independent etymological evidence is available from antiquity. Rather, all cases where verbal juxtapositions suggest etymology should be noticed. For example, it may not be accidental that in:

> ... iam Delia furtim
> nescio quem tacita *callida* nocte *fovet*   (1.6.5f.)

---

[16] The text breaks at *item syllabarum productione* but the universally accepted supplement ⟨... *correptione*, ... *adiectione*, ... *dectractione*⟩ restores at least the sense of the missing portion. Cf. *LL* 7.1: *Non reprehendendum igitur in illis qui in scrutando verbo litteram adiciunt aut demunt, quo facilius quid sub ea voce subsit videri possit.*

fovet involves 'warming' while *callida* 'cunning', by removal of the letter l (see above), becomes *calida* 'warm'. Similarly the conjunction of *pigra* and *frigora* in *non mihi pigra nocent hibernae frigora noctis* (1.2.29) might suggest itself as an etymology even if Seneca, *De Ira* 2.10.2: *pigrum est enim contractumque frigus* were not available to strengthen the view that the conjunction is not fortuitous. That *tunderet* and *unda* in *naufraga quam vasti tunderet unda maris* (2.4.10) is etymological is confirmed not by a textbook but by the use of the same learned etymology in another Roman Hellenistic poem, Catullus 11: *litus ut longe resonante Eoa | tunditur unda* (3f.). It can hardly be doubted that *tenero* and *continuisse* – the compound of *cum* and *tenere* – in *et dominam tenero continuisse sinu* (1.1.46) and both *veniant . . . Venus* and *optat opes* in *iam veniant praedae, si Venus optat opes* (2.3.50) are similar etymological complexes.

One or other ancient text-book of etymology may or may not have made some explicit link between pairs of words like these; and Tibullus may or may not have known the textbook. But it is clear that normally Tibullus starts from the rules of etymology and hypothesises links which must in many cases have been new to him and to his readers. Just as the reader actively apprehends poetic etymologies, so the poet does not merely allude to known etymologies but actively etymologises and sets himself up as an independent authority on the subject. It is for this reason that, whether they are attested independently or not, Tibullan etymologies should not be passed over in silence. It goes without saying that there should be no hesitation whatsoever about accepting the presence of etymologising when genuine philological links exist between the words juxtaposed by Tibullus. E.g.

    nec potuit curas *sanare salubribus* herbis   (2.3.13)

    adsideat custos *sedula* semper anus   (1.3.84)

(cf. Isidore, *Etymologiae* 10.24.4)

    fortis *arat* valido rusticus *arva* bove   (2.2.14)

Naturally there is a limit to the degree of allusive complexity which can readily be hypothesised. A borderline case is:

    urantur pia tura focis, urantur odores
        quos *tener* e terra divite mittit *Arabs*   (2.2.3f.)

Here it is obvious that *e terra divite* is an allusive way of referring to the north of Arabia which the Greeks and Romans knew as *Arabia Felix* (Εὐδαίμων). Much less obvious in the same line is a possible link between *tener* and *Arabs*. In Greek *tener* (or *mollis*, a synonym often used of Arabs) is ἁβρός. The Greek language is never far away in Roman Hellenistic poetry; and explanations of Latin words in terms of a Greek derivation are a

Verbal learning

standard type in Roman etymology;[17] in addition proper names are always more likely to be etymologised than other types of word. Tibullus can therefore be suspected of deriving *Arabs* from *habros* – *h* being a breathing not a letter – by one change of letter and by reordering of the letters, both of which are standard means of derivation.[18] The link may seem difficult; but in this short elegy, in addition to this and the *dives–Felix* etymology, there is yet another allusive etymology involving a proper name:

> nascitur, *Eoi*[19] qua maris unda *rubet*   (2.2.16)

where the *Rubrum Mare* is in question.

But leaving aside such examples as might be questioned, there seem to be indisputable cases where an etymological problem is posed by Tibullus in an allusive and riddling form. The case of *fictilia* at 1.1.39f. has already been noticed (above, p. 94) and two examples in Tibullus 2.5 have been discussed above in Chapter 3 (pp. 80f. and 81). Two further cases where Tibullus goes very far beyond the verbal in his etymologising and invites his readers to take part in a process of ratiocination may now be added:

(1)   hoc precor, hunc illum nobis Aurora nitentem
         Luciferum roseis candida portet equis   (1.3.93f.)

This couplet involves verbal echoes of a kind which will be discussed below (p. 100). *nitentem* and *candida* echo the *luci* element in *Luciferum*, while *portet* similarly echoes the *-ferum* element. But in addition Tibullus is alluding to what appears to have been the well-known problem of the derivation of Aurora. The ancient etymological material consists of

> Humor hinc [i.e. *humus*]. Atque ideo Lucilius: 'Terra abit in nimbos humoremque.' Pacuvius: 'Terra exhalat *auram* atque *auroram humidam*.'   (Varro, *De Lingua Latina* 5.24)
> Apud Accium: 'Iamque Auroram procul rutilare | cerno.' *Aurora* dicitur ante solis ortum ab eo quod ab igni solis tum *aureo* aer *aurescit*. Quod addit rutilare, est ab eodem colore: *aurei* enim rutili, et inde etiam mulieres valde rufae rutilae dictae.
> (Varro, *De Lingua Latina* 7.83)
> Haec et Aurora quae solem praecedit. Est autem *aurora* diei clarescentis exordium et primus splendor aeris, qui Graece ἠώς dicitur; quam nos per derivationem *auroram* vocamus, quasi *eororam*.   (Isidore, *Etymologiae* 5.31.13f.)
> ab *aura* enim dicitur *aurora*. proprie enim ipse ascensus solis, id est

---
[17] Cf. e.g. Varro, *LL* esp. 6.96; 7.88f.; also e.g. 5.21; 6.12; 6.61; 6.84; 7.37; Isidore, *Etym.* 1.29.4.
[18] Cf. Varro, *LL* 5.6 and see above, p. 95 and n. 16.
[19] See also below, p. 98.

> prima pars diei, *aurora* dicitur, in qua solet pulsa solis aer commotus *auram* facere. alii autem a splendore solis dictam putant.
>
> (Priscian: *Grammatici Latini* ed. Keil III 509.28)

Three separate possible derivations are mentioned or alluded to in these passages.

(a)   *ros* – this being the implication of Pacuvius' association of Aurora with moisture (*De Lingua Latina* 5.24). Other places where the view is alluded to are: cum primum gelidos *rores aurora* remittit (Cicero, *Aratea* (ed. Soubiran) p. 194: *Progn.* Fr. IV); *roscida* luciferos cum dea iungit equos (Ovid, *Ars Amatoria* 3.180).

(b)   *aurum*. This association is intended to cover the ruddy aspects of dawn light as well as the golden ones, since Varro goes on to claim (*De Lingua Latina* 7.83) that gold and red are the same colour.

(c)   *aura* (Varro, *De Lingua Latina* 5.24; Priscian, *loc. cit.*)

(d)   Greek ἠώς (Isidore, *loc. cit.*)

It is clear from these passages that the derivation was disputed in antiquity. This may be why Tibullus, instead of presenting options, appears rather to adopt one view strongly and to urge it against its unmentioned rivals. Tibullus lays great stress on light. The morning-star is called 'light-bearer', it is described as 'glittering' and the dawn who is qualified by the adjective 'bright' is said to have 'rosy' horses. Tibullus then is opting for the kind of view found in Varro, *De Lingua Latina* 7.83, which also associates dawn with light and colour. But he is not in fact adopting the precise etymology found there. *Aurum* plays no part in the Tibullan couplet; instead the word *roseis* containing the element *ro* in common with *Aurora* seems to be the key term. Roses in antiquity were either white or red. Thus *rosa* as a derivation for *candida Aurora* had the same colour ambivalence which also allowed *aurum* to be a plausible derivation. It looks then as though Tibullus is offering *rosa* as his solution. This is not found in professional etymologists – although it must have been a common one because of the stock Homeric phrase ῥοδοδάκτυλος ἠώς (rosy-fingered dawn). It seems to be alluded to in

> . . . *roseam* Matuta per oras
> aetheris *auroram* differt et lumina pandit
>
> (Lucretius, *De Rerum Natura* 5.656f.)

and in *Gloss.* on *Aeneid* 3.589:

> aurora nubes *rosea* ante solem

(2)

In the second example Tibullus does give the alternative derivations for his problem word. It is the problem word itself which the reader is left to deduce from the context.

Verbal learning

> Quis fuit, horrendos primus qui *protulit* enses?
>   quam *ferus* et vere *ferreus* ille fuit!
> tum caedes hominum generi, tum proelia nata,
>   tum brevior dirae mortis aperta via est.
> an nihil ille miser meruit, nos ad mala nostra
>   vertimus, in saevas quod dedit ille *feras*?   (1.10.1–6)

The discussion centres round the unmentioned word *ferrum*, which as well as meaning iron, also signifies anything made from iron, including the *enses* which appear in line 1. Tibullus proposes several possibilities in his allusive way. The first is a widely current derivation: *ferrum* from *ferus*. Cf.

Ennius, *Annales* 183f. (V):	feroque | ... ferro
Varro, *Menippean Satires* 405:	fera manu ... ferreo ensi
Cicero, *ad Quintum Fratrem* 1.3.3:	ferus ac ferreus
Lucretius, *De Rerum Natura* 2.103f.:	fera ferri | corpora
Ovid, *Metamorphoses* 13.444:	ferus ... petit ... ferro.

The word *vere*, which means 'literally', stresses that Tibullus is thinking in etymological terms. Having thus in line 2 made it quite clear that he is etymologising, Tibullus goes on to suggest another possibility: *feras* (6) – wild beasts – because the original use or intended use of iron weapons was against *ferae*. The reader who is really paying attention to Tibullus' text is intended however to realise that a third possibility has lain hidden since line 1. *protulit* (1) hints at the present tense of *proferre* – *profero* – which gives another alternative derivation, namely *ferrum* from *profero*, because the first inventor of iron weapons 'produced' them. Roman poets thought of *tulit* as coming from *fero*. Cf. Ovid, *Amores* 3.11.4: *et, quae non puduit ferre, tulisse pudet*. Here then Tibullus does not adopt a single etymological solution but leaves the matter open. Oddly enough Varro has nothing to say on *ferrum*: and Isidore (*Etymologiae* 16.21.1) speculates that it derives from *farra*, because *ferrum* is used to put the seeds of grain crops (*farra*) into the earth. The frequency of the *ferrum–ferus* link in poetry may mean that here Tibullus is playing the *doctus poeta* even more than usual in propounding two new solutions.

So much for 'etymology' proper: the cognate field of 'semantics' is if anything even more important for an understanding of Tibullus' artistic purposes. The methods adopted by Tibullus in his semantics are much the same as in his etymology: he brings together words which in combination may raise questions about their meaning in his readers' minds. Ancient poets do not necessarily employ 'semantics' in a scientific spirit any more than 'etymology', but the same interest in the universe as revealed through words lies behind both. This can be seen from the first aspect of semantics to be treated, a phenomenon found in many ancient poets and sometimes known as 'verbal tensions'.[20] It consists in the proximate use of at least two words which are near synonyms or near antonyms.

A few examples of Tibullus' 'verbal tensions', with the words corresponding or opposed to each other linked typographically, are:

Synonyms or near synonyms (probably the more frequent case):

1.1.3	quam labor *adsiduus vicino* terreat hoste
1.2.1	*adde* **merum vino**que *novos* compesce dolores
1.2.6	**clauditur** et *dura* ianua *firma* **sera**
1.3.33f.	at mihi contingat *patrios* **celebrare Penates** **reddere**que *antiquo* menstrua tura **Lari**
1.3.39f.	nec vagus **ignotis** repetens *compendia* terris presserat **externa** navita *merce* ratem
1.3.43f.	non domus ulla fores habuit, non *fixus* in **agris** qui regeret *certis finibus* **arva**, lapis.
1.3.48	*inmiti saevus* duxerat arte faber
1.3.69f.	Tisiphoneque inpexa *feros* pro crinibus angues *saevit*, et huc illuc inpia turba fugit
2.3.5f.	o ego, cum adspicerem dominam, quam *fortiter* illic versarem *valido* pingue bidente solum
2.3.14b–c	et miscere novo docuisse *coagula* lacte lacteus et mixtus *obriguisse* liquor

Antonyms or near antonyms:

1.1.7f.	ipse seram *teneras maturo* tempore vites rusticus et **facili grandia** poma manu
1.1.12	seu *vetus* in trivio *florida* serta lapis
1.3.52	non dicta in *sanctos impia* verba deos
1.5.16	vota *novem Triviae* nocte silente dedi
1.9.10	ducunt *instabiles sidera certa*[21] rates

(cf. Varro, *De Lingua Latina* 7.14: *sidera* quae quasi *insidunt*)

2.1.20   non timeat *celeres tardior* agna lupos

Tibullus sometimes goes further: he can build upon such 'tensions' and so create a complex verbal and conceptual pattern. An example is

> carior est auro iuvenis, cui levia fulgent
> ora nec amplexus aspera barba terit.   (1.8.31f.)

The pun on *carior* – 'more beloved' or 'valuable' – is followed by several verbal tensions: *auro* = *fulgent*, *levia* ≠ *aspera*, *ora* ≠ *barba*, *terit* = *aspera*.

Tibullus and other ancient poets who place synonyms or antonyms in close proximity are involved in the stylistic area known to the Greeks as

---

[20] For a study of verbal tensions in relation to Horace's *Odes* cf. D. West, 'Horace's poetic techniques in the *Odes*' in *Horace* ed. C. D. N. Costa (London 1973) pp. 29ff.

[21] Also etymological: cf. DS on *Aen.* 5,42, *STELLAS FUGARAT poetice dixit. nam si stellae ab stando dictae sunt, non fugantur; semper enim fixae sunt praeter planetas.*

ὄγκος (loftiness).[22] The close placing of synonyms and antonyms is one of the commonest of ancient poetic practices, going back to Homer and early Greek lyric. It was regarded by some ancient critics simply as a stylistic device; but others wished to detect subtle differences between the synonyms so placed and in particular they treated the more comprehensible word of the pair as a gloss upon the less comprehensible. It was in this way that synonymity became associated with some of the types of learning characteristic of Hellenistic poets – Homeric scholarship, lexicography and glossography. Complex mechanisms for the explanation of difficult glosses, some involving links with synonymity, are mentioned by ancient rhetorical writers and scholiasts.[23] But even in Greek Hellenistic poets it is not easy to say when synonyms and antonyms are being used for these learned purposes and when their employment is simply stylistic. It would be even harder to relate Tibullus' use of synonyms and antonyms to glossography, since like most Roman poets he avoids obscure words, and his learning in the use of synonyms and antonyms is etymological rather than glossographical. Synonymity and antonymity involve the concepts of *analogia* and *anomalia*, 'similarity and dissimilarity', 'analogy and irregularity', which are of great importance in ancient thought about language in general and etymology in particular.[24] But in Tibullus the stylistic function of synonymity and antonymity is foremost.

Another aspect of Tibullus' interest in the meaning of words is his thoughtful and effective use of adjectives. This falls under several headings, some of which (cf. esp. pp. 107f.) seem to be related to the so-called *enallage adiectivi* and kindred phenomena.[25] Modern discussion of this stylistic area is bedevilled by problems of definition and distinction; and it is mentioned here only to indicate that the Tibullan uses of adjectives (and sometimes participles) discussed below are in no way idiosyncratic but are part of the learned diction particularly associated with Hellenistic poetry.[26] The first heading is Tibullus' use of adjectives of general significance in a context which imposes on them a more limited and specific import. Juxtapositions of synonyms or antonyms sometimes help to draw the reader's attention to such limited use of adjectives. This phenomenon is well understood in the erotic field, where common words of all kinds have specialised senses, but it is not confined to this area. It is hard to know when such specialised senses are lexicographically distinct; but they are a striking feature of the Latin language frequently exploited by Tibullus and other Roman poets.

[22] Cf. L. Bottin, 'Retorica e lessicografia', *Università di Padova: Bollettino dell'Istituto di Filologia Greca* 3 (1976) 38ff.
[23] Cf. *id.* pp. 44f.; 46ff.
[24] Cf. Steinthal, *Geschichte der Sprachwissenschaft* I pp. 357ff.; Dahlmann, *Varro und die hellenistische Sprachtheorie* pp. 11f.; 52ff.
[25] Cf. V. Bers, *Enallage and Greek Style* (*Mnemosyne* Suppl. 29, Leiden 1974).
[26] Cf. G. Giangrande, *Ant. Class.* 46 (1977) 514f.

Three common adjectives so used by Tibullus are *durus*, *mollis* and *tristis*. Some instances of each are:

(1) *durus*

1.2.5f.   Nam posita est nostrae custodia saeva puellae
          clauditur et *dura* ianua firma sera

1.1.55f. Me retinent vinctum formosae vincla puellae
          et sedeo *duras* ianitor ante fores.

In neither case does the literal rendering 'hard' make much sense. In the first the juxtaposition of *saeva* and *dura* points to the fact that the 'hardness' of the bolt refers not to its metallic composition, but to its unyieldingness: it will not open to the lover. In the second case the meaning of *duras* is the same; but the reader must use the context and the metaphor, in which Tibullus wryly assimilates himself to a slave-doorkeeper bound in chains at his post, to realise that the *fores* are *durae* because they will not open.

(2) *mollis*

1.2.19f.   illa docet *molli* furtim derepere lecto,
           illa pedem nullo ponere posse sono

Beds can be soft; but there is no particular reason why the bed of the lovers should be soft in a literal sense. The context and the sequence of events described in 1.2.13ff. show that Tibullus calls the bed soft in part at any rate because the girl and her *vir* have made love on it.[27] *mollis* often has erotic associations. They are present also at

1.2.55f.   ille nihil poterit de nobis credere cuiquam,
           non sibi, si in *molli* viderit ipse toro

Here Tibullus is promising Delia that her *vir* will not be able to believe that she and Tibullus are having an affair 'even if he sees us in bed making love'. Similarly a little later in the same poem Tibullus says

  et te dum liceat teneris retinere lacertis,
   mollis et inculta sit mihi somnus humo   (1.2.73f.)

Now sleep can be 'soft' in antiquity with no erotic sense.[28] But here the erotic sense is also present: and *mollis somnus* implies sleep 'subsequent to love-making'. At 1.2.95f. however

  hunc puer, hunc iuvenis turba circumterit atra,
   despuit in *molles* et sibi quisque sinus.

mollis suggests 'young'.

(3) *tristis*

At 1.2.49f.

  cum libet, haec *tristi* depellit nubila caelo:
  cum libet, aestivo convocat orbe nives

---

[27] Cf. for the concept Cat. 68.145: *sed furtiva dedit rara munuscula nocte | ipsius ex ipso dempta viri gremio* (and see Kroll *ad loc.*).   [28] Cf. *OLD s.v. mollis* 10b.

the juxtaposition of *tristi . . . caelo* and *aestivo . . . orbe* implies that *tristi* means 'wintry'. But at 2.4.11f.

> nunc et amara dies et noctis amarior umbra est:
> omnia nam *tristi* tempora felle madent.

the conjunction of *amara, amarior* and *tristi* indicates that *triste fel* is the 'bitter bile' of ancient medicine (πικρὰ χολή or less probably μέλαινα χολή. Cf. LSJ *s.v.* χολή). At 1.5.9

> ille ego cum *tristi* morbo defessa iaceres

the context and comparison with Ovid, *Amores* 2.13 where a similar situation arises, may suggest that the *tristis morbus* is an abortion.

This usage shades into another, where the 'meaning' of a fairly colourless word certainly remains lexicographically the same, but the word is used much more precisely and has a greater allusive force than is generally realised. In 1.2.70

> insideat *celeri* conspiciendus equo

the *celer equus* is a 'fast horse' and Tibullus means the reader to think specifically of a war-horse, a charger. So the adjective really does fit the military picture which Tibullus is painting of his amatory rival. At 1.2.77f.

> nam neque tunc plumae nec stragula picta soporem
> nec sonitus *placidae* ducere posset aquae

the *placida aqua* is not just 'calm' water, it is the 'tamed' water of a stream channelled to flow through a rich man's house. Tibullus is envisaging something like the stream that flowed through the villa of Manilius Vopiscus in Statius, *Silvae* 1.3.20ff. esp. 37. When Tibullus writes

> pace bidens vomerque nitent, at tristia duri
> militis in tenebris occupat arma situs.   (1.10.49f.)

he is describing a precise traditional scene[29] which derives ultimately from two passages of Homer's *Odyssey* (16.284ff.; 19.4ff.). In peacetime weapons and armour are left lying about in dusty and sooty corners (*in tenebris*)[30] near the fire where smoke and rust may dirty them. They are *tristia* in part because they are 'black' as opposed to the *bidens vomerque* which are 'bright'.

Another verbal point in this last couplet illustrates how failure to grasp Tibullus' precise shade of meaning destroys not just the finer points of a passage but also its basic sense. Tibullus 1.10 is ostensibly an anti-war

---

[29] For other examples cf. Smith *ad loc.*
[30] Actual hanging up of objects in the smoke was normally restricted to wooden ones which would season there (e.g. Hes. *WD* 45; 629; Virg. *Georg.* 1.175). The notion of hanging up a shield in the smoke at Arist. *Ach.* 279 is a joke (see Rennie *ad loc.*).

poem. But this couplet shows Tibullus' discretion. The near-synonymity of *tristia duri* is not ornament: it draws attention to what *tristis* seems sometimes to mean additionally when used of war, that is 'civil' or 'fraternal':[31] and it underlines that it must be a *durus miles*, one hard and unfeeling, who does not shrink from civil war. Thus, although Tibullus throughout the elegy is playing the lover unfit for war, in his praise of peace he singles out freedom from civil war as one of its blessings, so that his praise of peace could be read as praise of what Augustus had achieved for Italy, despite the wars still going on abroad.

A few more examples of the need to grasp Tibullus' specific intent are:

(1)   *verba*que aratoris *rustica* discit Amor   (2.3.4)

Here the love-god is not learning to speak in a rustic dialect. He is becoming a ploughman and is learning the words of command used to oxen.

(2)   nec quisquam flammae *sedulus* addat aquam   (2.4.42)

The *sedulus* is not someone who is 'carefully' adding water to the fire, he is a 'busybody'.

(3)   abstineas, Mors atra, precor: non hic mihi mater
        quae legat in *maestos* ossa perusta *sinus*,
        non soror, Assyrios cineri quae dedat odores
        et fleat effusis ante sepulcra comis   (1.3.5–8)

The *maestos sinus* are not 'sad breasts' or even 'the breasts of sad people'. They are the breasts which mourners have torn or beaten. Thus these lines contain three of the main manifestations of ancient funerary grief – weeping (8), loosened hair (8), and beaten breasts (6).[32]

(4) In 1.8.35f., a couplet of disputed significance,

        at Venus inveniet puero concumbere furtim
        dum timet et teneros conserit usque sinus

there is, to begin with, one creative etymology – *Venus/inveniet*. There is also another allusive verbal complex: *teneros sinus* refers to the folds of a boy's toga – a *toga praetexta*, which was associated with abstinence from sex. Cf. *ut mihi praetexti pudor est* †*velatus*† *amictus* | *et data libertas noscere amoris iter* (Propertius 3.15.3f.). The fact that he *conserit* them – 'pulls them together' – is an indication of his suitably modest character. In antiquity loose clothing meant loose character and vice versa.[33] The boy's tight toga

---

[31] Notably in Virgil (*Ecl.* 6.7; *Aen.* 7.325; 545; 8.29). This may be connected with its augural use to mean something like 'ill-omened': cf. Pease on Cic. *De Div.* 2.25; Ernout–Meillet *s.v.*   [32] Cf. Daremberg–Saglio *s. v. funus* esp. p. 1391.

[33] Cf. e.g. Tib. 1.6.39f.: *tum procul absitis, quisquis colit arte capillos,* | *et fluit effuso cui toga laxa sinu*; 2.3.77f.: *nunc si clausa mea est, si copia rara videndi,* | *heu miserum, laxam quid iuvat esse togam?* and Smith on Tib. 1.6.40; Hor. *Sat.* 1.5.5f.; Sen. *Epp.* 33.2; 114.6f.

Verbal learning

also goes with his fear (*dum timet*) – the timidity of youth in matters of love – since his fear is cold (Varro, *De Lingua Latina* 6.45: *quod frigidus timor, tremuisti timuisti*) and this makes him draw his garments together.

Another aspect of Tibullus' concern with meaning relates to adjectives and participles which might appear ornamental, equally applicable to every object named by their noun, but which in fact distinguish the object referred to from others which could be denoted by the same noun. In

> Divitias alius fulvo sibi congerat auro
> et teneat culti iugera magna soli. (1.1.1f.)

fulvo (1) seems at first sight purely ornamental. But just as *culti* in line 2 distinguishes arable – and so valuable – land from other, less valuable, sorts, so *fulvus* emphasises the purity of the gold Tibullus has in mind. When Pliny classifies Corinthian bronzes into three types in accordance with the colour they had due to the metals with which the bronze was alloyed, he speaks of one class which contains *auri fulvi natura* (*Natural History* 34.8).[34] In 1.1.25ff. Tibullus counts as one of the blessings of rural life the cool repose of summer:

> iam modo, iam possim contentus vivere parvo
> nec semper longae deditus esse viae,
> sed Canis aestivos ortus vitare sub umbra
> arboris ad *rivos praetereuntis aquae*.

Here the triple mention of water – *rivos*, *praetereuntis* and *aquae* – is not otiose. Many Mediterranean streams dry up in summer – a fact which had legal effects in Roman law.[35] A Mediterranean countryman lying by a river at mid-summer might well see nothing but hot stones. Tibullus then is painting an attractive picture when he imagines himself sprawled by an ever-flowing and so cooling stream; and *praetereuntis* points to and negates the opposite situation. At 1.8.49f.

> neu Marathum torque: puero quae gloria victo est?
> in veteres esto dura puella senes.

Tibullus is not simply recommending that the girl be nasty to old men. Nor is *veteres* otiose. The *veteres senes* are 'old men who are veterans', that is veterans of love, since Tibullus is drawing on the common love/war equation of erotic poetry introduced in the previous line. Such men, unlike young men, are tough enough to be worthy opponents for the girl.[36] So line 50 means 'act the unyielding mistress towards men of mature years with plenty of experience in love'.

---

[34] See *TLL* s.v. *fulvus* 1c1.
[35] I.e. the distinction between *aqua quotidiana* and *aqua aestiva*, cf. *TLL* s.v. *aestivus* p. 1109.10ff. and esp. Tib. 1.7.22: *fertilis aestiva Nilus abundet aqua*.
[36] For such concepts see Smith on Tib. 1.6.3.

In cases like the last the poet is redeemed from what might at first look like folly or insensitivity by a proper understanding of his language. Another such case is

> quam bene Saturno vivebant rege, priusquam
>   tellus in longas est patefacta vias!
> nondum caeruleas pinus contempserat undas,
>   effusum ventis praebueratque sinum.   (1.3.35–8)

Some critics assume, when they see the signs of an impending commonplace, that the poet will inevitably trot out the usual platitudes without thinking. So here Tibullus is supposed to be reproducing the old topos that in the Golden Age men did not travel by land or sea. But the seemingly otiose adjectives *longas* (36) and *caeruleas* (37) tell a different story. What Tibullus says is that in the Golden Age men did not make *long* land journeys and that *ships* did not venture boldly onto the *deep-blue* waves, that is the mid-sea waves. This is a sensible modification of the old commonplace. It allows primitive man to have made short journeys by land and along the sea coast, not in ships – *pinus* is a large vessel and specifically the *Argo*, the first ship – but perhaps in little boats. It was believed in antiquity that before the *Argo* such voyages had been made:

> Nave primus in Graeciam ex Aegypto Danaus advenit; ante ratibus navigabatur inventis in mari Rubro inter insulas a rege Erythra. reperiuntur qui Mysos et Troianos priores excogitasse in Hellesponto putent, cum transirent adversus Thracas. etiam nunc in Britannico oceano vitiles corio circumsutae fiunt, in Nilo ex papyro ac scirpo et harundine. longa nave Iasonem primum navigasse Philostephanus auctor est, Hegesias Parhalum etc.
>   (Pliny, *Natural History* 7.206f.)

Tibullus may have been motivated to refer to such topics by the role of sea-faring in two famous descriptions of well-ordered societies: Homer, *Odyssey* 19.109ff. and Hesiod, *Works and Days* 225ff. In the former fishing is part of the way of life, in the latter the people are said not to travel on ships. These descriptions influenced later social thinking.[37]

A final amusing example is

> at tu casta precor maneas, sanctique pudoris
>   adsideat custos sedula semper anus.
> haec tibi fabellas referat positaque lucerna
>   deducat *plena* stamina *longa* colu.   (1.3.83–6)

---

[37] Notably in the kingship treatises; cf. O. Murray, 'Philodemus on the Good King according to Homer', *JRS* 55 (1965) 161ff. esp. 169, 177; I. M. Le M. Du Quesnay, 'Vergil's Fourth *Eclogue*', *PLLS 1976* pp. 61ff.

Verbal learning

At first sight it might appear that *plena* and *longa* in line 86 are just 'fillers'; but their juxtaposition alerts the reader to their semantic value. Tibullus hopes that, if Delia is occupied listening to the stories of the old woman doing her spinning, she will remain faithful to him. Naturally therefore he specifies that the old woman should have long threads and a full distaff, that is lots of spinning to do. The vignette is thus not only an oblique example of the domestic virtues motif,[38] but it underlines in a delicate and telling way the fragility of the elegiac mistress' fidelity to her lover and his fear of losing her to a rival.

Some brief remarks about Tibullus' syntax and grammatical practices will end this chapter. As was noted above (p. 88) Tibullus' syntax does not have the vigour and irregularity of Propertian syntax. This is of course a deliberate choice and part of Tibullus' attempt to be *tersus et elegans*. But this aspect of Tibullus must not be overstated. Streifinger's detailed examination of Tibullus' language[39] reveals that he makes very considerable use of the poetic resources of Latin grammar and syntax. Among the features detailed by Streifinger are a large number of irregular usages in both areas. Many of these are directed towards the elegant Hellenistic *variatio* of which Tibullus is a master, especially in his catalogue and quasi-catalogue passages. *Variatio* of course need not involve grammatical irregularity. It can be achieved with regular usage, as can be seen from

> *neu* comes ire *neges*, quamvis via longa paretur
>   et Canis arenti torreat arva siti,
> quamvis praetexens picta ferrugine caelum
>   † venturam amiciat imbrifer arcus aquam. †
> *vel si* caeruleas puppi volet ire per undas,   45
>   ipse levem remo per freta *pelle* ratem.
> *nec te paeniteat* duros subiisse labores
>   aut opera insuetas atteruisse manus;
> *nec*, velit insidiis altas si claudere valles,
>   dum placeas, umeri retia ferre *negent*.   50
> *si* volet arma, levi *temptabis* ludere dextra;
>   saepe *dabis* nudum, vincat ut ille latus.   (1.4.41–52)

Only one part of Tibullus' grammatical practice needs further comment: some phenomena connected with adjectives and particles not noted by Streifinger. An adjective or particle can be chosen and placed so that, although from a strict grammatical viewpoint it refers to only one noun,

---

[38] Cf. Daremberg–Saglio *s.vv. fusus* p. 1427; *lana* p. 920. Prop. 1.3.41; R. Lattimore, *Themes in Greek and Latin Epitaphs* (Illinois Studies in Language and Literature 28, 1942) pp. 293ff., 297ff.; J. Esteve Forriol, *Die Trauer- und Trostgedichte in der römischen Literatur* (Diss. Munich 1962) pp. 122f.

[39] J. Streifinger, *De Syntaxi Tibulliana* (Diss. Würzburg 1881).

the reader wishes to think of it as referring or alluding to another noun also. For example, in the line

>   Martia cui somnos classica pulsa fugent (1.1.4)

the unusual participle *pulsa* agrees with *classica*.[40] But *pello* and *fugo* are almost synonymous so that, in addition to reading the line as it actually is, the reader is almost compelled by the oddity of *pulsa* to understand the line as the unmetrical but conceptually acceptable:

>   Martia cui somnos classica pulsos fugent.

An easier pair of such 'shadow references' can be seen a few lines later:

>   flava Ceres, tibi sit nostro de rure corona
>   spicea, quae templi pendeat ante fores
>   pomosisque ruber custos ponatur in hortis (1.1.15–17)

flava agrees with *Ceres*; but its force extends in addition to *corona*. The *custos* (Priapus) is strictly speaking *ruber*; but the juxtaposition of *ruber* with *pomosis* naturally brings to mind the colour of ripe fruit. In

>   sit modo casta, doce, quamvis non vitta ligatos
>   impediat crines nec stola longa pedes. (1.6.67f.)

it is the *stola* which is *longa*. But in disassociating Delia from a *matrona* with her ordered 'bound' hair and her 'long' garment covering her feet Tibullus also recalls the real Delia with her bare feet and her disordered 'long' hair. Cf.

>   tunc mihi, qualis eris, longos turbata capillos,
>   obvia nudato, Delia, curre pede. (1.3.91f.)[41]

This double allusive use of adjectives is fairly common in Tibullus; and it is also one of the most noticeable characteristics of the style of Virgil and is found in Horace and Propertius. Its importance from the viewpoint of ancient poetic style is that it offers an objective and controllable literary insight into the imaginative world of the poets.

Tibullan adjectives can carry a great deal of weight in other ways too. Predicative uses such as

>   elicit et *tepido* devocat ossa rogo (1.2.46)

'while it is still warm';

>   Tantalus est illic, et circum stagna: sed *acrem*
>   iam iam poturi deserit unda sitim. (1.3.77f.)

---

[40] On the rarity of the expression cf. K. F. Smith *ad loc*.
[41] The presence in both passages of an *anus* (1.3.84; 1.6.63) who is identified as Delia's *mater* at 1.6.57 and who in both protects Delia's 'chastity' (1.3.83f.; 1.6.67) is another link.

'when it reaches its peak'; and proleptic uses such as

> *effusum* ventis praebueratque sinum (1.3.38)

and

> quid tibi nunc *molles* prodest coluisse capillos? (1.8.9)

are well within the normal range of adjectival meaning. Also within this range but more remarkable are such cases as

> lucra petens *habili* tauros adiungit aratro (1.9.7)

where *habili* seems to express purpose – 'so that he can use it'.[42] Similarly in

> et *placidam* soleo spargere lacte Palem (1.1.36)

placidam almost means 'so as to placate her'.

However Tibullus' main resource in this area is his use of adjectives more frequently intransitive in an active sense. In

> quaerebam *tardas* anxius usque moras (1.3.16)

the *tardae morae* are 'retarding' delays. In

> ipseque te circum lustravi sulpure *puro* (1.5.11)

the sulphur is 'purifying'. In

> lena necat miserum Phryne furtimque tabellas
> *occulto* portans itque reditque sinu. (2.6.45f.)

occultus means 'concealing'. Some further examples are:

> sternitur, hic *apta* iungitur arte silex (1.7.60): *joining, fitting*
> num te carminibus, num te *pallentibus* herbis
>   devovit tacito tempore noctis anus? (1.8.17f.): *which cause pallor*
> ne iaceam clausam *flebilis* ante domum (2.4.22): *weeping*[43]
> *naufraga* quam vasti tunderet unda maris (2.4.10): *shipwrecking*
> mixtaque *securo* est *sobria* lympha mero (2.1.46): *which makes carefree, sobering*

As has been emphasised, the categories used in this chapter – etymology, semantics, verbal juxtapositions, specific, distinguishing or allusive uses of words – are artificial. The field of study is in fact the continuum of Tibullus' interest in words and their meaning; and the point of it is to arrive at a fairer assessment of Tibullus' use of words. This must be that, although Tibullus is less dramatic and colourful verbally than Propertius or the Hellenistic poets, he is equally rigorous and careful in his choice and

---

[42] On *habilis* cf. M. Leumann, *Die lateinischen Adjectiva auf -lis* (Untersuchungen zur indogermanischen Sprach- und Kulturwissenschaft 7, Strasburg 1917) pp. 41ff.
[43] *Id.* p. 99.

use of words. Tibullus' etymological and semantic techniques are one means whereby in a typically Augustan way he handles, varies and comments upon commonplace Hellenistic material in a detailed and intelligent fashion. These techniques also retain the reader's interest and compel him to make fine distinctions, verbal and real.

5
EXPOSITION

So far, in Chapters 2–4, aspects of Tibullus' content have been discussed. In Chapters 5–8 his techniques of communicating it will be examined. Just as the verbal and conceptual aspects of learning analysed in Chapters 2–4 were not sharply distinct, so the techniques discussed in Chapters 5–8 overlap and are distinguished simply as different facets of the complex process whereby Tibullus communicated his material. In Chapters 2–4 the types of learning treated were all recognised as such in antiquity. In Chapters 5–8 however the discussion will not draw on ancient, or indeed modern, notions of style. Antiquity did have categories of style, but they contribute little to the interpretation of ancient poetry. Even an apparently detailed treatment such as Demetrius *On Style* has at present few practical applications because its details are not precise and numerous enough. The frequently made statement that Tibullus' poetry belongs to the *genus tenue* exemplifies the unhelpfulness of ancient stylistic labels. Most if not all ancient elegy and lyric also belongs to the *genus tenue*, so that this label does not help to distinguish Tibullus from his fellow elegists. The ancient divisions of style may at some future time be pressed to yield better insights. But meanwhile an objective treatment of Tibullus in ancient stylistic terms could only be a catalogue of easily observed phenomena like figures of speech and length of sentences and clauses, which would offer little more than would a careful reading of his text. This is why the emphasis in these three chapters will be on the modes in which Tibullus presents his material, although ancient literary theory offers little help here and recourse must be made in each chapter to the Greek literary context in which Tibullus was working. Considerable space will be devoted in this chapter in particular to discussing Greek techniques of exposition, because they serve also as an introduction to most of the second half of the book.

The most frequent form of exposition in ancient poetry is narrative. Tibullus has no wholly narrative elegies, although two have narrative portions. But the expository techniques of ancient narrative poetry are important for the understanding of Tibullus' elegies for three reasons. First, Greek narrative poetry, as will be illustrated in this chapter and Chapter 9, has several important literary-historical links with Roman elegy. Second, there is evidence that at least some Roman non-narrative elegies derive from Hellenistic narrative poetry in the sense that the Roman poet has put himself in the place of a mythical character in

Hellenistic poetry. I have tried for example to show elsewhere that this has happened in Propertius 1.18: Propertius has imagined himself in the situation of Acontius as portrayed by Callimachus in *Aetia* Frr. 67–75 (Pf.), and he displays in his own person the reactions of the mythological hero.[1] Similarly it is more than probable that Tibullus in 2.3 is adopting Apollo's role as lover of Admetus as well as comparing himself explicitly to the god in 2.3.11ff. The erotic version of the story of Apollo and Admetus is referred to by Callimachus (*Hymns* 2.47ff.). Rhianus may have given a fuller account of it (Fr. 10 Powell),[2] and this version may stand in the same relation to Tibullus 2.3 as does Callimachus, *Aetia* Frr. 67–75 (Pf.) to Propertius 1.18. The third reason why Greek narrative expository techniques are important for Tibullus is that his techniques of non-narrative exposition can most easily be understood if they are viewed as variations on narrative techniques, even though this may not be historically a correct viewpoint.

Students of Hellenistic and Augustan poetry are familiar with the so-called 'Alexandrian' or 'Hellenistic' ways of telling a story.[3] They involve such devices as flashback, anticipation, learned allusion, syntactical variation, digression, vivid sensory emphasis, abrupt transition, compression of some aspects of a narrative and expansion of others, and so forth. They are of course found also in early Greek epic and lyric poetry; and the sophistication of the Hellenistic narrative technique consists in the enhancement of an already sophisticated approach by earlier Greek poets to the problems of relating a story. Homer, in this as in all areas, displays the maturity of a writer at the end of a long epic tradition. *Iliad* 3.1–37 shows a typically Homeric narrative pattern which already has some Hellenistic tendencies. The narrative does not proceed simply and in a straight line. Instead in each section description is encapsulated within narrative in a self-consciously artistic way. In the first verse-paragraph (1–14) line 1 relates that the armies were drawn up. Then the Trojans and the Greeks are each described as advancing, the Trojans noisily (2), the Greeks silently (8). The two descriptions are followed by two similes but there is a subtle *variatio* in their arrangement and application. The first (3–7) follows immediately after the description of the Trojans; its point of comparison is the previously mentioned cries of the Trojans; and it applies only to them. The second (10–12) is separated from the description of the Greeks by one line referring to both sides, and it refers to the subsequently described dust (13f.) raised by both armies. Both similes contain the sort of material to which a Hellenistic audience was also partial: in the first this is interest in natural phenomena, like cranes

---

[1] Cf. F. Cairns, 'Propertius 1.18 and Callimachus, *Acontius and Cydippe*', *CR* N.S. 20 (1969) 131ff.

[2] Cf. Smith on Tib. 2.3.11ff.

[3] Cf. J. Heumann, *De epyllio Alexandrino* (Diss. Leipzig 1904) pp. 50ff.; Fordyce, introd. to Cat. 64; B. Otis, *Ovid as an Epic Poet* (2nd ed. Cambridge 1970) Ch. 2.

rising before a storm, plus learned geographical information; in the second it is visual interest and 'low' characters like the shepherd and the thief. The contrast between the South Wind, mentioned explicitly in the second simile, and the North Wind which by implication wings the cranes south in the first simile is also worth noting. The second verse-paragraph, 15–20, contains two narrative items: Paris was out in front of the Trojan army (16); and Paris challenged the Greek leaders to single combat (19f.). These items form a sandwich containing a description of Paris' equipment (17f.). This sandwich technique is combined in the third verse-paragraph (21–9) with something more elaborate, the repetition with appendages of a single narrative element: twice Homer declares, using the same word (ἐχάρη), that Menelaus 'was glad' when he saw Paris (23, 27). Between[4] this repeated narrative element there is a colourful simile in which Menelaus is compared to a lion finding a carcass. Moreover – a technique which will recur in this chapter – an additional piece of information is appended to the narrative element when it is repeated. In 28 a reason is given for Menelaus' joy: he now thinks he will get his revenge. Then the narrative is carried forward again with another appended narrative element in line 29 when Menelaus leaps down from his chariot. The fourth verse-paragraph (30–7) repeats the sandwich/repetition pattern, after which the text modulates into speeches.

This already sophisticated narrative technique was carried further by the archaic lyric poets, particularly when they reworked material from the epic cycle. They have two narrative types: first, brisk summary of epic action, which is highly selective and concentrates on incidents relevant to the moral, didactic, emotional and, if appropriate, encomiastic functions of the poem. Alcaeus Fr. 283 (LP) exemplifies this type. Its apparent simplicity conceals subtle and rigorous selection and pointed expression of the aspects Alcaeus wishes to emphasise. The departure of Helen for Troy is signalled in a few words (5f.). Her infatuation, caused probably by Love or Aphrodite, for Paris, described allusively as 'deceiver of his host' (5) occupies the rest of the first stanza which survives whole. The consequences fill the next three stanzas and they all make implicit moral statements. The scene is at first Helen's home in Sparta (7f.). Alcaeus pinpoints its desolation and her guilt by saying that she left 'her child in her house' and 'the bed of her husband'. The domestic void at Sparta is quickly followed by the slaughter of Paris' brothers 'because of her' (12–14). This item together with a mention of chariots and people (?) falling in the dust (15f.) do duty for a description of the Trojan War; and to crown them, Achilles, the grimmest avenger of Helen's seduction, appears in line 18.[5]

The second type of lyric narrative involves larger scale reworking of

---

[4] The first ἐχάρη (23) is placed inside the simile but everything else referring to Menelaus precedes it.
[5] Cf. D. Page, *Sappho and Alcaeus* (Oxford 1955) p. 277 (on l. 18).

epic material. In this type direct speech is frequently introduced. Of course the *Iliad* and *Odyssey* are also full of direct speech; but there its primary function is to forward the action or to serve the structural needs of the poem. In archaic lyric poetry however speeches serve primarily to vary the narrative mode and to convey material which in epic would have been narrated. In this second type of lyric narrative, as well as in the first type, the poets concentrate on descriptive elements and reduce the space devoted to action.

Sappho's single surviving narrative poem, Fr. 44 (LP),[6] is a good example. It begins with the arrival of the herald Idaeus, which is quickly signalled in lines surviving in mutilated form (1–4). Direct speech by the herald follows (5–10): he announces the imminent return to Troy of Hector, who is bringing home his bride Andromache. The speech has a distribution of narrative and descriptive material which is characteristic of such speeches in lyric. The first portion (5–8) announces in epic terms the return: the rest (8–10) is an ornamental catalogue of Andromache's bride-gifts with emphasis on the colourful and exotic. Lines 11f. record Priam's joyful response to Idaeus' speech and the spreading of the news of Hector and Andromache's coming throughout Troy. Eight lines (13–20) then describe the effect of this news, the harnessing of chariots and horses by different groups of Trojans. This passage is again full of visual, and probably antiquarian, interest. A lacuna follows in which Hector and Andromache actually arrive. Their arrival prompts a further tableau (21–34). In this they are escorted into Troy to the sound of various musical instruments, songs and shouts of joy, cups of wine and the burning of fragrant scents and incense. The sensuous emphasis is again notable.

The same techniques, used in an even more markedly 'Hellenistic' way, appear in narratives of epic material in the later lyric poets. Their use of speeches is even more contrived; their concentration on the descriptive is more noticeable; sensory emphasis continues; and the flashbacks, digressions and abrupt transitions usually associated with Hellenistic poetry can be seen clearly. Good examples of all these features can be found in Pindar, *Pythian* 4 and in Bacchylides, *Dithyramb* 17 (Sn.–Mae.). To take only the first part of *Pythian* 4 (1–69), the following pattern of material and of speech mode can be seen:

A^1	1–4	Address to Muse (narrative about Arcesilas and his victory)	Pindar's own account	Present
B^1	4–10a	Narrative about Battus (including)	Pindar's own account	Past
	6–10a	Oracle given by the Pythia to Battus	Indirect speech (referring to future)	

[6] For an excellent account of this poem cf. Page, *Sappho and Alcaeus* pp. 63ff.

Exposition

C¹	10b–12	Introduction to Medea's speech (narrative about Argonauts)	Pindar's own account	Past
D¹	13–20a	Medea's prophecy	Direct speech by Medea (given in the remote past and referring to Medea's future, Pindar's past)	Present and Future
E¹	20b–33a	Narrative by Medea	Direct speech by Medea (about the past)	Past
F	33b–34a	Speech of Eurypylus	Indirect speech	
E²	34b–49	Narrative by Medea	Direct speech	Past
D²	50–6	Medea's prophecy	Direct speech	Future
C²	57f.	Ending of Medea's speech to Argonauts (narrative about Argonauts)	Pindar's own account	Past
B²	59–64	Address to Battus about Battus	Pindar's own account	Past
	(including) 61–4	Brief summary of Pythia's Oracle	Substitute for indirect speech	Past
A²	64–9	Narrative about Arcesilas and his victory: he and Argonauts commended to the Muses	Pindar's own account	Present Future Aorist (indicative tenses)

In addition to employing this variegated but symmetrical structure of content and speech mode[7] Pindar enlivens his material further by introducing genealogy (e.g. 33ff., 44ff.); colourful geography (e.g. 6ff., 14ff., 43ff.); foundation learning (e.g. 6ff., 19ff., 38ff., 53ff., 61ff.); etymology (27); and vivid poetic diction (e.g. 3ff., 11ff., 17ff., 63, 67ff.). In Bacchylides 17 similar effects are aimed at but in a more muted context: the seemingly facile pattern of Bacchylides' narrative counteracts his frequent changes of speech mode and ornate descriptions.

Hellenistic narrative poetry to some extent blends the function of Homeric epic with the narrative techniques of lyric. Homeric epic sets out

[7] On similar structures in ancient poetry see below, Ch. 8.

primarily to tell a story, whereas in lyric epic subjects were treated in order to eulogise gods, individuals or states. So for example in Sappho Fr. 44 (LP) the myth of Hector and Andromache was used to celebrate a cult occasion or a wedding; and the myth of the Argonauts in *Pythian* 4 is part of the praise of Cyrene and Arcesilas. In Homer therefore everything was subordinate to the story, while in lyric, narrative techniques were refined to a point where they could sustain interest without allowing the listener to become too caught up in the story and so be diverted from the ceremonial, occasional or celebratory function of the poem. In Hellenistic narrative poetry the story is again primary and the functional aspects are usually fictional or subordinate. But the techniques of lyric, not epic, narratives are used. The difference between the Homeric and Hellenistic concepts of narrative is that Homer wanted his audience to gain pleasure and profit from the story, and his techniques made his art compelling and effective, while Hellenistic poets expected to be appreciated not only for the story they told but also for their narrative skills as such.

Many Hellenistic writers concentrated on episodic narrative poems brief in comparison with Homeric epic but longer than most lyrics. Nevertheless, since they were consciously imitating lyric narrative technique, its characteristic devices appear in their work with greater frequency and in greater concentration than they did in their models. The narrative elements are even more vestigial, the descriptive elements proportionately greater. There is constant emphasis on the colourful, the emotional and the exotic. Since these lyric devices are generally being used by Hellenistic poets in hexameter and elegiac poetry rather than in lyric metres, the poets are thus implicitly challenging the earlier writers of strophic and stanzaic poetry: they are claiming the ability to achieve through stylistic and metrical virtuosity, within very limited metres, the same effects as their predecessors achieved with much greater metrical resources. The metrical restriction of much Hellenistic poetry has of course an economic basis: it avoided for the most part types of poetry which appeared to require choral delivery, dance and elaborate musical accompaniment in favour of minimally accompanied forms. But the Hellenistic poets made a virtue of this necessity.

Thirdly Hellenistic poets had a different attitude to grammar, syntax and vocabulary from earlier Greek poets. In Homer there is little striving after variation in these areas for its own sake. It occurs as part of the natural progress of the narrative. In early lyric a deliberate variation in the subjects of sentences and in some other features becomes apparent.[8] But there is no abnormal striving after variety in vocabulary and in tense and clause structures. In later lyric the greater complexity of sentences produces a more variegated syntactical appearance, but this does not clash with the

---

[8] Cf. F. Cairns, '*Splendide Mendax*: Horace Odes III.11', *Greece and Rome* 2nd ser. 22 (1975) p. 131 and n. 24.

Exposition

natural flow of speech and narrative. But in Hellenistic poetry continual variation in all these aspects is an end in itself:[9] the less the logic of the discourse demands such variation, the greater the poet's efforts to import it.

The largest surviving fragment of Callimachus' *Aetia* (Fr. 75 (Pf.)) is a useful example of Hellenistic narrative for analysis. It is the end of the love-story of Acontius and Cydippe.[10] Acontius fell in love with Cydippe and inscribed on a large apple 'I swear by Artemis to marry Acontius.' Cydippe read these words aloud and so unwittingly swore to marry Acontius. Cydippe's father unknowingly arranged for her to marry another man, while Acontius bewailed his fate in the countryside. Fr. 75 (Pf.) begins at the point where Cydippe's marriage to the other man is about to take place:

> ἤδη καὶ κούρῳ παρθένος εὐνάσατο,
> τέθμιον ὡς ἐκέλευε προνύμφιον ὕπνον ἰαῦσαι
> ἄρσενι τὴν τάλιν παιδὶ σὺν ἀμφιθαλεῖ.
> Ἥρην γάρ κοτέ φασι – κύον, κύον, ἴσχεο, λαιδρέ
> θυμέ, σύ γ' ἀείσῃ καὶ τά περ οὐχ ὁσίη·
> ὤναο κάρτ' ἕνεκ' οὔ τι θεῆς ἴδες ἱερὰ φρικτῆς,
> ἐξ ἂν ἐπεὶ καὶ τῶν ἤρυγες ἱστορίην.
> ἦ πολυιδρείη χαλεπὸν κακόν, ὅστις ἀκαρτεῖ
> γλώσσης· ὡς ἐτεὸν παῖς ὅδε μαῦλιν ἔχει.

Already the maiden had been bedded with the boy, as custom bade that the bride should sleep her pre-nuptial sleep with a boy whose parents were both alive. For they say that once Hera – dog, dog, check yourself, rabid spirit, you would sing even of forbidden things. Lucky for you that you have never seen the mysteries of the dread goddess, otherwise you would have been vomiting out an account of them too. Ah knowing too much is a terrible trouble, when a man cannot control his tongue. Truly this is a boy with a knife.

It appears that this passage sets out to alarm the reader. Line 1 relates that Cydippe was already bedded with the 'boy'. The reader was probably meant to assume that all was lost, since Cydippe had already slept with Acontius' rival. This false alarm is deliberately contrived[11] and it allows Callimachus to introduce local religious antiquarianism (2f.) in the form of an ancient Naxian pre-marriage custom paralleled in other primitive cultures.[12] She was spending a pre-marriage night with a 'child', that is, the

---

[9] Cf. G. Giangrande, 'Aspects of Apollonius Rhodius' language', *PLLS 1976* p. 288 and the works listed in n. 47; 'Dorische Genitive bei Homer', *Glotta* 51 (1973) 1ff.; and on the beliefs of Hellenistic grammarians about Homer in this area 'Der stylistische Gebrauch der Dorismen im Epos', *Hermes* 98 (1970) 257ff.

[10] Lost sections of the narrative can be reconstructed from secondary sources. See Pfeiffer *ad locc.*

[11] On such features in ancient poetry see below, Ch. 7; on this example p. 190.

[12] See Pfeiffer *ad loc.*

'boy' was pre-pubertal. In line 4 Callimachus launches into a flashback narrative, an explanation of the custom. But he immediately checks himself in abusive self-apostrophe. The explanation, he implies, is secret, perhaps part of the restricted material imparted to initiates of a mystery cult. To emphasise this, he refers in lines 6f. to the mysteries of Demeter at Eleusis, the most famous initiation cult in ancient Greece. These further pieces of erudition suggest to Callimachus a general reflection (8f.) at the end of which he appends a brief asyndetic remark giving final clarification to lines 1–3: the 'child' he has mentioned was armed with a knife. Syntactical variation is prominent throughout. First come indicatives: aorist (1) is followed by imperfect (2) and then present (4). The subject of the verb changes each time.[13] At line 4 an imperative in apostrophe abruptly breaks the run of indicatives to be followed immediately by a subjunctive (5). Five further indicatives expressed and one understood follow (6–9), with four changes of subject and three of tense, and with variation from particular to general statement and back again. The changes of mood and mode – from straight narrative at 1 to exposition of a custom in 2f. to the beginning of an aetiological explanation in 4, which is immediately interrupted by apostrophe; then back to generalisation in lines 8f., to the custom in 9 and finally all the way back to the main narrative at the beginning of the next paragraph (10) – these are the product of and combine with the syntactical variation to generate an impression of continuous and boundless intellectual energy. This weaving, complex tissue of material contains only one narrative item, compressed into the first misleading line. The rest is a digression cunningly hooked onto this fact. An illusion is created that the narrative is moving forward; but in fact the movement is one which takes place within the descriptive material and consists in correcting a deliberately created misapprehension on the part of the reader.

The next paragraph (10–21) is introduced by the temporal link ἠῶοι (10). Hellenistic poetry is very heavily paragraphed; and the paragraphing is frequently underlined by the contrived triviality of the link established by the poet between one paragraph and the next. Logical links inherent in the material tend to be suppressed: instead temporal conjunctions or particles without strong logical content are preferred. Asyndeton, which ostensibly repudiates a link altogether, is frequent. The first two lines (10f.) of the second verse-paragraph move the reader into the future. They anticipate the pre-nuptial sacrifice, which was to take place, but in fact did not. This indirect manner, paradoxically combined with a visually vivid description of a non-event which further frustrates the reader's expectation, is characteristic of Callimachus. In contrast lines 12ff. relate what actually happened. Three lines (12–14) describe how epilepsy seized Cydippe: but two of them refer learnedly to the contrasting medical and superstitious attitudes towards the disease.[14] At this point the narrative

---

[13] See above, p. 117 and n. 9.   [14] The *locus classicus* is Hippocr. *Morb. Sacr.* 1ff.

Exposition

speeds up dramatically. The first attack of disease and its effects take four lines (12–15). The reader assumes that Cydippe recovers from it, although no space is actually given to this recovery. A second marriage preparation and a second attack of illness causing seven months of fever occupy only two lines (16f.). A third attempt at marriage and a third seizure with chill occupy another couplet (18f.). The decision on the part of Cydippe's father not to make a fourth attempt and his consultation of the Delphic god occupy just over one line (20f.). The detailed syntactical and conceptual variety employed by Callimachus in the narration of the three identical attempts to marry off Cydippe and her three bouts of illness is worth noting:

(1) In the morning the oxen were going to . . .
(2) A second time the couches were being spread . . .
(3) A third time they considered the marriage . . .

(1) In the afternoon a pallor seized her and the disease came . . . the disease then wasted her almost to Hades
(2) A second time the girl was ill for seven months with a quartan
(3) Again a third time a baleful chill came upon Cydippe.

Such variation can be observed throughout the whole fragment and need not be commented upon further.

The cumulative compression of lines 10–21 leads directly into a passage which, in its diffuseness, is a deliberate contrast to it. This is the expansive sixteen-line direct speech of Phoebus to Cydippe's father Ceyx (22–37).

In it only three lines (22, 26f.) actually inform Cydippe's father of what has, unknown to him, happened to his daughter. Two lines (28f.) tell him what to do, namely marry Cydippe to Acontius. But three lines (23–5) are expended on relating what Artemis was not doing at the time Cydippe swore the oath to her, and eight lines (30–7) are given to praise of Acontius and to elaboration of his genealogy. This non-narrative material is typical of what Hellenistic poets liked: mythological, historical, aetiological, religious and genealogical topics, the stock in trade of civilised antiquarianism. It is interwoven with colourful and allusive visual interest – rush-weaving, the bath of Artemis, the alloying of lead and silver, electrum and gold, quail-netting. The return of Cydippe's father to Naxos and the marriage of Acontius to Cydippe occupy only six lines of clipped narrative (38–43) which is followed by a passage of equal length (44–9) in which Acontius is apostrophised and congratulated through mythological comparisons.

To cap the tale Callimachus relates the 'ancient history' of Ceos in twenty-five lines (50–74) containing quintessential Alexandrian learning, both secular and religious. Aetiology and etymology, *ktisis* and *archaeologia*, local antiquarianism and erudite myth are all present. First the

Cean tribe Acontiadae, who claimed Acontius as their eponymous ancestor, are introduced (50f.). Callimachus next gives as his source the local historian Xenomedes' Cean history (53ff.). Then Callimachus goes backwards in time and begins with purely mythical material (56–9), subsequently moving forward again, entering prehistory and introducing the Carians and another pre-Greek people, the Leleges (60ff.). Both peoples are not infrequently found in the Greeks' accounts of their antiquity. With the prehistory comes an allusion to a local religious peculiarity – sacrifices to Zeus of the War Cry accompanied by trumpet blasts (60f.) and also a mention of how the island changed its name to Ceos (63f.).[15] Six lines (64–9) on a mythical version of a famous prehistoric Aegean disaster, which may have been the eruption of Thera,[16] are followed by five (70–4) on the foundations of the four cities of Ceos. Finally Callimachus gracefully returns to the love-story of Acontius and Cydippe (74–7) which he underscores with another reference to his source Xenomedes and typical Hellenistic emphasis on that source's reliability (76).

Hellenistic narrative technique as exemplified in Callimachus' *Acontius and Cydippe* is thus much more sophisticated than that of Homer, although there are shared characteristics. In Homer, because the narrative itself was in every sense dominant and the attention of the audience was applied primarily to following the story, each stage of the story was presented clearly and for the most part in the order of its occurrence. Where the narrative was interrupted by similes, speeches, descriptions and so forth, these were carefully sign-posted. But by the third century BC educated men knew Homer, lyric poetry, and much else besides. As experienced readers they welcomed the stimulation of epic narrative in which the story was constantly tangled, broken, expanded and contracted in the fashion of lyric poetry, and in which the story had been subordinated to large amounts of descriptive and allusive material.

In his two brief narrative passages (2.3.11–28 and 2.5.39–64) Tibullus shows himself conversant with all the standard Hellenistic techniques. The first passage tells how Apollo pastured Admetus' cattle. Syntactically it conforms to Hellenistic practice. There is frequent change of subjects and of the tense, voice and mood of verbs throughout. So *pavit Apollo* (11) is followed by *cithara . . . profueruntve comae* (12), *nec potuit* (13), and *quidquid erat* and *vicerat . . . amor* (14). The lacunose section 14a–c employs perfect infinitives active while 15f. use perfect passive indicatives. Exclamations at 17–20 carry the story forward and introduce more variation in verb forms: *gestante* (17); *dicitur . . . erubuisse* (18); *caneret* (19); *ausae . . . rumpere* (19f.). The narrative resumes as plain statement at 21ff. but subjunctives appear in 25f. in both principal and subordinate clause, and 27 is a double rhetorical

---

[15] For this type of learning cf. Call. Frr. 412; 601 (Pf.); and Pfeiffer *ad locc.*
[16] On the myth see Pfeiffer *ad loc.* On the possible connection of events in Ceos with the Thera eruption see J. V. Luce, *The End of Atlantis* (London 1969) pp. 118ff.

Exposition   121

question answered in 28. Only one essential fact is narrated in this passage, and this right at the beginning of the paragraph: *pavit et Admeti tauros formosus Apollo* (11). The rest is ornamental expansion and development of this fact. First, lines 12–14 list the divine attributes of Apollo which did not relieve his plight – his musical and verbal skills. Here Hellenistic learning is combined with emotional piquancy. Then lines 14a–16 list his rustic tasks in vivid detail – herding, milking, cheesemaking and basket weaving. Then come the social effects on and the emotional reactions of Apollo's sister (17f.), the cows (19f.), his important human worshippers (21f.), his mother (23f.) and finally any chance passer-by (25f.). The last couplet (27f.) sums up the whole pitiful situation. Hellenistic learned bucolic interest and concern for vivid detail are combined with humour, with the humanising of gods and the injection of human social standards into divine life, and with touches of grotesquerie and pathos. Irony and self-distancing on Tibullus' part are also in play. The other narrative passage, the prophetic speech of the Sibyl (2.5.39–64), could be analysed in similar terms.

It was emphasised above that no Tibullan elegies are wholly narrative. But a second important type of poetry, well exemplified in the Hellenistic period, is much better represented in Tibullus. This is 'dramatic' or 'ceremonial' or 'mimetic' poetry, in which an ongoing scene or situation is described. This type of poetry has been discussed by other scholars.[17] Their findings will be expanded briefly in connection with Callimachus, *Hymn* 2 which can serve as a model for the understanding of the Tibullan dramatic elegies, 1.7, 2.1, 2.2 and 2.5. *Hymn* 2 is usually described by scholars as a commentary on sacred events, or the poet is supposed to be some sort of master of ceremonies.[18] In fact *Hymn* 2 is a choric hymn imagined by Callimachus as sung at the Karneia by a chorus of boys or young men.[19] Confusion has arisen because certain conventions of ancient choric poetry employed in the *Hymn* have not been recognised, namely choric self-address and self-fulfilling injunction and the choric speaker's *persona*, the ἐγώ (I)-figure, which is a mobile compound of chorus, chorus-leader and poet.[20] As a result of failure to understand these conven-

---

[17] Cf. P. Pöstgens, *Tibulls Ambarvalgedicht* (Kieler Arbeiten zur Klassischen Philologie 6, 1940) esp. Chh. 2, 6.; E. Fraenkel, *Horace* (Oxford 1957) pp. 180ff., with bibliography; G. Williams, *Tradition and Originality in Roman Poetry* (Oxford 1968) pp. 194ff.; A. L. Wheeler, 'Tradition in the epithalamium', *AJP* 51 (1930) esp. 217ff.

[18] E.g. G. Williams, *Tradition and Originality* pp. 211f. The same incorrect view is adopted of other ancient choric poems. For further discussion see F. Cairns, 'Five "religious" odes of Horace (I,10; I,21 and IV,6; I,30; I,15)', *AJP* 92 (1971) 440ff.; *GC* p. 192.

[19] 'Imagined' must be stressed. It is disputed whether some or all of Callimachus' *Hymns* had a first 'performance' (on the question cf. É. Cahen, *Callimaque et son oeuvre poétique* (Bibliothèque des Écoles françaises d'Athènes et de Rome 134, Paris 1929) pp. 245ff. esp. 260ff.); but the form of the poem and not historical fact is in question here.

[20] Cf. W. J. Slater, 'Futures in Pindar', *CQ* NS 19 (1969) 86ff.

tions, the virtually explicit revelation of the choric nature of *Hymn* 2 in line 8 – οἱ δὲ νέοι μολπήν τε καὶ ἐς χορὸν ἐντύνασθε (young men, strike up the song and the dance) – has been missed. What might appear to be a personal digression at the end of the poem (lines 105–13ff.) is of course quite consistent with its hymnic and choric character. Such 'personal' digressions can be paralleled both in the *Homeric Hymns* and in Pindaric *epinikia*.[21]

In general dramatic poems are less curt than narratives in their exposition. A sophisticated audience, which could readily perceive a narrative thread, needed more help with a dramatic situation, except in cases where the order of presentation of material, as well as the material itself, was generically dictated.[22] Therefore in *Hymn* 2 the expository material is not so compressed as it was in the narrative *Aetia* Fr. 75 (Pf.), and in fact a fair proportion of the hymn is given over to it. But in *Aetia* Fr. 75 (Pf.) the facts were conveyed in a fairly straightforward, if highly abbreviated, fashion, whereas in *Hymn* 2 the expository details are hinted at several times rather than conveyed directly once: or alternatively they are first hinted at and then conveyed more directly at a later point. Thus the indirectness of the communication compensates for its expansiveness. The process does not seem repetitive to the reader because each repetition adds a little more to the overall picture and because the very success of the exposition depends on such reiteration. *Hymn* 2 therefore consists largely of accumulations of tangential and peripheral but, in combination, informative details. Digressions are inserted into this material but the mode of insertion is specific to dramatic poetry. Whereas digressions in a narrative like *Aetia* Fr. 75 (Pf.) were hooked onto the compressed narrative material as appendages, in *Hymn* 2 a subtler technique is frequently used: digressions involving learned or sensuous material are interwoven with the repeated allusive expository elements. These repeated elements are of course varied throughout with all the resources of grammar and syntax, particularly with apostrophe, interrogation, command and quotation. Occasionally in *Hymn* 2 a technique resembling narrative exposition is found: information is given fairly simply at the beginning of a verse-paragraph, and sometimes also again at the end, while the central portion consists of digression.

In narrative, events are usually related, however briefly, in temporal sequence. If the sequence is broken, this is made clear and, whether straightforward or not, the temporal sequence is often signalled explicitly. Thus in *Aetia* Fr. 75 (Pf.) the stages of the narrative are marked by 'already' (1), 'next morning' (10), 'in the afternoon' (12), 'then' (14), 'a second time' (16), 'a third time' (18) and 'no longer a fourth' (20). The reader receives no

---

[21] Cf. E. L. Bundy, 'The "Quarrel between Kallimachos and Apollonios"', Part I 'The epilogue of Kallimachos's *Hymn to Apollo*', *CSCA* 5 (1972) 66ff.

[22] On this question and the distinction between *logos* and *lalia* see *GC* p. 40; on 'order' in general see *GC* pp. 113ff.

'logical' assistance with the story since stages in the narrative are not marked by connective particles; but at least a time-scale is provided. In *Hymn* 2 help is even more limited, neither temporal nor logical links being given. Of its ten verse-paragraphs, eight begin with asyndeton and two with the weak additive δέ.[23] The reader must therefore deduce for himself the conceptual bonds between the verse-paragraphs. The absence of explicit connections between the blocks of repetitious expository detail naturally sharpens the reader's deductive bias; and for the questioning mind of the Hellenistic reader it is a substitute in 'dramatic' poetry for the discontinuity and compression achieved in narrative poetry by abridgement of expository elements.

Finally, *Hymn* 2 exemplifies the ability of Hellenistic dramatic poetry to achieve another hermetic effect beyond the reach of narrative. A narrative poem by its nature requires a preliminary scene-setting, however brief. But a dramatic poem can, if the poet wishes, erupt into the middle of the situation it treats. Explanations follow later. This is what happens in *Hymn* 2. The reader's interest is sharpened by the need to work out the very subject-matter of the *Hymn*, which, with its abrupt transitions, contrives to tease understanding as long as possible.

Two passages of *Hymn* 2 (1–31 and 97–113) can exemplify different aspects of the techniques described. At the beginning the hearer is transported immediately into the dramatic framework of the Karneia. But there are no explicit statements about the setting. Although the first verse-paragraph in effect reveals that a sacred rite is in progress, that Apollo is the object of worship and that his epiphany is expected, for the most part this is conveyed obliquely. Two omens are exclaimed over in quick succession (1f.). These stimulate the utterance of a ritual formula used at the beginning of religious ceremonies (2). Apollo is then said to be at the door (3). Two more omens follow (3–5). The first pair of omens and the ritual formula that follows imply a forthcoming divine epiphany on a sacred occasion; and the bay is said to be Apollo's attribute (1), which suggests that it is he who will appear. These expectations are confirmed by the information that Apollo is at the door (3), which in turn is supported by the second pair of omens involving 'the Delian palm' and the 'swan' (4f.).

Once this oblique exposition has been completed, excitement is maintained by commands to the bolts and bars of the door (6f.). At the end of the paragraph the proximity of Apollo is confirmed (7); and the third command which follows, a self-address by the chorus of youths envisaged as singing this hymn (8), tells the reader that the poem is a hymn, and specifically a choric hymn.[24] The introductory paragraph thus ends by

[23] The paragraphing used agrees with that of Pfeiffer except that one extra paragraph division is introduced at l. 25 and the last line of the *Hymn* is not treated as an independent paragraph.

[24] Naturally if *Hymm* 2 had a first performance at the Karneia (see above, n. 19) the original audience would have known these facts before the poem began. But the

focusing attention on the central unifying theme of *Hymn* 2 – the praise of Apollo in song. The pattern of piecemeal allusive exposition in repeated form combined with more explicit confirmation of the setting is characteristic of Hellenistic dramatic poetry. The syntactical variety and the learned and antiquarian content is of course typical of all Hellenistic poetry.

The second verse-paragraph (9–16) begins asyndetically. This is partly because lines 9f. are gnomic and partly because Callimachus is introducing a deliberate logical discontinuity to retain his reader's attention. To understand the connection between the two paragraphs, the reader must pay close attention to the implied run of thought: 'Apollo is coming, he only appears to the good. Because he will appear to us we are among the good.' With the comforting thought that they will be blessed by Apollo (11), the chorus now resume their preparations for his epiphany with another self-injunction like that of 8: since Phoebus is coming they must greet him with song and dance (12f.). Now the thought weaves back. Just as the young chorus assured themselves in 11 that the presence of Apollo would ensure their future material prosperity, so now at 14f. they reflect that their future longevity and large families depend on their greeting Apollo in suitable fashion and in 15 they congratulate themselves on having begun to do so. Such thematic interweaving is yet another way by which the reduplication characteristic of dramatic exposition can be achieved. The second paragraph now stands revealed as an amplification of the scene set in the first paragraph. In it further hints add to the reader's picture of the young chorus and fill out the emotional background to the hymn with suitable pious reflections.

The third verse paragraph (17–24) begins with an injunction which, like the ban on the uninitiated in 2, indicates that a sacred ritual is in progress. This is the call for holy silence on the part of the congregation (17). It is reinforced in the rest of this paragraph by a series of parallels for this kind of silence. Hellenistic dramatic poetry often amplifies on a theme and introduces learned material into the text through such *paradeigmata*. The parallels here also aptly continue the praise of Apollo. The celebration by bards of his attributes silences the sea (18f.) and the cry of *paean* stops Thetis' mourning for her son, Achilles, killed as a young man through Apollo's agency (20f.). At the cry the petrified and fecund Niobe, whose children were shot by Apollo and his sister Artemis, ceases her weeping (22–4).

To balance the injunction to holy silence with which this verse-paragraph begins, the next (25–31) begins with another command – a self-injunction to the chorus to sing ἰὴ ἰή, the cry sacred to Apollo. Just as the earlier injunction introduced a series of positive *exempla* of silence, so the second injunction is followed by negative reinforcement. The chorus

Hymn is primarily 'book-poetry' and Callimachus has the needs of a reader foremost in his mind.

state that 'it is evil to fight against the blessed gods' (25). This statement of course relates to the previous group of *paradeigmata*, where both Achilles and Niobe had in their different ways fought against the gods. But it also reinforces the injunction to praise Apollo, since it is implied that failure to praise Apollo is tantamount to fighting against the gods. Callimachus cleverly associates this with opposition to his patron, King Ptolemy (26), who is thus introduced in a quasi-divine role, and then associates opposition to Ptolemy explicitly with opposing Apollo (27). Next follows positive reinforcement of the injunction: since the choir is singing ἰὴ ἰή, powerful Apollo will reward it (28f.); and Apollo is in any case an excellent theme for a song (30f.).

These two verse-paragraphs are constructed in a masterly way. The clear logical thread underlying them is never explicit in the text. On a surface reading the lines seem typically repetitive, hieratic and hymnic formulae expressing naive piety. But in fact the whole section of the hymn is united by an underlying conceptual framework: you (the congregation) must keep holy silence (17); we (the chorus) must sing of Apollo (25); and the intervening and succeeding lines argue subtly and learnedly for these injunctions.

The second exemplary section of *Hymn* 2 – lines 97–113 – uses slightly different techniques of discursive exposition. It consists of the two final paragraphs of the *Hymn*, which have no syndetic links, either with each other or with the preceding paragraph. After a series of reflections on the deeds and titles of Apollo, the chorus finally come in 97ff. to repeat from 21 and consider the sacred cry honouring Apollo ἰὴ ἰὴ παιῆον. They utter the cry again in 97 and then move from this ritual act into a learned explanation of its origin. This allows the introduction of the legend of Pytho, a monster killed by Apollo when the god occupied his shrine at Delphi. In the last two lines of the paragraph (103f.), within this narrative, the cry occurs again – this time in quotation, in the mouths of the Delphians. The paragraph, which begins and ends with its key theme of the sacred cry, is structured like a narrative paragraph. But whereas a narrative paragraph has narrative elements at beginning and end and descriptive material in the middle, this 'dramatic' paragraph has a miniature narrative in the centre acting as a learned digression, and 'dramatic' elements at its beginning and end.

The last section of *Hymn* 2 displays the technique of 'tangential ending' which is also found in Roman poetry modelled on Hellenistic prototypes.[25] *Hymn* 2 ends in a mythological digression, a common form of

---

[25] E.g. Cat. 11.21ff.; Tib. 1.4.73ff.; Hor. *Od.* 1.5.13ff. (with D. West, *Reading Horace* (Edinburgh 1967) pp. 104f.); 2.19.29ff.; 3.4.69ff.; 3.14.25ff.; Prop. 2.3.51ff. The description 'tangential' applied to Call. *Hymn* 2.105ff. is not in opposition to the findings of Bundy, *CSCA* 5 (1972) 66f., who shows that these lines are hymnic and an integral part of the poem. An ending tangential on one level may be integral on another.

tangential ending. Envy personified speaks to Apollo and attacks the type of poetry which Callimachus favoured (105f.) This 'myth' is of course a learned invention on the analogy of similar stories in which Envy, or Blame, spoke maliciously to a higher god.[26] Envy's attack is then answered by Apollo in the vivid metaphor of the great river Euphrates (108–112).[27] Callimachus' defence of his poetry and his counter-attack on his literary rivals is thus put into the mouth of Apollo. Callimachus is trying to add strength to his views by representing Apollo, whom he claims here and elsewhere as his literary protector,[28] as their champion. There is also an implied compliment to Apollo's literary taste in that he espouses the right, that is, the Callimachean, cause. In this way Apollo's repudiation of Envy becomes yet another of the divine achievements celebrated in the Hymn. This fact allows Callimachus to end the hymn with a single line of greeting to Apollo (103) in which the final *chaire*, which is characteristic of the Homeric and other hymns, is balanced by a combined attack on Envy and Blame. Thus on one level the last paragraph is integrated with the *Hymn* while on another its tangential ending achieves a final discontinuity typical of dramatic poetry.

Many of the characteristics of Hellenistic dramatic poetry can be found in one of the Tibullan dramatic elegies, which has some resemblance also in subject-matter to Callimachus, *Hymn* 2. This is Tibullus 2.1, another hymn, the setting of which is the Roman rustic festival of the Ambarvalia.[29] It is quite certain that this festival is the scene of the elegy, since in line 1 *fruges* lustramus et AGROS = amb*i* – ARVALIA, and the festival is defined in remarkably similar language by Macrobius, *Saturnalia* 3.5.7:

> ambarvalis hostia est, ut ait Pompeius Festus, quae rei divinae causa circum arva ducitur ab his, qui pro frugibus faciunt. huius sacrificii mentionem in bucolicis habet Vergilius, ubi de apotheosi Daphnidis loquitur:
> > haec tibi semper erunt, et cum sollemnia vota
> > reddemus Nymphis, et cum lustrabimus agros.
> > > (*Eclogue* 5.74f.)
> ubi lustrare significat circumire, hinc enim videlicet et nomen hostiae adquisitum est, ab ambiendis arvis, sed et in Georgicorum libro primo:
> > terque novas circum felix eat hostia fruges
> > > (*Georgics* 1.345f.)

---

[26] Cf. on the tradition Fraser I pp. 757ff. and esp. n. 302.
[27] The identification has recently been upheld by Williams on Call. *Hymn* 2.105–13.
[28] Notably in the programmatic *Aet*. Fr. 1.21ff. (Pf.).
[29] See Pöstgens, *Tibulls Ambarvalgedicht*, esp. Ch. 4. Ball (pp. 217f.) is unduly sceptical: *lustramus* is decisive (cf. *TLL s.v. ambarvalis*). See further below, esp. p. 129.

Exposition

Tibullus 2.1. is addressed to the gods of the countryside – Bacchus, Ceres and a group of unnamed deities referred to as *di patrii* (17), *rurisque deos* (37) and perhaps *agricolis caelitibus* (36). This unnamed group is presumably the small gods of the countryside, important to the farmer but not of sufficient social status to gain entry to an elegy individually.[30] Tibullus adds Amor and Messalla to this group to make it clear that he is a love-poet under Messalla's patronage. Messalla is virtually deified by the invocation to him at 35, just as Ptolemy was obliquely included among the gods in Callimachus, *Hymn* 2 (see above, p. 125).

It is not at first clear whether Tibullus thought of 2.1 as a choric hymn or whether he imagined himself, in his individual poetic *persona*, as the hymnic speaker. The ritual instructions: 'keep holy silence' (1); 'impure persons depart' (11); and the command 'sing' (83), which resembles the self-fulfilling self-injunctions to song of a Greek chorus,[31] imply a chorus; and the placing in the speaker's mouth of formal prayers (17–24, 35f., 81f.) and of a prophetic statement (25f.) appears to provide confirmation. The singular verbs *precor* (25) and *cano* (37), and the singular pronoun *mihi* (27, 35, 70) are not inconsistent with this notion: Greek choruses often refer to themselves in the singular,[32] either because each member is thinking of himself individually or because at that point the *persona* of the poet predominates and the chorus is speaking for him.

On the other hand there are no elements in Tibullus 2.1 which can only be explained on the supposition that it is a choric hymn. This raises the question how, if 2.1 is a choric hymn, Tibullus' original readers recognised it as such. Again, Cato represents the Roman *paterfamilias* as himself presiding at the *lustratio* of his own fields at the Ambarvalia and acting as sacrificing priest,[33] and it might be argued that a Roman reader would have identified the speaker of Tibullus 2.1 as the poet *qua paterfamilias*, giving appropriate instructions and offering poetic refinements of prayers such as those found in Cato, *De Agri Cultura* 141.

The decisive factor is historical. If choruses did in fact play a prominent part in the rustic Ambarvalia, then Tibullus could have expected his readers to realise that a chorus was speaking in 2.1 without making this totally explicit inside the elegy. The most informative source for the festival besides Cato and Tibullus is Virgil in *Georgics* 1.338ff., where three

---

[30] For a probable parallel suppression of the name of a vulgar deity see F. Cairns, 'Propertius 3.10 and Roman birthdays', *Hermes* 99 (1971) 153.

[31] On these conventions see above, pp. 121f. and nn. 18–20.

[32] The plural is also used. The conventions, which are complicated and which may well await a fully satisfactory formulation, are discussed by: M. R. Lefkowitz, 'ΤΩ ΚΑΙ ΕΓΩ: The first person in Pindar', *HSCPh* 67 (1963) 177ff.; Slater, 'Futures in Pindar'; M. Kaimio, *The Chorus of Greek Drama within* (sic) *the Light of the Person and Number Used* (Commentationes Humanarum Litterarum 46, Helsinki 1970); R. Hamilton, *Epinikion: General Form in the Odes of Pindar* (De Proprietatibus Litterarum, Series Practica 91, The Hague/Paris 1974), pp. 113ff.

[33] *De Agri Cult.* 141; see Smith introd. to Tib. 2.1.

rustic festivals are described. Of these the central festival is the Ambarvalia:

> cui tu lacte favos et miti dilue Baccho
> terque novas circum felix eat hostia fruges,
> omnis quam chorus et socii comitentur ovantes
> et Cererem clamore vocent in tecta;   (344–7)

Augustan poetry is not the easiest source for historical data. But the hendiadys *chorus et socii*, the participle *ovantes* with its implications of song, and the phrase *clamore vocent* expressing prayer and formal summons must refer to the singing and dancing of a chorus. A chorus could then play a part in the private Ambarvalia and Tibullus and his readers must have known this. The hints that 2.1 is a choric hymn must therefore be seen against this background and its choric nature acknowledged. The allusions to tragic song and dance in Tibullus 2.1.51–6 and to the stars as a playful chorus in 87f. can now be interpreted as learnedly underlining the choric aspect of the pôem.

Tibullus 2.1 can now be examined in the light of Hellenistic 'dramatic' exposition. The first 'verse-paragraph' (1–16) consists mainly of a series of commands regulating the preliminaries of the festival. Certain of these commands are addressed to all or some of the worshippers; one is addressed to Bacchus and Ceres; one to the ritually impure; and some are choric self-injunctions. The commands are interspersed with statements explaining or expanding them. The mood used in the commands varies between imperative, iussive subjunctive and indicative. The pattern is as follows:

Lines

1	Keep holy silence (subj.), whoever is present.
1f.	We are performing the ritual lustration (indic.).
3f.	Bacchus come (imper.) with the grape-bunch hanging from your horns (subj.). Ceres, garland your head with corn ears (imper.)
5f.	Land and ploughmen, rest (subj.)
7	Unyoke the oxen (imper.)
7f.	The oxen must be idle today (indic.)
9	Everything must be dedicated to the god (subj.)
9f.	No one is to spin (subj.)
11f.	Impure persons, keep away (indic./subj.)
13	Pure things please the gods (indic.)
13f.	Come ritually purified (imper.)
15f.	Look at the sacrifice and its attendant worshippers (imper. with dependent subjunctive).

The variety of subjects, tenses and moods is immediately reminiscent of Hellenistic practice; and its disjunctive effect is intensified by the internally asyndetic character of the paragraph. Latin of course uses fewer connective

Exposition

particles than Greek, but here the frequency of syndetic linkage is intentionally lower than normal; and this combines with the varied syntax, the imperatives and the assumption that the reader can see what is happening, to make him feel present at the ceremony. Callimachus of course achieves parallel vividness in the indirect scene-setting of *Hymn* 2 through similar devices.

Again, in *Hymn* 2 there was no initial announcement of the nature of the rite; and it was only later that the reader became aware that it was the Karneia. Similarly Tibullus begins abruptly with a call for holy silence (1). The mention of lustration in line 1 of Tibullus 2.1 is more specific than the beginning of *Hymn* 2. But it is only through accumulation of details that the reader learns the exact nature of the rite by the time it begins at line 17. The lustration, the invitation to Bacchus and Ceres (3f.), the emphasis on rest from labour for the whole rural community, men, animals and women (5–10), the information about a sacrifice and its attendant procession (11–17), all these hints together characterise and describe a performance of the Ambarvalia by a whole rustic community.

In another respect also the paragraph employs Hellenistic 'dramatic' exposition. Learned antiquarian material is hooked onto the repeated oblique expository elements. In line 2 the festival is characterised as an ancient one. Its particular institutions are lovingly detailed: Bacchus and Ceres are to come along with attributes of their godhead, which in turn imply that one aim of the Ambarvalia, the protection of the crops, will be achieved; the cattle are to be garlanded and remain in their stalls; another purpose of the rite, fertility, demands that no one present has had sexual intercourse the night before; finally the procession is olive-crowned. These antiquarian and religious details have a contemporary point. Tibullus' rustic Ambarvalia is his indirect poetic tribute to the restoration by Augustus of the priestly college of the Arval brothers, whose main task was to carry out the urban lustration of Rome.[34]

The second verse paragraph of Tibullus 2.1 (17–26) begins asyndetically with a prayer to the *di patrii* (17). The repeated *purgamus* (17) at the start echoes sacerdotal language.[35] The grammatical variation seen in the first paragraph reappears: the subjects change with each clause; and the verbs are varied, with present indicative first person plural (17), plural imperative (18) and singular third person iussive subjunctive (19f.). At line 21 this goes further. There is an abrupt temporal transition to an imagined fulfil-

---

[34] The exact date of the Augustan restoration of the Arvals is not known but it was in the first ten years of the reign. Cf. *R-E s.v. Arvales fratres* p. 1468.

[35] Cf. E. Norden, *Aus altrömischen Priesterbüchern* (Lund/Leipzig 1939) pp. 232f.; *Agnostos Theos* (Leipzig/Berlin 1913) pp. 169f.; G. Appel, *De Romanorum Precationibus* (Religionsgeschichtliche Versuche und Vorarbeiten 7,2, Giessen 1909), pp. 142ff.; D. Fehling, *Die Wiederholungsfiguren und ihr Gebrauch bei den Griechen vor Gorgias* (Berlin 1969) pp. 169ff.; H. Meyer, *Hymnische Stilelemente in der frühgriechischen Dichtung* (Diss. Würzburg 1933) p. 17.

ment of the prayers of 17–20 with the future indicatives of 21–4. The only warning of this is *tunc* (21). This anticipation of the future is a characteristic Hellenistic device already noted in Callimachus (see above, pp. 118, 124f.). After this four-line vignette (21–4) of the happy countrymen at their future harvest festival, the elegy returns to the present: it states that this fantasy will be fulfilled and a good omen is cited in support (25f.). In the oblique fashion of Hellenistic discourse, this omen alludes to the ongoing ceremony. It must be derived from inspection of the entrails of a sacrificial animal – the lamb approaching the altar in line 15. The sacrifice therefore has been made and the rite carried one stage forward.

The third verse paragraph (27–36) begins asyndetically with another change of speech mode: an order for the production of wine is given first in imperative (27 and 28) and then in iussive subjunctive (29). This is immediately followed by a justification of wine-drinking upon this festival day (29f.). The festal scene thus gains a new dimension and the train of thought is again forwarded in an indirect fashion. Since wine is flowing someone may be toasted: Tibullus introduces his patron Messalla as that person.

> sed 'bene Messallam' sua quisque ad pocula dicat,
>   nomen et absentis singula verba sonent. (31f.)

But Messalla has another relevance to the festival, and this is yet another place where Tibullus relies on his readers' knowledge of something not explicitly mentioned (see above, Chapter 2). Among his many other distinctions Messalla was a *Frater Arvalis*.[36] This fact was denied by historians when the evidence for it first appeared, but is now generally accepted. However, its importance for the interpretation of this elegy does not seem to have been recognised. Messalla is absent (*absentis*, 32) because he is at Rome celebrating the *Amburbium* in his official capacity as *Frater Arvalis*. The toast to him at the rural Ambarvalia unites that ceremony in spirit with the great urban celebration, the conjunction *sed* (31) having of course no adversative significance but being additive and injunctive.[37] Since Messalla is to be toasted (31f.) his victories and triumph can be mentioned (33). This topic is learnedly appropriate to the Ambarvalia given that the ancient Roman Arval Hymn was addressed to Mars in his capacity as a god of agriculture and that it ended with the quintuple cry of '*triumpe*'.[38] The mention of Messalla's triumph leads to an invocation of him as a semi-deity to inspire the hymn being sung. This is an easy

---

[36] For recent discussions cf. M. W. H. Lewis, *The Official Priests of Rome under the Julio-Claudians* (Papers and Monographs of the American Academy in Rome 16, Rome 1955) p. 121; J. Scheid, *Les Frères Arvales* (Bibliothèque de l'École des hautes Études, Section des Sciences religieuses 77, Paris 1975) pp. 13ff., 55. Cornutus, the addressee of Tib. 2.2 and 2.3, may well be M. Caecilius M.f. Gal. Cornutus, associate and fellow Arval of Messalla (see Scheid pp. 34ff.).

[37] Cf. Leumann–Hofmann–Szantyr, *Lateinische Grammatik* II (p. 487 §260b).

[38] Cf. Norden, *Aus altrömischen Priesterbüchern* pp. 114ff.

Exposition

transition given the link mentioned with the Arval Hymn and the half-divine status of the *triumphator*.

The technical skill with which Tibullus thus introduces Messalla as the person toasted, converts him into a 'divine' addressee[39] and injects an encomiastic couplet between is characteristic of Hellenistic poetry. Characteristic also is the way in which Tibullus implies other conceptual links. One is the learned link wine–toasting–triumph, with its allusion to the connections between Dionysus and the triumph.[40] This is of course more eulogy of Messalla: Dionysus was deified for his achievements and benefits to man, including victories on earth. Messalla by implication is another Dionysus whose 'godhead' has been achieved in the same way. More eulogy of Messalla is linked with the antiquity of the ceremony. The Ambarvalia was said at line 2 to be a ritual derived from the Romans' remote ancestors (*prisco . . . avo*); at 34 Messalla is said to be a great glory to his long-haired, that is, remote, ancestors (*intonsis . . . avis*). The honouring of Messalla at the Ambarvalia therefore implies that he reproduces the virtues of his ancestors.[41] In this oblique method of eulogising his patron Tibullus is again comparable to Callimachus in *Hymn* 2.

The introduction of Messalla and his triumph are an invitation to the reader to remember 1.7. The reader who does so finds the structures of the two poems fascinatingly similar:

1.7		2.1	
		Ambarvalia	1–30
Messalla's triumph and campaigns	1–28	Messalla's triumph and campaigns; invocation of him	31–6
Inventions of Osiris/Bacchus	29–48	Inventions of rustic gods and rustics	37–80
Invocation of Bacchus along with Genius	48–54	Invocation of Amor	81–6
Messalla and his triumphal fame	55–64	Back to the Ambarvalia	87–90

---

[39] Cf. Stat. *Silv.* 1.4.19 with Vollmer *ad loc.*; S. Commager, *The Odes of Horace: A Critical Study* (New Haven and London 1962) pp. 4ff.; [Germanicus] *Aratea* 2ff.

[40] See above, pp. 41ff. and *GC* pp. 95ff.

[41] Tibullus may here be employing the standard topos whereby a man is said to add to (i.e. by continuing) his ancestors' distinction (cf. Tib. 1.7.55f. and Smith on 1.56). It is possible however that he is alluding to the rare Roman concept that distinction can be conferred retrospectively by someone on his ancestors. Cf. Stat. *Silv.* 1.4.68f. (of Rutilius Gallicus): *permissaque retro | nobilitas*. The latter notion may also lie behind Hor. *Od.* 1.12.45f., i.e. the 3rd-century BC Marcellus may be implied to be gaining in glory through the achievements of his descendant, Horace's contemporary Marcellus, Octavia's son and Augustus' son-in-law. Cf.

It appears that 2.1 imitates with variation the train of thought of 1.7. The triumph and birthday of Messalla, which are the festal occasions of 1.7, are replaced in 2.1 by the rustic Ambarvalia. It is therefore to this festival that 2.1 returns at its end, whereas in 1.7 the final couplets go back to the objective result of Messalla's triumph, road-mending (57–62), and a wish for long life for Messalla (63f.). In 2.1 the triumphal material is compressed into two lines (33f.) and the inventions which led to civilisation are attributed not to Bacchus and deities identified with him but to the *ruris dei* and countrymen. The *ruris dei* replace Bacchus as the benefactors of mankind because Messalla is now being celebrated primarily as a *Frater Arvalis* rather than as a *triumphator*. This choice allows Tibullus to end the catalogue of inventions by invoking Amor, an inventive god dear to his own heart, who recurs in a similar location in 2.5.106ff.

The remainder of Tibullus 2.1 can be analysed more briefly by omitting mention of the syntactical *variatio* which has been fully enough exemplified. The Messalla passage is followed by a long section which fulfils the preliminary undertaking made at line 37: *rura cano rurisque deos*. It lasts until line 80 and within it there are three verse-paragraphs: 37–50 celebrating the inventions and blessings of the *ruris dei* in general; 51–66 treating the inventions of rural man; and 67–80 describing the role of Cupido in the countryside.

The technique in this section is that of ancient catalogue poetry in general, modified and enlivened by the Hellenistic method of repeating themes with added details. So at 37f. Tibullus states that the gods of the countryside were responsible for mankind abandoning its original diet of acorns; and at 39f. that they taught men to build their first houses. The first of these achievements is amplified at 41ff. where these deities are credited with taming oxen in the plough and inventing the wheel (41f.), whence (43) *tum victus abiere feri*. The full implication comes after four more lines (43–6) about fruit trees, gardens and wine: *rura ferunt messes* (47); and the ploughing motive then provides a link with the beginning of the next verse-paragraph at 51: *agricola adsiduo primum satiatus aratro*. Similarly the motif of wine which is carried over into 45f. from the preceding verse-paragraph (27ff.) is hinted at again in 55f. and the topic of spring flowers occurs both at 49f. and at 59f. In addition to such repetitions, Tibullus is continually reinforcing his picture of the countryside and its gods by accumulation of congruent details: the many aspects of husbandry and agriculture invented by gods and men; the different kinds of animals kept and exploited in the countryside (bulls 41f.; goats 57f.; sheep 61f.); and the rustic products, wine, honey, wool.

In the third verse paragraph Cupido is naturalised in the countryside first by the assertion, backed it is claimed by learned authority (*dicitur*, 68),

> Norden on Virg. *Aen.* 6.875f. for further discussion of concepts in this area; also Quint. *Inst. Or.* 3.7.8; 10; 18; 21; 26.

that he was born there, and then by a brief allusive reference to his growing up in a rustic setting. Tibullus then relates the inventions and teaching of this last of the rustic deities in terms which clearly and ironically refer more to the urban experience of the love-poet. There is a pointed and moving antithesis here: on the one hand the other rustic deities, who provide wealth and happiness, teach man to exploit the beasts for his own uses and offer a number of blessings ending in the female arts of spinning and weaving which characterise and protect female chastity in antiquity; on the other hand we have the activities of Amor. Far from providing man with wealth and comfort, Cupido strips the youth of his wealth and the older man of his dignity. Love has given up practising his arts on cattle and instead exploits and torments human beings. The girl in love is not chaste and home-loving but wanders away from home alone at night in the dark. It is small wonder that Tibullus, when, at the beginning of the next verse-paragraph, he invokes Love to come to the Ambarvalia, begs him to leave his arrows and torches behind (81f.) and emphasises his role with respect to the cattle (83f.).

The piquant accumulation of detail throughout this section adds up to a description of the blessings of the countryside and of primitive society which stands alongside those of Tibullus 1.1, 1.3 and 2.5. This example is outstanding in its discreet and self-effacing use of learned material. Apart from two explicit touches, 55ff. where the Dionysia and the origins of tragedy are linked,[42] and 59f. where the spring offering of flowers to the Lares is mentioned, the details about the inventors, primitive man and the cult-festival are only hinted at. It is clear however that Tibullus meant his reader to recollect specific names associated with the inventions he details; and he or his source may have been working on the basis of a list of such inventors and inventions.[43] Similarly Tibullus' account of primitive man here, as in 1.3 and elsewhere, is clearly drawing on learned traditions.[44] As regards the cult-festival, Tibullus, like other Roman poets, makes complex use of traditional material in describing it. It cannot be assumed for example that all the details will be factual:[45] it may be that the poet has in

---

[42] See Smith on Tib. 2.1.57–8.
[43] On such lists cf. Fraser I pp. 455f. and nn.; II Ch. 11 n. 439; on the tradition of 'inventors' A. Kleingünther, ΠΡΩΤΟΣ ΕΥΡΕΤΗΣ: *Untersuchungen zur Geschichte einer Fragestellung* (*Philol.* Suppl. 26,1, Leipzig 1933); for the inventor motif in Roman poetry cf. R. Müller, *Motivkatalog der römischen Elegie* (Diss. Zürich 1952) p. 21.
[44] See above, pp. 47ff. On learned ancient thought about early man cf. W. K. C. Guthrie, *In The Beginning* (London 1957) Chh. 4, 5; E. R. Dodds, *The Ancient Concept of Progress and other Essays on Greek Literature and Belief* (Oxford 1973) Ch. 1.
[45] See e.g. A. Hardie, 'Horace *Odes* 1,37 and Pindar *Dithyramb* 2', *PLLS 1976* pp. 113ff., on Hor. *Od.* 1.37, where the Salian celebration, Greek dithyramb and Roman triumph are blended; Fordyce, introd. to Cat. 61, where the marriage ceremony is 'a fantasy in which the traditional topics of the genre and Hellenistic formulae are combined with a vivid and colourful representation of some of the

mind one or more Greek festivals in addition to the Roman festival under discussion. So for example in 2.5.91f. Tibullus seems to have the Attic feast of Χύτροι, the thirteenth day of the Anthesteria, in mind as well as the Roman Parilia;[46] and he may be drawing in part in 2.1 on the Ἀλῷα and the Dionysia[47] as well as on the Ambarvalia in order to place the Ambarvalia in a Graeco-Roman cultural and religious context. The last brief verse-paragraph of Tibullus 2.1 (81–90) rounds off the poem and the festival with a final set of injunctions by the chorus. The method is again accumulation of details: the invocation of the god; the revels and flute-playing; the dancing of the chorus implied by the dance of the stars; the coming of night and sleep upon the festivities. The final pair of couplets have a distinctly iconographic appearance. Tibullus may be indulging, in the manner of Hellenistic poets,[48] in a brief learned *ekphrasis* of a famous sculpture or painting or artistic type in which the goddess Night and her *komos* of subordinate deities, Somnus and the Somnia, were represented.

Tibullus therefore employs an expository technique in 2.1 which is thoroughly Hellenistic. But, as was noted above, the majority of Tibullan elegies are not 'dramatic'. They are 'personal monologues' and lack even the residual narrative and temporal structure which, for example, an ongoing religious ceremony gives to a poem like 2.1. A suitable Hellenistic model for this type of poetry must be sought not in the surviving portions of Greek elegy, which are inadequate for this purpose, but in Theocritean hexameter poetry.[49]

The speech of Polyphemus in *Idyll* 11 is a useful example of a 'personal monologue' of the Tibullan type. As will be seen, it depends even more on apparent redundancy in exposition and on general repetitiousness than do Callimachus, *Hymn* 2 and Tibullus 2.1, where a residual temporal sequence survived. Such repetitiousness in exposition is accompanied by skilful *variatio* and is in no way a fault. On the contrary, it shows a poet's

---

main features of a Roman wedding' (p. 236); and *GC* pp. 183ff. on Hor. *Epod.* 16, where a similar blend is present.

[46] I.e. if the 'jug kiss' (on which see Smith on Tib. 2.5.92) is an allusion to this festival.

[47] On the Haloa see Pöstgens, *Tibulls Ambarvalgedicht* p. 3; ll. 51ff. appear to allude to the Dionysia, although it is arguable whether the Great, the Lesser or both is meant.

[48] On Greek Hellenistic descriptions of works of art cf. Dover on Theocr. *Id.* 1.29–63; cf. also Call. *Iamb.* 6 (Pf.) and *AP* Book 16 where this ecphrastic tradition is exemplified from most periods. On ecphrasis of works of art in the whole of ancient literaure cf. J. Bompaire, *Lucien écrivain: imitation et création* (Bibliothèque des Écoles françaises d'Athènes et de Rome 190, Paris 1958) pp. 707ff. For Propertius cf. K. Keyssner, 'Die bildende Kunst bei Properz' (Würzburger Studien 13, Stuttgart 1938) pp. 169ff. (repr. in *Properz* ed. W. Eisenhut (Wege der Forschung 237, Darmstadt 1975) pp. 264ff.); M. Hubbard, *Propertius* (London 1974) pp. 164ff.; 173; for Ovid cf. H. Herter, 'Ovids Verhältnis zur bildenden Kunst' in *Ovidiana: Recherches sur Ovide* ed. N. I. Herescu (Paris 1958) pp. 49ff. = *Kleine Schriften* ed. E. Vogt (Munich 1975) pp. 493ff.

[49] On the relevance of Theocritean hexameter poetry to Roman elegy see above, Ch. 1 and below, Ch. 9.

Exposition

skill at expanding his material (*macrologia*), an essential aspect of poetic craft. In *Idyll* 11, before the actual speech of Polyphemus begins, there are eighteen lines of scene-setting in which Theocritus addresses his patron Nicias. In Callimachus, *Hymn* 2 and Tibullus 2.1 there was no scene-setting and the reader was brought straight into the middle of the action. Non-narrative poems, both 'dramatic' and 'personal', differ among themselves in this respect; in some scene-setting is necessary, in others it is not. Narratives however always require it.

In *Idyll* 11 the scene-setting for Polyphemus' speech (1–18) links Nicias with the 'myth' and says a fair amount about Polyphemus; but it says nothing about Galatea except that Polyphemus is in love with her. Thus Galatea is seen only through the eye of Polyphemus. This reinforces the point of the poem, which is that Polyphemus sees her through the eye of love.

The first verse-paragraph of Polyphemus' speech (19–24) is a highly ornate and repetitious apostrophe of Galatea. It tells us that she is beautiful and that she rejects Polyphemus. It also contains an etymology on her name (19f.) (Galatea = 'milky-white'); and a vivid and colourful description of her in rustic terms, which the poet has selected as appropriate to the *persona* of Polyphemus. In addition the emotional depth of Polyphemus' affection for Galatea and hence his bitter sorrow at her rejection of him as a lover is demonstrated. The pain of Polyphemus' situation is particularly emphasised in the responsive repetitions of lines 22f.

The second verse-paragraph (25–9) begins with one of those sudden flashbacks so characteristic of Hellenistic poetry. It is a highly coloured sentimental vignette – again something typical of the Hellenistic period. Polyphemus fell in love with Galatea when he was a boy and she a young girl picking hyacinths. Then the paragraph returns to the present with a reiteration of Polyphemus' earlier complaint (19ff.) that he is in love with Galatea but she rejects him (28f.). The illusion that this repetition has a summarising function both conceals its otioseness and allows Theocritus to reinforce the pathos of the vignette by juxtaposing its happier scene with Polyphemus' present unhappiness.

The third verse paragraph of the Cyclops' speech (30–53) begins with an abrupt asyndeton at 30. Polyphemus turns to himself. He declares that he knows why Galatea rejects him: it is because he is ugly. The same pictorial vividness is present in his unflattering self-description (31–3) as in his flattering description of Galatea (19ff.). The contrast between the two depictions reinforces that typical Hellenistic feature,[50] the grotesqueness of lines 30–3. Then, in contrast to his ugliness, the Cyclops goes on to describe his wealth and his pleasant way of life (34–49). This description of

---

[50] Cf. e.g. G. Giangrande, 'Theocritus' Twelfth and Fourth Idylls: a study in Hellenistic irony', *Quad. Urbin.* 12 (1971) 95ff.; F. Williams, 'A theophany in Theocritus', *CQ* 21 (1971) 141.

Polyphemus' circumstances gives Theocritus an opportunity to indulge in an elaborate and convincing bucolic fantasy enhanced by the antiquarian interest of the life-style of this primitive and prehistoric rustic. Thus in typically Hellenistic manner, Theocritus gives verisimilitude to the fantastic. The animals and plants mentioned come from the sphere of Hellenistic zoological and botanical learning (40–6) and there is also pronounced visual and aural aestheticism of the type favoured in Hellenistic poetry (38ff., 45ff.).

The elaborate escapism of lines 34–49 is brought back to reality by a return in 50 to the question of the Cyclops' own revolting physique with which the paragraph began (30ff.). This is followed by another pathetic evocation of the depth and strength of his passion (51–3). It is clear that at least one function of the many reiterations of this last motif is to unify the meditation of Polyphemus. At 52f. a sophisticated ironic note is heard: the burning of the Cyclops' eye is an allusion to a mythical event in Polyphemus' future, the arrival of Odysseus at his shores; and this allusion is picked up again at 61 where the Cyclops speaks of 'a stranger' coming in his ship. Such reflections in one myth of a wider mythological world are typical of learned Hellenistic poets.[51]

At 54 a sudden asyndetic exclamation initiates a new verse-paragraph. Polyphemus bewails the fact that his mother did not bear him with gills. The Hellenistic grotesquerie and contrived naivety of this notion is obvious. Elaboration follows in 55–9, where Polyphemus claims that had his mother done so, he would have come to kiss Galatea's hand and bring her flowers. The botanical emphasis of these lines is again learned, and the colour contrasts show Hellenistic visual interest. This learning, like that of lines 40ff., is structurally possible because it is supported by the repetitive exposition.

Just as lines 25ff. were a flashback into the past, so in the next paragraph (63–6) in equally typical Hellenistic fashion Theocritus projects the reader with the same abruptness into an imagined future. This technique of rapid temporal alternation is of course also characteristic of Tibullan elegy; and this Theocritean example of it is of particular interest for Tibullus since it is remarkably similar in content to one passage of Tibullus. In his fantasy Polyphemus imagines that he and his beloved will together lead a happy country life and pursue the work of country folk. The same fantasy is expressed at Tibullus 1.5.19–34.

At line 67 Polyphemus' fantasy abruptly ends; and in the succeeding lines Theocritus draws the Cyclops' discourse to a close. These final lines are marked by constant asyndeton: at 67 where Polyphemus suddenly

---

[51] Cf. Prop. 1.1.9ff.; Call. *Hymn* 6.72ff.; Virg. *Ecl.* 6.74ff. Poetic interest in variant legends, synchronisms and incongruous elements in myths goes back of course to Hesiodic catalogue poetry and to lyric poets' 'revisions' of myths.

Exposition 137

blames his mother for his plight; at 68 where he explains why he does so; at 70 where he thinks of a device to punish his mother; at 72 where he suddenly begins a self-apostrophe; at 73 where he begins to envisage possible alternatives to his love for Galatea; at 75 where he employs proverbial self-injunction; at 76 where he speculates about an alternative girlfriend; at 77 where he claims he is a favourite of the girls; and finally in the last line of his speech (79) where he sums up in a self-congratulatory fashion. Syntactic variation makes this asyndetic complex even more jerky and exciting, with the main verbs of the sentences constantly changing in tense, voice, number, person and mood. This jerkiness goes hand in hand with and reinforces the emotional tensions of the lines. Thus it emphasises towards the end of the poem the sufferings of Polyphemus, which the reader may have been lured into neglecting because of the strength and vividness of his previous hopes and fantasies.

The repetitiveness of the expository elements – even within a section where the trend of thought changes often – is again marked; and as usual it allows Theocritus to introduce the favourite concepts of the Hellenistic poet. So in 67ff. the grotesque confrontation of Polyphemus and his mother with its overtones of abnormal psychology sums up the two earlier mentions of this lady; one sentimental (26), one macabre (54). The confrontation also allows the unfortunate monster to be portrayed as sulking like a child and as inventing imaginary pains – an excellent example of the Hellenistic technique of humanising the heroic.[52] The girls in 78 'giggle', in Greek also an onomatopoeic word; and throughout the paragraph visual interest is notable. At 73ff. the bucolic side of Polyphemus, prominent throughout the idyll, surfaces for the last time aptly in a context infused by the typical Hellenistic concern with the humble and lowly, particularly as introduced into heroic contexts.

1.8, a typical example of a Tibullan personal monologue, displays many of the same techniques as Theocritus, *Idyll* 11. Like *Idyll* 11, Tibullus 1.8 contains even more repetition *cum variatione* than Callimachus, *Hymn* 2 and Tibullus 2.1. But there is less jerkiness and discontinuity in Tibullus 1.8 than in either Callimachus or Theocritus, while at the same time Tibullus contrives to begin the elegy with less 'scene-setting' than Theocritus. This is in fact a general feature of Tibullus, principally because he employs the particular technique of information conveyance to be discussed in Chapter 6. Tibullus' mode of concealing and varying repeated elements is of some interest; and 1.8 exemplifies this well.

[52] Cf. e.g. P.-E. Legrand, *Étude sur Théocrite* (Bibliothèque des Écoles françaises d'Athènes et de Rome 79, Paris 1898, repr. 1968) pp. 184ff.; H. Herter, 'Kallimachos und Homer', *Xenia Bonnensia* (Bonn 1929) pp. 57ff. = *Kl. Schriften* pp. 377ff.; repr. in *Kallimachos* ed. A. D. Skiadas (Wege der Forschung 296, Darmstadt 1975) pp. 354ff.; H. White, *A Textual and Stylistic Commentary on Theocritus Idyll XXIV* (Classical and Byzantine Monographs 5, Las Palmas de Gran Canaria, forthcoming).

138   Exposition

In its first verse-paragraph (1–8) Tibullus declares that he is a *magister amoris* well qualified to give erotic advice.[53] He begins (1f.) with a general statement that the significance of love's signs and flirtations cannot be concealed from him. The next couplet (3f.) denies that this situation comes about in certain ways, so reiterating that it does come about. The third couplet (5f.) relates how it does come about, so repeating that it does for a third time. In the fourth couplet (7f.) the paragraph is ostensibly summed up in a prohibition: 'stop pretending you are not a lover'. This in fact repeats the original proposition of lines 1f.: 'the meaning of a lover's actions cannot be concealed from me'. But 7f. also clarify the setting of the elegy by revealing that Tibullus is addressing a single person who is a lover. This additional revelation palliates the repetitiveness of the verse-paragraph and also rouses the reader's excitement at its end. Thus it enhances the interest of the transition between this paragraph and the next.

The fact that some of the topoi are varied from their normal forms also enlivens the paragraph. In the first couplet Tibullus does not claim to know that one specific person is in love with another, as a *magister amoris* may do.[54] Rather he says he knows the significance of a lover's signs and whispers. This is at once a less self-important and more practical stance. Tibullus does not in 3f. compare himself with oracles, as the *magister amoris* sometimes does.[55] Instead he claims he has received no help from oracles, divination or prophetic birds. But then, in the third couplet he admits a divine instructor: Venus, like the *magistra* of a mystery-cult group, has initiated a bound Tibullus with the usual flogging, and has taught him this arcane knowledge. In this form the topos is enlivened with touches of comedy and magic. In the last couplet of the paragraph (7f.) Tibullus makes a conceptual jump from *dissimulare* to *invitos*. He assumes something by no means obvious, that someone who denies that he is in love does not want to be in love. This assumption is another amusing touch which gives Tibullus, as *magister*, an initial unfair advantage over his pupil.

The first verse paragraph thus provides a scene-setting for the elegy, but only a partial one. It is worth emphasising for example that, although by the end of line 8 the reader is aware that Tibullus is addressing a single person in love, it is not yet clear whether his addressee is male or female, or who he or she is in love with. The second paragraph works rather like the first. Two couplets (9–12) interrogate the addressee, asking if various

---

[53] For erotodidaxis cf. A. L. Wheeler, 'Propertius as Praeceptor Amoris', *CPh* 5 (1910) 28ff.; 'Erotic teaching in Roman elegy and the Greek sources. Part I', *CPh* 5 (1910) 440ff.; '*id.* Part II', *CPh* 6 (1911) 56ff.; *GC* index *s.v.* and F. Cairns, 'Horace on other people's love affairs (*Odes* I 27; II 4; I 8; III 12)', *Quad. Urbin.* 24 (1977) 121ff. On the 'retention' of the names Marathus and Pholoe in this elegy see below, pp. 148f.

[54] Cf. Herodicus ap. Athen. *Deipn.* 5.219c; Prop. 1.9.3ff.; Heliodor. *Aeth.* 3.17.2.

[55] Cf. e.g. Call. *Iamb.* 5.31f. (Pf.); Prop. 1.9.5f. cf. *GC* p. 73 and n. 7; 2.21.3; Heliodor. *Aeth.* 3.17.2.

Exposition

cosmetic items are not useless, a third (13f.) states that yet other cosmetics are useless. The final couplet of the second verse paragraph (15f.) states a contrasting confirmatory circumstance: *illa* attracts affection without make-up. This final couplet also adds another touch to the scene-setting. But *illa* is still ambiguous: she could be a general example or a girl Tibullus loves or a girl the addressee loves. This concealment of the true situation for as long as possible is typically Tibullan and gives the elegy a further comic flavour (see below, Chapter 6). The reader, even at line 16, still does not know what the situation is. Only at lines 23ff. does it become clear that the addressee is a former beloved boy who is in love with *illa* and whose cosmetics, once useful in attracting male lovers, do not impress the girl whom he now loves.

Within the first two verse-paragraphs many Hellenistic aspects of technique and content can be noted. Syntactical variation is prominent. Although lines 1–6 are made up entirely of statements, tense is varied (1–4 present, 5f. perfect) as is mood (1 and 3–6 indicative, 2 subjunctive) and the subjects of the clauses and hence the persons of the verbs (1 first singular, 2f. third plural, 4–6 third singular). The lengths of the individual clauses in these lines are also varied. Line 7 introduces a command and lines 9–12 interrogations with statements intervening at 7f. and returning in 13–16. Between the verse-paragraphs there is deliberate abruptness with asyndeton. As regards content, topical *variatio* has already been mentioned in lines 1–6; and in these lines the learned interest in omens and magic is also notable. Here Tibullus is in a favourite area of Hellenistic poetry.[56] In the second verse-paragraph another Hellenistic concern, the uselessness of cosmetics,[57] is involved. Tibullus handles this topic with a wealth of vivid detail about hairdressing, make-up, manicuring, high-fashion clothing and tight footwear. Both paragraphs suggest the emotional conflict inherent in the situations they describe. In the first the teacher of love is confidently proclaiming his skill and prescribing for his addressee. The very air of confidence hints that, as elsewhere,[58] the teacher has an axe to grind and is in love with his addressee. In the second paragraph an even more open and variegated emotional conflict is revealed: the one-time beautiful boy with his effeminate appearance is now, paradoxically, in love with a girl who does not rely on cosmetics. Here is a practical example of the standard Hellenistic precept that girls who do not wear make-up are

---

[56] On the poetic tradition cf. Smith on Tib. 1.2.42ff.; A. A. Day, *The Origins of Latin Love Elegy* (Oxford 1938) pp. 96ff.; Gow and Dover on Theocr. *Id.* 2; Prop. 1.1.19ff. and Enk *ad loc.*; L. Fahz, *De Poetarum Romanorum Doctrina Magica* (Religionsgeschichtliche Versuche und Vorarbeiten 2,3, Giessen 1904) esp. Ch. 2; and most recently A.-M. Tupet, *La Magie dans la poésie latine*: I *Des origines à la fin du règne d'Auguste* (Paris 1976).

[57] For a full collection of material cf. *Gregor von Nazianz: Gegen die Putzsucht der Frauen* ed. A. Knecht (Heidelberg 1972) esp. pp. 39ff. Cf. also A. L. Wheeler, 'Erotic teaching II', 70ff.

[58] Cf. e.g. Prop. 1.2; Tib. 1.6.

more attractive than those who do,[59] rendered even more poignant by its combination with another, that former beautiful boys grow up and fall in love with girls.[60]

The remainder of the poem functions in the same way. The following division into verse-paragraphs may be adopted as the basis of a brief analysis: (3) lines 17–26; (4) lines 27–38; (5) lines 39–48; (6) lines 49–54; (7) lines 55–66; (8) lines 67–78. In each paragraph the same type of repeated exposition can be observed along with parallel care to alter the syntactical basis of the repetitions and to enliven them with pointed and varied Hellenistic topical material. Paragraph 3 begins with asyndeton and can be analysed thus:

17f.	Surely you have not been bewitched into loving? (Interrogative)
19f.	The power of witchcraft ⎫
21f.	The power of witchcraft ⎬ (Statements with initial anaphora)
23f.	You have not been bewitched into loving (Interrogation plus statement)
25f.	Physical contact has made you fall in love (Statement with triad of dependent perfect infinitives)

Here again the ending of the verse-paragraph with a fuller reiteration of its initial theme can be seen. Marathus has actually been making love with the girl and this is the cause of his condition. There is also an amplification of that Hellenistic interest in magic which was hinted at in the first verse-paragraph and which is frequent in Tibullus' work.[61] The emotional intensity is heightened by the contrast between the grandiloquent assertions of the power of magic and the denial of its efficacy in the case of Marathus.[62] Vivid sensory impressions permeate this paragraph: the witch at the dead of night casting her spells, the beating of bronze echoed in the words of line 22, the sensual details of lines 25f.

The fourth paragraph (27–38) begins with *nec* (27) which is the first syndetic link between verse-paragraphs in this elegy. But the link is deliberately combined with sudden change of addressee from the boy to the girl. It is thus an example of the pseudo-syndetic technique of Hellenistic writers already commented on.[63] The paragraph consists of:

27–30	Two precepts to the girl not to be unkind to Marathus (Imperative plus supporting indicative statement; and second person iussive subjunctive plus supporting third person iussive subjunctive)

---

[59] Cf. Smith on Tib. 1.8.15–16; Knecht, *Gregor von Nazianz* pp. 52f.
[60] Cf. e.g. *AP* 12.31 (Phanias); Prop. 1.20; varied, i.e. he falls in love with a boy: *AP* 12.12 (Statilius Flaccus); Theocr. *Id.* 13 (a dramatisation of the topos, as was understood by Propertius); Hor. *Od.* 1.4.19f. (implied).
[61] See above, p. 139 and n. 56.
[62] Cf. Prop. 1.1.19ff.   [63] See above, pp. 118, 123.

Exposition

31f. The value of Marathus (Indicative statement)
33f. Precept to be kind to Marathus (Imperative plus iussive subjunctive)
35–8 Love will find a way (Gnomic perfect indicative – reading *invenit* with A – with dependent infinitives giving details)

The plan of the paragraph – repetitions together with the introduction of a new note towards the end of it – is by now familiar. So is the syntactical variety, although here it may be noted that Tibullus is exploiting the particular richness of the Latin language in varieties of command. *Memento* is chosen because of its unusual form; and variation continues in *ne poscas* (29), *det* (29), *suppone* (33), and *despiciantur* (34), before the gnomic perfect *invenit* (35) leaves the area of command altogether. The protreptic tone of moralising in the passage is of course appropriate to the *magister amoris* and in the light of Tibullus' own love for Marathus it is emotionally interesting. Notable also is the strong visual content of lines 29–33 where colour and tactile contrasts are combined with verbal play. Again in lines 35–8 there is lively sensual detail.

The fifth verse-paragraph (39–48) is the centre-piece of the poem and it begins with asyndeton. It consists of

39f. Old women have no pleasure in riches without a man (Indicative)
41–6 That is the time for make-up (Indicatives)
47f. Employ your youth properly (Imperative with supportive indicative statement)

The centre-piece thus sums up what the poem is about and its relatively low level of syntactical variegation is compensated for by its conceptual importance. The first and last couplets convey the same sentiment, expressed first negatively and then positively. The central trio of couplets take up once more the notion of artificial aids to beauty last mentioned in line 16 and declare that the appropriate age for using cosmetics is old age. This discussion of make-up is even more vivid than the first: the colour contrasts of *cana* (42), *viridi* (43) and *albos* (45), and the grotesque visual concepts of plucking out hairs and sloughing off old skin like a snake (45f.) are most striking. The contrast between Youth and Age, the central theme of the elegy, is thus achieved with maximum effect at this point of central structural importance.

The rest of the elegy can now be treated even more briefly by neglecting syntactical variation, which has been illustrated sufficiently. Lines 49–54 constitute a linking paragraph between the centrepiece of the elegy and the speech of Marathus (55–66). In it Tibullus begs the girl to cease tormenting Marathus: he is a boy (49, 51); she should torment older men (50). He is not guilty of any offence (51): his appearance is due to the ravages of love (52) and to his complaints and tears (53). Repetition is again a prominent aspect; and it is notable that Tibullus' precepts echo those of lines 27–38. Thus the two passages on either side of the centrepiece are variations on the same theme. The notion of *sontica causa* which appears at 51 is a typical piece of Tibullan learning. It is a term rooted in legal language, the significance of which was debated in antiquity.[64] Whatever the primary meaning of the phrase, the half line *non illi sontica causa est* must have at least a secondary sense of something like: 'he is not a guilty party', i.e. 'his appearance is not due to guilt'. But the learning and difficulty of the concept gives colour and interest to the paragraph.

At 55 Tibullus in abrupt Hellenistic fashion introduces a direct speech of Marathus (55–66). This is a change of speech mode so far unparalleled in the elegy. Marathus' speech has a particular piquancy in that Tibullus puts into the boy's mouth remarks which include an erotodidactic precept (55f.) analogous to the lore which Tibullus and Venus taught girls at 1.2.16ff., which Tibullus taught Delia at 1.6.9ff. and which Venus has already been credited with in this elegy at 35ff. Such precepts are typical instructions of the experienced *magister amoris*. The irony of this is patent. Tibullus is drawing an implicit comparison between himself, taught by Venus painfully (lines 5f.) to be a *magister amoris*, and the boy Marathus, his erotic pupil, who is already through bitter experience gaining sufficient knowledge of love to begin to instruct his girlfriend. But the erotodidactic theme is only fleeting. Marathus turns from instructions to the girl back to his own experiences as a lover, which have convinced him that furtive love is possible (57ff.). But like Tibullus himself at 1.4.81ff. lamenting the fact that his erotodactic arts were no help to him in his love of Marathus, so with striking similarity, Marathus here laments that his *artes* (61) do not help with his girl friend. The paragraph is constructed as follows:

55f.	Girls in love can evade their guards and reach their lovers
57–60	Marathus' own experiences in *furtivus amor*
61–6	But the girl does not come to Marathus.

As usual, accumulation of detail is the expository method: the quietly drawn breath, silent kisses, creeping about at night and noiseless opening of doors in 57–60, the two ways in which a lover can be disappointed in 61–6.

In the final verse paragraph (67–78) Tibullus first addresses Marathus in 67f. and then turns for the rest of the elegy to address the girl, now finally named (69) as Pholoe. The structure of the paragraph is

67f.	Marathus, your efforts are useless
69f.	Pholoe, the gods dislike such pride
71–6	Marathus once maltreated his lovers, but now he detests this kind of behaviour.
77f.	Stop being arrogant or you will be punished.

[64] See Smith and André *ad loc.*

Exposition

Lines 71–6 contain an illustration of the precepts given at the beginning and end of the paragraph. In this respect it exemplifies a type already discussed in connection with dramatic exposition and found also in personal monologue poetry, in which dramatic or monologue material makes up the beginning and end while the centre is a brief narrative.

The changes of direction both at the beginning of the verse paragraph (67) where Tibullus replaces Marathus as speaker and again, equally abruptly, at 69, where Pholoe takes Marathus' place as addressee, combine with the temporal changes at 71 and 77 and with the two different sorts of counsel at 67 and 69 to give interest and excitement to this paragraph, which sums up the whole elegy in brief. Equally striking is Tibullus' tact. He makes his point without exaggeration. Having portrayed with verve the nasty glee of Marathus in the old days when he was maltreating his lovers, including Tibullus, with great enjoyment (71–4), Tibullus follows up this portrait with a mild complaint which understates Marathus' present misery (75f.). Moreover, instead of threatening Pholoe in detail with torments like those at present suffered by Marathus, Tibullus merely repeats the theme of 27f., warns her of divine anger twice (69f., 77), and ends: *quam cupies votis hunc revocare diem*. The lesson is all the more impressive for its understatement.

Tibullus' expository techniques have therefore general similarities to those of Callimachus or Theocritus. If all Hellenistic poets survived entire, then perhaps a clear analogue could be detected. But it may be more likely that Tibullus, writing in a different language and in a different age, based himself on Hellenistic models but created out of them an individual and original style of exposition.

6
INFORMING

Chapter 5 dealt with Tibullus' technique of exposition in general. Chapters 6 and 7 will deal with one aspect of it, the conveyance of information about the scenario of an elegy. This is a vital part of exposition, since without knowing the situation the audience cannot understand the poem. This chapter will examine how Tibullus gives such information; the next will treat cases where he appears to be doing so, but it turns out not to be genuine. The distinction made in Chapter 5 between narrative poetry on one hand and dramatic and personal monologue poetry on the other will also prove useful in this chapter. In a narrative poem the reader must follow the story-line to understand the poem, including any elaborations, descriptions, similes and digressions. But the whole story is not told at the beginning: new facts and incidents are introduced regularly at opportune points – an easy process, since narrative involves time-lapse. The recurrent introduction in a narrative of essential new information has the slight disadvantage that a reader whose concentration lapses at a single point can lose his place. On the other hand, he is not burdened by a large initial conveyance of data; and the writer has the advantage of an audience alert to each new stage of the narrative, and hence to other levels also.

But some non-narrative poems are constructed differently. The audience is told all the facts necessary for understanding the situation at or near the beginning. The poem then amplifies or comments upon these facts. There is a simple reason for the difference: an interesting story can start from a small factual base; but a non-narrative poem often requires a more complex starting-point. Some elegies of Propertius and Ovid work in the way described. Propertius 1.14 for example starts with six lines in which wealth is associated with Tullus and declared to be a less potent force than love, which is linked with Propertius. The remaining eighteen lines of the elegy amplify this theme. Again in *Amores* 1.2.1–10 Ovid wonders why he cannot sleep, decides that it is because he is in love, and therefore resolves that he must yield to love. In the remaining forty-two lines of the elegy Ovid justifies this decision and describes the consequent triumph of Love. There are no new twists or turns and no new information about the situation is provided.

However other elegies of Propertius and Ovid and most elegies of Tibullus are constructed in a different way. At the beginning the reader is given only as much information as he needs to understand the first section.

Later, at various convenient points, new, essential information is presented. As a result the elegies of Tibullus are vivid and mobile. They change course, often dramatically, and the reader's reactions also change in response to the new information and its implications.

Before the literary history and affiliations of this technique are discussed, some cases will be examined in detail. It is found, like many other characteristic features of Tibullus' work, in 1.1. In 1–6 Tibullus rejects war and its reward, wealth, and opts for a life of humble sufficiency in the countryside. Lines 7–24 elaborate on this choice, describing the rustic tasks with which Tibullus will occupy himself and his pious attitudes and observances, which will ensure that his toil is fruitful. At this point new information is given:

> iam modo, iam possim contentus vivere parvo
>   nec semper longae deditus esse viae   (25f.)

The pentameter obliquely reveals that Tibullus has been a soldier. So his rejection of war as a way of life is not merely a philosophical and rhetorical commonplace[1] but the considered opinion of a man with personal experience of both peace and war. The reader's understanding and evaluation of Tibullus' sentiments is altered by this new information; and the retention of it to this point intensifies its effect.

Lines 27–44 elaborate yet further upon the activities of Tibullus in his role as countryman. But then a new note appears:

> quam iuvat immites ventos audire cubantem
>   et dominam tenero continuisse sinu.   (45f.)

Tibullus is revealing for the first time that he is a lover. For Tibullus' original readers this really was new information: they did not know their poet's *persona*; and his elegiac form, although implying an erotic element, did not entail that he was a lover. So far all they knew was that Tibullus, an ex-soldier, had turned farmer. The new information that he is a lover has two sets of implications. First, it focuses more sharply the picture of Tibullus as an ex-soldier: there was already in New Comedy a standard antithesis between the lover and the soldier which also became standard in Roman elegy.[2] Tibullus now stands revealed as a man who has abandoned one of the two antithetic ways of life for the other. Secondly, as has been

---

[1] Cf. F. Cairns 'Horace, *Epode* 2, Tibullus 1,1 and rhetorical praise of the countryside', *Mus. Phil. Lond.* 1 (1975) 79ff.; and on the detailed background H. Kier, *De Laudibus Vitae Rusticae* (Diss. Marburg 1933) and R. Vischer, *Das Einfache Leben* (Studienhefte zur Altertumswissenschaft 11, Göttingen 1965).

[2] Cf. R. Müller, *Motivkatalog der römischen Elegie* (Diss. Zürich 1952) pp. 47ff.; 66f.; and e.g. Tib. 1.2; Prop. 1.8; 2.16; Ov. *Am.* 3.8; cf. Gallus in Virg. *Ecl.* 10; W. Steidle, 'Das Motiv der Lebenswahl bei Tibull und Properz', *WS* 75 (1962) 100ff. On the comic soldier in general see W. Hofmann and G. Wartenberg, *Der Bramarbas in der antiken Komödie* (Berlin 1973).

described in Chapter 1, the revelation that Tibullus is a lover is a novel refinement upon the rustic element in his *persona*, which stresses his paradoxical claim to moral rectitude as a lover.

The fresh information of lines 45f. is further illuminated by lines 53f. Here for the first time the reader is introduced to Messalla, Tibullus' patron and the dedicatee of his two books of elegies, and told that Messalla is a famous general. Tibullus 1.1 can now be seen to exemplify what became a standard type of Augustan poem.[3] In it the poet and his patron adhere to different life-styles; and the sincerity of the poet's praise of his patron is ostensibly guaranteed by this difference in personal ideology. Tibullus' praise seems particularly sincere: as a former soldier, he knows how unpleasant and difficult war is, and so, when he lauds Messalla's martial achievements, he speaks from personal knowledge. In addition, as an *agricola* enjoying *pax*, he depends on the achievements of Messalla as a general, while as a lover he relies on the kindness and understanding of a patron who will not insist on his going to war but will allow him freedom to live as he wishes. Thus the virtuous patron has a virtuous dependant, whose choice of life is in accordance with rhetorical and other conceptions of the countryside as a place of high personal morality.[4]

At lines 55–8 the last new information given in 1.1 makes its appearance. It consists of first the identity and social status of Tibullus' mistress Delia, and second the explicit link made by him between erotic *inertia* and the rustic *inertia* of line 5. This link once more contradicts the standard rhetorical view of the countryman as hard-working by bringing to the fore that arch-symptom of love, *otium*,[5] and reiterates the attachment to elegiac love already proclaimed by Tibullus at 45f. The mention of Delia's *fores* (56) shows that she is a *hetaira*, someone specifically excluded from the rustic scene in the rhetorical tradition.[6] Tibullus then is, in contrast to the rhetorical farmer, attached to a demi-mondaine and living a life of *otium*. These factors do not weaken his aspiration to the admirable moral status of the farmer. They mean that Tibullus is claiming moral rectitude not just for love but for that type of love characteristic of New Comedy, Hellenistic epigram and Roman elegy. This is a bold and interesting view, and one which dominates the rest of the poem. Indeed it recurs, not always dominantly, but continually, in the elegiac love poetry of both Tibullus and Propertius. To end 1.1 in a conceptually symmetrical way Tibullus,

---

[3] Cf. e.g. Hor. *Od.* 1.6; Prop. 2.7 and F. Cairns, 'Propertius on Augustus' marriage law (II,7)', *Grazer Beiträge* (forthcoming); Prop. 1.6 and *GC* pp. 4ff.; Prop. 3.4 and *GC* pp. 185ff.

[4] Apart from rhetorical sources, on which see above, n. 1, Virgil's *Georgics* had made the farmer a noble figure, thus confirming a traditional view. Cf. e.g. Cato, *De Agr. praef.* 2: *et virum bonum quom laudabant, ita laudabant, bonumque agricolam bonumque colonum.*

[5] Cf. J.-M. André, *L'Otium dans la vie morale et intellectuelle romaine* (Paris 1966) index rerum notabilium *s.v. Amor*.

[6] Cf. esp. Libanius, Ἐγκώμιον Γεωργίας (ed. Foerster) VIII p. 263 ll. 13ff.

employing an Augustan topos,[7] describes as warfare his whole life and death as a lover, and reiterates his moral rejection of real war (75–8).

The same technique of delayed information can be seen also in Tibullus 1.8, which was studied from the viewpoint of exposition in Chapter 5 (see above, pp. 137ff.). As was noted there, Tibullus in lines 1–16 declares himself a teacher of love, advises someone to admit to being in love, attacks cosmetics as useless, and introduces an unexplained *illa*. But only in line 23 is the addressee identified as male (*misero*); and only in 27 is *illa* identified as the girl whom the *miser* loves. He is now seen to be a former beloved boy who has fallen in love with her. The situation is piquant, relying as it does on the standard ancient distinction between lover and beloved and between the different needs and advantages of the two roles, a distinction particularly and naturally clear in homosexual relationships. The notion of the beloved turned lover was therefore of great psychological interest to an ancient reader.

Lines 27ff. also offer new information in another way in that they confirm something the reader might already have guessed. From the erotodidactic nature of the elegy, as proclaimed in 1f., and from lines 7f., it might have been surmised that the young man was having some problems in his love. But only here is this surmise ratified, and the cause revealed: the girl is rejecting him. This information throws new light on what precedes. It explains why the youth's finery (9–14) is useless – not merely because his role as a *puer delicatus* is at an end with the onset of maturity, but because it makes no impression on the girl. Moreover it clarifies Tibullus' position as *magister amoris*. The task of a teacher of love is not just to give general advice but to act as a practical counsellor in individual cases. The revelation of the young man's inability to win the girl thus explains why Tibullus has undertaken the role.

Acting primarily on behalf of the boy, Tibullus therefore addresses and counsels the girl in 27ff. Lines 29f. are teasingly vague. Tibullus speaks of a *canus amator* (29) but it is not clear whether or not this is a specific individual. The same ambivalence is continued in line 50 where the plural *senes* underlines it. The full picture, namely that a single person who is older than Marathus is keeping the girl – and with it implications about the girl's mercenary character – is sketched first by the hint in line 35 where we learn that the girl will have to conduct her affair with the youth in secret, and then fully in lines 55–60 where she is under surveillance. These facts further explain why Tibullus is acting as teacher of love. Love poets acting in this role counselled against greed and in favour of true non-mercenary love for poor persons. It was also part of their duty to teach a girl how to trick a lover.[8] It is because the girl has an old lover that Tibullus continually

---

[7] Cf. A. Spies, *Militat Omnis Amans: Ein Beitrag zur Bildersprache der antiken Erotik* (Diss. Tübingen 1930).
[8] Cf. e.g. Tib. 1.2.15ff. and 1.8.35ff., places where Venus joins in the instruction.

contrasts youth and age, first in lines 29–32 (boy and old man as lovers), then in lines 39–48, where the girl is told to enjoy her own youth before she becomes old, and finally in the injunction:

> neu Marathum torque: puero quae gloria victo est?
> in veteres esto dura, puella, senes. (49f.)

The contrast is strengthened by the continual stress on the boy's youth throughout the elegy, not only in the description of him as a *puer delicatus* (9–14) but in the application to him of the terms *puer* (27, 35, 49, 67), *iuvenis* (31) and *tener* (36, 51). Tibullus' general injunctions to the girl to treat old men harshly can be seen in retrospect, if not also in prospect, to refer in particular to her lover, who is to be maltreated and frustrated while the young man is indulged and treated well (see also above, Chapter 4, p. 105). The age of the girl's lover also changes our attitude to the boy. As a former *puer delicatus*, he might have seemed to deserve the girl's treatment of him, since beautiful boys behaved in the same way towards their own lovers. But once he is seen as the rival in love of a rich old man he becomes worthy of sympathy.

At line 49 the name of the *puer* is first revealed – as the girl's name will be first revealed at 69. The retention of proper names is a longstanding feature of ancient poetry (see below, p. 156). But here there is a special significance in the retention of the name Marathus. Tibullus organised his first book as a collection; and he intended his readers to remember the name Marathus from an earlier poem. In 1.4 Marathus was the beautiful boy who tormented Tibullus and forced him to seek the advice of Priapus. The final four lines of 1.4 sum up the position there:

> eheu quam Marathus lento me torquet amore!
> deficiunt artes, deficiuntque doli.
> parce, puer, quaeso, ne turpis fabula fiam,
> cum mea ridebunt vana magisteria. (81–4)

When the reader comes to 1.8.49 and learns, aided by its echo (*Marathum torque*) of 1.4.81 (*Marathus . . . torquet*), that the former *puer delicatus* of 1.8, who is now in love and who is himself being maltreated by a *dura puella*, is none other than the unfeeling Marathus of 1.4, this has two effects. First the reader's earlier unsympathetic reaction to the *puer*'s fate is reinvoked and the sympathy generated by the intervening portion of the elegy is dampened. But more important, the scenario is clarified. Tibullus the former lover of Marathus, now his teacher in love, is trying to persuade the girl to be complaisant to Marathus, and so is using his erotodidactic powers not upon Marathus on his own behalf, but upon the girl on Marathus' behalf. But Tibullus' real interest in the whole matter, that is, whether he is genuinely acting on behalf of Marathus or, paradoxically, for his own benefit, is not yet clear.[9]

The resolution of the two problems – what the reader's attitude to Marathus should be, and where Tibullus in fact stands in all this – comes in the latter part of the elegy, in the description and speech of Marathus (49–68), and in Tibullus' apostrophe to the girl (69–78). Up to 49, as has been indicated, the reader has see-sawed between a feeling that Marathus deserves his fate and pity for him in his plight. Now a pathetic picture is drawn of Marathus' erotic misery. He speaks to the girl *absenti* (53), and so he does not even have the good fortune *praesenti flere puellae* (Propertius 1.12.15). He is ready to observe all the discretion of *furtivus amor*, but the girl frustrates him (55–66). The pathos of this speech swings the balance finally in favour of Marathus. He has, as it were, redeemed his cruelty as a beloved through his sufferings as a lover.

At line 67 Tibullus declares that Marathus' pleas are ineffectual, a declaration intentionally parallel to his admission in 1.4.81 ff. that his own efforts to win Marathus were useless. Tibullus then turns to the girl and addresses her for the first time by name – Pholoe – a name conventionally attached to a harsh and uncomplaisant girl.[10] Its introduction here both stresses the cruelty of her behaviour and makes Tibullus' apostrophe of her more direct and personal, which is appropriate since it is his final appeal to her. He asks her to relent towards Marathus on the ground of Marathus' own experiences, and spells these out as follows:

> hic Marathus quondam miseros ludebat amantes
>   nescius ultorem post caput esse deum;
> saepe etiam lacrimas fertur risisse dolentis
>   et cupidum ficta detinuisse mora:
> nunc omnes odit fastus, nunc displicet illi
>   quaecumque opposita est ianua dura sera. (71–6)

The reader and Pholoe know that Tibullus himself is one of the lovers whom Marathus maltreated. But Tibullus rises above his own past disappointments over Marathus and sees Marathus' sufferings as an injustice for which Pholoe, if she really does refuse to relent, will be accountable. The final couplet spells out the warning explicitly:

> at te poena manet, ni desinis esse superba.
>   quam cupies votis hunc revocare diem! (77f.)

Unless she is kind to Marathus, Pholoe will one day find herself a lover

---

[9] For a case where the poet pretends to be acting on his addressee's behalf but has his own axe to grind cf. Hor. *Od.* 3.11 and F. Cairns, '*Splendide Mendax*: Horace *Odes* III.11', *Greece and Rome* 2nd ser. 22 (1975) 137.
[10] Cf. Nisbet–Hubbard on Hor. *Od.* 1.33.7.

unloved. The authority of the teacher of love is one guarantee that the prophecy will come to pass; another is the present experience of Marathus.

The scenario for 1.8 as a whole may still seem somewhat puzzling, even though by its final section Tibullus has supplied enough information for an ancient reader to grasp it in its entirety. This is because Tibullus has in mind an ancient moral ideal associated with homosexual relationships, the existence of which I have tried to establish elsewhere.[11] Ancient male homosexual relationships of the kind usually celebrated in literature were between a man and a boy. When the boy grew up the sexual relationship was over; and while the boy was still young the pleasure of the older partner was by far the greater. There arose therefore a view that it was the older person's – the lover's – duty to reciprocate the favours bestowed by the younger – the beloved – when the latter had grown up, by remaining his friend and helping him as needed. This view is expressed clearly in Plato, *Phaedrus* 232e3ff., 233e5ff., 240e8ff.; *Symposium* 181d3ff.; Xenophon, *Symposium* 8.14, 8.30ff.; and Theocritus, *Idyll* 29.31ff.; and I have argued that it lies behind Pindar's description of the love-affair between Poseidon and Pelops in *Olympian* 1.[12] This last example is particularly relevant to Tibullus 1.8. Pelops as a boy gratified his lover Poseidon. Poseidon duly reciprocated when Pelops became a man and lent him practical assistance towards winning his bride. In Tibullus 1.8 Tibullus is trying to do exactly the same thing, to help his former beloved Marathus win the girl with whom he has fallen in love. There is a difference however between the circumstances of Poseidon and Tibullus which is much to Tibullus' credit. Poseidon was gratified by Pelops; but Marathus spurned Tibullus. However Tibullus does not react as the neglected lover of *Idyll* 29 does:

> αἰ δὲ ταῦτα φέρην ἀνέμοισιν ἐπιτρέπῃς,
> ἐν θύμῳ δὲ λέγῃς, 'τί με, δαιμόνι', ἐννόχλης;'
> νῦν μὲν κἀπὶ τὰ χρύσια μᾶλ' ἕνεκεν σέθεν
> βαίην καὶ φύλακον νεκύων πεδὰ Κέρβερον,
> τότα δ' οὐδὲ κάλεντος ἐπ' αὐλείαις θύραις
> προμόλοιμί κε, παυσάμενος χαλέπω πόθω.   (35–40)
>
> *But if you let these words be carried off by the winds and say in your heart 'Fellow why are you bothering me', although now for your sake I would seek the golden apples and go down for Cerberus, guardian of the dead, then I would not come to the door of my house even if you called me, once my harsh desire had come to an end.*

He does not now refuse to help Marathus because Marathus treated him ungenerously, but shows his moral superiority to Marathus (and to the lover in *Idyll* 29), by acting like a generous and grateful lover in spite of

[11] Cf. F. Cairns, "Ἔρως in Pindar's First Olympian Ode', *Hermes* 105 (1977) 129ff.
[12] *Id.*

Marathus' failure to gratify him. This is of course appropriate, since Tibullus is a teacher of love in this elegy – a role implying superior status. It is not however without ironic undertones: the threats to Pholoe are an implied reminder to Marathus that his own former harsh treatment of Tibullus has been repaid in kind.[13]

The succeeding elegy, 1.9, is an equally complex homosexual poem. In it Tibullus is renouncing his love for Marathus;[14] and he relies for his moral superiority on different grounds, notably his own services to Marathus, Marathus' perfidy, and the sordidness of Marathus' alternative love-life. It is clear that there is common ground between 1.8 and 1.9: the reader does not come to 1.9 completely ignorant of Tibullus' love-life. For this reason Tibullus does not even have to name the *puer* of 1.9; once a *puer* is mentioned there, he must be Marathus. However this does not imply that Tibullus must be in exactly the same position in 1.9 as in 1.8. In Roman elegy sharp changes of situation can take place, even between adjacent elegies, as the first four elegies of Propertius' Monobiblos clearly illustrate. What does however remain constant between different love-elegies, whether homosexual or heterosexual, is the ensemble of characters and their general relationships. But differences in their detailed relationships can be expected; and other new characters may enter the scene. Therefore when Tibullus introduces his male beloved in 1.9.1 (*laesurus*) the reader identifies him as Marathus. But the relationship between Tibullus and the boy is changed. Tibullus begins by attacking him for perfidy (1f.). At line 11 he adds: *muneribus meus est captus puer*. This reveals that the perfidy involves sexual infidelity and that the boy has defected from Tibullus to a rich rival. From this point on nothing new is revealed up to lines 39f. In the first thirty-eight lines Tibullus simply elaborates on his condition as stated and the reader's interest is kept alive partly by the element of deception discussed in the next chapter.

At lines 39f. Tibullus reveals a new aspect of the scenario:

>   quid faciam, nisi et ipse fores in amore puellae?
>   sit precor exemplo sit levis illa tuo.

Here Tibullus is confirming that, in 1.9 as in 1.8, the *puer* is in love with a girl. The reader might at first be puzzled at finding Marathus both gratifying a rich rival of Tibullus and still in love with a girl. But of course these are not really inconsistent factors. Tibullus himself presumably still had some erotic interest in Marathus in 1.8, even though it was unreciprocated. In 1.9 then the *puer* is simultaneously the lover of a girl, the beloved of Tibullus, and possessed by a rich rival of Tibullus. He might well have needed money from his own rich lover to buy presents for his girlfriend.

In the scenario as revealed by 39f. Tibullus' own right to be indignant at

---

[13] Cf. *GC* p. 86.
[14] On the genre *renuntiatio amoris* and its relation to Tib. 1.9 cf. *GC* pp. 80ff.

Marathus is not weakened by the revelation that the boy is in love with a girl. If he had simply been in love with a girl and had abandoned Tibullus for her, then his action would have been in ancient terms both natural and free from guilt.[15] But he has been attracted away from Tibullus to another man by cupidity; and in Tibullus' mind the girl's role is primarily to punish Marathus by maltreating him, not to excuse his action. Tibullus rather exploits the information given in 39f. that Marathus is in love with a girl to introduce in 41ff. an account of his own past services to the boy. These are not like the lover's services of 1.4.39ff., where the homosexual relationship was uncomplicated. Rather they involve Tibullus acting as he did in 1.8, namely forwarding his beloved boy's love for the girl but doing so at the same time as being himself in love with the boy. The synchronous nature of Tibullus' services further enhances his moral stature as a homosexual lover and further points up the ingratitude of Marathus in deserting him for another male lover.

Tibullus then for the first time renounces his love for Marathus (47–52) and adds to his renunciation a long attack on his rival, who has corrupted the boy. Within this attack two new, or seemingly new, characters enter the elegy. The first is the rival's *uxor* (54); the second her *soror*[16] (59). As the *puella* of lines 39f. was introduced as a scourge upon Marathus, so the rival's *uxor* is supposed to be going to torment him with her infidelity and to equal her *soror* in drunkenness and sexual depravity. But two specific lines in this passage raise a further question:

> et cum furtivo iuvenem lassaverit usu   (55)
> non tibi sed iuveni cuidam vult bella videri   (71)

It could of course be argued that 55 simply refers to young men in general and that 71 refers to an unspecified young lover who plays no other part in the elegy. But the lines give rise to a suspicion that Tibullus is revealing yet another new aspect of the scenario: there is both economy and elegance in the hypothesis that the *iuvenem* and the *iuveni cuidam* is none other than the *puer* Marathus, and in its corollary, that the *puella* and the *uxor* are the same person. There is some support for this view in the parallel expression *quidam* at Tibullus 1.5.71: *non frustra quidam iam nunc in limine perstat*. The interpretation of this line is also in dispute. But there too the scenario is much more meaningful if *quidam* refers not to some new person as yet unmentioned in the elegy, but to Tibullus himself. That the *puer* and the *iuvenis*, the *puella* and the *uxor*, are the same persons is again supported by a further piece of new information which surfaces in lines 69–74. It is most clearly conveyed at line 74, where the rival is described as a *senex*, and where the *uxor* is specifically said to be a *culta puella*. With this final

---

[15] See above, Ch. 5 n. 60.
[16] As in Tib. 2.6.29 the mistress's *soror* is in question. Cf. also Ter. *And.* 117ff. A Hellenistic topos may be behind these passages.

revelation that the rival is an old man the reader is meant to conclude with certainty that he is indeed faced with almost the same set of characters as in 1.8. There, to put it schematically, Tibullus loves the *puer* Marathus who loves the *puella* Pholoe who is involved with an old *amator*. In 1.9 Tibullus loves the *puer* Marathus who is involved with the same old man (now therefore Tibullus' rival also) and who at the same time is in love with the *puella* who is the old man's *uxor*. Between 1.8 and 1.9 the situation has stabilised in that whereas the old man was the *puella*'s *amator*, now she is his *uxor*, that is, at least his concubine. Marathus then is in a similar situation to Trimalchio as a young slave-boy, except that there is no indication that he is a slave:

> tamen ad delicias ipsimi annos quattuordecim fui . . . ego tamen et ipsimae satis faciebam.   (Petronius, *Satyricon* 75.11)

The scenario of 1.9 is therefore even more complex and sophisticated than that of 1.8. The group portrayed are so depraved that Tibullus can safely rely on them to inflict on each other mutual punishment for their offences against himself. At the same time their depravity allows Tibullus most aptly to disassociate himself from them in his *renuntiatio*.[17]

Tibullus 2.3 will provide a final and particularly useful example of Tibullus' technique of information conveyance. Unlike 1.1 and 1.8, where some element of deception (see below, Chapter 7) is also involved, 2.3 does not deceive but simply retains information. The text of this elegy is somewhat corrupt and lacunose. The corruptions however do not affect the interpretation offered below; and as for lacunae, a working assumption has been made that they are present only at the two points where this is certain, namely after 14a and after 74. The extent of these lacunae is again unknown; but it has been assumed that nothing with a significant bearing on the train of thought has been lost.

As with 1.9 the reader does not come to 2.3 completely uninformed. The vocative *Cornute* in 2.3.1 reintroduces the addressee of 2.2, a good Roman citizen, happily married, probably the Arval colleague of Messalla.[18] The rest of the poem implicitly contrasts this respectable figure remaining in Rome with Tibullus going off to the countryside in an effort to be with his mistress; and the initial address to Cornutus allows the easy inference that Cornutus has been advising Tibullus to stay in Rome and not degrade himself by chasing after her.

The first six lines reveal the basic situation. Tibullus' *puella* has gone off into the country; Tibullus is justifying to Cornutus his decision to leave Rome also, in the hope of being with her. Lines 5ff. with their vivid details emphasise that Tibullus would endure even the hard labour of a realistic countryside in order to be with his mistress. This statement is reinforced

[17] For an elegist's disgust at an *examen stuprorum* cf. Prop. 2.32 esp. l. 41.
[18] See above, Ch. 5 n. 36 *ad fin*.

by the myth of Apollo and Admetus (11ff.) (see above, Chapter 5, pp. 120f.). Tibullus relates how Apollo, like Tibullus a cultured poet (12), went into the countryside and did rustic tasks because of his love for Admetus. The reactions of his worshippers and relatives are amusingly recorded (21ff.) and the contrast between Apollo's civilised shrines at Delos and Delphi and the squalor of his life in the countryside tellingly made (27f.). Presumably these places stand for Rome in Tibullus' own life and the reactions of Diana and Leto are being equated with those of Cornutus. The myth closes with Tibullus' reflection that it belongs to the Golden Age of the past: *felices olim* (29) is opposed to the iron age (*ferrea . . . saecula*, 35) of the present, to underline this point.

At lines 33f. Tibullus reveals for the first time that he has a rich rival. An implication of this confirmed at line 61 and possibly anticipated in a lost couplet here is that this rival has taken Tibullus' mistress off with him to the countryside. The wealth of the rival stimulates Tibullus to an elaborate attack on *praeda* (35–46) in which he combines the concepts of wealth and *praeda* in order to discredit him and to suggest that the *puella*'s motives for going off with the rival are unworthy.[19] However this attack on wealth is followed by a surprising change of mind:

> heu heu divitibus video gaudere puellas:
>   iam veniant praedae, si Venus optat opes   (49f.)

Tibullus says that since girls like rich men he will embrace wealth, so that he can give his girlfriend all she wants that money can buy – and do so in town (50f.). This is striking new information, not about the situation in Tibullus' imaginary universe, but about his own response to it; and in the midst of this volte-face, for the first time in this poem and in Book 2, the name of the girl who has produced this change in Tibullus is revealed (51). She is Nemesis, a different class of girl from Delia, who appears nowhere in Book 2. Nemesis is more mercenary and less admirable than Delia. Her presence in Book 2 allows Tibullus to express some attitudes which contradict those of Book 1 and are in opposition to the standard views of the lover in Roman elegy. She also allows Tibullus to contrast his own *persona* with hers. He is clearly morally superior to her, but his character is by no means unambivalent, and this permits Tibullus to portray complex moral dilemmas in an intriguing way.

More new information comes at lines 59f., where Tibullus explains the reason for his reversal of attitude to wealth: Nemesis' lover, his rich rival who has taken her off to the countryside, is a barbarian ex-slave of bad character. The rival's possession of her is therefore purely the result of his wealth, and Tibullus' higher social status is worthless. All this confirms Nemesis' low moral condition and provides a partial ironic justification for Tibullus' own espousal of a wealth ethic in 49ff. Moreover it allows

[19] Cf. e.g. Prop. 1.8 and *GC* pp. 151f.; Prop. 2.16 and *GC* pp. 206ff.

Tibullus to take an even more extreme view of the countryside (61ff.): if the country means for Tibullus loss of Nemesis to such a rival, then he spurns it and looks back, as he did before at lines 29ff., to the pre-agricultural Golden Age when men ate acorns but love was unmercenary. However at the end of the elegy Tibullus realises that it is pointless to attack the countryside and to wish for the great wealth of an urban magnate if all the time Nemesis is shut away from him out of town. So he decides that he will go to the country after all and live like a rustic, indeed like a rustic slave doing hard labour. Thus he voluntarily chooses for Love's sake a life which even for an urban slave would have been a punishment.[20] This change of mind and fresh return to the intent of lines 2 and 5ff. rounds off the elegy in an elegant manner.

The technique of gradually releasing new information which has been analysed in 2.3 allows Tibullus to achieve in the elegy a set of paradoxical reworkings both of facets of his own *persona* of Book 1 and of common-place elegiac material. The first paradox is that for Tibullus the countryside is an unsafe place for his mistress to be – contrast Propertius 2.19. The second involves his whole attitude to it. In Book 1, particularly in 1.1 and 1.10, he had a firm commitment to an idealised countryside which he saw as a place of happiness and love, in contrast to *militia*, the alternative way of life to which his attachment to Messalla constantly drew him. But in 2.3 – and this may be something to do with Cornutus not Messalla being its addressee – Rome is for Tibullus the ideal location, and the countryside is a harsh place of realistic labour (2.3.5ff., 79f.). Tibullus moves from acceptance of it in these terms in the initial part of the elegy to antipathy to it in 61ff. and a wish for the pre-agricultural Golden Age. He then moves back to a renewed acceptance at the end of the poem. But this acceptance is merely because Tibullus can be with Nemesis only at the price of enduring the countryside as it is.

A third paradox is that at 2.3.49ff. Tibullus desires the wealth which he has just been attacking and which is diametrically opposed to his normal moral values. These paradoxes express the strength of Tibullus' devotion to Nemesis; if the countryside opposes his love, then he is ready to attack it; if wealth helps him, he will espouse it. Love therefore has the power to override, at any rate for a time, other aspects of his *persona*. At the same time the paradoxes demonstrate the power of love to degrade the ideals which Tibullus claimed in Book 1. The result is that he incorporates in 2.3 a subtler complex of moral ideas than those of Book 1. The force of temptation is shown in his lapses from his earlier elegiac *persona*; the ideals of Book 1 have gone and the true status of the elegiac lover, degraded and humiliated by his emotions, is revealed without disguise.

In Chapter 7 the question of the origin and history of certain deception

---

[20] Cf. e.g. Plaut. *Most.* 15ff.; *Pers.* 21f.; Ter. *Phorm.* 249f.; Hor. *Sat.* 2.7.118; and cf. W. and G. G. Ramsay, *The Mostellaria of Plautus* (London 1869) pp. 256ff.

techniques used by Tibullus will be raised. Here a more general attempt will be made to discuss the literary background of Tibullus' technique of information retention as a whole. This background seems to consist of a number of analogous and related devices which show that sophisticated methods of withholding information are of long standing in ancient literature but were consciously exploited with great frequency by Hellenistic and Roman poets, particularly in non-narrative poetry. First, a widespread ancient literary practice, that of withholding for a time proper names, must be considered. This practice goes back to early Greek lyric.[21] A succession of clues is given to the identity of the person under discussion, but the actual name is only revealed after the clues. The alert and informed hearer could thus guess the name before it came and so could enjoy the double pleasure of guessing and of being proved correct. Proper names continue to be withheld in this way throughout ancient poetry; and Tibullus makes use of the device in a highly sophisticated form: examples have been noted above (pp. 148f.) where the retention has a powerful effect on the way the reader reacts to the poem.

Another relevant technique is one generally regarded as an archaic Greek literary device.[22] It consists in the postponement of important details in narrative. As was noted above (p. 144) narrative does not normally require an initial conveyance of all the aspects of the situation which will be relevant to the whole story. These can be conveyed as and when convenient. But the technique under discussion involves more than this: it is the deliberate displacement of certain important details. These are not related at the most convenient and natural point but are held back until they can be revealed with maximum effect. Examples are known in Pindar, Aeschylus and Herodotus.[23] It is clear that this technique is closely related to that found in Tibullan non-narrative poetry and may well stand in direct line of ancestry to it.

It may also be appropriate to stress one further piece of literary history and two theoretical literary considerations. In literary-historical terms the frequency of information retention in Tibullus may have something to do with the nature of the Theognidean corpus. It will be suggested in Chapter 9 that this work probably had some influence in the development of elegy. The corpus may not at all times in its history have appeared, as it does now, to be a collection of separate short pieces.[24] Some of the pieces may once have been longer; and the layout of the collection may have given the

---

[21] Cf. F. Dornseiff, *Pindars Stil* (Berlin 1921) pp. 107f.; Fraenkel on Aesch. *Ag.* 156f.; 681ff.; 687. See also R. Führer, *Formproblem–Untersuchungen zu den Reden in der frühgriechischen Lyrik* (Zetemata 44, Munich 1967) pp. 5; 6 for related techniques.

[22] Cf. E. Fraenkel, *Aeschylus: Agamemnon* (Oxford 1950) III Appendix A (p. 805): 'On the postponement of certain important details in archaic narrative', relating to *Ag.* 59 (cf. II *ad loc.* and on 190f.) and referring to Hdt. 1.110–12 and L. Illig, *Zur Form der pindarischen Erzählung* (Diss. Kiel 1932) p. 25 n. 3 (on Pind. *Nem.* 1.35ff.).

[23] *Id.* [24] See below, pp. 218f.

impression that some separate pieces were in fact linked. Now the layout, in terms of information conveyance, of a Tibullan elegy, tends to be that ten to twenty lines of meditation and expansion of previously given information are followed by new information and further meditation upon it. This layout is similar to what can be conjectured about the appearance of the Theognidean corpus in the fourth and third centuries BC.[25]

The two relevant theoretical considerations are the generic principle of 'reaction' and the length of Tibullan elegies. Reaction, discussed fully in *GC* chapter 6, naturally involves presenting the reader with new information either about the imaginary situation of the poem or about the poet's responses to it. For this reason some of its effects are identical to those of Tibullus' retentions of information. However these go far beyond the limits of generic 'reaction'. Information retention is more characteristic of Tibullus than of the other Roman elegists whereas all equally use 'reaction'; and in addition the belated new information which Tibullus presents is found at many points in the same poem, and not only at one point, as happens with reaction. In Tibullus the technique amounts to the full scale employment in non-narrative poetry of the normal pattern of information conveyance found in narrative.

As regards the length of Tibullus' elegies, it is obvious that to some extent his information-conveyance techniques must relate to this. Tibullan elegies are, on the whole, longer than those of Propertius and Ovid; and a longer non-narrative poem may for structural reasons need to include dramatic devices like withholding facts from the reader and then revealing them at an appropriate point. In this way the constant audience alertness which a narrative poem achieves by natural means can also be created in a non-narrative poem. That this is part of the reason for Tibullus' practice is confirmed by its occurrence also in Catullus 68, a very long elegy (see below, pp. 162ff.). But this aspect should not be overstressed. There are other ways of raising the level of tension within a long elegy besides importing new information into it. In any case, in Tibullus' work the structural function of the device is always ultimately subordinated to literary effects. In fact the constant interplay between expectation and fulfilment in Tibullus' conveyance of the information essential to the understanding of an elegy is the mainspring of his communication with his reader, whether the information is doled out throughout the elegy in small quantities, as in the examples in this chapter, or is actually false information, as in those in the following chapter.

These particular and general aspects of the background to Tibullus techniques of information conveyance need to be supplemented by an

---

[25] For an examination of coincidences of content between Theognis and Tibullus cf. A. Foulon, 'Une «source» peu connue de Tibulle dans le *Corpus Tibullianum*: Théognis', *Latomus* 36 (1977) 132ff.

examination of Hellenistic Greek practice. Since so little non-narrative poetry from this period survives, recourse must again be made to Theocritus' *Idylls*, which display a large number of information-retentions quite similar to those of Tibullus. Notably, in several instances, the genre is concealed for some time. *Idyll* 11.19ff., the song of Polyphemus (see pp. 134ff.). is not clearly identified as a komos until line 42 when Galatea is asked to leave the sea.[26] Similarly the song of Simichidas (*Idyll* 7.96–127) does not reveal itself as a komos until lines 122–4, where Simichidas speaks of the watching at the beloved's door.[27] Again the komastic nature of *Idyll* 6 does not become obvious until line 32.[28]

These parallels between Theocritus and Tibullus might be thought to have more to do with the behaviour of the genre komos than the practice of the two poets.[29] But in these same Theocritean komoi there are also in a number of instances non-generic retentions of information. For example, in *Idyll* 6 most of the poem simply amplifies the situation as outlined in the first two lines of Daphnis' song:

> Galatea is throwing apples at your sheep, Polyphemus, and calling you bad in love and a goat-herd. (6f.)

But at line 31ff. new information appears: Polyphemus' rejection of Galatea is, he claims, a deliberate device to win her love:

> Perhaps when she sees me do this often, she will send a messenger; but I will shut my door until she swears to spread her fair bed for me here in this island. (31–3)

This revelation alters the reader's view of the whole komastic setting and thus neatly reverses the roles of Polyphemus and Galatea.

Again in *Idyll* 7.96ff. non-generic information is retained and, when it is revealed, the revelation changes the reader's view of the situation. Aratus the lover and Simichidas his friend are outside the door of a beautiful boy, Philinus. The usual komastic attempts to win him fail; so Simichidas tries to abandon the komos (122f.).[30] But at this point a new character enters the song:

> ... and may Molon for one be choked in that wrestling school, my dear friend. (125)

The reader learns for the first time that Aratus has a rival, Molon. The reasons for Aratus' komos, and for its failure, suddenly become clear.

---

[26] Cf. *GC* pp. 144ff.   [27] Cf. *GC* pp. 201ff.   [28] Cf. *GC* pp. 194ff.
[29] Cf. also e.g. Hor. *Od.* 3.7 and *GC* p. 209; Prop. 2.17 and F. Cairns, 'Further adventures of a locked-out lover: Propertius 2.17' (University of Liverpool Inaugural Lecture Series, Liverpool 1975); and to a lesser extent Prop. 1.3 and 2.29: cf. F. Cairns, 'Two unidentified *komoi* of Propertius: I 3 and II 29', *Emerita* 45 (1977) 351ff.   [30] Cf. *GC* pp. 201ff.

In *Idyll* 11.19–79 two pieces of information are kept back. Lines 20–66 amplify the first line:

> White Galatea, why do you reject a lover? (19)

But at line 67 a new piece of information is introduced:

> My mother, and she alone, does me wrong, and I blame her for it: she has never said a good word to you on my behalf, although she sees me growing thinner daily. I shall tell her that my head and both my feet are sore, so she may be troubled, since I am troubled.
> (67–71)

This information, that the Cyclops' mother is to blame for his failure with Galatea, is not meant to convince the reader. It is a fantasy of Polyphemus; and it shows him to be an immature lover. The gibe addressed to the lover, Bucaeus, by the mocker of love Milon[31] at *Idyll* 10.57f., shows the significance of the mother in such contexts. But imagination or not, Polyphemus' attack on his mother has, as well as its structural function of anticipating the 'reaction' of lines 72ff.,[32] a semantic function: it gives the reader a new and less flattering view of the Cyclops' emotional condition and so diminishes the sympathy he receives as a lover. A few lines later another new piece of information crops up which again probably derives from Polyphemus' imagination:

> Many girls ask me to spend a night with them, and they all giggle when I pay attention to them. (77f.)

This information both explains the earlier 'reaction' of Polyphemus and once more alters the reader's attitude to the whole *Idyll* by giving its final section a touch of humorous pathos.

Moreover Theocritus' use of the techniques of information retention go beyond the komos. *Idyll* 16[33] is a good example. This poem conceals its real theme for many lines. There is a long build-up, the purpose of which is kept from the reader. In it Theocritus says (1–4) that the proper function of mortal poets is to sing of their fellow-mortals; he asks who will be his patron, and concludes that nowadays men prefer to keep their money; he reflects (22–31) on a good man's duties, which include generosity to poets and the consequent possession of fame after death; he then reminisces (34–57) about great men of the past who would have been unknown in his own day had not poetry conferred fame on them. Finally Theocritus

---

[31] Cf. F. Cairns, 'Theocritus Idyll 10', *Hermes* 98 (1970) 38ff.
[32] Cf. *GC* pp. 143ff.
[33] The view of *Id.* 16 offered here is contrary to orthodox interpretations, for which see Gow and Dover introd. to *Id.* 16. W. Meincke, *Untersuchungen zu den enkomiastischen Gedichten Theokrits* (Diss. Kiel 1965) pp. 73ff. insists correctly that *Id.* 16 is an encomium and not a 'Betellied'. Further on *Id.* 16 see F. Cairns, 'The distaff of Theugenis – Theocritus *Idyll* 28', *PLLS 1976* pp. 303f.

dismisses greedy men (58–65), announces that he is looking for a generous patron (66–72), one who will be as great in deeds as Achilles or Ajax (73–5).

It is only at this point that the import of everything which has gone before in this long introductory section is revealed, when a new character enters the poem:

> Even now the Phoenicians who live on the farthest edge of Libya beneath the setting sun are trembling; even now the Syracusans grasp their spears by the middle and load their arms with shields of wicker-work. Among them Hieron, the equal of the heroes of old, arms himself; and the horse-hair crest shades his helmet.
> (76–81)

For the first time Hieron II, tyrant of Syracuse, stands forth as Theocritus' desired patron, the man of great deeds whom Theocritus will celebrate and the paymaster who will fulfil the duty of a good man and patronise Theocritus. It is Hieron who will be remembered after death through Theocritus' poetry, like another Achilles or Ajax. The whole point of the introductory section and of the idyll itself is now manifest. The idyll continues with prayers for Hieron's victory and for the subsequent peace, prosperity and good fame of his realm (82–103); and right at the end another new piece of information clarifies the whole context of the poem's composition, by showing that Theocritus is not an impertinent poet singing about Hieron unbidden. He has in fact been authorised to do so by a commission from Hieron:

> ὦ 'Ετεόκλειοι Χάριτες θεαί, ὦ Μινύειον
> Ὀρχομενὸν φιλέοισαι ἀπεχθόμενόν ποτε Θήβαις,
> ἄκλητος μὲν ἔγωγε μένοιμί κεν, ἐς δὲ καλεύντων
> θαρσήσας Μοίσαισι σὺν ἁμετέραισιν ἴοιμ' ἄν.
> καλλείψω δ' οὐδ' ὔμμε· τί γὰρ Χαρίτων ἀγαπατόν
> ἀνθρώποις ἀπάνευθεν; ἀεὶ Χαρίτεσσιν ἅμ' εἴην.   (104–9)
>
> Graces, Eteokleian goddesses who love Minyan Orchomenos, foe once to Thebes, I would stay at home if I were not invited abroad. But I would happily go with my Muses to the houses of those who invite me. You too I shall never abandon. For what is pleasant for mankind without the Graces? May I always be in their company.

Idylls 1 and 2 provide further examples of Theocritean information retention. The song of Thyrsis in Idyll 1 (64–145) is a lament for the dead Daphnis. It consists mainly of an account of Daphnis' death. At the beginning of the account the reader is told only that Daphnis was wasting away (66) and died (72). Daphnis receives various visitors on his deathbed. As each god among the visitors comes and speaks to Daphnis, the reader learns more and more about the reasons for his plight. First Hermes comes and reveals that Daphnis is in love (77). Then Priapus discloses that the girl whom Daphnis loves is also frenzied with love for him:

> (Priapus came) and said 'Poor Daphnis, why are you wearing away? Your girl goes wandering afoot by every spring and grove ... searching' (82–5)

Finally Aphrodite comes and gloats that she has defeated Daphnis:

> 'Surely you boasted, Daphnis, that you would throw Love! But have you not yourself been thrown by cruel Love?' (97f.)

Only now is it known that Daphnis had previously been hostile to love.[34] Daphnis answers Aphrodite with equal animus; and then he bids farewell to the countryside and dedicates his pipe to Pan. This passage (115ff.) provides the final clarification of Daphnis' situation. It shows that Daphnis had been one of those anti-love heroes who, like Atalanta and Milanion, resorted to the countryside as a means of expressing their hatred of love. The address to the countryside and the dedication to Pan are thus a final defiance of Aphrodite.

In *Idyll* 2 Simaetha is carrying out a magic ritual in the hope of compelling her lover to return to her. As she does so she meditates on her love, her lover, the beginnings and causes of their love-affair, and so on. This meditation informs the reader of her situation by a process of continuous revelation. The basic initial information is given in lines 2–7:

> Crown the bowl with red wool, so that I can bind my lover with a spell, my lover who is cruel to me. It is eleven days since the wretch has come here; and he does not know if I am alive or dead; he feels nothing for me and has not knocked at my door. Love and Aphrodite must have carried his quickly changing heart off elsewhere. (3–7)

The lover's name, Delphis, is withheld until line 21; his nationality, Myndian, until 29. These items give verisimilitude to the lover but they are not essential information. Much more important is the revelation at line 40f.

> But I am consumed with the fires of love for that man who made me, poor wretch that I am, not a wife but a miserable girl no longer a virgin.

This couplet shows that Simaetha is not a prostitute but a free chaste girl whose chances of marriage have been ruined by her affair. This is confirmed by what is later revealed about the circumstances of her falling in love (66ff.): she met and fell in love with Delphis on her way to a festival, a

---

[34] I intend to treat Daphnis' condition in *Id.* 1 at greater length in a forthcoming article.

typical focus in ancient literature and life for such an event,[35] since it was one of the few occasions when such girls could leave home, meet young men and fall in love. Further details add greater pathos to her position. She tried to escape her love by typical magical means (90ff.).[36] Her maid acted, characteristically,[37] as go-between (94ff.). When the maid went to fetch Delphis for her mistress, he came to her and claimed that he had been in love with Simaetha before she fell in love with him, and would, if not summoned, have come to her on a *komos* anyhow (114–38).

The picture of Simaetha is now complete. She is neither a low woman nor a love-struck girl who has fixed her affections on someone indifferent to her. She was a free virgin; her path to destruction was made easy by circumstances and by a lover who was either insincere or fickle. Simaetha is therefore a woman deceived. Her plight calls for pity rather than censure; and even her dangerous magical practices are more justified than they might at first have seemed. Final new information comes at 145–9:

> But the mother of Philista our flute-player and of Melixo came to me today, when the horses were racing up, carrying rosy dawn from the ocean up the sky, and she told me among other things that Delphis is in love.

Simaetha does not know whether Delphis is in love with a boy or a girl but knows for certain he is in love with someone other than herself. The hint of line 7 is thus confirmed and the tale is now complete. It is the well-worn story of the lover ousted from the beloved's affections by a rival. The pathetic impact of the whole situation, once it is revealed fully, is an apt prelude to and partial palliative of the final piece of witchcraft in the *Idyll* – Simaetha's threat to poison Delphis (159–62).

From Theocritus these techniques found their way into Virgil's *Eclogues*[38] which may well have influenced Tibullus in his turn. But even more valuable as a testimony to Hellenistic influence on Tibullus in his own field of elegy is Catullus 68, the first long Latin elegiac poem. It is a controversial piece: some scholars divide it into two; the name or names of the addressee(s) are disputed; and many details have also caused disagreement. For present purposes it will be assumed that it is a single poem addressed to Allius.

Catullus 68 employs complex thematic ring-composition and many other devices of sophisticated Hellenistic poetry.[39] Among them are some prominent information-retentions which can be discussed briefly and

---

[35] See above, Ch. 3, p. 67 and n. 10.
[36] For magic and love see the works cited above, Ch. 5 p. 139 and n. 56.
[37] Cf. e.g. Ov. *Am.* 1.11; 12; 2.19 (20) 41; 3.1.55f.; *AA* 1.383f.; 3.470; Alciphr. *Ep.* 3.26.3 (= 3.62.3); 4.8.1 (= 1.35.1); 4.10.2 (= 1.37.2).
[38] Virgil's use of these techniques will be discussed by I. M. Le M. Du Quesnay, 'Vergil's First *Eclogue*' (forthcoming).
[39] Cf. esp. Kroll and Fordyce, introd. and commentaries.

dogmatically because they have been partly elucidated by other scholars concerned primarily with the unity of the elegy and the significance of its myth.[40] Lines 1–10 virtually announce that Catullus will be using such techniques. 1–4 read

> quod mihi fortuna casuque oppressus acerbo
>   conscriptum hoc lacrimis mittis epistolium,
> naufragum ut eiectum spumantibus aequoris undis
>   sublevem et a mortis limine restituam

If these lines alone had survived and the question were asked what misfortune Catullus' addressee had suffered, the unhesitating answer would be that he had lost a loved one through death. This is implied by *fortuna* and *casuque . . . acerbo* (1) and by *a mortis limine* (4). But the next few lines dispel this illusion. Allius is said to be kept awake in an empty bed by Venus (5f.); he gains no satisfaction from old poetry (7f.) and he asks Catullus for new love-poetry (10).[41] Through this anticlimax the reader realises that Allius has not lost a beloved to death but has been abandoned by a living mistress. The anticlimax increases the impact of lines 17ff. when Catullus reveals his excuse for inability to help Allius, namely that he has indeed suffered a loss through death – that of his brother. The reader is thus confronted with the two kinds of loss and is meant to judge which of the pair – Catullus or Allius – is really in need of consolation. This initial deception eases the blending and contrast in Catullus 68 of the concepts of love and death, familial, friendly and sexual affection. It also gives Catullus enough moral status to allow him to counsel Allius indirectly as well as to console, eulogise and thank him.

This particular way of presenting a scenario verges on the type of deception treated in Chapter 7; and the whole poem is in a sense a gigantic deception of the reader. Catullus responds to Allius' request (17ff.) by saying that although he once could write love-poetry he cannot now do so: first, because the death of his brother has withdrawn him from such activities (19–26); and second, because he is writing from Verona, not Rome, and so has only a few books with him (33–6). But at line 41 Catullus launches asyndetically into what he has in fact written for Allius. The lay-out of the poem up to this point is a macrologic version of a standard

---

[40] The secondary literature on this poem is very extensive. Recent major treatments of it include B. Coppel, *Das Alliusgedicht* (Bibliothek der klassischen Altertumswissenschaften N.F. 2, 48, Heidelberg 1973) and T. P. Wiseman, *Cinna the Poet and Other Roman Essays* (Leicester 1974) pp. 70–103. In the discussion of it which follows I have drawn freely on the valuable contributions of: H. W. Prescott, 'The unity of Catullus LXVIII', *TAPA* 71 (1940) 473ff.; G. Williams, *Tradition and Originality in Roman Poetry* (Oxford 1968) pp. 229ff.; 464ff.; 478f.; and C. W. Macleod, 'A use of myth in ancient poetry', *CQ* N.S. 24 (1974) 84ff.

[41] Cf. G. Jachmann, *Gnomon* 1 (1925) 211; Lenchantin de Gubernatis *ad loc.*; Macleod, *CQ* N.S. 24 (1974) p. 84 n. 5.

flexible formula: the writer begins with a programmatic prooemium, which may be addressed to the patron; he then launches into an asyndetic apostrophe to or statement about the Muses, or an equivalent, which begins the poem proper. Virgil, *Eclogue* 6, where a patron is also addressed within a brief recusatio in the initial part (7–11), immediately followed by asyndetic address to the Muses and the beginning of the poem proper in 12, may be compared.[42] So may the *Aeneid*, with its programmatic prooemium (1.1–7) and invocation of the Muses in asyndeton (8ff.), as may the *Culex* with its initial address to patron (1–10) and asyndetic description *cum* invocation of Phoebus, Naiads and Pales (11ff.). It becomes apparent at 67ff. that Catullus' refusal in lines 1–40 to write love-poetry for Allius is a hoax of a standard type. The elegy is a eucharistikon – a *gratiarum actio* which begins with an included recusatio: and as with other recusationes[43] the refusal is a means whereby what is refused is indirectly granted. The erotic material which now begins to appear – about Catullus' own mistress, his feelings for her, their terms of love, the love of Laodamia and Protesilaus – makes this quite clear. Of course, this material is introduced under the guise of amplifying his first excuse, his brother's death. Catullus 68.1ff. is an unusual recusatio in one way. Normally recusationes refuse to praise a great man, offering as their excuse inability to perform the task adequately because their authors are lovepoets or something similar. Then the excuse is elaborated into an implicit version of the praise ostensibly refused. Horace, *Odes* 1.6 is a good example, where Horace interweaves praise of Agrippa with discussion of his status as lyric poet, which, he claims, makes him unfit to write the epic which Agrippa's deeds demand. Catullus has done the exact opposite in 68. He refuses to write love-poetry for Allius on the ground of his bereavement and lack of books and instead professes to thank Allius. Nothing more is heard of the lack of books; and the learned mythological material of the poem implies recourse to Hellenistic texts. But the thanks to Allius in fact introduce the very love-poetry which Catullus professes to be unable to write, the story of Protesilaus and Laodamia and of Catullus' own love-affair. As a recusatio then Catullus 68.1ff. is an interesting variation upon the normal type.

As well as these deceptive aspects, Catullus 68 has informationretentions of a non-deceptive kind. In line 12 Catullus had spoken of his obligation to Allius as *hospitis officium*. The particular application of the word *hospes* is only revealed at lines 68f.:

> isque domum nobis isque dedit dominae
> ad quam communes exerceremus amores

Allius had provided Catullus and his mistress with a house of assignation.

[42] Noted as a parallel by Kroll on Cat. 68.41.
[43] Cf. e.g. Prop. 3.9; Hor. *Od.* 1.6; 4.2.

In this way he was Catullus' *hospes*; and the revelation, from a structural point of view, allows Catullus, by describing his indebtedness to Allius, to fulfil in yet another way Allius' request for *munera Veneris et Musarum*.

From the account of Allius' help to him, Catullus moves into the myth of Protesilaus and Laodamia (73ff.). It is only at lines 91f. that the full relevance of this myth appears: like Protesilaus, Catullus' brother also died at Troy. This further explains the choice of the Protesilaus/Laodamia myth as an illustration of the emotions associated with Catullus' own love-affair. Her relationship with Protesilaus involved Laodamia in love and mourning, which are Catullus' sentiments too. From Allius' point of view there is also a consolatory element in this mythical *paradeigma*, as is confirmed by the similar purpose of lines 135ff. (see below, pp. 224f.). The love of Laodamia and Protesilaus was ended by death, which divided them finally. Allius is therefore being offered the consolatory reflection that his love-affair has not necessarily ended permanently, since a quarrel and not death has intervened.

After the myth of Laodamia Catullus moves back to his own mistress (131f.). Here another piece of retained information is revealed:

> quae tamen etsi uno non est contenta Catullo
> rara verecundae furta feremus erae (135f.)

Catullus states that his mistress is not always faithful to him, and that he tolerates this. This information brings into sharp focus for the first time the dominant theme of the elegy, which is the different kinds of human relationship which in Greek could fall under the heading of $\varphi\iota\lambda\acute{o}\tau\eta\varsigma$ – family relationships, friendship, love. Between Catullus and his brother there was noble and unbroken fraternal affection. Between Catullus and his mistress, as between Allius and his former beloved, there is sexual love. Between Catullus and Allius there is friendship. Laodamia's love for Protesilaus conjoined sexual and familial affection. Catullus' revelation of the nature of his own sexual love combines consolation for Allius with implied advice to him: Catullus is suggesting that Allius should be more tolerant and allow his mistress a freer rein; in this way his breach with her will be healed. That Catullus is thinking in these terms is confirmed by line 155 where Allius and his mistress are imagined together and are wished well.

Catullus 68 therefore contains information-retentions of the type found in Tibullus and in Theocritus. They have the same semantic and structural functions and their frequency is relatively high. It is clear therefore that, although the process of influence and development cannot be traced because texts have been lost, the devices found in Tibullus are yet another Hellenistic aspect of his work.

7
DECEIVING

It is well known that lines 1–4 of Tibullus 1.2 pose a problem about the setting of the elegy: Tibullus seems to be at a symposium, but a little later he turns out to be on his mistress's doorstep. A similar difficulty is caused by Tibullus 1.3.1–4: these lines contain many signals which suggest falsely that the whole elegy will be a propemptikon. I have dealt with such initial misdirections of the reader elsewhere in a specifically generic context.[1] Here they will be examined as a preliminary to a study of Tibullus' more widespread habit of 'deceiving' his reader. The information Tibullus gives is frequently not what it appears to be: he induces his reader to arrive now at false, now at correct conclusions, and then he reverses the wrong impressions and reinforces the true ones. The result is highly enlivening in that the reader must remain constantly alert and the poet can achieve striking effects of control over his audience's emotions, particularly when he deceives them into one emotional response only to undeceive them into a doubly powerful opposite response.

Tibullus 1.2 opens (1–4) with the poet calling for more wine so that he can fall asleep and thus escape the pain of love. The implication of these lines seems unmistakable: the poet must be at a symposium. But three lines later (7) Tibullus is apostrophising his mistress's door, having stated in the intervening couplet (5f.) that it is closed to him. Such an apostrophe implies Tibullus' physical presence. The reader is thus forced to revise his notion of the elegy's setting. Tibullus is not, after all, at a symposium. He had doubtless been to one beforehand, since the lover's komos normally began at a symposium. But he is now actually standing at his mistress's door. He is accompanied, probably by a slave, as is common in komoi,[2] and he asks his slave to give him more wine. The drinking of wine at a mistress's door, odd though it may appear to a modern reader, must have been familiar enough as a komos topos to Tibullus' contemporaries to allow them to move from their first conception of the setting as a symposium to the door setting. Amusing evidence[3] of this is found in Chari-

---

[1] Cf. *GC* pp. 202f. and n. 45; F. Cairns 'Further adventures of a locked-out lover: Propertius 2.17' (University of Liverpool Inaugural Lecture Series, Liverpool 1975) pp. 9ff.; and, with particular reference to Tib. 1 3, *GC* p. 165.

[2] Cf. e.g. Xen. *Symp.* 2.1; *p. Teb.* 2(d); Plaut. *Curc.* 1ff.; Prop. 1.3.10 (cf. F. Cairns, 'Two unidentified *komoi* of Propertius: I 3 and II 29', *Emerita* 45 (1977) 331); for flute-girls, also slaves, accompanying komasts see Headlam–Knox on Herodas 2.34–7.

[3] The scene at Plaut. *Curc.* 88ff. is presumably also related to this concept.

ton's *Chaireas and Callirrhoe* (1.3.2) where various unpleasant failed suitors who wish to tarnish the reputation of a respectable married woman, Callirrhoe, by pretending that they have been on a komos to her in her husband's absence do various things specifically designated by Chariton as 'signs of a komos' to simulate such an event. One is pouring wine on the street outside her house.

In 1.2 therefore the poet's seemingly symposiastic commands to his slave modulate into a komos-scene. In 1.3.1 the first word (*ibitis*) appears to herald a propemptikon. Three other propemptic commonplaces in lines 1–4, *Aegeas . . . per undas* (1), the *memor sis* topos of 2 and the 'excusatory' second couplet (3f.) seem to confirm that this is the genre of the elegy. Moreover lines 5–8 appear to expand the excusatory material of lines 3f.; and in lines 9–14 Tibullus seems to be recalling, in a passage resembling the similar account of Cynthia's pleas, tears etc. in the propemptic Propertius 1.6.5ff.,[4] schetliasmos on Delia's part when he left Rome. But in Tibullus 1.3 propemptic themes lapse after line 14 and the elegy is as a whole an inverse epibaterion, a common variant of another travel genre, the arrival poem. In the inverse epibaterion the speaker laments his separation from home and family[5] and lines 5–20 can be seen in retrospect as a bridge passage between propemptikon and epibaterion, equally at home, as such passages are,[6] in both genres, where danger encountered far from home and absence from loved ones play a part.[7]

A fairly elaborate generic hoax is carried out in 1.9, which begins with a strong attack on the oath-breaking of a beloved boy, who once swore fidelity to Tibullus and has now perjured himself. Two *paradeigmata* lead to new information: *muneribus meus est captus puer* (1.9.11). The reader deduces, correctly, that a rival has lured the boy away from Tibullus. Now one of the *paradeigmata* concerned travel:

> lucra petituras freta per parentia ventis
> ducunt instabiles sidera certa rates   (1.9.9f.)

and the punishments which Tibullus subsequently prophesies for the boy's perjury also seem to imply travel:

> iam mihi persolvet poenas, pulvisque decorem
> detrahet et ventis horrida facta coma;
> uretur facies, urentur sole capilli,
> deteret invalidos et via longa pedes.   (1.9.13–16)

The first section of the elegy thus has some characteristics of a propemptic schetliasmos. The beloved going off with a rival for gain is paralleled in the

---

[4] Cf. *GC* pp. 3ff.   [5] Cf. *GC* pp. 60ff.
[6] Cf. *GC* p. 161; I. M. Le M. Du Quesnay, 'Vergil's First *Eclogue*' (forthcoming) §3.
[7] Cf. *GC* index *s.v.* propemptikon esp. propemptikon: fear of dangers etc. and pp. 60ff.

genre[8] and the attack on the beloved's oath-breaking is a propemptic topos.[9] But this conclusion is not reinforced in the succeeding lines; and finally at 51 in: *tu procul hinc absis* etc. (1.9.51) the elegy identifies itself as a renuntiatio amoris.[10] This allows the topoi of lines 17–50 to be identified as belonging in fact to the renuntiatio amoris; and likewise lines 1–16 are seen as portraying another commonplace of that genre, the beloved's infidelity, and sometimes perjury, which cause the lover to reject him.[11]

An even more interesting example of generic deception occurs in Tibullus 1.5, which is usually said simply to be a komos.[12] It is true that its overall genre is komos, but it should be added that its beginning suggests that it will be a palinode. This genre is first found in Stesichorus, whose work is still controversial, since it is not clear whether he wrote one or two palinodes attacking Homer and perhaps Hesiod.[13] But the controversy does not affect our view of Tibullus 1.5. Post-Stesichorean palinodes were based as much on the pseudo-biographical accounts of his life as on his poetry. Such accounts survive in Plato and Isocrates, the Platonic version, which is fuller, being as follows:

> Ἔστι δὲ τοῖς ἁμαρτάνουσι περὶ μυθολογίαν καθαρμὸς ἀρχαῖος, ὃν Ὅμηρος μὲν οὐκ ᾔσθετο, Στησίχορος δέ· τῶν γὰρ ὀμμάτων στερηθεὶς διὰ τὴν Ἑλένης κακηγορίαν, οὐκ ἠγνόησεν ὥσπερ Ὅμηρος, ἀλλ' ἅτε μουσικὸς ὢν ἔγνω τὴν αἰτίαν καὶ ποιεῖ εὐθὺς·
> Οὐκ ἔστ' ἔτυμος λόγος οὗτος·
> οὐδ' ἔβας ἐν νηυσὶν εὐσέλμοις
> οὐδ' ἵκεο πέργαμα Τροίας.
> Καὶ ποιήσας δὴ πᾶσαν τὴν καλουμένην Παλινῳδίαν, παραχρῆμα ἀνέβλεψεν.   Plato, *Phaedrus* 243a–b
> *There is an old means of purification for those who commit an offence concerned with mythology, which Homer was not aware of but Stesichorus was. He was blinded because he spoke evil of Helen and he was not unaware of the reason, as Homer was, but being a man of culture he recognised it and immediately wrote 'this story is untrue. You did not go in the well benched ships; nor did you come to the citadel of Troy' and when he had written the entire poem called the Palinode he immediately recovered his sight.*

The story also lies behind the three lyric palinodes (*recantationes*) of Horace,

---

[8] Cf. Prop. 1.8; Hor. *Od.* 3.27.
[9] *GC* index *s.v.* propemptikon: breach of faith topos.   [10] Cf. *GC* pp. 80ff.
[11] Cf. *GC* p. 80 – element B3 (ii). It might appear that Tibullus is relating the non-rhetorical renuntiatio amoris to the rhetorical propemptikon – in each separation is envisaged – as he seems to be relating palinode and komos in 1.5 (see below, n. 21) and propemptikon and komos in 2.6 (see below, pp. 181ff.).
[12] Cf. Copley pp. 107ff.
[13] Cf. *Euripides Helena* ed. R. Kannicht (Heidelberg 1969) I pp. 26ff.; G. Devereux, 'Stesichoros' palinodes: Two further testimonia and some comments', *RhM* N.F. 116 (1973) 206ff.

Epode 17, *Odes* 1.16 and *Odes* 1.34, which are the only non-Stesichorean examples of the genre hitherto identified by scholars. On the basis of what remains of Stesichorus – including the pseudo-biographical material – and of these known Horatian examples, I have elsewhere[14] reconstructed a preliminary outline of the generic 'formula':

Primary Elements
- A^1 The speaker/retractor
- A^2 The addressee (about whom the speaker has expressed views)
- A^3 The former views
- A^4 The retraction of the former views

Secondary Elements (topoi)
- B^1 The views formerly held were impious
- B^2 They were expressed in poetry
- B^3 They attacked:
    - (i) a woman
    - (ii) the divine
- B^4 Madness
- B^5 Punishment
- B^6 Explicit acknowledgement of the opposite to the former views
- B^7 A relevant powerful force:
    - (i) the addressee
    - (ii) another entity
- B^8 The 'surrender' of the speaker
- B^9 Anger:
    - (i) of addressee
    - (ii) of speaker

Although Tibullus 1.5 ultimately proves to be a komos, the poet initially gives clear signals that it is a palinode, the primary elements all appearing in the first couplet. In line 1 Tibullus the speaker (A^1) states his former views (A^3). They concern separation from his beloved (A^2) and in line 2 he recants them (A^4). At line 9 it becomes clear that Tibullus' beloved is a woman (B^3(i)). Lines 5f. imply that madness was the cause of Tibullus' former views (B^4): *ure ferum et torque, libeat ne dicere quicquam | magnificum post haec: horrida verba doma*. This is because Tibullus described himself as *ferus* and prescribes for himself a treatment which is a specific treatment for madness. Cf.

>   fortiter et ferrum saevos patiemur et ignis
>   sit modo libertas quae velit ira loqui   (Propertius 1.1.27f.)[15]

Tibullus is alluding, like Propertius, to contemporary medical practice.

---

[14] Cf. F. Cairns, 'The genre palinode and three Horatian examples: *Epode*, 17; *Odes*, I, 16; *Odes*, I, 34', *Ant. Class.* 47 (1978) 546ff.

[15] Cf. F. Cairns, 'Some observations on Propertius 1.1', *CQ* N.S. 24 (1974) 102ff.

The Tiberian writer Celsus emphasises the importance of preventing the madman from saying anything amiss. Cf.

> Si vero consilium insanientem fallit, tormentis quibusdam optime curatur. Ubi perperam aliquid dixit aut fecit, fame, vinculis, plagis coercendus est. (Celsus 3.18.21)

This treatment is of course also part of Tibullus' punishment (B^5) and the employment of fire for this purpose is reminiscent of the burning of Horace's iambs at *Odes* 1.16.3. Another aspect of Tibullus' punishment is his harsh handling by Love in lines 3f. The *turben* of 3 recalls the *turbinem* with which Canidia punished Horace at *Epode* 17.7. Tibullus then surrenders and pleads (7f.) for forgiveness (B^8). At several places near the beginning of the elegy, in *asper* (1), *ferum* (5), and *horrida* (6), Tibullus is implying that anger (B^9) closely related to and sometimes synonymous with madness (B^4), was the cause of his offence.

The anger topos introduces a long account of the reason for it. Tibullus had performed many services for Delia when she was sick (9–17), but on recovery Delia gave her favours to another man (17f.). It was this 'betrayal', coming as it did after Tibullus' hopes of a happy life with Delia had flowered (19–34), which caused Tibullus to become *asper* and to declare in his chagrin that he could do without Delia (1). Since this declaration, which constituted his offence, was caused by *ira/furor*, the whole account of Tibullus' services, hopes and disillusion also functions as an excuse for his offence (cf. Horace, *Odes* 1.16). The adjective *demens* in line 20 is an unmistakable glance at the 'madness' topos (B^4) already evoked more obliquely at the beginning of the poem. As such it confirms that the whole account of Tibullus' self-deceptive optimism is intended to have an excusatory effect.

It is no objection to this analysis of the first section of Tibullus 1.5 that the generic commonplaces appear in sophisticated forms. Examination of the Horatian palinodes reveals in them equally oblique and varied use of the same topoi.[16] However the whole of Tibullus 1.5 is not palinodic since after line 20 unmistakably palinodic elements cease to appear. But only at lines 67f. does Tibullus explicitly reveal that he is speaking at his mistress's door and that the elegy is a komos. Such delayed generic identifications are of course particularly frequent in the komos, partly because that genre is so common.[17] Once Tibullus 1.5 is identified as a komos two major komastic themes which occur before 67f. can be recognised. These are the *rivalis*,[18] introduced at lines 17f. and reintroduced at lines 47f. and the attack on the *lena*[19] in 48ff. Tibullus' bucolic fantasy of his future happy life with Delia (19ff.) may be another komos topos. It is reminiscent of Theocritus, *Idyll*

---

[16] Cf. Cairns, *Ant. Class.* 47 (1978) 547ff. [17] See above, n. 1.
[18] Cf. *GC* pp. 203 and n. 51; 225 and n. 18.
[19] Who here replaces the standard komastic *custos*: cf. Copley p. 111.

11.65f., 42ff. and parts of Polyphemus' speech, which is also komastic,[20] and also of Virgil's imitation of the same Theocritean passage in his komastic second *Eclogue* (28ff.). If Tibullus' original readers remembered either of these passages, then 19ff. may have given them the first hint that 1.5 is a komos including a palinode.[21]

Examination of a fifth Tibullan example of initial deception will not only add to the number of cases on record but will allow the elegy in question to be described more accurately. The poem is 1.7, and in *Generic Composition* I wrote (p. 167) 'Tibullus 1.7 is a genethliakon which includes a triumph-poem.' These two genres are indeed involved in the elegy, but in fact the overall including genre is the 'triumph-poem' = dithyramb, and the genethliakon is the included genre. This new formulation is not an empty technicality but affects the interpretation of the elegy. The signals of the first couplet led me to think that the genethliakon was the overall genre[22] but I was in fact deceived, like the original audience, by the deliberate contrivance of the poet, who here, as in 1.3 and 1.5, begins with a misleading generic announcement. There is a certain similarity in lay-out between 1.3 and 1.7. In 1.3 the brief deceptive propemptikon of Tibullus to Messalla introduces Tibullus' inverse epibaterion; and at the end of it another passage, probably also epibateric, but concerned now with Tibullus' return to Rome, rounds off the elegy. In 1.7 a deceptive couplet, which looks at first as though it will introduce a birthday poem, in fact introduces the triumph-poem/dithyramb; and at the end a birthday scene closes the poem with an included genethliakon.

This version of what is happening in Tibullus 1.7 has at least two advantages. First it removes a problem caused by my former view. The genethliakon certainly became a major epideictic genre,[23] but it treats a private occasion, albeit often the birthday of a public man. On the other hand the triumph is the most significant event in the politico-military life of the Roman State. If there is a status difference between including and included genre, it is the less important which seems normally to be included. It would be odd then to find the less important genethliakon including the more significant triumph-poem. Now the roles of the genres have been reversed, this problem vanishes; and indeed this consideration

---

[20] Cf. *GC* pp. 144ff.
[21] On the concept of inclusion cf. *GC* Ch. 7. See also above, n. 11. The contiguity of subject-matter often found in including and included genres may here consist in the division of the two parties in both palinode and komos and the eagerness of one to overcome this.
[22] The *dies* of l. 1 is Messalla's birthday rather than the day of his triumph (see *GC* p. 167), if a distinction is to be made, i.e. if M. did not hold his triumph on his birthday. Against the latter view is the past tense of *vidit* (6) and *portabat* (8). But for parallels for this practice and argument about Tib. 1.7 see Weinstock pp. 207ff. Other possibilities are that M. conquered the Aquitani on his birthday or that the victory is linked with M.'s birthday because it brought the victor into the world.
[23] Cf. Ps.-Dionysius of Halicarnassus (ed. Usener–Radermacher) VI, 2, pp. 266ff.; Menander Rhetor (ed. Spengel) III pp. 412f.

of generic status may help to explain how Tibullus' original readers understood the relations of the two genres. They would have been deceived only momentarily at the beginning of the elegy, and when the birthday themes appeared in the latter part of the elegy, the genethliakon would have been recognised without hesitation as the included genre.

The second advantage of the new view of Tibullus 1.7 is that it clarifies beyond doubt the role of the Osiris hymn. One of the more embarrassing features of 1.7 on my former view was that the 'included' triumph-poem/dithyramb seemed to occupy much more of the poem than the 'including' genethliakon, since the long hymn to Nile–Osiris–Bacchus (23–48) is clearly part of the triumph-poem/dithyramb (see *Generic Composition* p. 168). It was partly to diminish this difficulty that I stressed, and indeed overstressed, the link-function of the hymn between triumph poem and genethliakon. However now that the length of the triumph-poem/dithyramb is no longer a problem, the role of the hymn to Nile–Osiris–Bacchus in 1.7 can be seen more clearly. The equation of the triumph-poem with the dithyramb was Roman[24] and the first surviving poem embodying it is Horace, *Odes* 1.37, a dithyramb associated with the *triplex triumphus* of Octavian in 29 BC.[25] Tibullus combines in 1.7 Roman triumph material with an invocation to Nile–Osiris–Bacchus which is dithyramb of the Greek type. He is thus incorporating the literary history of a genre grafted from one culture onto the other, as Virgil does in *Eclogue* 4.[26] There Virgil makes it clear that he is using the Greek genre basilikon to deal with a purely Roman event, the inauguration of a consul. He does so partly by setting purely Greek basilikon material side by side with purely Roman description of matters relevant to the inauguration of a consul.

Another example of generic deception, Tibullus 2.6, will be discussed at the end of this chapter. Here a related device may be considered. Tibullus sometimes begins an elegy with material which belongs to a rhetorical progymnasma[27] but then modulates into another genre. It is not useful to speak of progymnasmata being included since, although they can be genres in themselves, it is also one of their functions to be assimilated as topoi into higher genres.[28] But when a poem starts with a progymnasma, this raises the reader's expectation that it may continue to exemplify

---

[24] Cf. *GC* pp. 95ff.
[25] Cf. A. Hardie, 'Horace *Odes* 1.37 and Pindar *Dithyramb* 2', *PLLS 1976* pp. 113ff.
[26] Cf. I. M. Le M. Du Quesnay, 'Vergil's Fourth *Eclogue*', *PLLS 1976* pp. 43ff.
[27] On rhetorical progymnasmata cf. G. Reichel, *Quaestiones Progymnasmaticae* (Diss. Leipzig 1909); on their influence on ancient poetry cf. *GC* index *s.v.* progymnasmata; J. T. Underwood Jr, *Locus Communis, Laus Legum and Laus Locorum: Rhetorical Exercises as a Model for Propertius, Book III* (Diss. The Ohio State University 1971); F. Cairns, 'Horace, *Epode* 2, Tibullus I, 1 and rhetorical praise of the countryside', *Mus. Phil. Lond.* 1 (1975) 79ff. and 'Propertius on Augustus' marriage law (II, 7)', *Grazer Beiträge* (forthcoming)); J. C. McKeown, 'Ovid *Amores* 3 12', *PLLS 1979* pp. 163ff.
[28] Cf. *GC* pp. 88ff.; 158f.

that progymnasma throughout. If it then alters course, then something similar to, although not so violent as full-blown generic deception is occurring.

Two brief examples will suffice. Tibullus 1.10 begins with the progymnasma *psogos polemou* (attack on war). Lines 1–10 censure the inventor of swords, blame greed as the cause of war and describe the idyllic world before wars. But at lines 11–13 the elegy is revealed as a syntaktikon and the psogos polemou as a topos of that genre. Similarly Tibullus 1.1.1–6 are a psogos ploutou (attack on wealth). But at line 7 Tibullus begins to describe his farming activities. Eventually Tibullus' successful and wealthy soldier-patron Messalla appears (53ff.) as an antithesis to the 'poor' farmer Tibullus. Although the themes of wealth and poverty continue throughout the elegy, its main emphasis is on the ways of life which generate them, and it is a *synkrisis biōn*, a *comparatio vitarum*, in which warfare and agriculture are compared and Tibullus opts for agriculture.[29] The modulation from a minor progymnasma to a more complex one in 1.1 might have seemed even less striking to Tibullus' original readers than a modulation from a progymnasma to a full-blown epideictic genre, as in 1.10; and indeed warfare was mentioned in 1.1 as early as lines 3f. But there is still some surprise-value in the way the poem develops.

As was noted, initial misleading generic signals are only one way in which Tibullus deceives his reader. Another is the Tibullan trick ending, the most celebrated example of which occurs in 1.4. There the poet appears for a long time to be soliciting on his own behalf advice from Priapus on matters of homosexual love. He questions Priapus in lines 1–8; and Priapus responds in an extensive speech of generalised erotodidaxis (9–72). It is only at line 73, a mere eleven lines before the end, that the whole complexion of the elegy is altered by a surprising new turn of events. Tibullus declares: *haec mihi quae canerem Titio, deus edidit ore.* Thus Priapus' whole performance was, according to Tibullus, not for the poet's benefit at all, but for that of Titius, and Tibullus was only an intermediary. This surprise is immediately compounded in the pentameter which follows: *sed Titium coniunx haec meminisse vetat.* Titius' wife forbids him to pay attention to the account Tibullus gives him of Priapus' advice, so, although Titius is now supposed to be the person receiving the erotodidaxis, he is not in fact allowed to benefit from it. Instead, Tibullus claims, the whole class of 'lovers of boys' will benefit, since they will regard Tibullus, the pupil of Priapus, as their teacher of love (75f.). Lines 73f., with their mention of Titius, turn out to have been a humorous misdirection of the reader, the real pupil being all the time Tibullus.

Who is the Titius suddenly introduced by Tibullus as the supposed intended recipient of the erotic instructions given to the poet by Priapus? He may be a straw character, a mere name without substance. If so,

[29] See Cairns, *Mus. Phil. Lond.* 1 (1975) 79ff.

Tibullus' naming of him is parallel to Theocritus' occasional habit of introducing and immediately discarding bucolic characters[30] so as to fill out the background and make the reader believe that his poems are partial eavesdroppings upon a richly populated world with an independent continuing existence of its own. Another possibility is that 'Titius' is 'John Doe'; and indeed the name M. Titius is used in this way in legal texts.[31] But some names are used as legal fictions which are also the names of real Romans. There is no reason therefore to think that 'Titius' would immediately have been apparent to Tibullus' readers as a legal fiction.

It may be more fruitful to think of the appropriate context for a Roman poet to write both of a man being interested in boys and of his wife as being opposed to that interest. As has been understood, this is an 'allusion aux mignons abandonnés par les jeunes gens à leur mariage et aux plaisirs désormais interdits aux maris; cf. CATULLE, 131–145'.[32] This context then is probably marriage; and it might be guessed, although it is only a guess, that Titius is M. Titius, an important contemporary of Tibullus. Titius and his uncle L. Munatius Plancus were, like Tibullus' patron M. Valerius Messalla Corvinus, important ex-Antonians who had gone over to Augustus. Messalla was appointed consul in place of Antonius for the year 31 BC. When he demitted office, he was succeeded in the consulship by M. Titius. M. Titius married Fabia Paullina, daughter of the Caesarian *cos. suff.* of 45 BC and sister of Paullus and Africanus Fabius Maximus, two strong Augustan supporters (*coss*. 11 BC and 10 BC). It is not impossible that M. Titius married her around the time the elegy was composed: Paullina, whose brothers were presumably born around 50 BC, was herself born not later than 44 BC. Her father died in his consulship, doubtless around 42 years of age; and she is honoured as Titius' wife in a Samian inscription probably dating from 32 BC, when Titius was at Samos as Antonius' admiral.[33] This would make her at least twelve at the time and probably older. Titius is likely to have been in his late thirties or early forties in 31 BC and the marriage may well have been fairly recent.[34] Indeed, the marriage and the political relationship it created with the Fabii could have contributed to Titius' eventual defection from Antonius to Augustus; and it may be that Messalla in 31 BC asked Tibullus to pay a compliment to his consular successor and his marriage to the daughter of this important family seemed a good topic for it. Other poetic compliments to consuls in the period are *Eclogue* 4, written for C. Asinius Pollio's consulship, and Horace, *Odes* 1.4, written for L. Sestius, suffect consul of 23 BC, when the

---

[30] E.g. Theocr. *Id.* 3.2ff., 26, 31ff., 35f.; 4.1, 2, 21, 25f., 31, 33f., 38f., 132f., 134; 5.11f., 62f.; imitated by Virg. e.g. *Ecl.* 2.14ff.; 3.3f., 10, 67, 81.

[31] E.g. Gaius, *Inst.* 1.149; 2.165, 174, 209, 216, 250.

[32] André on Tib. 1.4.74–5.

[33] *SEG* I 383.

[34] Titius was probably around 30 in 43 BC when he and his father were proscribed since he raised a force independently in 40 BC. Cf. Dio 48.30,5f.

first three books of Horace's *Odes* were published as a collection. The tradition continues throughout the Empire.[35]

To return to Tibullus 1.4: after the double deception and restatement of Tibullus' status as teacher of love, six lines (75–80) proclaim Tibullus' proficiency in this role; but another surprise follows at lines 81–4:

> eheu quam Marathus lento me torquet amore!
>   deficiunt artes, deficiuntque doli.
> parce, puer, quaeso, ne turpis fabula fiam
>   cum mea ridebunt vana magisteria.

For all his expertise, Tibullus confesses that he is helpless in his own love-affair with Marathus: he is reduced to begging Marathus in 83f. not to make a public fool of him by exposing the contrast between the poet's theoretical proficiency and his practical inefficiency.

In 1.4, not once but three times the reader is forced to re-assess the situation presented in the elegy. The three new turns each involve ironic comment upon himself by Tibullus; and the poetic *persona* presented at the end of the elegy is a compound of these ironies. Tibullus means us to realise that, in spite of a half-serious attempt to involve Titius in the action of the elegy, he, Tibullus, is the real pupil of Priapus; he is therefore fully responsible for putting to proper use the education he has received from the god. As a poet and educator of the young lovers he is indeed competent (75–80). But in his personal love-life he is a failure. The reader's attitude is changed by each new revelation.

It is not so easy to produce examples of surprise-endings in Tibullus as it was to find surprise beginnings. But the end of 1.3 is to some extent parallel to the end of 1.4. In 1.3 Tibullus is lying sick at Corcyra and up to line 82 the dominant theme is his death. Lines 83–8 urge Delia to remain chaste during his absence and they may imply that she should do so in the event of his death. The lines depict Delia sitting together with her old female *custos* and a slave-girl, the other two women spinning and the old woman telling Delia stories. At this point the elegy takes a surprising turn when Tibullus suddenly declares

> tunc veniam subito, nec quisquam nuntiet ante,
>   sed videar caelo missus adesse tibi. (89f.)

Of course it is not surprising if someone abroad anticipates returning home. But in 1.3 Tibullus has been all the time at death's door, so that his sudden vision of return to Rome and Delia is a shock. It is intended to clarify the relationship between Tibullus and Delia and Tibullus' real view of it. Earlier in the elegy Delia was unwilling that he should leave Rome (9ff.) and later on he gave precepts to Delia to be *casta* (83ff.). But women

---

[35] Cf. A. J. Woodman, 'Questions of date, genre, and style in Velleius: some literary answers', *CQ* N.S. 25 (1975) 274f.

176   Deceiving

like Delia have in Roman elegy a limited loyalty to their lovers. Their *castitas* is conditional – and their lovers are aware of it.[36] Tibullus expresses the matter more openly elsewhere:

> sit, modo, casta, doce, quamvis non vitta ligatos
>   impediat crines nec stola longa pedes.   (1.6.67f.)

Here Tibullus does not assume that Delia will heed the injunctions to fidelity. The irony of Tibullus envisaging his sudden return to Rome is that his return is a precautionary move which reveals that his confidence in Delia is not as firm as he might pretend, even to himself.

Techniques of surprise and deception in Tibullus are not confined to the beginnings and ends of elegies. They also occur elsewhere, often inextricably combined with retentions of information such as were described in Chapter 6. This will be demonstrated first by further examination of Tibullus 1.5, and then by a study of his final elegy, 2.6. These illustrate internal deceptions and retentions of information, associated sometimes with typically Hellenistic flashbacks and anticipations of the future.[37] The simplest way of clarifying Tibullus 1.5 is to list its events in their 'historical' order and in their order of presentation.

'HISTORICAL' ORDER

1. Tibullus was having a clandestine affair with Delia (7 (*per* . . .)–8).
2. Delia fell ill (9).
3. Tibullus employed religious and magical means to assist Delia in her illness (10–16).
4. Tibullus imagined that, if Delia recovered, she would, out of gratitude to Tibullus, leave her *vir* and go off with Tibullus into the countryside. There they would live an idyllic life as lovers and Messalla would visit them (19–35 (*fingebam*)).
5. Delia recovered from her illness through Tibullus' actions (10, cf. 17 (*persolvi*)).
6. A *lena* intervened and introduced Delia to a *dives amator* (47 (*quod* . . .)–58).
7. Tibullus' dreams were shattered (35(*quae* . . .)–36).
8. Delia took up with this *dives amator* and she is now his mistress (17 (*fruitur* . . .)–18).
9. Tibullus in chagrin declared that he did not care about his loss of Delia (1).
10. He tried to solace himself with wine and with other women, but unsuccessfully (37–40).

---

[36] See above, pp. 106f.
[37] Some of these features of Tib. 1.5 have been studied in K. Vretska, 'Albius Tibullus: Elegie 1 5 Interpretation', *Das altsprachliche Unterricht* 6 (1963) 111ff., reprinted in *Antike Lyrik* ed. W. Eisenhut (Darmstadt 1970) pp. 293ff.

Deceiving

11. The women left him saying that he was bewitched but Tibullus realised that Delia's beauty had damaged him (41–7 (*mihi*)),
12. and he is now tormented by love for her (2–4);
13. so he accepts punishment that will prevent a repetition of his offence and begs her for forgiveness (5–7 (*parce*)).
14. He begs Delia to abandon the *lena*'s teaching and urges the benefits of a poor lover (59–66).
15. Tibullus' singing at Delia's door receives no response (67–8).
16. He warns the *dives amator* in possession to beware of a reversal. One of these days his *komos* will succeed (69–76).

ACTUAL ORDER OF PRESENTATION

9. Tibullus in chagrin declared that he did not care about his loss of Delia (1).
12. He is now tormented by love for her (2–4),
13. so he accepts punishment that will prevent a repetition of his offence and begs her for forgiveness (5–7 (*parce*)).
1. Tibullus was having a clandestine affair with Delia (7 (*per* . . .)–8).
2. Delia fell ill (9).
5. Delia recovered from her illness through Tibullus' actions (10, cf. 17 (*persolvi*)).
3. Tibullus employed religious and magical means to assist Delia in her illness (10–16).
8. Delia took up with a *dives amator*, and is now his mistress (17 (*fruitur* . . .)–18).
4. Tibullus imagined that, if Delia recovered, she would, out of gratitude to Tibullus, leave her *vir* and go off with Tibullus into the countryside. There they would live an idyllic life as lovers and Messalla would visit them (19–35 (*fingebam*)).
7. Tibullus' dreams were shattered (35 (*quae* . . .)–36).
10. He tried to solace himself with wine and with other women, but unsuccessfully (37–40).
11. The women left him saying that he was bewitched but Tibullus realised that Delia's beauty had damaged him (41–7 (*mihi*)).
6. A *lena* intervened and introduced Delia to a *dives amator* (47 (*quod* . . .)–58).
14. He begs Delia to abandon the *lena*'s teaching and urges the benefits of a poor lover (59–66).
15. Tibullus' singing at Delia's door receives no response (67–8).
16. He warns the *dives amator* in possession to beware of a reversal. One of these days his komos will succeed (69–76).

It goes without saying that such a poem could only have been written within a literary context such as Roman elegy, where the repertoire of characters and incidents was limited and already well-known from Hellenistic and earlier Roman literature. For Tibullus' readers a great part of the intellectual enjoyment of his poetry lay in the demands made on them: they had to detect the exact situation of the lover in each elegy, his precise response to it, the genre of the elegy, the true time-scale of the events, and so forth. The author's task in this area was to tease the readers by paucity of information and by misdirection, thus postponing detection as long as was reasonable, and more important, manipulating the readers' emotional reactions.

In the latter area Tibullus' deceptions and distortions of the temporal sequence have a very important apologetic function. A Roman elegiac poet observes a dual morality. Although he confesses that simply by being a lover he is in terms of normal social morality worthless, nevertheless he insists that in terms of the morality of love, he is virtuous. In 1.5 Tibullus is trying to convince first Delia, and second his readers, that he is a virtuous lover. He is trying to show Delia and his readers that he really deserves her love in spite of everything; and he is trying to save Delia's reputation, as far as this is practicable, in the eyes of the reader. Admittedly Tibullus does have to cast a temporary slur upon Delia in order to justify his own folly in rejecting her. But, as soon as possible, this odium is, as will be explained, transferred first to the *lena* and later, obliquely, to the *dives amator*.

The elegy begins with Tibullus admitting actions contrary to the usual disposition of the elegiac poet. He was *asper* rather than, as an elegiac poet usually is, *mollis*, and he declared that the break-up of his love-affair with Delia would not trouble him. The reader is intrigued by this anti-love stance and unusual self-presentation of Tibullus, but naturally suspects that this is not the whole story. Line 2 immediately confirms his suspicion: the elegiac poet was not able to maintain this attitude for long. Tibullus now speaks as a disillusioned *asper*. His rejection of Delia was nothing more than a vainglorious and unsubstantiated boast about his powers of endurance. Now he is whirled about by Love like a boy's top (3f.). Even in this second couplet the reader's, and Delia's, sympathy is being enlisted on Tibullus' side. When in 5f. Tibullus offers himself voluntarily for the punishment *cum* treatment normally given to madmen, and when in 7f. he begs forgiveness of Delia in the name of their past love, this combination of confession and plea increases the pathos of his situation.

So far Tibullus has not offered any direct excuse for his behaviour. He has hinted at madness in 5f.; but this is a characterisation of his action, rather than a cause of it. In lines 9ff. he describes a service he has performed for Delia. These lines seem, in context, not to be offering excuses for Tibullus' offence, but merely to be advancing facts in mitigation of his offence. They relate how Delia was sick and how Tibullus, by vows and by magical practices, brought about her cure. It is this deliberately low key presentation of the facts of lines 9–16 which makes lines 17f. come as such a shock. There we are told that Delia, immediately on being cured through

Tibullus' good offices, rejected him and went off with another man. The reader now realises that Tibullus' cure of Delia was not just described to mitigate his crime; more importantly it is the explanation and excuse for the crime. Poor Tibullus, having devotedly slaved to restore Delia's health, was treated to a display of gross ingratitude and rejected by Delia. No wonder he reacted by trying to give up Delia altogether.

By postponing this information until lines 17f. the poet reverses his previous build-up of the expectations and sympathies of the reader. The reader, on learning that an elegiac poet has tried to abandon love, will naturally regard him as having behaved in an improper way and therefore as deserving punishment. But when the reason for Tibullus' behaviour is finally given, the reader's previous disapproval is reversed all the more effectively because he is made to feel that he has wronged Tibullus, who can now be seen clearly as a man more sinned against than sinning. It is now Delia who appears in the reader's eyes to be the offender, a notion which Tibullus does not immediately try to dispel. Rather Tibullus embarks (19ff.) on an account of one of his former fantasies, which, in the light of the way things actually turned out, is at once touching and compelling. Tibullus hoped that Delia's cure would be followed by their life together in the bliss of the countryside. The reader's sympathy for Tibullus is doubled. But something odd happens in the midst of this description of their imagined rural felicity. Messalla, Tibullus' patron, is introduced into the fantasy, when Tibullus claims that he hoped Messalla would visit Delia and himself in their country retreat (31ff.). This is a bold concept: the elegiac poets normally kept their patrons, who are real personages of contemporary Rome, apart from their mistresses, who are imaginary composites of Hellenistic literature and life. Here Tibullus has broken the rule; and in doing so, he makes his patron interesting to the reader and brings him into the elegy in a most ingenious way. But in order to do so without casting a slur on Messalla's consular dignity, Tibullus has altered the image of Delia, as he presents it in his fantasy, from her normal image in his elegies. Delia is no longer the *meretrix* mistress;[38] instead she acts in every respect like a Roman *materfamilias*. The use of the term *custos*, which has associations with the *materfamilias*,[39] at the beginning of the vignette in 21 sets the tone for the rest of the portrayal, in which Delia does all the things which characterise a wife in the Roman conception of that role. Of course marriage with a woman of Delia's class was socially impossible for a man of Tibullus' standing. But only by thinking of her as a

---

[38] The view that the elegiac mistresses are, in general, imagined as *meretrices* of one sort or another has been challenged by G. Williams, *Tradition and Originality in Roman Poetry* (Oxford 1968) pp. 529ff., but it remains the consensus. For a later, more flexible view which seeks to explain some of the conflicting evidence cf. A. S. Hollis, *Ovid: Ars Amatoria Book 1* (Oxford 1977) introd. pp. xvff.

[39] Cf. T. E. V. Pearce, 'The role of the wife as CUSTOS in ancient Rome', *Eranos* 72 (1974) 16ff. (on Tib. 1.5.21ff. see 29f.).

wife in his fantasy can he venture to bring her into conjunction with Messalla – and it is only a fantasy anyhow.

The portrayal of Delia in a wifely role does however have another deliberately sought effect: it partly swings audience sympathy back to her and detracts from the odium which her ungrateful rejection of Tibullus has brought upon her. This effect is continued in the next passage (37ff.) where another displaced piece of information is revealed, once more changing the reader's view of the situation. The reader already knows that Tibullus rashly underestimated the effects upon himself of giving up Delia (1) and that subsequently he experienced them in full and was tormented by love (2–4). What the reader does not yet know is that Tibullus, on comprehending the strength of his attachment to Delia, had not simply sat around moping miserably. He had in fact first tried to console himself with wine (37f.), an indulgence which might well be regarded by a reader as venial, but then, finding himself still unconsoled, had turned to other women (39ff.). In doing so he was adopting a remedy for love recommended in serious philosophical works in antiquity.[40] But in an elegiac context he has betrayed the elegists' ideal of fidelity to one woman and so revealed himself to be not simply a hopeless passive victim of love for Delia. He has thus forfeited a little of the reader's sympathy and respect. The balance of moral rectitude between Tibullus and Delia is therefore shifted a little towards Delia; and the humorous aspects of Tibullus' psychological impotence detract from his heroic sufferings. The withholding and late revelation of these facts again makes them more influential in conditioning the reader's emotional view of the situation.

The final swing of sympathy and the final absolution of any odium attaching to Delia come at last in lines 47ff. At this point information, which in fact belongs temporally to an earlier part of the sequence of events, and which has again been withheld in order to trick the reader, is at last revealed. Lines 47f. read

> haec nocuere mihi. quod adest huic dives amator,
> venit in exitium callida lena meum.

Here Tibullus first sums up the previous four lines (43–6), in which he has been making the point that Delia's physical attractions have brought him to his present condition: 'these are the things that have done me harm'. Then he suddenly reveals everything in a single sentence: 'As for her having a rich lover, a cunning procuress has ruined me.' The introduction of the sinister figure of the *lena* has considerable impact. The third scene of Plautus' *Mostellaria* (157ff.) shows how influential *lenae* could be in Hellenistic literature dealing with erotic matters. It shows also how valid in practical terms were the arguments which a *lena* could put to a *meretrix*

---

[40] Cf. Lucr. *DRN* 4.1063ff.; Cic. *Tusc. Disp.* 4.35.75; cf. also Ov. *Rem. Am.* 441ff.; 485ff.; Nonnus, *Dionys.* 9.356ff.

against her committing herself to a poor lover and in favour of her accepting his rich rival. Since Tibullus has said nothing about the intervention of the *lena* before this point, he has in effect deceived his reader into believing that the action of Delia in deserting him was voluntary and not, as is now made clear, the result of pressure from a stock bad and strong character of Hellenistic literature. Because the audience has been mistaken in this way and has misjudged Delia, its sympathies flow back to her with redoubled force. But they do so – and this is very important for Tibullus' standing in the elegy – without turning against him. For now a third figure has appeared against whom all the hostile feelings of the reader can be turned. Tibullus' curses upon the *lena* (49ff.) express and stimulate the emotional release which the structure of the poem demands from both poet and reader at this point.

There are no more temporal distortions in the elegy. By now the sympathies of the reader are fully committed to Tibullus and Delia. The two lovers are seen as victims of the *lena* and, in a sense, as united in spirit against her. Tibullus follows the curses with another appeal to the girl – to reject the advice of the *lena* and to consider the advantages, albeit non-financial, of a poor lover like himself. There is a final touch of pathos when he declares his appeals unavailing (67f.). But renewed hope immediately follows. The *dives amator*, who has so far been a shadowy character, is addressed and solemnly warned. Outside the door is an excluded lover – Tibullus – who, if not now, will at least one day gain admission.

Tibullus is thus evoking in succession a series of emotional responses in the reader, first doubt and self-congratulation, then pity, then moralising, then shock, then sympathy, then disapproval, then hatred, then pathos, and finally hope. These are variegated and mobile emotions because the excitement of a Tibullan elegy often lies in its ability to compel the reader into transient and perhaps incorrect reactions to the events as they are presented to him, not chronologically but in the most emotionally effective order.

The final Tibullan elegy, 2.6, will provide a last example both of generic deception and of other internal deceptions. As was the case in 1.5, the deception techniques found in 2.6 merge with the technique of retaining essential information discussed in Chapter 6. In fact 2.6, more than any of the other elegies previously treated in this respect, will emphasise that deception is only one part of a more general process of communication.

The elegy begins with a couplet containing clear signals that a propemptikon is beginning:

> Castra Macer sequitur: tenero quid fiet Amori?
> sit comes et collo fortiter arma gerat? (1f.).

The situation outlined in line 1 immediately suggests that Macer is a propemptic addressee going off on a journey and abandoning the 'logical' propemptic speaker Amor (see below).[41] Line 2 relates to the propemptic commonplace that the speaker may accompany the departing traveller.[42] Such generic signals were unmistakable for Tibullus' readers, and more topoi may have reinforced their impression. It is possible that the idea of Amor accompanying a departing traveller was a Hellenistic commonplace;[43] and there was certainly a well-worn propemptic topos whereby kindly deities escorted travellers.[44]

2.6 is like 1.3 in beginning with propemptic signals. However different signals are used in the two poems. Part of the reason for this is that the propemptikon in 1.3 is a normal bi-personal example involving only Tibullus and Messalla, while the one in 2.6 is a tri-personal example in which Macer is 'addressee' and Tibullus, the 'actual' speaker, speaks on behalf of Amor the 'logical' speaker.[45] Such tri-personal examples of genres are common[46] and there is an Augustan propemptic parallel, Propertius 3.12, where Propertius, the 'actual' speaker, speaks on behalf of the 'logical' speaker Aelia Galla, and addresses her husband Postumus who is going off as a soldier.[47] Tibullus 2.6 seems to be influenced by Propertius 3.12[48] and the concept of the poet speaking on behalf of Amor in dissuading the departing traveller is more sophisticated than the notion of the poet speaking on behalf of the traveller's wife. 2.6 is certainly influenced by another Propertian propemptikon, 1.6 (see below).

The second couplet of Tibullus 2.6 continues with another propemptic commonplace, the division between land and sea in the traveller's route:[49]

> et seu longa virum terrae via seu vaga ducent
>   aequora, cum telis ad latus ire volet? (3f.)

Cf. Propertius 1.6.33f.

> seu pedibus terras seu pontum carpere remis
>   ibis . . .

and more relevant, part of the Ovidian propemptikon of Alcyone to Ceyx:

> iam via longa placet? iam sum tibi carior absens?
> at, puto, per terras iter est, tantumque dolebo,
> non etiam metuam, curaeque timore carebunt.
> aequora me terrent et ponti tristis imago.
>   (*Metamorphoses* 11.424–7)

---

[41] Cf. *GC* pp. 52 and n. 28; 121; 141; 186; 199.
[42] Cf. *GC* pp. 4ff.; 115ff.; 123; 141ff.; 239.
[43] See Cairns, *CQ* n.s. 24 (1974) 108ff.
[44] Cf. *GC* p. 121 and n. 23f.; 117; 150; 190.
[45] On the concepts of 'logical' and 'actual' speakers cf. *GC* Ch. 8.
[46] Cf. *GC* pp. 192ff. [47] Cf. *GC* pp. 198ff.
[48] Tib. Book 2 was probably published posthumously. Prop. Book 3 is dated 25–20 BC. Cf. *Propertius: Elegies Book III* ed. W. A. Camps (Cambridge 1966) p. 1.
[49] The division is also found in Menander Rhetor's propemptikon prescription – *R.G.* (ed. Spengel) III p. 398 l. 29–p. 399 l. 10.

The sea was always a dangerous place to be in antiquity, particularly in propemptika.⁵⁰ Lands could vary in danger. Tibullus is alluding to the topos in order to emphasise that, because he is 'going to war'. Macer's heroism (*virum*) is not diminished whether he is travelling by land or by sea. Another propemptic topos follows in the third couplet: Tibullus turns to Amor, the logical speaker, and urges him to 'burn' and 'call back to your standard' the deserter Macer. Here Tibullus is alluding to the perjury topos of the propemptikon,⁵¹ as well as playing on the love/war opposition/ equation omnipresent in Roman elegy. A soldier took a formal oath of allegiance to the standards. If he deserted, he was an *erro* (cf. 6). This concept of the runaway lover as a deserting soldier is related to the Hellenistic topos whereby the lover seeking to escape love was described as a runaway slave.⁵² The link is helped by the fact that the word *erro* in Latin covers both a runaway slave and a deserting soldier.⁵³ A lover who was an *erro* was then automatically foresworn and so committed, in the eyes of the speaker, the standard sin of the propemptic addressee, breach of a compact of friendship and association with the speaker.⁵⁴

After the first six lines of 2.6, Tibullus' thoughts turn from Macer to himself: if Amor spares soldiers, Tibullus declares that he too will be one (7f.), and indeed in the next couplet (9f.) he boldly declares that he is turning soldier. But immediately the *clausae fores* of his girlfriend shatter his resolve (12). With the introduction of Tibullus' own beloved and her closed door, his military fantasies and the propemptic portion of the elegy come simultaneously to an end. The reader is undeceived and realises that 2.6 is in fact going to be not a propemptikon but a komos. As is normal with generic inclusion, the lines (7–11) linking the clear propemptic topoi and the clear komastic announcement of 12 are a bridge passage, with topoi capable of being seen as belonging to both genres.⁵⁵ In the propemptikon they relate to the speaker's decision or wish to accompany the addressee⁵⁶ and the excuses which he sometimes offers for his inability to do so.⁵⁷ By introducing these concepts Tibullus amusingly alludes in his schetliastic propemptikon to the other, the excusatory, variant of the genre. He probably has in mind Propertius 1.6, a propemptikon addressed to Tullus, also a young aristocratic⁵⁸ state functionary off on *militia*. There

---

⁵⁰ Cf. e.g. *GC* p. 150 and n. 17; 191 and n. 27; 199 and n. 38.
⁵¹ Cf. above, n. 9.
⁵² See F. Cairns, 'Propertius 2 29A', *CQ* N.S. 21 (1971) 455ff.; *Emerita* 45 (1977) 344ff.
⁵³ Cf. *TLL s.v.* The double sense of *erro* may also be one of the many links between Ov. *Am.* 2.9 and 3.11. Cf. F. Cairns, 'Self-imitation within a generic framework: Ovid *Amores* 2.9 and 3.11 and the *renuntiatio amoris*' in *Creative Imitation and Latin Literature*, ed. D. West and T. Woodman (Cambridge 1980) pp. 121ff.
⁵⁴ Cf. above, n. 9.
⁵⁵ Cf. above, n. 6.
⁵⁶ Often envisaged and sometimes actually happening: see above, n. 42.
⁵⁷ Cf. *GC* pp. 11ff.
⁵⁸ Cf. also *GC* pp. 3ff. and F. Cairns, 'Some problems in Propertius 1.6', *AJP* 95 (1974) 156ff.

is one conspicuous difference between Tullus and Macer: Tullus is explicitly represented as a non-lover while Macer is portrayed as a former lover. In literary terms the Tibullan propemptikon is the subtler: while Propertius simply contrasts himself as lover with Tullus the non-lover, Tibullus plays with the *personae* of the former lover Macer who becomes the successful soldier, of himself, still a lover wanting to become a soldier but unable to do so, and of the love god, who might turn soldier to accompany the former lover Macer on his campaigns. The characterisation of Macer may be a bow to the taste of the late twenties, when Propertius' portrayal of Tullus may have come to seem too austere. The treatment of Macer also has an interesting encomiastic aspect lacking in Propertius 1.6. Tibullus, a failure both as a lover and in his attempts to escape from Love, contrasts himself with his patron Macer, who is credited with past success as a lover, with prospective success as a soldier, and with the moral strength to abandon the inferior way of life for the better.

Lines 7–11 relate to the komos as well. At line 12, when the komos is explicitly announced, the reader in retrospect identifies Tibullus' attempt to abandon love as a komastic topos: the lover tries to leave his beloved but love drags him back.[59] The confirmatory couplet 13f., in which Tibullus recognises his present experience as something which has often happened to him before, repeats the topos in a specific form, which again has links with the 'runaway soul' and 'runaway lover' themes of Hellenistic literature.[60] Since Propertius had already in another komos, 2.29,[61] given the motif large-scale allegorical rendering with the lover as a runaway slave and the Loves as *fugitivarii* (slave-catchers), it may be suspected that the designation *erro* applied to Macer in line 6, together with lines 12–14, constitutes *imitatio cum variatione* of Propertius.[62]

Tibullus moves next into a four-line attack on Love (15–18), a typical example of the verbal abuse which disappointed komasts deploy when attacking the mistress/door/*custos*/Love.[63] Excuses or pleas in mitigation can accompany such attacks.[64] But here the nearest equivalent to excuses amounts in fact to further attacks on Love (17f.). Love is blamed for the curses which Tibullus heaps, not on Love, as would be normal, but on himself. Love is also accused of causing Tibullus *insana mente nefanda loqui*, which is as much of a retraction of his accusations as Tibullus makes and which may refer primarily in any case to lines 7–10. All this is part of Tibullus' especially adverse portrayal of Love in this elegy.

At line 19 the first really daring variation upon a komastic topos is

---

[59] Cf. e.g. Cairns, *Emerita* 45 (1977) 351ff. and *CQ* N.S. 21 (1971) 455ff.
[60] *Id.* [61] *Id.*
[62] See above, p. 183 and n. 53.
[63] Cf. Copley pp. 19 and nn. 44–53; 33f. and nn. 25–33. Copley rightly stresses that the lover is usually a helpless victim – but verbally he remains fairly aggressive.
[64] Cf. e.g. Ov. *Am.* 1.6.59f.; Tib. 1.2.11ff.; Copley p. 19 and n. 48 and p. 34 and n. 31.

introduced. A komast can threaten suicide;[65] and sometimes a komast actually killed himself.[66] Here Tibullus varies on this topos by declaring 'I would have killed myself, had not . . .'. This bold topical sophistication allows Tibullus to introduce the notion of *spes*. *Spes*, he declares, is the cause of his decision to continue a life of love. He amplifies on *spes* (20–6) ending with an account of her power over a chained slave, a notion suggested by the common equivalence of lover and slave in elegy in general, and paralleled in the komos.[67] This long account of *Spes* is introduced because Tibullus' mistress is called Nemesis. When this information is revealed for the first time in line 27 Tibullus juxtaposes the two words *Spes* and *Nemesim* to make the word play unmistakable (cf. *AP* 9.146 (Anon.)).

The fact that the reader learns of Nemesis only in line 27 is an important factor in Tibullus' manipulation of his feelings. It is true that lines 11–14 imply that Tibullus is in love with at least one girl. But in line 9, in his attempted renunciation of love, Tibullus deliberately spoke in general terms of *puellae*. The withholding of information about Nemesis allows Tibullus to achieve in 2.6 what he achieved by different means in 1.5: to end the elegy with less discredit cast upon his mistress, because it has been deflected elsewhere. The method Tibullus uses is as follows: in 2.6 *Amor* is cast as a protagonist from the first line on. To begin with he is portrayed fairly sympathetically. He is a boy (1, 5) and Macer is trying to desert him (6); Tibullus pretends to be on the side of *Amor*. This pretence is yet another deception and it is with surprise that the reader learns in lines 15f. how things really stand. Far from having felt sympathy with Love in lines 1ff. Tibullus has been simply envious of Macer for his ability to flout Love (see especially line 7). What seemed to be Tibullan advocacy of Love's cause in connection with Macer was really veiled reproach of Love for being indulgent with Macer and strict with Tibullus. This only becomes clear at line 15, when Tibullus launches into his extravagantly severe attack upon Amor.

Thus 2.6 works like 1.5; there Tibullus began by building up a hollow case against Delia and, when the *lena* was disclosed as the real culprit, the case against Delia fell. But in 2.6 the deception is more complex. First Amor is treated by Tibullus almost as a colleague or protégé and then he is

[65] Cf. Theocr. *Id.* 3 (and see Copley p. 17 and n. 35; pp. 134ff. and n. 33); Prop. 2.17 and Cairns, 'Further adventures of a locked-out lover'. See also below, n. 66.
[66] Cf. [Theocr.] *Id.* 23; Ov *Met.* 14.698f.; – and see Copley *locc. citt.* above, n. 65; F. O. Copley, 'The suicide-paraclausithyron: a study of Ps.-Theocritus, *Idyll* XXIII', *TAPA* 71 (1940) 52ff.
[67] For elegy in general cf. F. O. Copley, '*Servitium amoris* in the Roman elegists', *TAPA* 78 (1947) 285ff. For the komos cf. e.g. Powell p. 178 ll. 27f.; Tib. 1.2.97f.; Prop. 2.29A (on which see Cairns, *Emerita* 45 (1977) 344ff.). The analogous images of the komast as suppliant or prisoner are found e.g. at: Powell p. 177 ll. 11ff.; *AP* 5.191.5f. (Meleager); *AP* 12.23 (*Id.*); *AP* 12.119 (*Id.*); Hor. *Od.* 3.10.16f.; Tib. 1.2.13f.; 85f.; Prop. 1.16.13f.; Ov. *AA* 2.527; *Met.* 14.702.

attacked as a cruel tyrant. The reader feels at 15ff. that he is being undeceived and admitted to the real truth about Amor. But when Nemesis makes her appearance at 27, and is immediately called *dura puella* in 28 and compared in harshness with the implacable goddess whose name she bears, the odium which attached to Amor is transferred by implication to her. A komastic commonplace, the harshness of the mistress,[68] is followed by an appeal to her by Tibullus which combines characteristically Hellenistic sentimentality and grotesquerie (29–40). Tibullus begs Nemesis in the name of her dead sister to have pity on him. If Nemesis resists his love, he will pray to her sister and she will haunt Nemesis in her death guise, fresh from her fall from a high window. The speech has the flavour of New Comedy;[69] and the pathos it evokes further contributes towards representing Nemesis in unfavourable terms.

However Tibullus has a further surprise in store. Having exploited the komastic topoi mentioned to cast blame upon Nemesis, he once more changes the moral emphasis of the poem. As Amor was first cherished and then attacked, so Nemesis, having initially been blamed for Tibullus' suffering, is finally absolved. Tibullus first softens a little when he acknowledges (41) that his words are liable to awaken Nemesis' sense of loss for her sister. Then he contradicts his earlier stance: *non ego sum tanti, ploret ut illa semel* (42). This surprising change of direction demands explanation. The reason for it and for Tibullus' expressions of renewed sympathy for Nemesis is disclosed at 44. Here the true villain of the piece, a *lena* as in 1.5, at last stands revealed. The reader is now and for the last time undeceived. The result is that, as in 1.5, the accumulated odium of the elegy is discharged upon the *lena* as the elegy moves into its final section, and the identification of the real culprit helps to absolve in retrospect both Amor and Nemesis. The description of the *lena* and her villainy also brings the elegy back to the komastic scene which is the background to all that has preceded. The *lena* among her other crimes

> saepe, ego cum dominae dulces a limine duro
>   agnosco voces, haec negat esse domi:
> saepe, ubi nox mihi promissa est, languere puellam
>   nuntiat aut aliquas extimuisse minas.   (47–50)

Tibullus, as he stands at Nemesis' door, meditates on the tricks and lies which the *lena* deploys against his komoi and on the misery and jealousy which they arouse in him. These komastic commonplaces[70] bring the

---

[68] Cf. Copley pp. 19 and nn. 43–7; p. 33 and nn. 25–30.
[69] Cf. e.g. Ter. *Andria* 70ff.; *Adelph.* 455ff. (both from Menander).
[70] Deceit is usually attributed to the beloved: cf. Copley p. 19 and n. 47; p. 33 and n. 25. However, there is a sporadic tendency in Roman literature to focus komoi wholly or partly on the *ianua* or the *ianitor custos* instead of the beloved: cf. e.g. Plaut. *Curc.* 147ff.; Prop. 1.16.17ff.; Tib. 1.2.7ff.; Ov. *Am.* 1.6. Here the *lena* acts as *custos* – see above, n. 19.

poem to its climax in which Tibullus curses the *lena*. It will be clear that 2.6 is not attempting to reach the level of moral seriousness which 1.5 achieves. Its choice of a more complex and dramatic background shows that Tibullus' interest is more in technical virtuosity than in a moral message. But it is a most interesting example of the self-imitation and imitation of literary predecessors which Roman elegy delighted in.

A pendant to this discussion of Tibullus 2.6: in all cases so far analysed of generic inclusion in this book and elsewhere, if the two genres are different, some congruity, real or apparent, between the including and the included genre has been manifest. In Tibullus 2.6 something unusual and interesting can be observed: a *komos* includes a propemptikon. Not only is this a combination hitherto unparalleled but it offers an interesting sidelight on the way Tibullus might have speculated about the komos. The komos is a non-rhetorical genre and it could hardly have been otherwise. But there seems to have been a tendency in the ancient world to associate, if necessarily falsely, non-rhetorical genres with rhetorical ones. In Tibullus 2.6 the non-rhetorical komos is found associated with the epideictic rhetorical genre propemptikon. The factor in the komos which made this possible must have been its processional element – *komos* could *inter alia* mean 'procession'. Cf. especially lines 13f.

> iuravi quotiens rediturum ad limina numquam!
> cum bene iuravi, pes tamen ipse redit.

This must have made the komos seem in one way analogous to a travel genre and thus capable of being included by a propemptikon. The attempt to assimilate the komos to the propemptikon is aided by Tibullus' allusion in 2.6 to Propertius 1.6, where one variant of the propemptikon includes another (cf. *GC* pp. 12ff.).

The deception techniques exemplified in this chapter have a long history in antiquity. They originate in early Greek poetry and were used in the classical period. They were then employed in different contexts in Hellenistic poetry; and Tibullus in adopting them is imitating Hellenistic exemplars. Even in Homer there are examples of false preparation. The account given by Zeus at *Iliad* 15.63ff. of the future course of the Trojan war does not in fact correspond with its course. Similarly Achilles' statement to Hector about the future fate of the latter's body (*Iliad* 22.345ff.) is not borne out by events.[71] A famous early lyric example of reader deception occurs in Archilochus. Aristotle gives an account of a poem by him beginning 'I care not for the wealth of golden Gyges' (Fr. 22(D)), which is the model for Horace, *Epode* 2 and which attacks wealth and power.[72]

---

[71] Cf. also Hom. *Od.* 11.100ff. where the unfulfilled notion that Odysseus' men might also return home is raised and *Od.* 19.1ff. – the plan to deprive the suitors of weapons, foiled at *Od.* 22.135ff. [72] Arist. *Rhet.* 1418b.

From Aristotle's description and from Horace's imitation, it is clear that Archilochus did not reveal until a late point in the poem the identity and occupation of his speaker, Charon the carpenter. This involved both surprise and deception of the audience since a rejection of wealth and empire might have been expected to come from someone with at least a moderate status in society. The eventual revelation that it was a mere craftsman who spoke in this way must have been startling. In Horace's second *Epode* in imitation of this device the identity and occupation of the speaker, Alfius the moneylender, is made known only at the end. The reader is both surprised and undeceived, since the whole epode, a laudation of the countryside, is hardly a normal speech for such a person. The fact that in retrospect, or indeed for a shrewd reader, in prospect, Alfius' praise has many suspicious aspects, is neither here nor there.[73]

Deception techniques are of wider occurence in early Greek lyric. Some of the confusion over a famous passage in *Olympian* 1 is caused by Pindar's deliberate deception of his audience and subsequent revelation of the true facts. In telling the story of Pelops, Pindar relates that Poseidon fell in love with him:

ἐπεί νιν καθαροῦ λέβητος ἔξελε Κλωθώ,
ἐλέφαντι φαίδιμον ὦμον κεκαδμένον. (26f.)

The natural interpretation of this line on first hearing is 'when Klotho took him from the purifying (or pure) cauldron, endowed with a shoulder gleaming with ivory'; and the obvious conclusion is that Pindar is telling the story of how Pelops was cooked and served up to the gods, how Demeter ate his shoulder and how it was replaced with an ivory one when he was brought back to life.

But Pindar goes on to meditate on the true and the false in myth and poetry, to attack impious statements about the gods and to present an alternative account in which Pelops is carried off by Poseidon to heaven and an envious neighbour makes up a lie about Pelops being eaten by the gods. The audience now realises that lines 26f. actually meant: 'because Klotho took him from the purifying cauldron with a shoulder gleaming white as ivory'. Klotho therefore functions as the goddess of birth, not just as a Fate; she is washing the new-born child; he is beautiful in that he is white as ivory;[74] and Poseidon falls in love with him at birth, in accordance with the commonplace that enduring affection of a god for a mortal begins early in life.[75]

---

[73] Cf. Cairns, *Mus. Phil. Lond.* 1 (1975) 79ff.
[74] Cf. K. Jax, *Die weibliche Schönheit in der griechischen Dichtung* (Innsbruck 1933) pp. 76f. and nn. 311, 332, 333. The canons of beauty for women were also applicable to boys: cf. G. Giangrande, *L'Humour des Alexandrins* (Classical and Byzantine Monographs 2, Amsterdam 1975) pp. 22ff.
[75] Cf. Call. *Aet.* Fr. 1 37f. (Pf.) and Pfeiffer *ad loc.*

Another Pindaric deception occurs in *Pythian* 3. There Pindar relates how Apollo learnt of the marriage of Coronis:

οὐδ' ἔλαθε σκοπόν· ἐν δ' ἄρα μηλοδόκῳ
Πυθῶνι τόσσαις ἄϊεν ναοῦ βασιλεύς
Λοξίας, κοινᾶνι παρ' εὐθυτάτῳ γνώμαν πιθών,
πάντα ἴσαντι νόῳ· (27–9)
Nor did she escape the notice of the watcher: King Loxias, who was in his temple at Delphi receiver of sheep, heard this and persuaded his heart with that surest of witnesses, his all-knowing mind.

Initially the reader is deceived into interpreting the 'watcher' as the crow which, in the pre-Pindaric tradition, acted as Apollo's informant. But by line 29 it becomes clear that Apollo, in Pindar's version, needed no informant other than his own all-knowing mind.[76] By deceiving his audience in this way, Pindar leads them to give assent to a version of a myth which he then demonstrates to be untrue, or even impious. Their former association with this version leads them all the more easily to reject it in revulsion when a better version is offered.

Bacchylides also knew the technique of suggesting a false conclusion and then undercutting the suggestion. In *Dithyramb* 18 the Attic chorus starts in a panic caused by trumpet blasts. They fear invaders or pirates and in terror question their king Aegeus (1–15). Aegeus replies with a catalogue of mighty deeds of a man who is approaching Attica (16–30). This catalogue gradually undeceives the audience, who come to recognise the man as Theseus, the great Attic hero. But the chorus and king remain in ignorance throughout the dithyramb. Again, Attic tragedy makes use of similar devices. This has been demonstrated for Aeschylus,[77] Sophocles and Euripides: deception was clearly a standard practice understood as such by poets and audiences.

In the Hellenistic period there are further examples of deception techniques analogous to those of Tibullus. In the epodic tradition Callimachus seems to have used in his *Iambus* 9 (Pf.), of which only the first two lines survive, a technique resembling that of Archilochus Fr. 22(D) and Horace, *Epode* 2. The *diegesis* shows that an ithyphallic Herm, asked for an explanation of its condition, started with a serious sounding *aetion* but ended with a jeering attack on its interrogator and his motives. This iamb has been associated with Tibullus 1.4;[78] and indeed the speakers, ithyphallic Herm

---

[76] Cf. R. W. B. Burton, *Pindar's Pythian Odes: essays in interpretation* (Oxford 1962) p. 84.
[77] Cf. O. Taplin, *The Stagecraft of Aeschylus* (Oxford 1977) pp. 94ff.; W. G. Arnott, 'Euripides and the unexpected', *Greece and Rome* 20 (1973) 49ff.; 'Red herrings and other baits: a study in Euripidean techniques', *Mus. Phil. Lond.* 3 (1978) 1ff.
[78] Cf. C. M. Dawson, 'The iambi of Callimachus', *YClS* 11 (1950) 95; 'An Alexandrian Prototype of Marathus?' *AJP* 67 (1946) 12f.

and ithyphallic Priapus, are very similar. Callimachus is also capable of other deceptions: his tricking of his readers at *Aetia* Fr. 75.1 (Pf.) into believing that Cydippe has already slept with someone other than Acontius has already been noted in Chapter 5 (pp. 117f.).

In addition the epigrammatic tradition often relies on deception. The 'sting in the tail' technique inevitably involves revealing that the situation in the poem was not as the reader thought; and it goes back at least to Anacreon.[79] A Theocritean epigram (4) exemplifies the technique in an elaborate way. Like Tibullus 1.4 it is addressed to Priapus. It takes the form of a prayer and it is an interesting example of the generic complexity favoured in the Hellenistic period. The 'logical speaker', a lover, employs a goatherd as a 'substitute speaker' on his behalf.[80] There is humorous and practical intent here: the lover believes that the goatherd, with tastes and personality closer to those of Priapus, will have more success as an intercessor on his behalf than he himself would if he approached the god directly. In the epigram the 'logical speaker' gives instructions to the 'substitute speaker'.[81] The directions given to the goatherd to enable him to reach the shrine of Priapus amount to a description of that shrine and its setting (1–12); and at lines 13f. the actual prayer begins. The lover wants the god to release him from his love for Daphnis. The surprise ending, which comes in lines 15ff., is not a surprise in terms of ancient commonplaces about love, for it involves a known thought-pattern of love-poetry.[82] But its sudden appearance in this epigram runs contrary to the previous train of sense:

> κευθὺς ἐπιρρέξειν χίμαρον καλόν. ἢν δ' ἀνανεύσῃ,
>   τοῦδε τυχὼν ἐθέλω τρισσὰ θύη τελέσαι·
> ῥέξω γὰρ δαμάλαν, λάσιον τράγον, ἄρνα τὸν ἴσχω
>   σακίταν. ἀῖοι δ' εὐμενέως ὁ θεός. (15–18)
>
> *And at once sacrifice a fine young he-goat. But if he refuses, I am willing if I win him to make three sacrifices. I will sacrifice a calf, a hairy billy and a fold-reared lamb which I possess; and may the god give kindly hearing to me.*

The lover prays that, if Priapus will not release him from his love, then he should help him win Daphnis. The lover makes different vows to be fulfilled in the event of his alternative petitions succeeding. The size of the sacrifices shows that the second plea is not a *pis-aller* but the preferred outcome; and the surprise ending compounds the humour of this gradated scale of vows.

---

[79] Cf. G. Giangrande, 'Symposiastic literature and epigram' in *L'Épigramme grecque* (Entretiens sur l'Antiquité classique 14, Vandoeuvres– Genève 1968) pp. 109ff.; 'Anacreon and the Lesbian Girl', *Quad. Urbin.* 16 (1973) 129ff.

[80] For parallels cf. *GC* pp. 216f.

[81] This gives the poem the initial appearance of being an epistaltikon, although in fact it is not. [82] Cf. e.g. Tib. 1.2.59ff.; Prop. 1.1.

Finally some interesting Hellenistic cases of deception occur in Menander.[83] In *Aspis* 1–69 Menander induces his audience to believe that Kleostratus has died in battle. Only in 106ff. is the truth revealed, that Kleostratus is not dead. In the *Epitrepontes* the audience is first led to believe that Onesimos' suspicions about Habrotonon's motives may be justified. But eventually these suspicions prove totally unjustified. Finally in the *Samia* Moschion and the audience expect his father Demeas to appear on stage (670ff.). This expectation is disappointed when Parmenon in fact appears. The same thing now happens again (687ff.) and again the expectation is disappointed. But after two deceptions Menander produces what is now the unexpected: Demeas does appear (690). This technique, which of course derives in part at least from tragedy[84] and is echoed in Roman Comedy,[85] is clearly very similar to that of Tibullus; and it is particularly interesting that it appears in Comedy because of the many links between Comedy and Roman Elegy.[86] Finally it may be noted that Catullus begins a long elegiac poem (68) with the deception explored at the end of Chapter 6 (p. 163).

None of the earlier parallels offered for Tibullan practice involves generic deception, and this raises the question whether it might be his original invention. Delay in providing generic information is certainly a Hellenistic device: Theocritus in his komastic idylls withholds for a time information about the genre, as does Propertius in 2.17.[87] But this is not the same as deceiving the audience about the genre of a poem. Again neither Propertius nor Ovid have yet been detected in generic deception and if it were a Hellenistic device then they would have been likely to have used it, particularly since delay in generic identification, which is known to be a Hellenistic technique, appears at least in Propertius. All this suggests, although it does not prove, that Tibullus himself in the innovating spirit of Hellenistic poetry developed this technique, which Propertius and Ovid perhaps found too novel and difficult to imitate.

---

[83] Cf. A. G. Katsouris, 'Menander misleading his audience', *Liverpool Classical Monthly* 1 (1976) 100ff. K.'s dissertation referred to there (100) is published as *Tragic Patterns in Menander* (Hellenic Society for Humanistic Studies, International Centre for Classical Research, Second Series: Studies and Researches 28, Athens 1975) and *Linguistic and Stylistic Characterization: Tragedy and Menander* (University of Ioannina, Philological Periodical of the School of Philosophy, Dodone Suppl. 5, Ioannina 1975).

[84] See above p. 189 and n. 77; n. 83.

[85] Cf. G. E. Duckworth, *The Nature of Roman Comedy* (Princeton 1952) pp. 200f., 227.

[86] A. A. Day, *The Origins of Latin Love Elegy* (Oxford 1938) Ch. 5 with bibliography; J. C. Yardley, 'Comic influences in Propertius', *Phoenix* 26 (1972) 134ff.

[87] See above, p. 166 n. 1.

8
ORDERING

The examination in Chapters 5, 6 and 7 of Tibullus' techniques of exposition may unintentionally have reinforced a common view of his elegies, namely that they are linear, proceed from one idea to another as their internal dynamics lead them, and involve no overall organisation of material. Such a view is mistaken. Far from being loosely written meditations following no dictates except those of Tibullus' roving imagination, they are in thematic terms tightly and symmetrically organised compositions. In one respect modern understanding of Tibullus' thematic organisation has improved. It is now generally realised that the transitions between his verse-paragraphs are made in an unobtrusive but telling way. The standard pattern is that a verbal or conceptual link bridges the two verse-paragraphs. A word or concept in the first couplet of the new verse-paragraph echoes a similar word or concept in the final portion of the old verse-paragraph. This is a thoroughly Hellenistic linking device: it is found in Menander as a means of joining scenes[1] and between sections in Theocritus and Callimachus.[2]

A few examples will suffice to illustrate Tibullus' technique of linking verse-paragraphs:

(1)   non acies, non ira fuit, non bella, nec ensem
           immiti saevus duxerat arte faber.
        nunc Iove sub domino caedes et vulnera semper,
           nunc mare, nunc leti mille repente viae.
        parce, pater. timidum non me periuria terrent,
           non dicta in sanctos impia verba deos.
        quodsi fatales iam nunc explevimus annos   (1.3.47–53)

Here a section contrasting the Golden Age with the Iron Age meets a section in which Tibullus envisages his own death. The link is made through *Iove sub domino* (49), *pater* (51) and the concept of death in both passages.

(2)   nam mihi tenduntur casses: iam Delia furtim
           nescio quem tacita callida nocte fovet.

---

[1] Cf. G. Arnott, 'The modernity of Menander', *Greece and Rome* 2nd ser. 22 (1975) 140ff. with bibliography at 153 n. 2.
[2] *Id*. 143 and 154 nn. 8f.

Ordering

> illa quidem iurata negat, sed credere durum est:
>   sic etiam de me pernegat usque viro.
> ipse miser docui, quo posset ludere pacto
>   custodes: heu heu nunc premor arte mea.
> fingere tunc didicit causas ut sola cubaret, (1.6.5–11)

Here a new theme begins at line 9. Tibullus reveals that he is responsible for his own deception by Delia because he taught her to deceive her *vir*. The link is conceptual and is between *viro* (8) and *custodes* (10). The *vir* had set *custodes* to watch Delia. Sometimes the link is subtler. E.g.

(3)   te bellare decet terra, Messalla, marique,
>   ut domus hostiles praeferat exuvias:
> me retinent vinctum formosae vincla puellae,
>   et sedeo duras ianitor ante fores. (1.1.53–6)

Here the *domus* of Messalla is implicitly contrasted with the *domus* of Delia where Tibullus sits as an excluded lover before the doors (56).

(4)   illic sit quicumque meos violavit amores,
>   optavit lentas et mihi militias.
> at tu casta precor maneas, sanctique pudoris
>   adsideat custos sedula semper anus. (1.3.81–4)

Line 81 talks about people who have violated Tibullus' love. The first line of the next verse paragraph begins by enjoining on Delia that she remain chaste.

In organising his material over whole elegies Tibullus employs the principle known as 'ring-composition'. This term is used both in a minor and a major sense. In its minor sense it refers to the poet's return at the end of a poem or section of a poem to the initial theme or words of that poem or section. In its major sense, in which it will be used in this chapter, it refers to a mode of composition in which, within a poem or section of a poem, a number of themes are handled one after the other until a central point is reached; then the same themes are rehandled in reverse order. This gives a pattern of the type $A^1 B^1 C^1 D^1 E D^2 C^2 B^2 A^2$. Many variations are possible within rings. For instance the central point may take up one of the themes in the surround, e.g. $A^1 B^1 C^1 B^2 C^2 B^3 A^2$; or the order of two items may be reversed, e.g. $A^1 B^1 C^1 D^1 E D^2 B^2 C^2 A^2$, or $A^1 B^1 C^1 D^1 E D^2 C^2 A^2 B^2$. Another symmetrical arrangement of themes sometimes used by ancient poets is 'parallel-composition'.[3] A set of themes is handled and then rehandled in the same order: e.g. $A^1 B^1 C^1 D^1 A^2 B^2 C^2 D^2$. Parallel-composition admits of the same sorts of variation and refinement as ring-composition; and subtle combinations of the two are possible (for

---

[3] Called 'linear-construction' by T. P. Wiseman, *Cinna the Poet and Other Roman Essays* (Leicester 1974) pp. 64ff.

an example see below, p. 202). Tibullus does not appear to use this pattern, which in general is much less common than ring-composition.

Formal structures and ring-composition in particular have been observed intermittently by scholars since the twenties in many ancient poets and prose-writers from Homer on.[4] D. Lohmann's recent investi-

---

[4] The following bibliography is not complete but may be useful:
Beck, I. *Die Ringkomposition bei Herodot und ihre Bedeutung für die Beweistechnik* (Spudasmata 25, Hildesheim/New York 1971)
Brink, C. O. *Horace on Poetry* II *The 'Ars Poetica'* (Cambridge 1971) pp. 453ff.
Cairns, F. *GC* pp. 117, 145ff., 154, 172f., 185ff., 194, 197ff.
'Theocritus Idyll 10', *Hermes* 98 (1970) 38ff.
'Propertius on Augustus' marriage law (II 7)', *Grazer Beiträge* (forthcoming)
'Two unidentified *komoi* of Propertius: I 3 and II 29', *Emerita* 45 (1977) 351ff.
'Further adventures of a locked-out lover: Propertius 2.17' (University of Liverpool Inaugural Lecture Series, Liverpool 1975);
'The distaff of Theugenis – Theocritus *Idyll* 28', *PLLS 1976* pp. 303f.
Copley, F. O. 'The suicide-paraclausithyron: a study of Ps.-Theocritus, *Idyll* XXIII', *TAPA* 71 (1940) 52ff.
Hamilton, R. *Epinikion: General Form in the Odes of Pindar* (De Proprietatibus Litterarum, Series Practica 91, The Hague/Paris 1974) index of terms *s.v.* Ring Composition
Hanslik, R. 'Tibulls Elegie 1 3' in *Forschungen zur römischen Literatur* ed. W. Wimmel (Wiesbaden 1970) I pp. 138ff.
Illig, L. *Zur Form der pindarischen Erzählung* (Diss. Kiel 1932) pp. 56ff.
Lesky, A. *A History of Greek Literature* (2nd ed. English trans. London 1966) index *s.v.* Ring composition
Lohmann, D. *Die Komposition der Reden in der Ilias* (Untersuchungen zur antiken Literatur und Geschichte 6, Berlin 1970)
Moulton, C. *Similes in the Homeric Poems* (Hypomnemata 49, Göttingen 1977) Ch. 2
Myres, J. L. *Herodotus Father of History* (Oxford 1953) pp. 81ff.
Otis, B. *Virgil: A Study in Civilised Poetry* (Oxford 1963) esp. Chh. 5, 6, 7
Van Otterlo, W. A. A. *Beschouwingen over het archaïsche Element in den Stijl van Aeschylus* (Diss. Leiden 1937)
'Untersuchungen über Begriff, Anwendung und Entstehung der griechischen Ringkomposition' (Medeelingen der Nederlandsche Akademie van Wetenschappen, Afd. Letterkunde, N.R. 7, Amsterdam 1944)
'Die Ringcompositie als Opbouwprincipe in de Epische Gedichten van Homerus' (Verhandelingen der Koninklijke Nederlandsche Akademie van Wetenschappen, Afd. Letterkunde, N.R. 7, Amsterdam 1944)
Richardson, L. Jr. *Poetical Theory in Republican Rome. An Analytical Discussion of the Shorter Narrative Hexameter Poems written in Latin During the First Century Before Christ* (Undergraduate Prize Essays: Yale University Vol. 5, New Haven/London 1944)
Whitman, C. H. *Homer and the Heroic Tradition* (Harvard 1958) esp. Chh. 11, 12
Willcock, M. M. 'Mythological paradeigma in the *Iliad*', *CQ* N.S. 14 (1964) p. 142 n. 2
Williams, G. *Tradition and Originality in Roman Poetry* (Oxford 1968) General index *s.v.* Ring-composition
Wiseman, T. P. *Cinna the Poet and Other Roman Essays* (Leicester 1974) Ch. 3
Woodman, A. J. 'Remarks on the structure and content of Tacitus *Annals* 4. 57–67', *CQ* N.S. 22 (1972) 150ff.
'Actium in Velleius', *Latomus* 25 (1966) 564ff.
Velleius Paterculus The Tiberian Narrative (2.94–131) (Cambridge Classical Texts and Commentaries 19, Cambridge 1977) Indexes I: General *s.v.* ring composition

gation of ring-composition in the speeches of the *Iliad* (see n. 4) has been of particular importance. Surprisingly enough, however, there is little sign of ancient recognition of the practice. The aspects of rhetorical theory which come nearest to ring and parallel structures are the figures of speech chiasmus, antithesis and antistrophe. Fairly elaborate forms of these figures could be practised in antiquity – especially in 'Gorgianic' and later 'Asiatic' oratory; but figures are essentially small-scale features of discourse, and it is hard to extrapolate from them to large-scale modes of arranging material in whole poems or sections of poems. Apart from the lack of a theoretical basis for formal structures in rhetoric, there are few signs of conscious recognition of them in ancient literature and literary criticism. In Latin literature there are a number of resumptive formulae which show an awareness of the practice of returning to the initial theme at the end (e.g. Cic. *Pro Marc.* 33; Hor. *Sat.* 1.1.108 and Lejay *ad loc.*); and the use of similar material for ancient prologues and epilogues is common knowledge. As regards literary criticism, the passages from the *Iliad* scholia and from Eustathius noted by W. Schadewalt and by D. Lohmann (*Komposition der Reden* pp. 2f.) in connection with ring-composition certainly refer to this mode of handling themes, but the scale in which the ancient critics are thinking is small. Proof of the validity of this concept and of its usefulness must therefore derive from analysis of literary texts.

But here there are some further problems. The first is that scholars may well disagree about what the dominant themes are. This is principally because ancient literature is limited in its thematic range, and sometimes in its vocabulary, but is very sophisticated, so that structurally significant and non-significant themes are often hard to distinguish. In future it may be possible to arrive more often at generally accepted structural divisions by relating thematic structure to verse-paragraphs, with which they sometimes coincide; but there remains the difficulty that in some cases at least two different thematic structures may overlap (see below, pp. 208f.). The second problem is that the formal thematic analysis of poetry runs the risk of becoming a dull and uninformative cataloguing of the obvious, with no value except to guarantee the poet's craftsmanship at a mechanical level. To be worth doing, it must be used as an interpretative tool to throw light on what the poet is saying. Demands of space prevent all the analyses in this chapter being exploited fully in this way, but this should not obscure the fact that formal analysis is only a preliminary to something more important. The third problem is to understand the historical role of formal thematic structures in ancient literature. They are not an obscure quasi-mathematical activity, but are, in origin, mnemonic features of oral poetry. They helped the poet to marshal his material, particularly in short

> Young, D. C. *Three Odes of Pindar* (*Mnemosyne* Suppl. 15, Leiden 1971) general index *s.v.* Ring composition and pp. 121 ff. esp. the bibliography at p. 122 n. 1. See also pp. 201ff. and nn. 13, 17 and 18.

non-narrative sections or over longer sections of narrative, and they helped the audience to follow the poet. For a long time all ancient literature continued to be, at least from its audience's point of view, oral, so that the role of thematic structures in assisting the hearer continued to be important long after writing was introduced. By the Hellenistic period formal structures were an integral part and guarantee of literary craftsmanship and this is why they are universal in Hellenistic and Roman poetry.

Thematic structures are used in different ways at different times. In narrative poetry they inevitably alter the narrative order, and in this sense they replace the logic of narrative as early as Homer, although the scale on which this happens is so large that the replacement is unobtrusive.[5] In non-narrative poetry, formal structures can co-exist with and reinforce the inherent logic of the material, as they do in the speeches of Homer;[6] or they can take primacy of place and organise subject-matter which lacks a necessary order, as happens in some Pindaric epinikia (e.g. *Pythian* 10). In the Hellenistic period the use of formal structures as an organising principle was carried one stage further. Some Hellenistic writers, followed by some of the Augustans, ignored the inherent logic of non-narrative material and imposed a formal structure on it arbitrarily, making transitions between different verse-paragraphs on a purely verbal basis. This is why some Hellenistic and Augustan poems, like Pindaric epinikia, may appear to lack unity if the presence and function of their formal structures is not understood. This Hellenistic use of formal structures was partly an imitation of early Greek lyric, and Pindar in particular, and partly a reaction against rhetorical canons. In the fifth and fourth centuries BC rhetoricians concentrated on *logoi*, public or forensic speeches whose order of material was fixed on logical grounds at an early date. The poets rebelled against this order in an effort to differentiate poetry from rhetoric.

Of course poets quickly learned to make the formal sequence of themes appear also to be logically necessary. The new substitute logic compelled readers to compare and contrast the two forms in which a theme was presented and to react emotionally as the poet wished. Augustan poets, and among them Tibullus, are very ingenious at exploiting formal structures in this way. As ancient poetry developed there was a growing tendency to asymmetry in the length of the corresponding sections and of the two halves of formal structures and to a great frequency of minor sophistications in the arrangement of the themes. Both asymmetry and variation in order became frequent by the Hellenistic period. In general, the later an ancient poem, the less obvious the thematic structure is likely to be, up to the Latin Silver Age when this tendency was reversed. All these trends were naturally relative and affected by the needs of different

[5] Cf. Whitman *Homer and the Homeric Tradition* and Moulton, *Similes in the Homeric Poems*. [6] Cf. Lohmann, *Komposition der Reden, passim*.

Ordering

types of poetry.[7] For example, Catullus 64 and 68 have clear structures but this does not mean that they are early examples of the 'epyllion' and elegy, but only that Catullus was experimenting in these poems with two literary types which were fairly new in Roman poetry.

Before Tibullus' use of formal thematic structures is examined, some earlier examples will be analysed. In this way some further aspects of the development of thematic structures in ancient literature may become clearer. First, *Iliad* 6.343–68 will demonstrate how Homer uses ring-composition not just to provide a memorable and pleasing pattern of themes, but for powerful semantic and emotional purposes.[8] This passage consists of a speech made by Helen to Hector together with his reply to her:

> τὸν δ' Ἑλένη μύθοισι προσηύδα μειλιχίοισι·
> 'δᾶερ ἐμεῖο κυνὸς κακομηχάνου ὀκρυοέσσης,
> ὥς μ' ὄφελ' ἤματι τῷ ὅτε με πρῶτον τέκε μήτηρ   345
> οἴχεσθαι προφέρουσα κακὴ ἀνέμοιο θύελλα
> εἰς ὄρος ἢ εἰς κῦμα πολυφλοίσβοιο θαλάσσης,
> ἔνθα με κῦμ' ἀπόερσε πάρος τάδε ἔργα γενέσθαι.
> αὐτὰρ ἐπεὶ τάδε γ' ὧδε θεοὶ κακὰ τεκμήραντο,
> ἀνδρὸς ἔπειτ' ὤφελλον ἀμείνονος εἶναι ἄκοιτις,   350
> ὃς ᾔδη νέμεσίν τε καὶ αἴσχεα πόλλ' ἀνθρώπων.
> τούτῳ δ' οὔτ' ἂρ νῦν φρένες ἔμπεδοι οὔτ' ἄρ' ὀπίσσω
> ἔσσονται· τῷ καί μιν ἐπαυρήσεσθαι ὀΐω.
> ἀλλ' ἄγε νῦν εἴσελθε καὶ ἕζεο τῷδ' ἐπὶ δίφρῳ,
> δᾶερ, ἐπεί σε μάλιστα πόνος φρένας ἀμφιβέβηκεν   355
> εἵνεκ' ἐμεῖο κυνὸς καὶ Ἀλεξάνδρου ἕνεκ' ἄτης,
> οἷσιν ἐπὶ Ζεὺς θῆκε κακὸν μόρον, ὡς καὶ ὀπίσσω
> ἀνθρώποισι πελώμεθ' ἀοίδιμοι ἐσσομένοισι.'
>   Τὴν δ' ἠμείβετ' ἔπειτα μέγας κορυθαίολος Ἕκτωρ·
> 'μή με κάθιζ', Ἑλένη, φιλέουσά περ· οὐδέ με πείσεις· 360
> ἤδη γάρ μοι θυμὸς ἐπέσσυται ὄφρ' ἐπαμύνω
> Τρώεσσ', οἳ μέγ' ἐμεῖο ποθὴν ἀπεόντος ἔχουσιν.
> ἀλλὰ σύ γ' ὄρνυθι τοῦτον, ἐπειγέσθω δὲ καὶ αὐτός,
> ὥς κεν ἔμ' ἔντοσθεν πόλιος καταμάρψῃ ἐόντα.
> καὶ γὰρ ἐγὼν οἰκόνδε ἐλεύσομαι, ὄφρα ἴδωμαι   365
> οἰκῆας ἄλοχόν τε φίλην καὶ νήπιον υἱόν.
> οὐ γὰρ οἶδ' εἰ ἔτι σφιν ὑπότροπος ἵξομαι αὖτις,
> ἦ ἤδη μ' ὑπὸ χερσὶ θεοὶ δαμόωσιν Ἀχαιῶν.'
> *Helen spoke to him with honeyed words: 'Brother-in-law to me, who am an evil-devising, horrible bitch, I wish that on the day that my mother bore me a harsh squall of wind had carried me off to the mountain or to the*

---

[7] The problem is akin to that of generic development. Cf. *GC* Ch. 3.
[8] This passage is treated by Lohmann, *Komposition der Reden* pp. 101f. with somewhat different thematic divisions.

wave of the billowing sea and that the wave had carried me away before these things had come to pass. But since the gods have decreed that these evils should take place, then I wish I had been the wife of a better man who took some account of the anger and the insults of men. But my husband's mind is not firm nor will it ever be and I think he will reap his reward from it. But come now and sit down on this chair, brother-in-law, since troubles have gathered round you thick and fast because of me, bitch that I am, and because of the deceitful behaviour of Paris — we two upon whom Zeus has placed an evil fate so that men may sing of us in time to come.' Great Hector of the flashing helmet replied to her 'Do not ask me to sit down, Helen, although it is kind of you. You will not persuade me, for my spirit is already eager to help the Trojans who have great need of me in my absence. But you arouse your husband and let him make haste so that he may catch up with me inside the city. For I will go to my house so that I may see my servants and my dear wife and my little child, since I do not know whether I shall come back to them from war or whether the gods will now lay me low at the hands of the Greeks.'

It can be analysed as follows, omitting the 'stage directions', 343 and 359:

Helen:	A¹	(344–8)	I wish I had *died* at birth
	B¹	(349–51)	I wish I had a better *husband* than Paris
	C¹	(352f.)	Further attacks on *Paris*
	D¹	(354–6)	Hector's *weariness/trouble*
	E	(357f.)	The eternal fame of Helen and Paris in generations to come
Hector:	D²	(360–2)	The Trojans' *trouble*
	C²	(363f.)	Rouse *Paris* to meet me inside Troy
	B²	(365f.)	I shall go home to see my *wife* and *child*
	A²	(367f.)	I do not know whether I shall return from battle or *die* in battle

Several aspects of this passage are worth examining from the general viewpoint of thematic structures. First, the question whether the same word or words appear in two treatments of the same theme. In this particular passage it is clear that Homer is sometimes deliberately avoiding the repetition of the same word in corresponding sections. The words for death in the two A passages are different. In the B passages the word for wife in the first is ἄκοιτις (350), in the second is ἄλοχον (366). The word πόνος (trouble) in D¹ (355) is not repeated in D², although the concept is again evoked. In this way the poet ensures that the audience is not bored by a large number of verbal correspondences coming on top of the thematic correspondences. This is not to say that there are no verbal correspondences in this passage. Paris is referred to as 'this fellow' with two forms of οὗτος in the two C passages (τούτῳ, 352 and τοῦτον, 363). The word 'sit down' in 354 (D^1) – ἕζεο – is cognate in form to 'do not sit me down' – κάθιζ' in 360 (D^2). In general the most influential factor is clarity. Where the correspondence is obvious conceptually, additional verbal help is less likely to be required. The more difficult the thematic symmetry is to establish in conceptual terms, the more likely it is that the poet will assist his audience with a verbal clue. Another relevant factor is date, since as time went on, poets and audiences became more sophisticated and sensitive in this area and the need for verbal correspondences was reduced. This is why Hellenistic and Roman thematic correspondences rarely offer a verbal clue.

Another aspect too is characteristic of formal structures. Homer deliberately creates verbal correspondences which are outside his thematic structure. For example in line 344 (A^1) and line 355 (D^1) the repeated address to Hector with the word δᾶερ (brother-in-law) may be noted. Again in line 349 (B^1) Helen says of the gods 'they so ordained these evils'. In line 357 (E) she reiterates this notion in reminiscent terms which like 349 include a form of κακόν – 'to whom Zeus has assigned this evil destiny'. Such verbal cross-currents are clearly intended to provide variety and a counter-interest to the thematic structure. The audience is expected not only to detect the underlying conceptual symmetry, but to do so in spite of deliberately trailed red herrings in the form of aberrant verbal correspondences. The poet's procedure is interestingly reminiscent of the 'irrational correspondences' between simile and narrative which have been detected as a phenomenon of some ancient poetry.[9]

Another technical subtlety of this Homeric passage lies in the quantitative relationships of the parts of the thematic structure. They are as follows: the central theme (E) is two lines long. D^1 and D^2 are both three lines long. C^1 and C^2 are both two lines long. The central portion of the ring thus involves exact numerical responsions. But at the beginning and end of the ring the situation changes. B^1 has three lines, B^2 two lines. A^1 is five or, if 347 is an interpolation, four lines long, while A^2 is only two lines long. This is of course a simple-minded way of looking at a passage of ancient poetry; but, has been noted (above, p. 196), regularity in quantitative response seems to be more characteristic of early thematic structures.

Finally, Homer's structure is not only an organisational or mnemonic device but is also meaningful. He never represents Helen as an out-and-out villain but always as a victim of the gods or fate or circumstances. In Dorian cities Helen was a racial heroine, if not a goddess, and rhapsodists telling the story of the Trojan War in these places had to exercise caution in their treatment of her. Literary considerations also demanded in an epic principal characters of rounded dimensions, perhaps prone to fault, but

---

[9] Cf. D. West, 'Multiple-correspondence similes in the *Aeneid*', *JRS* 59 (1969) 40ff.; and 'Virgilian multiple-correspondence similes and their antecedents', *Philol.* 114 (1970) 262ff.

always great and always retaining audience sympathy. But at the same time Homer and his audience could not simply regard Helen as an unfortunate woman afflicted by the gods and they would not have wished to commend her behaviour to their own wives as a model. That is why Homer makes Helen condemn herself out of her own mouth, shows that as a sinner she suffers unhappiness in her sinful state and places her in situations where her underlying lack of moral worth demonstrates itself. So here, he juxtaposes her with Hector and uses his structure to imply judgements about their relative worth and the sufferings Helen has caused.

Homer's method is one of slow build-up from line 360. D^2 begins a process of contrast. In D^1 Helen had commiserated with Hector for the trouble which he suffered because of the sins of herself and Paris. In D^2 Hector first pushes aside Helen's concern for himself (360) and then makes an open-hearted declaration of sympathy, not for his own troubles but for those of his people, the Trojans. C^2 reinforces this contrast in the attitudes of Helen and Hector. In C^1 Helen had inveighed bitterly against Paris, but in C^2 Hector, who has been put to mortal suffering and danger because of Paris and Helen, simply tells Helen to rouse Paris. There is no word of direct reproach of Paris, although indirectly his words are a riposte to Paris' last utterance at 341. B^2 is even more telling. Helen in B^1 wished that she had a better husband than Paris while Hector in B^2 mentioned his faithful wife and his little child. Homer's audience knew the story of the fall of Troy before they heard the *Iliad*, so that Hector's mention of his wife and child is a master-stroke of dramatic irony and pathos. On one side we have a woman of dubious morality who wishes she had a better husband, by which she means a better lover, since her husband was not Paris but the abandoned Menelaus. On the other side we have a good man, whose faithful wife will be carried off into slavery and whose helpless child will be dashed to death from the walls of Troy. A^2 sets the seal on the implicit criticism. In A^1 Helen self-indulgently wished that she had died at birth, but in A^2 Hector calmly and unsentimentally lays down the two possible results of his own impending foray into war. Either he will return, or he will die at the hands of the Achaeans. The audience know that eventually Hector will in fact die in this way.

At no point here or elsewhere does Hector reproach Helen and indeed, later in the *Iliad* when Hector's body is brought back to Troy, Helen bewails his death saying 'You never spoke a harsh word to me' (*Iliad* 24.767). But Hector's speech, contrasting thematically point by point with hers, conditions the audience's view of Helen. Her empty self-reproach, her hostility to her lover, Paris, her attempts to sentimentalise Hector's role in the war and to obtain his favour by suggesting that he is particularly troubled by the war and by contrasting him with Paris, are set against Hector's refusal to reproach anyone for the difficulties he endures, his thought for the sufferings of others rather than for his own sufferings, his failure to reproach Helen and his anticipation of his own death with courage and without sentimentality. The central theme (E), here as often in ancient formal structures,[10] contains the most significant item in the passage. It emphasises the moral implication of the dialogue: Helen's words about the 'evil destiny' of herself and Paris underline that most common of all Greek moral notions, that the sinner must suffer. This passage is also, of course, self-referent and anachronistic. When Helen speaks of herself and Paris being sung of by future generations, she is referring to the *Iliad* itself. Homer is stressing that the heroic deeds glorified in epic are also, for the agents, suffering and horror: the epic is both κλέα ἀνδρῶν and κήδεα.[11] It was because of such lessons that Homer was regarded throughout antiquity as the supreme moral instructor.[12]

As well as using ring-composition in speeches, Homer uses it in narrative, both in large blocks[13] and in *exempla*, which are small sections of narrative.[14] Hesiod and the lyric poets again appear to use it. A Hesiodic example is *Theogony* 720–819;[15] and in Alcaeus it is found, for instance, in Frr. 129 and 130 (13–39) (LP). Among the later lyric poets ring-composition is particularly clear in Pindar (e.g. *Olympian* 7; and see above, Chapter 5, pp. 114f.) where it involves both narrative and non-narrative material. In Attic tragedy it occurs in narrative (e.g. Aeschylus, *Agamemnon* 184–205)[16] and in speeches (e.g. the speech of Polyneices at Euripides, *Phoenissae* 469–96). This latter passage deserves brief examination:

A¹	(469–72)	Truth is simple
B¹	(473–80)	I once made a just agreement to avoid war and departed from Thebes
C	(481–3)	Eteocles broke the agreement
B²	(484–93)	I am willing again to make a just agreement to avoid war and send my army away from Thebes
A²	(494–7)	My words are simple truth

To some extent the passage works like the Homeric ring examined above. C is the crux of Polyneices' case: its brevity and finality stress this. In B¹ the emphasis is mainly on Polyneices' voluntary withdrawal and on the agreement between him and his brother (lines 473–8). Avoidance of strife occupies only two lines (479–80). B² again emphasises the new agreement which Polyneices says he is now willing to make (lines 484–7) but more space is given to the warfare and destruction which will ensue if Polyneices does not obtain his rights (lines 488–91). Although he is arguing about

---

[10] Cf. on this topic L. A. Moritz, 'Some "central" thoughts on Horace's *Odes*', *CQ* N.S. 18 (1968) 116ff.
[11] Hom. *Od.* 8.73 and 9.15. [12] Cf. Ch. 1 p. 29 and n. 126.
[13] See Whitman, *Homer and the Homeric Tradition* and Moulton, *Similes in the Homeric Poems*. [14] E.g. *Il.* 24.602–13 and Eustathius *ad loc.*
[15] Cf. West *ad loc.* and General Index *s.v.* ring-composition.
[16] See Fraenkel *ad loc.*

justice and about the agreement between himself and his brother, his case in fact relies very much on the threatening presence of the army which accompanies him. The repetition of B therefore comments implicitly on Polyneices' speech, gives an insight into his character and reveals the true nature of the debate in progress. The repetition of A has other functions. It softens the impression of iron-fistedness given by the principal part of B^2; it re-emphasises the justice of Polyneices' case and leaves this final notion in the hearer's mind. Thus it reinforces the end of B^2, the implication that Polyneices' exile is contrary to the laws of gods and men. A^2 also reintegrates Polyneices' speech into the play by its address to Jocasta in line 494. The Euripidean ring might appear simpler than that of Homer, in that the number of discrete sections is smaller. But this is a question of division: it might be possible to analyse B^1 and B^2 in greater detail and so split them into more sections. In general terms Polyneices' speech is, like the Homer passage, more or less quantitatively symmetrical: A^1 has four lines and A^2 three; B^1 eight and B^2 ten. Thus twelve lines precede and thirteen follow the central section, a type of arrangement which seems to be characteristic of some such speeches in Attic drama (cf. Euripides, *Hippolytus* 433–85).

A brief inspection of some Hellenistic poems employing formal structures will lead in to an examination of Tibullus' elegies in the same terms. First, Theocritus, *Idyll* 28:[17]

A^1	(1f.)	The distaff
B^1	(3–5)	Miletus and Theocritus
C^1	(6–9)	Nicias and Theocritus
D^1	(10–14)	Theugenis
A^2	(15f.)	The distaff
B^2	(17f.)	Syracuse
C^2	(19–21)	Nicias and Miletus
D^2	(22f.)	Theugenis and Theocritus
A^3	(24f.)	The distaff

In many Hellenistic and Roman poems one half of the structure is noticeably longer than the other. *Idyll* 28 does not have this characteristic, but it does exemplify another feature of post-classical thematic structures in combining the ring and parallel form. It possesses the ring feature of having as its first, middle and last sections variations on the same theme, but it also contains a prominent parallel structure. The readers of *Idyll* 28 clearly had to be more sophisticated than earlier audiences in identifying formal

---

[17] This is a slightly more precise version of the analysis offered at F. Cairns, 'The distaff of Theugenis – Theocritus *Idyll* 28', *PLLS 1976* pp. 298f.

structures. But on the other hand, the actual correspondences are clear enough. The Miletus/Syracuse equivalence, where a reader might for a moment be uncertain, is confirmed by the mention of the founders of the two cities, Neleus and Archias. Moreover, it does not seem that the reader of *Idyll* 28 was meant to perceive semantic implications or overtones in the recurrence of themes, as he was obliged to do with Homer and Euripides. The repetitions are simply cumulative. They give more information about the distaff, Theocritus, Nicias and Theugenis, but they do not undercut or place in a new perspective the information previously given. This does not mean that Theocritus is a simpler writer than his predecessors, but only that since he is using the formal structure to impose an arbitrary order upon the themes he does not also aim at making the structure meaningful.

A longer Theocritean idyll (18), the Epithalamium of Helen, will illustrate Theocritus' use of a formal structure on a larger scale, and will also reveal a greater degree of asymmetry in the corresponding sections than did *Idyll* 28. But it shows a similar lack of interest in exploiting the structure to enhance meaning, except by accumulation of detail.

A^1	(1–8)	The chorus of maidens dancing and singing the epithalamium
B^1	(9–15)	The sleep of Menelaus
C^1	(16–21)	Congratulation of Menelaus who is to be son-in-law of Zeus; their children
D^1	(22–4)	The chorus' past exercises with Helen by the Eurotas
E	(25–37)	Eulogy of Helen
D^2	(38–48)	The chorus' gathering of flowers without Helen in the country tomorrow
C^2	(49–53)	Greeting to Menelaus and Helen; their children and descendants
B^2	(54f.)	The sleep of Menelaus and Helen
A^2	(56f.)	The chorus' *diegertikon* tomorrow

+ one line of Hymeneal song (58)

E, the central part, contains the all-important topic of praise of Helen; and two cross-currents are worth mentioning. These are the numbers 'twelve' at line 4 (A^1), and 'four times sixty' at line 24 (D^1); and the garlands at line 2 (A^1) and at line 40 (D^2). It is interesting that these appear in a simpler and more straightforward structure than was found in *Idyll* 28. There is asymmetry between occurrences of the same theme and between the two halves, but it is not achieved by consistent expansion of one group of themes. The count is: A^1 8, A^2 2(3); B^1 7, B^2 2; C^1 6, C^2 4; D^1 3, D^2 11.

Tibullus' use of ring-composition varies in complexity but is always highly meaningful.[18] A short and easy example can begin the examination, Tibullus 2.2:[19]

A^1	(1–4)	A well-omened and honorific reception for Natalis
B^1	(5–8)	Invocation of the Genius
C^1	(9f.)	May he grant Cornutus' birthday wish
D	(11–16)	The actual wish: the faithful love of Cornutus' wife for him
C^2	(17)	Cornutus' birthday wish will be fulfilled
B^2	(17–20)	Invocation of Amor
A^2	(21f.)	Prayer to Natalis

Here there is fairly pronounced asymmetry in the corresponding sections, the repeated themes C^2–A^2 occupying only six lines as against the ten lines which they occupy in their first appearance. B^2 and A^2 reveal Cornutus not just as a man celebrating his birthday but as a potential father whose celebrations and worship of his Genius are part of an activity seen essentially as a means of ensuring the continuity of his family. The central position given to the love of Cornutus' wife stresses this aspect further (cf. Theocritus, *Idyll* 17.40ff. for the concept). Tibullus is making pronounced use of the formal structure as a means of organising his ideas.

A more complex and longer Tibullan example is 2.5, already discussed in Chapter 3:

A^1	(1–10)	Phoebus, come and show favour to your new priest, Messalinus! Come in triumphal laurel and the dress of citharode!
B^1	(11–18)	Since you are patron of prophets (including the Sibyl) inspire Messalinus in his interpretation of the Sibylline books!
C^1	(19–38)	The Sibyl gave Aeneas her books before the foundation of Rome, when Pan and Pales were the gods of the rustics
D^1	(39–50)	She prophesied Aeneas' settlement in Italy and the successful wars he would fight,
E	(51–66)	and the foundation and future world domination of Rome,
D^2	(67–78)	to be followed by civil wars prophesied and portended by the Sibyls but now over

---

[18] Structural analyses of Tibullan elegies have been offered by various scholars but not always in terms of ring and parallel composition. Among recent works cf. e.g. Ball (*passim*); R. J. Ball, 'The structure of Tibullus 1 7', *Latomus* 34 (1975) 726ff.; J. M. Fisher 'The structure of Tibullus' first elegy', *Latomus* 29 (1970) 765ff.; R. Hanslik, 'Tibulls Elegie 1 3' in *Forschungen zur römischen Literatur* ed. W. Wimmel (Wiesbaden 1970) I, pp. 138ff.;H. Musurillo S.J., '*Furtivus Amor*: the structure of Tibullus 1.5', *TAPA* 101 (1970) 387ff.

[19] For a treatment of the content of this elegy cf. *GC* pp. 112f.

Ordering

C² (79–104)   A description of the rustic festival of the Parilia
B² (105–14)   Phoebus, assist my love!
A² (115–22)   so that I may celebrate Messalinus, when he will enjoy a victor's triumph. Hear my prayers, Phoebus!

The analysis has been made in such a way that the first and second descriptions of themes do not always instantly reveal their identity. Any other procedure would have been unfair to Tibullus. His poetic skill often lies in his ability to vary his two handlings of the same theme so as to leave the thematic identity recognisable, but only after the pleasurable difficulty of making the identification. A considerable degree of asymmetry between the two treatments of the same theme often, as here, accompanies this feature. The imagined future triumph of Messalinus, treated over six lines (115–20) in A², is anticipated in A¹ (5) by the single word *triumphali*, describing the bay Phoebus is to wear when he comes to show favour to Messalinus (cf. 117f.). More delicate and amusing is the contrast of B¹ and B²: in B¹ Phoebus, as the patron of prophets, is to authorise and instruct the *XVvir* Messalinus' interpretation of the Sibylline books; in B² Phoebus, as the patron of poets, is to promote Love and the love-affair of Tibullus. The connection between these two sections lies partly in the standard prophet/poet equivalence of antiquity. But Phoebus' protection of poets (B²) also provides an argument addressed to Tibullus' mistress Nemesis (113f.), who is essential to his poetry (111f.). Its purpose is to induce her to be kind to her poet, Tibullus, but only so that he can celebrate Messalinus (A²), who was, we remember, to be inspired by Phoebus (B¹). Tibullus helps his readers to grasp the connections by using the ambiguous word *vates* of the Sibyl at 18 in B¹, and again of her in the centre-piece E at 65, but of himself in B² at 114. The formal structure here helps to emphasise that commonplace notion of much ancient encomiastic poetry, the identity of interest of the speaker and addressee,[20] themes A and B being repeated in such a way as to stress it. In D¹ Tibullus is fairly specific about the wars of Aeneas which will precede the foundation of Rome. In contrast he is much less exact in his account of the Civil Wars (D²). One reason is obvious: Tibullus did not want to reopen old wounds. Another reason is that he wanted to concentrate attention on the whole troupe of Sibyls (see above, pp. 76f.). The connection which Tibullus is implying between the wars of Aeneas and the Civil Wars involves the concept which, as I have emphasised elsewhere,[21] is at the heart of Virgil's *Aeneid*, namely that the Trojans and Latins were one people who had been brought to civil strife by Turnus, an alien interloper. As the war between Latin and Trojan ended with the triumph of Aeneas, the establishment of *concordia* and the glorious

[20] Cf. *GC* pp. 222ff.
[21] F. Cairns, 'Geography and nationalism in the *Aeneid*', *Liverpool Classical Monthly* 2 (1977) 109ff.

rise of Rome, so, Tibullus is insinuating, the Civil Wars which have ended with the triumph of the *Iulii*, the family of Aeneas, will usher in a new *saeculum* of *concordia* in which Rome will again rise to world conquest. Messalinus will bring in the new age as a *XVvir* in charge of the Saecular Games, and he will also be one of Rome's new conquering heroes. The relationship between c^1 and c^2 has already been explored in Chapter 3 (see pp. 79ff.). The central point E is given to the all-important theme of the future greatness of Rome.

Tibullus 2.5 introduces several repeated words and concepts counterpointing the ring structure. There are five invocations of Phoebus by name in two different *sedes*, and he is addressed once as Apollo. Initial *Phoebe* (1, A^1) corresponds with fifth-foot *Phoebe* (121, A^2), while *Phoebe* occurs at the same initial *sedes* in 17 and 106 (B^1 and B^2). The fifth invocation occurs in the centre-piece E at 65, in the same fifth-foot *sedes* as at 121 (A^2). This is appropriate since the centre-piece often echoes the first and last sections. The address to Apollo (79, c^2) in final position is deliberately outside the symmetry. The many invocations of course remind the reader that the elegy is a hymn to Phoebus. The bay occurs at 5, 63, 81, 83 and 117. The occurrences at 5 (A^1) and 117 (A^2) are symmetrical, and that at 63 is in the central section (E), a phenomenon parallel to the invocations of Phoebus. But those at 81 and 83 are not part of the formal structure, occurring as they do again in c^2, but without a mate in c^1. *Amor* occurs at 39 and 106 (D^1 and B^2). His introduction at 39 as the brother of Aeneas is probably meant as an anticipatory justification of his later appearance.[22] It shows that the love-god is not a foreigner to Roman history: therefore the celebration of Roman greatness by a love-poet and his appeal for help to Phoebus, patron of Augustus, are not out of place. But the two references also counterpoint the ring. Two final significant thematic correspondences reinforce a point made earlier about the invocations to Phoebus. Wishes for perpetual virginity, expressed in syntactically identical clauses, supporting in one case an affirmation and in the other a prayer, occur at 64 (E) and 122 (A^2). Again, the long hair of Phoebus is mentioned at 8 (A^1) and 121 (A^2) and that of the Sibyl at 66 (E). It is clear that the hair and bay motifs and the invocations of Phoebus draw the elegy together at all its focal points and that the prayer for virginity links the centre section with the final one by anticipating the introduction of Diana. Thus the conceptual unity of the whole elegy is constantly stressed.

Tibullus 2.5 then is characteristic of his use of ring-composition. The themes are handled so as to highlight similarities and differences between their first and second occurrence and to convey implicitly the poet's sentiments about his subject-matter. There is a tendency to weight the second handling of a theme slightly in terms of size and significance; and

---

[22] The *Roma–Amor* palindrome may also be relevant. For a similar play on *Amor–Roma* cf. Ov. *Am.* 2.9.14; 15 and 17.

finally the formal structure is, as has been shown, counterpointed by correspondences which cut across the ring and also have their own intrinsic artistic function.

The same approach yields results with 1.4:

A^1	(1–6)	Tibullus asks Priapus, a successful lover, to act as 'teacher of love' and tell him how to win boys
B^1	(7–14)	Priapus expounds the dangerous attractions of boys
C^1	(15–26)	and advises their lovers to be persevering and ready to swear to anything
D	(27–38)	and above all timely, because youth passes quickly
C^2	(39–56)	The lover must do whatever the boy wishes and then he will be successful
B^2	(57–72)	Boys must favour poets, their immortalising songs and their love, rather than money
A^2	(73–84)	Tibullus proclaims that he too is a 'teacher of love' but an unsuccessful lover

There is even more asymmetry in length of corresponding sections in 1.4 than in 2.5, the second half of the ring consisting of noticeably larger sections than the first. The repetition of themes, as in 2.5, gives a subtle flavour of diversity in similarity. C^1 consists of general precepts to the lover: C^2 is particularised advice illustrating and adding to and putting into practice those general precepts. A^2 and B^2 clarify and comment upon A^1 and B^1 in an ironic fashion. The dangerous attractions of boys (B^1) turn out to be those which captivate love-poets like Tibullus (B^2), who offer their songs rather than cash. B^2 is so placed as to reinforce the irony of the revelation (A^2) that Tibullus' request to Priapus for erotic precepts (A^1) is made not so that Tibullus can act as a teacher of love towards others but because Tibullus, in contrast to Priapus, is an unsuccessful lover.

The central passage (D) is given its pride of place for two reasons. First, it is a particularly important consideration in homosexual as opposed to heterosexual love. Once the boy had matured he was no longer attractive and this increased the normal urgency of the lover's passion. Second, the prominence of the topic emphasises the unusual use to which Tibullus has put it. Normally the transience of youth is an argument put by the lover to the beloved boy on his own behalf.[23] Here however it is used to urge the lover not to delay his wooing until the boy has grown too old.

As usual there are recurrent themes which undercut the formal structure. The heat and dryness of the dog-days is mentioned at lines 6 and 42 (A^1 and C^2): Priapus, who endures the extremes of heat naked, advises the lover who wants to be successful to be prepared to endure heat. The

---

[23] Cf. e.g. *AP* 11.51 (Anon.); *AP* 11.53 (Anon.); *AP* 12.31 (Phanias); *AP* 12.33 (Meleager); *AP* 12.39 (Anon.); *AP* 12.197 (Straton); *AP* 12.215 (*Id.*); *AP* 12.224 (*Id.*). Cf. also *AP* 12.229 (Straton).

nakedness of Priapus (5f., A¹) implies that the god has no money.[24] Later at 57ff. (B²) the theme recurs when Priapus mounts an attack on money. Patience and the good effects of lapse of time are illustrated in 15–20 (C¹). But the reverse of this theme, that is, the need for timely action and the evil effects of lapse of time, are the subject of 27–38 (D). Finally there are contrasting vignettes of the formerly unyielding beautiful boy (33f.) in his sad old age (D), the former mercenary beautiful boy who later becomes a castrate priest of Cybele (67–70) (B²), and the poet-lover in his old age, enjoying the honoured status of 'teacher of love' (79f., A²).

It should not be assumed that once a structure of this type has been identified in a Tibullan elegy, the last word has been said about the arrangement of material. For one thing, a single section or part-section may contain within itself a ring or parallel arrangement of material just as significant as those detected within the elegy as a whole. Tibullus 2.6.1–10 seems to fall into a small ring, the sections being picked out, as often, verbally:

a¹	(1f.)	Macer is off to war (*castra*): will Amor take *arma* and go with him?
b¹	(3f.)	Love imagined as equipped with weapons (*telis*) off on his journey to war (note: *aequora*)
c	(5f.)	Love, punish the runaway Macer
b²	(7f.)	If Love will not, Tibullus imagines himself off to war with his helmet (*galea*, note: *aquam*)
a²	(9f.)	Tibullus will go off to war (*castra*) – goodbye to Venus – he too has a *tuba*

Moreover, there can be cases where part or all of a poem could be analysed simultaneously on two different levels. This fact of course explains some scholarly disagreement over thematic questions. In overall terms Tibullus 1.9 could be divided up as follows:

A¹	(1–6)	Marathus' treachery which has caused a breach between him and Tibullus, and its punishment
B¹	(7–28)	Vituperation of wealth – the weapon used by Tibullus' rival – Marathus will be punished
C¹	(29–38)	Tibullus is ashamed of his former credulity
A²	(39f.)	May Marathus' girlfriend deceive him and thus punish him
C²	(41–50)	Tibullus is now ashamed of the credulous help he gave to Marathus over this girl
B²	(51–78)	Vituperation and curses upon Tibullus' rival who is already being punished

[24] Cf. Ov. *Am.* 1.10.15ff. and above, pp. 37f.

A³ (79–84) Marathus' punishment and Tibullus' renunciation of him

But if sections A¹ and B¹ are regarded as a single unit and analysed as such they break down into:

a¹ (1f.) Marathus' *concealed* treachery (infidelity) against Tibullus
b¹ (3–6) The *punishment* of treachery
c¹ (7–12) *Gain* as the cause of it
b² (13–16) Marathus will be *punished*
c² (17–20) *Gain* as the cause of infidelity
b³ (21–4) The *punishment* of treachery
a² (25–8) although it is *concealed*

This little ring has an extra refinement analogous to the major ring above. Its centrepiece is the same as the second and second last theme.

Again, if B² and A³ are analysed as one unit, the same kind of result is obtained; and naturally the theme of gain turns up again:

a¹ (51) Tibullus' renunciation of Marathus,
b¹ (51f.) because he seeks *gain*
c¹ (53) The rival who has corrupted Marathus with gifts
d¹ (54–8) May his wife constantly be unfaithful to him – with Marathus among others
e (59–64) The rival's drunken harlot of a sister
d² (65–74) The rival's wife – further evidence of her infidelity – with Marathus among others
c² (75f.) Marathus and the rival
b² (77f.) Marathus has left Tibullus for *gain*
a² (79–84) Tibullus' renunciation of Marathus

The fact that two overlapping analyses are possible does not show that the whole process of formal analysis is unsound. Rather it reveals how complex and highly wrought Tibullan elegy is, in this as in every other respect.

Some hint of further possible interpretative uses of formal analysis can be obtained by an examination of Tibullus 2.3 and 2.4. These two elegies resemble 1.8 and 1.9 in that, like them, they are contiguous poems sharing themes and situation. The character of Nemesis and its effects on Tibullus are identical, as is Tibullus' striking espousal of wealth and rejection of aspects of his standard *persona* (see pp. 154f.). The two elegies, when analysed, also turn out to have the same type of formal structure, that is ring-composition with one displacement of theme at the same point. They also present analogous themes at the same places in their structure. This shows that Tibullus wrote them as complementary poems to be read against each other. The reader thus derived pleasure from the subtle contrast not just of two treatments of a single theme in a single elegy but four treatments of the same, or of two analogous themes, in two elegies. The analyses can be set down side by side for ease of comparison:

		2.3		2.4
A¹	(1–10)	Tibullus will go off and work in the country since Nemesis is there	(1–12)	Tibullus wishes respite from his sufferings as a lover, which amount to slavery
B¹	(11–28)	Apollo became a rustic for love	(13–20)	Poetry as a path to a girl's favour is useless
C¹	(29–34)	Golden Age/Iron Age	(21–6)	So Tibullus will get money by resorting to crime and sacrilege
D¹	(35–48)	Attack on *praeda*	(27–34)	Attack on luxurious commodities which make women bad and cruel
E	(49–50)	Girls are won by wealth – Tibullus will become wealthy	(35–8)	Beauty combined with greed causes all the trouble and degrades love
D²	(51–60)	and give Nemesis luxurious goods	(39–44)	Attack on mercenary and cruel mistresses
B²	(61–8)	Rejection of countryside/ Invocation of Bacchus	(45–51)	The protreptic praise in poetry of a good woman is useless
C²	(69–76)	Golden Age/Iron Age	(52–4)	So Tibullus will sell his patrimony to get money
A²	(77–80)	But Tibullus must go to hard labour and slavery in the country since his mistress is there	(55–60)	Tibullus will accept any sufferings as a lover, provided that Nemesis looks favourably on him

2.3 is, initially at any rate, a more optimistic poem than 2.4. Over the pair Tibullus slips further and further into degradation and the structural parallelism emphasises this. At the beginning of 2.3 Tibullus, it appears, has simply been deprived of Nemesis' company by her departure; and it seems he only has to go into the countryside and endure hard labour there to remedy this loss (A¹). He can readily cite Apollo's service to Admetus for love's sake as a justification for going into the countryside (B¹). The beginning of 2.4 however is much darker: Tibullus is in a state of servile misery: he is chained and punished, whether he is at fault or not (A¹). Moreover instead of citing some action of Apollo to justify a proposed remedy for his situation, he has no cure in mind. Instead he wishes all kinds of sufferings on himself rather than his present position; and he follows these despairing fantasies up with a declaration that poetry and Apollo are useless to a lover (B^1) – a marked contrast to the role played by Apollo in the corresponding section of 2.3. The Apollo material in 2.3 is followed by Tibullus wistfully looking back to the Golden Age and contrasting it with modern times. However the corresponding section of 2.4 sees Tibullus deciding to obtain money by violence and sacrilege. Both elegies in D^1 share a closely contiguous theme. But in 2.3 it is a generalised attack on *praeda* in a high moral tone which shows a social interest, whereas in 2.4 Tibullus attacks luxurious commodities only within the narrow sphere of his own amorous concerns. This contraction of his horizon is a sign of his increasing degradation.

The centre points of 2.3 and 2.4 again show interesting differences. In 2.3 the trend of the elegy is shown by a sudden volte-face on Tibullus' part in E. He decides to become wealthy in order to win Nemesis. The place of greatest importance in the elegy is given to this theme because it is the first time it has occurred and this elegy is about the beginning of Tibullus' moral deterioration. However in 2.4 his degeneration has already reached such depths that it would have been anticlimactic to repeat the theme in the central place. Instead the leitmotiv of both elegies comes at E in 2.4, when Tibullus asserts that the real problem is the combination in women of beauty and greed. In 2.3 the change of attitude is followed up in D^2 where Tibullus contradicts D^1 and explains that he wishes to shower Nemesis with luxury goods. But in 2.4 greater suffering has embittered Tibullus so much that he continues in D^2 his attack on greedy beauty, begun in D^1. Again the particularisation and personal note of hostility is prominent: Nemesis is directly addressed and the details are unpleasant.

In 2.3, after his change of mind, Tibullus goes back to two themes from the first part of the elegy: the gods and countryside and the Golden Age. He first continues the trend of E and D^2 in B^2 which, as was noted, comes out of strict ring sequence. The countryside is rejected as an ideal place for lovers. But in C^2 Tibullus then returns to wistful thoughts of the Golden Age before concluding the elegy in A^2 with a return to his resolve to go into the countryside to see Nemesis. But the vision he now has of life in the countryside is even more realistic than that of A^1. He will be accepting there slavery and punishment. Pessimism has prevailed, and it is this pessimism which recurs at the beginning of 2.4. Whether *hic* or *sic* should be read in 2.4.1, Tibullus has tried the only remedy he knew and, as he expected, the result has been nothing but suffering.

As befits the developing situation, the last part of 2.4 is black without remission. Tibullus first (B^2) reiterates obliquely his earlier statements in B^1 that poetry is useless as a means of winning over a beloved. He again particularises, giving a sample of the kind of protreptic advice which a poet (*moneo*, 51) might give to a woman in order to encourage her to be faithful to him. But he immediately acknowledges that although true, such statements have no influence on love. This leads him to a fresh resolve to obtain money in order to forward his passion (C^2). This time he thinks not of crime and sacrilege but of selling his ancestral estate. He thus moves from criminal to socially unacceptable behaviour. But this should not be seen as a dampening of his ardour or as a check on his degradation. Rather it shows the progress of his immorality, because the latter course is more practical and realistic and his recourse to it is more likely. The final section (A^2) shows Tibullus accepting every and any degradation, provided only that Nemesis smiles on him. Thus it is the culmination of the process observed over the two elegies. The formal structures of the two elegies play a significant role in underlining and reinforcing the moral implications of the situation.

The emphasis placed so far on thematic structures should not disguise the possibility of detecting in Tibullus and other ancient poetry other kinds of structure. For instance some poems of Tibullus reveal a clear 'temporal' structure.[25] 1.5 can be seen in this way:

A	Past	(1)	Tibullus' boast
B	Present	(2–10)	His repentance
A	Past	(11–17)	Tibullus' services
B	Present	(17f.)	The rival has possession of Delia
A	Past	(19f.)	Tibullus' dreams
C	Future	(21–34)	As he expressed them then
B	Present	(35f.)	His dreams are shattered
A	Past	(37–47)	Tibullus' unsuccessful attempts to forget Delia
B	Present	(47f.)	The *lena*
C	Future	(49–58)	Curses on the *lena* (in subjunctive but note: *eveniet*, 57)
B	Present	(59f.)	The rich rival
C	Future	(61–6)	The poor and devoted lover
B	Present	(67–74)	The rich rival admitted, Tibullus excluded
C	Future	(75f.)	Tibullus threatens a reversal (although still in present tense)

This structure is meaningful not only in terms of Hellenistic interest in constant temporal change (see pp. 117ff.; 176ff.) but also in semantic terms. The temporal differences distinguish the harsh reality of the present to which Tibullus is constantly forced to return from his fantasies both in the past and in the future. The elegy shows a movement from the past to the future

---

[25] On such questions cf. H. Musurillo S. J., 'The theme of time as a poetic device in the elegies of Tibullus', *TAPA* 98 (1967) 253ff. On temporal structures in the *Odes* of Horace cf. P. H. Schrijvers, 'Comment terminer une ode?', *Mnemosyne* s.IV 26 (1973) 140ff. esp. 144ff.; 151f.

as present disillusion about the past is replaced by illusions about the future. The greater space usually devoted to the past and future as opposed to the present illustrates Tibullus' plight and balances the ruthless impact of reality which keeps forcing Tibullus' thoughts back to the present.

This temporal structure coexists with and reinforces a thematic structure of normal ring form in 1.5:

A^1	(1–8)	Tibullus' pangs of unrequited love
B^1	(9–18)	Tibullus' past unsuccessful services to Delia
C^1	(19–36)	Tibullus' past unfulfilled wishes about life with Delia
D	(37–46)	Delia's beauty makes a substitute impossible
C^2	(47–58)	Tibullus' future, and to-be-fulfilled, wishes for the *lena*
B^2	(59–66)	The *pauper*'s (i.e. Tibullus') future services to Delia, which Tibullus hopes will be successful
A^2	(67–76)	Tibullus is excluded, while his rival is admitted; but there is hope

This chapter leaves unanswered several major questions which could be asked about formal structures. For instance, how are the different types of thematic analysis applied to Tibullus 1.9 related? Are formal and temporal structures linked and if so, how? How consciously did poets use these structures or readers perceive them? Before the first two questions can be answered a great deal of further work needs to be done on these aspects of ancient poetry. As for the third, the very habituation of antiquity to formal structures may make it meaningless. On the other hand, it can be stated with confidence that the employment of formal thematic structures is the hallmark of a professional poet in antiquity and that from the critical viewpoint analysis of them can reveal the craftsmanship of the poet and many subtleties of his meaning. In Roman elegy in particular, formal analysis is an essential *ancilla* to the study of Propertian and Ovidian elegies where unity is in doubt. No argument about unity can afford to be without a section on thematic structure and conversely, any scholar arguing against the unity of an elegy which demonstrably has a symmetrical and complete thematic structure must do so at his peril. As for Tibullus, his formal structures guarantee that he cared for the form in which he wrote and that he was an organised craftsman in full control of his thought and of its expression. Thus they reveal in yet another area his status as a professional Hellenistic poet.

9
'THE ORIGINS OF LATIN LOVE-ELEGY'

Throughout this book an attempt has been made to link Tibullan elegy with the principles and practice of Hellenistic Greek poetry, which in turn has been seen as a concentrated reworking of early Greek poetry. In this final chapter the question of the historical relationship between Roman elegy, including the work of Tibullus, and the elegy of the Hellenistic and early Greek periods will be discussed. The chapter title is also that of A. A. Day's famous work.[1] Day, in his first chapter, dealt with the most intractable problem in ancient elegy. This is that the Roman elegists write about erotic matters in the first person and claim they are writing about their own experiences – the 'subjective' Latin love-elegy – while the Hellenistic poets, whom the Roman elegists regard as their predecessors, seem, on the basis of their surviving fragments, to be doing something completely different. Their erotic elegiac passages are third-person narrations of the emotions and experiences of mythical and historical characters, that is, they are 'objective' erotic elegy. In the nineteenth and early twentieth centuries, there was considerable controversy over this problem.[2] One side believed in a lost Hellenistic and earlier Greek subjective elegy in which Greek elegists had anticipated Roman elegy and told of their own loves. The other side maintained that Hellenistic love-elegy was always third-person and objective and that the Hellenistic elegists did not write subjective love-elegy. For them the Roman elegists were making an original contribution when they wrote subjective first-person elegy; and they were influenced to do so by a wide variety of Greek literature in addition to Hellenistic elegy.

Day reviewed the progress of the controversy up to his own time in an astringent and authoritative fashion. He came down heavily in favour of the second side, claiming that the hypothesis of a Greek 'subjective' love-elegy was both unfounded and unnecessary. He showed convincingly that the Roman elegists exploited a great many sources besides Greek elegy, for example New Comedy, rhetoric and epigram, in order to combine the length and imaginative wealth of Hellenistic 'objective' elegy with the personal character of Hellenistic epigram.

Day's work, with its clear-cut distinction between 'subjective' and 'objective' and its simple verdict, has won general approval. It had few

[1] *The Origins of Latin Love Elegy* (Oxford 1938).
[2] Summarised by Day, *Origins* pp. 1ff.

reviews, partly because its importance was not appreciated when it was published and partly because it appeared just before the outbreak of the Second World War. Some of the few reviews were mildly unhappy about Day's conclusions;[3] and there have been some later protests. But there has never been a full re-examination of Day's arguments.

Characteristic of the later protests[4] against Day's views is that of J.-P. Boucher.[5] Boucher claimed that the whole problem was a pseudo-problem, because the distinction between 'subjective' and 'objective' was false. He argued correctly that Roman elegy in not genuinely autobiographical. The Roman elegists are assuming a *persona*, that of the elegiac lover-poet, which is a self-conscious construct, and each poet gives this construct, or rather his own version of it, his personal name. Boucher concludes that in this sense Latin love-elegy is just as 'objective' as Hellenistic love-elegy, because in each the erotic heroes are characters and not the poets themselves. This is an ingenious view and one which certainly focuses the problem more accurately, but does not in fact remove or solve it. There remains the important distinction that Hellenistic elegists wrote in the third person about mythical and historical characters, while Roman elegists write in the first person about a construct to which they attach their own name. The problem of 'subjective' and 'objective' elegy in this sense therefore remains a real one and this chapter offers a new solution to it.

It must be made clear at the outset that this new solution will not involve denying the modern consensus about this problem. Some Latin 'subjective' love-elegy is certainly a reworking of Hellenistic 'objective' elegy.[6] Roman elegists do imagine themselves in the emotional situations of the heroes of Hellenistic elegy and so transform 'objective' into 'subjective' elegy (see above, p. 9). But this is only part of the truth and in isolation it offers an unsatisfactory account of the development of Roman elegy. Day dealt with each fragment of Greek elegy and *testimonium* for Greek subjective love-elegy individually and, quite naturally, found them wanting. His subsequent chapters treat other sources of inspiration for subjective Latin love-elegy, all correct and important. But his book is to some extent motivated by a desire to claim for Roman elegy originality and independence of Greek sources. However, there is overwhelming evidence that all Augustan literature is indebted to Greek literature and that the Augustans

---

[3] Cf. L. P. Wilkinson, *JRS* 29 (1939) 273f.; R. Helm, *Philolog. Wochenschr.* 59 (1939) 1000ff.; H. W. Prescott, *CPh.* 35 (1940) 102f.

[4] E.g. P. Fedeli, 'Properzio 1,3 Interpretazione e proposte sull' origine dell'elegia latina', *Mus. Helvet.* 31 (1974) 23ff.; D. O. Ross Jr, *Backgrounds to Augustan Poetry: Gallus, Elegy and Rome* (Cambridge 1975) pp. 51f.

[5] J.-P. Boucher, *Caius Cornélius Gallus* (Bibliothèque de la Faculté des Lettres de Lyon 11, Paris 1966) pp. 99f.; Newman (pp. 365ff.) also doubts the reality of the subjective–objective division.

[6] Cf. F. Cairns, 'Propertius i.18 and Callimachus, *Acontius and Cydippe*', *CR* N.S. 20 (1969) 131ff., and see above, pp. 111f.

knew this and believed it both inevitable and right. Horace, for example, did not try to claim that *satura quidem tota nostra est*, but attempted to point to Greek origins. Day then begins with the wrong presupposition and advances his position by brilliant advocacy. But his views do create serious literary-historical difficulties which are worth summarising before the evidence is re-examined.

First, Day's solution relied on a sharp distinction between subjective erotic elegy and other types of 'subjective' elegy, for which there is no ancient evidence. On the contrary, the Roman elegists treat erotic themes subjectively in addition to and in combination with political, social, literary, symposiastic, moral and other themes. Second, both sides in the controversy admitted that 'subjective' erotic epigrams in the elegiac metre were commonly written in the Hellenistic period. These are distinguished from elegies only by their length. Length was an important concept in Hellenistic poetry but there is no evidence that literary theory required writers composing elegiac poems of over ten or twelve lines to avoid subjective erotic content. Third, some of Theocritus' longer erotic poems in other metres make the distinction look frail, namely *Idylls* 2, 3, 12, 29 and 30 (cf. also Ps.-Theocritus 20 and 23). It is true that the speaker in these idylls is certainly or probably not Theocritus, but rather Simaetha (2), an unnamed goatherd (3), and unnamed lovers (12, 29, 30). But in the latter cases the gap between the *persona* of the speaker and the *personae* which Roman elegiac poets adopt is slight; and it is hard to see why we should believe that Theocritus could write in this way in other metres while no Hellenistic poet could use elegy for subjective erotic purposes. Fourth, it is difficult to understand why two of the Roman elegists constantly claim to be inspired by Mimnermus, Philetas and Callimachus if all the love-elegies of these Greek poets were narrative and if they never at any point wrote anything more like Roman love-elegy.[7] Fifth, in the absence of a Greek subjective erotic elegy, Catullus' elegiac poems, and in particular 68, have no literary context, no precedent and no place in the development of the form. Finally, if we deny that there was any Greek subjective love-elegy, then a suspiciously large part in the development of Latin love-elegy must be credited to Cornelius Gallus, of whose work almost nothing survives and about whom there is little reliable information.

These difficulties more than justify a fresh look at the evidence. Most of the surviving fragments of early Greek elegy treat military, political, social or moral themes and are attributed to Mimnermus, Callinus, Solon, Tyrtaeus and Theognis. Early Greek elegy often exhorts to bravery, propounds a view of the state or of the current condition of the city, urges to political action, or inculcates social *mores* and personal morality. The fragments are almost all subjective, some are erotic and certain individual elegies, especially those of Solon, are long. A few of the erotic pieces are by

[7] This point troubled some of Day's reviewers. See above, p. 215 and n. 3.

Mimnermus, while the majority are part of the Theognidean corpus.[8] Both are important for the question under discussion. Mimnermus was regarded as the originator of Greek subjective erotic elegy by those scholars who believed in its existence, an assessment founded primarily on four pieces of evidence: first Mimnermus Fr. 1(D); second, the fact that Mimnermus wrote an elegiac work named, after his mistress, *Nanno*; thirdly, six lines of the Hellenistic poet Hermesianax, which are part of his account of the loves of poets in his elegiac poem, the *Leontion*:

>   Μίμνερμος δέ, τὸν ἡδὺν ὃς εὕρετο πολλὸν ἀνατλὰς   35
>   ἦχον καὶ μαλακοῦ πνεῦμα τὸ πενταμέτρου,
>   καίετο μὲν Ναννοῦς, πολιῷ δ' ἐπὶ πολλάκι λωτῷ
>   κημωθεὶς κώμους εἶχε σὺν 'Εξαμύῃ,
>   ἤχθεε δ' 'Ερμόβιον τὸν ἀεὶ βαρὺν ἠδὲ Φερεκλῆν
>   ἐχθρόν, μισήσας οἷ' ἀνέπεμψεν ἔπη.   40
>   (Fr. 7.35–40 (Powell))

And Mimnermus who, after much endurance, invented the sweet sound and breath of the soft pentameter, fell in love with Nanno and afterwards, with the grey lotus-pipe bound to his lips, went on revels with Examues. He hated Hermobios who was always loathsome to him and Pherekles, his enemy, and in hating them what verse he used in his reply!

and fourthly, a Propertian reference to Mimnermus: *plus in amore valet Mimnermi versus Homero* (Propertius 1.9.11).

Day was sceptical about the evidence for subjective elegy by Mimnermus (pp. 3ff.),[9] but the passage of Hermesianax in particular cannot be brushed aside as Day does. It is undeniable that Hermesianax believed Mimnermus had loved a girl called Nanno, and had written verses against his enemies Hermobios and Pherecles. A further conclusion about Hermesianax's views can be drawn from the symmetry of thought between lines 37f. on one hand and lines 39f. on the other. In lines 39f. he refers to Mimnermus' written works attacking Hermobios and Pherecles; in 37f. he speaks of his love for Nanno and his komoi with Examues. Now there is a standard ancient poetic convention whereby a poet can be said to do something which he writes about.[10] Hence it is certain that lines 37f. also

---

[8] Cf. the excellent discussion of this material in M. L. West, *Studies in Greek Elegy and Iambus* (Untersuchungen zur antiken Literatur und Geschichte 15, Berlin/New York 1974) pp. 5ff.; 40ff. For Mimnermus cf. also S. Szádeczky-Kardoss, *Testimonia de Mimnermi Vita et Carminibus* (Acta Universitatis Szegedinensis, Sectio Antiqua 1959, Minora Opera ad studium antiquitatis pertinentia 2); and *R-E* Suppl. 11 *s.v.*

[9] It is interesting to contrast with Day's scepticism the statement of M. L. West, unbiased by preconceptions about Roman elegy, *Greek Elegy and Iambus* p. 12: 'Mimnermus is represented by Hermesianax ... as playing the pipes on many a κῶμος with Examyes, which presumably had some basis in his poems.'

[10] Cf. Thuc. 1.5.2; Virg. *Ecl.* 6.46; Hor. *Sat.* 1.10.36f.; 2.5.41; Prop. 2.30.19ff.; 3.3.39ff.; Stat. *Silv.* 2.7.77f.

refer to Mimnermus' work: Hermesianax believed that Mimnermus wrote poetry about his love for Nanno and about going on erotic komoi with Examues, just as he composed attacks on his enemies.

Now it might be objected that Hermesianax is an unreliable witness. But two considerations must be borne in mind. First, from our point of view, the beliefs of a Hellenistic writer about archaic Greek elegy are in many ways just as useful as facts. Even if they are invalid about archaic Greek poetry, they can tell us something about Hellenistic poetry. If Hermesianax believed that Mimnermus had written subjectively in his *Nanno*, it is all the more likely that Hermesianax himself did so in his *Leontion*. Secondly, although the value of Hermesianax's information about the loves of poets is admittedly variable – no one, for example, would take seriously what Hermesianax says about Homer having been in love with Penelope[11] – there is reason to take him seriously here. He was from Colophon, a town which claimed Mimnermus too as a citizen.[12] This makes it probable that Hermesianax was personally acquainted with Mimnermus' poetry and derived his 'facts' about Mimnermus from it. Another possible alternative or joint source for Hermesianax's knowledge of Mimnermus is worth mentioning. Mimnermus was a highly revered figure in Ionia. There was in the Roman period a gymnasium called the Mimnermeion at Smyrna, Mimnermus' place of birth.[13] Such cult centres were common in the late Classical and Hellenistic periods[14] and there would almost certainly have been one at Colophon in the Hellenistic period. A Mimnermeion would have contained works of the poet and a commemorative inscription. The inscriptional remains from the site of a parallel Hellenistic cult of an ancient poet, the Archilocheion at Paros,[15] give a clue about what the inscription might have been like; and Hermesianax would have known it. For various reasons then it is probable that Hermesianax was writing with more than his usual authority when he relates Mimnermus' love for Nanno and komoi with Examues, and hence that Mimnermus did write at least some subjective erotic elegy.

The Theognidean corpus confirms that archaic Greek elegy could easily handle erotic themes subjectively and at some length.[16] It is printed in modern editions as a series of short isolated poems, most of epigrammatic length, but M. L. West[17] presents a different view of its original form. He

[11] Fr. 7.27ff. (Powell).
[12] Cf. *R-E* Suppl. 11 p. 939. M. was a Smyrniote; but his ancestors came originally from Colophon and he himself lived there at the end of his life.
[13] Cf. Szádeczky-Kardoss, *Testimonia* p. 17 No. 31.
[14] Cf. Arist. *Rhet*. 1398b; Diog. Laert. 1.88; Fraser I p. 313 and II Ch. 6 nn. 56f. and the works cited by him; N. M. Kontoleon, 'Νέαι ἐπιγραφαὶ περὶ τοῦ Ἀρχιλόχου ἐκ Πάρου', Ἀρχαιολογικὴ Ἐφημερίς 1952 (1955) 50f.; M. Treu, *Archilochos* (Munich 1959) p. 207 and see above, nn. 12 and 13.
[15] Cf. Kontoleon, Ἀρχαιολογικὴ Ἐφημερίς 1952 (1955) 50f. and 'Zu den neuen Archilochosinschriften', *Philol*. 100 (1956) 29ff.; Treu, *Archilochos* pp. 40ff.; 205ff.
[16] Wilkinson, *JRS* 29 (1939) 273f.
[17] *Greek Elegy and Iambus*.

states that some of the pieces can be recognised as excerpts from what were originally longer poems and concludes: 'it is *a priori* very credible that Theognis composed extended elegies in the style of Mimnermus, Solon, Xenophanes, and others' (p. 40). West notes a fairly long fragment, 237–54, as an example of Theognis' capacity for extended writing and describes even it as 'hardly a complete poem' (p. 41). If West is right and the corpus originally contained longer poems or even if the present extracts were written down as if linked, then here was archaic subjective elegy which included erotic elegy in the love-poems addressed to the boy Cyrnus. If this form of the corpus survived to the Hellenistic period, then it could have stimulated Hellenistic subjective erotic elegy. The close association between erotic, political and moral themes in the corpus is worth stressing because the same combination of themes recurs in Roman subjective love-elegy.

To sum up: archaic Greek elegy is almost entirely subjective, it contains pieces of some length, and sometimes treats erotic subjects in combination with other themes. Theognis certainly did write subjective elegiac poetry about his love for the boy Cyrnus, and Mimnermus probably wrote it about his love for the Lydian flute-girl Nanno. When we move on to the Hellenistic period it is no surprise to find that the first candidate as a writer of subjective love-elegy is another Colophonian, Antimachus, who worked around 400 BC. On the testimony of Hermesianax and Plutarch[18] Antimachus composed a work, the *Lyde*, called after his wife, to console himself for her death. In this book he recounted the griefs of the heroes, presumably their erotic losses. Writing about Antimachus' *Lyde*, Day makes a concession which he quickly shrugs off but which not only undercuts his position but is the key to the new view which I shall offer. He writes: 'Part of the elegy, however, probably the introduction, may have been concerned with the poet's grief, real or imagined . . .' (p. 11). This concession had already been made by H. E. Butler and E. A. Barber when they briefly laid down in the introduction to their commentary on Propertius the position later amplified by Day. Speaking of Antimachus' *Lyde* they remark:[19] 'There is no evidence that the personal element extended beyond the frame of the poem.' It is indeed entirely probable that the function of the *Lyde* was revealed within the poem and was not merely known from external evidence; and a prologue or epilogue would be the natural place for such a revelation. As well as detailing his grief, Antimachus must also have rehearsed his love for his wife. This emerges from Ovid, *Tristia* 1.6.1: *nec tantum Clario est Lyde dilecta poetae* and from six more lines of Hermesianax, also from the *Leontion* 'loves of the poets' passage:

Λυδῆς δ' Ἀντίμαχος Λυδηίδος ἐκ μὲν ἔρωτος
πληγεὶς Πακτωλοῦ ῥεῦμ' ἐπέβη ποταμοῦ·

[18] Cf. Day, *Origins* p. 10.   [19] *The Elegies of Propertius* (Oxford 1933) intr. p. liii.

†δαρδανη δὲ θανοῦσαν ὑπὸ ξηρὴν θέτο γαῖαν
κλαίων, αιζαον † δ' ἦλθεν ἀποπρολιπὼν
ἄκρην ἐς Κολοφῶνα, γύων δ' ἐνεπλήσατο βίβλους
ἱράς, ἐκ παντὸς παυσάμενος καμάτου.   (Fr. 7.41–6 (Powell))
And Antimachus, struck by love of Lydian Lyde, went to the stream of the river Paktolos . . . and when she died he buried her beneath the dry earth weeping . . . and leaving . . . he went to high Colophon and filled his sacred books with lamentations and so escaped from all his toil.

When the opponents of Greek subjective elegy have conceded this point, it is perhaps unnecessary to argue it further. Certainly the onus of proof would lie with anyone who wanted to deny that there was at least a subjective frame to the *Lyde*; and if Antimachus wrote a subjective prologue or epilogue about his love and loss, it is even more likely that in a similar passage or passages of his *Nanno*, Mimnermus had done the same. Again, if at the very beginning of the Hellenistic period such a piece of subjective erotic elegy was possible, is there any reason to doubt that Philetas wrote at least one elegiac poem in which narrative material was preceded or followed or linked by a subjective erotic passage? In this way the *testimonium* of Hermesianax about Philetas becomes more comprehensible:

Οἶσθα δὲ καὶ τὸν ἀοιδόν, ὃν Εὐρυπύλου πολιῆται
Κῷοι χάλκειον στῆσαν ὑπὸ πλατάνῳ
Βιττίδα μολπάζοντα θοήν, περὶ πάντα Φιλίταν
ῥήματα καὶ πᾶσαν τρυόμενον λαλιήν.   (Fr. 7.75–8 (Powell))
And you know the poet whom the Coan citizens of Eurypylus set up in bronze beneath the plane tree, singing of his volatile Bittis, Philetas worn out with his research on every word and every dialect.

These lines refer to an actual statue on Cos – no doubt erected by the citizens in connection with a cult of Philetas of the type discussed above (p. 218). It would seem ultra-negative to insist that all Philetas' works about his love for Bittis were short epigrams if a hundred years before Antimachus has written a subjective elegiac passage in his *Lyde*. If the character 'Philetas' in Longus' *Daphnis and Chloe* reflects the poet Philetas, as was suggested in Chapter 1 (pp. 25ff.), then the reconstructed picture of Philetas' poetry can be filled out with further details.

What of Hermesianax himself, another Hellenistic poet? His *Leontion*, again named after his mistress, consisted mainly of love-stories. Again there seems little point in Hermesianax writing such a work if no portion of it explained for whom and why the book was so named and constituted, particularly if the book's predecessors had already done similar things or even if Hermesianax merely thought they had. In addition, the very nature of Hermesianax's long catalogue, to which Propertius 2.34 and Ovid,

Tristia 2 might be compared, suggests that Hermesianax was justifying through parallels his own combination of personal erotic poetry and myth. Of the *Apollo* of Alexander Aetolus, made up of stories of tragic love-affairs between men and women, and of the Ἔρωτες ἢ καλοί of Phanocles, a catalogue of the loves of heroes for beautiful boys, no specific information is available but the same general considerations apply.

The argument so far is this: once it is realised that some archaic Greek subjective love-elegy still survives and that more was written, then the *a priori* case against Hellenistic subjective love-elegy collapses. The two sides of the controversy can then be reconciled: the concession made by the sceptics about subjective frames can be accepted and amplified. Frames can involve not only prologue and epilogue sections but also link-passages; and together these can add up to a fair proportion of a work. It is these parts of objective Hellenistic elegies which constitute Hellenistic love-elegy. This means that there is no need to hypothesise discrete Hellenistic subjective elegies of the Roman type; or to assume that there was a large amount of Greek subjective erotic elegy.

It may be objected that frames, prologues, epilogues and link-passages are a somewhat vague answer to the question about Hellenistic subjective love-elegy, particularly when none of the ones hypothesised survive. In order to understand the nature of these passages it may be worth considering the most famous and best represented Hellenistic poetry book, Callimachus' *Aetia*. This work is not named after a woman nor are its link-passages etc. erotic, but it does consist of narratives linked by subjective passages and some of the narratives are erotic. The subjective portions of the *Aetia* are highly informative. In the prologue to the *Aetia* – Fr. 1 (Pf.) – Callimachus gives an account of a literary controversy in which he or, to avoid the biographical fallacy, the *persona* 'Callimachus' is taking part. This account includes criticisms made of Callimachus by others and his rebuttal of them (1–8, 17–20, 31f.). Callimachus states his own literary preferences in his predecessors' work (9–16). He also relates how at the beginning of his poetic career he was instructed by Apollo what to write (21–8) and how he obeyed the god (29f.). In addition Callimachus says that he is now old and is suffering from the weight of his years (33ff.). Secondary sources reveal that in the fragmentary *Dream*, Fr. 2 (Pf.), Callimachus described a Heliconian dream vision in which he met the Muses, just as Hesiod did in the *Theogony*. At one point, Fr. 7.13f. (Pf.), Callimachus requests the Muses to grant immortality to his elegies. The epilogue, Fr. 112 (Pf.), is fairly obscure; but it ends with a statement that Callimachus' next work will be his *Iambi* (9). All this material is subjective: Callimachus makes first-person statements about his literary experiences, feelings, intentions and preferences. In this respect the *Aetia* are exactly parallel to the Roman programmatic elegies influenced by them, e.g.

Propertius 2.1, 2.30A and B, 3.1, 3.2 and 3.3, Ovid *Amores* 1.1, 2.1 and 3.1, all of which are subjective literary elegies.

In another portion of the *Aetia*, the location of which cannot be determined, Callimachus appears in his own 'person' in a different but equally interesting context: in Fr. 178 (Pf.) he relates how at a celebration of a feast he found himself sharing a dining-couch with Theugenes of Icus. Callimachus noticed that his dining companion shared his own preference for moderate drinking. He then quoted a proverb about the pleasure of conversation over wine and went on to ask Theugenes questions about his native customs, to which the Ician replied. The whole scene is subjective and ostensibly autobiographical, and as well as being redolent of old Greek elegy, the symposiastic setting is reminiscent of the *convivium* which symbolises and is the background to Roman erotic elegy. Again the sententiousness of the discussion of wine and conversation both recalls the tone of earlier elegy and hints at Callimachus' adoption of a didactic role analogous to that of the Roman elegiac poets' role of teacher of love. Finally there are five fragments of the *Aetia* in which Callimachus is asking questions of the Muses: Frr. 3; 7.19ff.; 76; 79; 86 (Pf.), and one long passage in which the Muses and Callimachus conduct a dialogue: Fr. 43.46ff. (Pf.). The frequent appearance of the narrator as a linking device in this long narrative work and the framing of the objective *Aetia* within a 'subjective' prologue and epilogue suggests a pattern for reconstructing the books of erotic elegy discussed above.

Within the present context the *Aetia* is interesting in another way too. It reveals how Hellenistic narrative elegy is related not only to archaic narrative elegy but also to early Greek hexameter poetry. The appearance of the narrator himself at certain points in a narrative poem is of course as old as Homer.[20] But the real link between archaic hexameter works and Hellenistic elegy is Hesiod's *Theogony*, which is clearly designated as the *Aetia*'s model in its prologue, Fr. 2 (Pf.) and again in its epilogue, Fr. 112.5f. (Pf.). Callimachus chose the *Theogony* as a model for the *Aetia* for several reasons. One was clearly that the *Theogony* is both erotic and aetiological, consisting as it does of learned genealogies. Another was that he wished to revive the scene of Heliconian inspiration from the beginning of the *Theogony* (22ff.). A third must have been the fact that imitation of the *Theogony* gave him access to the whole field of Hesiodic catalogue poetry. This is hinted at in the *Aetia* epilogue, which, as was noted above, first makes a final bow to Hesiod and then closes with a terminal formula which at first seems to resemble that of many Homeric Hymns. However the Callimachean example is a real programmatic formula instead of a conventional one, as such formulae became or were considered in the Homeric Hymns:[21]

[20] Cf. e.g. *Il.* 1.1ff.; 2.484ff.; 11.218ff.; 14.508ff.; 16.112ff.; *Od.* 1.1ff.
[21] Cf. Richardson on *Hymn to Demeter* 495.

χαῖρε, σὺν εὐεστοῖ δ' ἔρχεο λωϊτέρῃ.
χαῖρε, Ζεῦ, μέγα καὶ σύ, σάω δ' [ὅλο]ν οἶκον ἀνάκτων·
αὐτὰρ ἐγὼ Μουσέων πεζὸν [ἔ]πειμι νομόν.
(Callimachus Fr. 112.7ff. (Pf.))
Farewell, and return with better fortune. Farewell to you also Zeus, preserve the whole house of the kings. But I am off to the Muses' prose pasture.

In addition, there seems little reason for Callimachus to allude at the end of the *Aetia* to the end of a Homeric Hymn, particularly since he ended none of his own hymns in this way. It may well be that Callimachus is alluding here not to Homer but again to Hesiod's *Theogony*. The *Theogony* in modern texts ends with

αὗται μὲν θνητοῖσι παρ' ἀνδράσιν εὐνηθεῖσαι
ἀθάναται γείναντο θεοῖς ἐπιείκελα τέκνα. (1019f.)
These are the goddesses who slept with mortal men and as immortals brought forth god-like children.

But in at least some ancient texts the first two lines of the *Catalogue of Women*, a long catalogue of heroines who loved gods or men, were tacked on to the *Theogony*:[22]

νῦν δὲ γυναικῶν φῦλον ἀείσατε, ἡδυέπειαι
Μοῦσαι Ὀλυμπιάδες, κοῦραι Διὸς αἰγιόχοιο.
But now, sweet-voiced Olympian Muses, daughters of aegis-bearing Zeus, sing of the tribe of women.

It may be that Callimachus knew such a text and modelled the end of the *Aetia* on it, ending as he did with an anticipation of his next work. It was of course the *Catalogue* which provided the pattern for Hermesianax, Alexander Aetolus and Phanocles.

There are then two main strands of influence on Hellenistic subjective love-elegy: the subjective but non-erotic frames of Hesiodic erotic catalogue poetry written in hexameters, which must have been the predecessors of Mimnermus' subjective erotic frame for his erotic narrative in elegiacs; and the Mimnerman, Theognidean and doubtless more widespread subjective erotic elegy with a strong symbouleutic bias. Originally this paraenetic aspect of elegy may have been prominent only in homosexual love-elegy, although it is not impossible that Mimnermus exploited it in heterosexual circumstances. Antimachus of Colophon appears to have combined Mimnerman form and Theognidean function – in his case specifically for self-consolation. Other writers doubtless fol-

---

[22] This is a complex problem. For a full discussion see Hesiod *Theogony* ed. M. L. West (Oxford 1966) pp. 48ff.; 397ff.; 437.

lowed suit, extending the paraenetic use of elegy fully to heterosexual as well as to homosexual poetry.

The importance of the subjective erotic frames of Hellenistic narrative elegies lies in their relationship with the narrative content. It is clear that the Greek elegists were emphasising analogies between themselves and their heroes and in doing so they created or implied poetic *personae* for themselves. It was this which encouraged the Roman elegists to go one stage further, to identify rather than analogise and to expand the process of subjectivisation by adding to their own erotic *personae* all the emotions and experiences of the love-sick heroes of Greek narrative erotic elegy.

The advantage of seeing Roman elegy not as a completely new departure but as a logical expansion and development of Greek subjective elegy is that the contribution of each Roman poet can be seen more clearly. The 'canon' of Roman elegiac poets set down first by Ovid and confirmed by Quintilian contains four names: Gallus, Tibullus, Propertius and Ovid himself. In spite of moribund controversies over the mutual influence of Tibullus and Propertius[23] the canon can be regarded as chronologically accurate. But it is not, and was never intended to be, a complete list of Romans who had written elegy, but only of those who had written a great deal of elegy or written it exclusively. The first extant Roman elegies are Catullus 65, 66, 67 and 68. 65 is a subjective elegy which forms an introduction to 66, an objective elegy translating a poem of Callimachus. It functions exactly like the hypothesised prologues of Greek narrative elegies. Although it is not erotic, it refers to Catullus' own loss of his brother and says that the translation of Callimachus is being offered to Ortalus in spite of Catullus' grief at his loss. 67 employs komastic themes and deals with clandestine love, but 68 is the most interesting from the viewpoint of subjective love-elegy. In the prologue we are told that Allius has lost his mistress to a rival and is seeking consolation from Catullus while Catullus himself has lost his brother through death and is also grief-stricken. In the body of the elegy Catullus consoles Allius, and incidentally himself, by writing a poem which includes much mythological material but is throughout a subjective erotic elegy. The myth concerns the tragic love of Protesilaus and Laodamia, cut short by death, and in this way Allius and Catullus are both consoled in their respective losses.

Catullus 68 thus contains the basic ingredients of Antimachus' *Lyde*: loss of a loved one, in Allius' case to another and in Catullus' case to death, and consolation of the grieving parties through the telling of a tragic love-story. Catullus 68 thus looks back to yet another function of the elegiac metre which probably influenced Antimachus to use it instead of the

---

[23] Esp. F. Jacoby 'Tibulls erste Elegie', *RhM* 64 (1909) 601ff.; *RhM* 65 (1910) 22ff. = *Kleine philologische Schriften* (Berlin 1961) II pp. 122ff. and R. Reitzenstein, 'Noch einmal Tibulls erste Elegie', *Hermes* 47 (1912) 60ff. (much more sensible on the general relationship between the two poets).

hexameter for his *Lyde* – its association with death, mourning and consolation. What is clearly new in Catullus 68 as opposed to the hypothesised Hellenistic Greek subjective erotic elegy is that from a structural point of view it subordinates myth to reality. In Hellenistic Greek elegy the erotic material must have been structurally subordinate to the narrative elements. But in Catullus 68 the Laodamia myth illustrates subjective erotic material which revolves around it but has primacy of place. The twin griefs and consolations of the speaker and addressee dominate the thematic pattern and meet in the mythical centre-pieces. The characteristics of Catullus 68 can be appreciated more accurately once it is seen as the first Roman refinement upon a Greek subjective erotic elegy. The careful structural symmetry, the heavy trappings of simile and the learning and ornate language are appropriate to its forebears while the bold *macrologia* of subjective erotic themes, the novel abbreviated and subordinated treatment of myth and the striking juxtaposition of erotic and familial love[24] are Catullus' own contributions.

It is not absolutely certain of course that Catullus was the first Roman elegiac poet to write subjective love-elegy. Varro Atacinus, born in 82 BC, who wrote among other works an elegiac poem entitled *Leucadia* after his mistress, is another possible candidate: Ovid's description of his work suggests that it too was a work with subjective erotic elements, perhaps of the Greek 'frame' type:

> is quoque, Phasiacas Argon qui duxit in undas,
>   non potuit Veneris furta tacere suae.   (Ovid, *Tristia* 2.439f.)

But this question is not particularly important and, from a literary-historical viewpoint it is perhaps more worthwhile to stress the role of Parthenius of Nicaea in influencing his younger contemporary Gallus, the first of the Roman canon, and perhaps Propertius too. Parthenius wrote an *Epikedion* for his dead wife Arete and an *Encomium of Arete* in three books. The latter work, and possibly the former also, contained myth, otherwise it could hardly have filled three books. Parthenius was regarded by later critics as a Hellenistic poet in direct line of descent from Callimachus and Philetas and this work must have resembled the hypothesised Hellenistic elegies with subjective frame and narrative content. Parthenius was Virgil's teacher and was also closely linked with Cornelius Gallus. He dedicated to Gallus a collection of synopses of tragic love stories (*Erotika Pathemata*) which had been treated by Hellenistic poets:

> Μάλιστά σοι δοκῶν ἁρμόττειν, Κορνήλιε Γάλλε, τὴν ἄθροισιν τῶν ἐρωτικῶν παθημάτων, ἀναλεξάμενος ὡς ὅτι μάλιστα ἐν βραχυτάτοις ἀπέσταλκα. τὰ γὰρ παρά τισι τῶν ποιητῶν κείμενα τούτων, μὴ

---

[24] See C. W. Macleod, 'A use of myth in ancient poetry', *CQ* N.S. 24 (1974) 82ff. and cf. Cat. 72.3f. and Kroll *ad loc.*

> αὐτοτελῶς λελεγμένα, κατανοήσεις ἐκ τῶνδε τὰ πλεῖστα· αὐτῷ τέ σοι
> παρέσται εἰς ἔπη καὶ ἐλεγείας ἀνάγειν τὰ μάλιστα ἐξ αὐτῶν ἁρμόδια.
> (Erotika Pathemata ad init.)
> I thought, Cornelius Gallus, that this collection of unhappy love stories
> would be particularly suitable for you and that is why I collected them and
> set them out as briefly as possible. The collection will inform you of most
> aspects of those of them which are narrated in certain of the poets in an
> allusive and fragmentary form; and it will be possible for you to introduce
> into your hexameter and elegiac poetry those of them which are most in
> keeping with it.

There is no need to take this dedication literally and think that Gallus actually used this handbook's synopses when composing his own poetry. It seems very likely that Gallus knew the Hellenistic originals and that Parthenius is simply commending his own handbook, and Gallus and Gallus' work, to the general public, by declaring it to have been written 'by appointment to Cornelius Gallus'. But the influence of Parthenius upon Gallus must have been strong. Gallus wrote four elegiac books of which one line has survived and which may have borne the title *Amores*.[25] Under the old view of Roman subjective elegy he had to be credited with most of the development of Roman elegy. Under the view now proposed he need not be credited with the invention of subjective love-elegy, which the Greeks already wrote. It goes without saying that he was not the first to subordinate mythical to subjective elements, since this is already found in Catullus 68. What he did contribute is less easy to say. The history of elegy would suggest that his work contained mythical narrative, and this is confirmed to some extent by the dedication to him of the *Erotika Pathemata*. That Gallus' elegies also contained subjective erotic elements is implied by the probable echoes of Gallan elegy in Virgil's tenth *Eclogue*.[26] The pastoral setting in which Gallus is placed there need not reflect Gallus' poetry. It may be no more than the means by which Virgil adapts the *persona* of Gallus to his own bucolic poetry. But at lines 22f. there is a reference to Lycoris leaving Gallus to go off with her soldier and to Gallus' sorrow at being deserted. These lines may allude to a propemptikon of Gallus to Lycoris, which is known to have existed, and which two Propertian propemptika, 1.8 and 2.19, imitate, and this propemptikon is certainly referred to later in *Eclogue* 10 (47–9). Another theme in which Gallus may have anticipated a subsequent Roman elegy – Tibullus 1.10 – is found in lines 44f.: the love-poet is perforce a soldier. The material attested by Servius as Gallan begins at line 46 (cf. Propertius 1.8.6ff.). More description of Lycoris' journeyings (47–9) is succeeded by Gallus' retreat to mope in the wild countryside singing and cutting his love's, that is, Lycoris' name,

---

[25] For discussions of this question cf. Boucher, *Gallus* pp. 72f.
[26] I leave *Ecl.* 6 out of consideration. For the extensive literature on echoes of Gallus in the *Eclogues* see Boucher, *Gallus* pp. 84ff.; and Ross, *Backgrounds* Chh. 3; 5.

into the trees (50–4). The carving on bark notion, derived from Callimachus' *Acontius and Cydippe, Aetia* Fr. 73 (Pf.), recurs in Propertius 1.18.22. Next follows a hunting scene: Gallus becomes the huntsman in an attempt to soften the pangs of his love (55–61) – a notion found again in Propertius 2.19.17ff. Finally Gallus becomes an Orpheus figure wandering the world in a futile flight from love (62–9) – cf. Propertius 2.30.1ff.

Since these incidents derive from Gallus' love-poetry, it may be concluded that there was a good deal of subjective love-elegy in the poetry of Cornelius Gallus – more, it would seem, than in Hellenistic erotic elegy. Historical considerations confirm this view: that Gallus merely copied Greek elegy would appear unlikely in the light of Catullus' prior composition of at least one long subjective elegy of a more highly developed type. The very sophisticated and almost wholly subjective love-elegies of Tibullus Book 1 also imply that Tibullus is building on the work of a predecessor – Gallus – who had gone far beyond the Greek achievement. Gallus' work need not of course have been homogeneous. His four books could well have contained several different sorts of elegies.

Three further possibilities about Gallus have more plausibility than many suggestions made about him. The first is that he may have been the first among those working in the Hellenistic elegiac tradition to regard as non-essential the strong association between love and death which Antimachus' *Lyde* had established. He may have developed the hints given by Catullus in this direction and concentrated on separation from a living mistress instead of from a dead one. The second is that he was the first elegiac writer (again following Catullus' lead?) to place 'himself' fully in the situation of a mythical character. The coincidences between Callimachus' Acontius, the Propertius of 1.18 and Gallus as seen in *Eclogue* 10 are strong indications that Gallus, like Propertius, played an Acontius role in one of his elegies. Thirdly Gallus may well have been the first elegiac poet to write books made up of separate elegies. Hellenistic elegy books had to be united poems because there was no precedent for works made up of unlinked narratives. The subjective portions held them together and in fact the subjective portions could only be introduced in this role. Once Catullus had shown how myth could be subordinated within a long subjective elegy, the need for an elegy book to be a single united poem had passed. Each small subjective elegy could introduce itself; and the collection could consist of elegies either mainly subjective or mainly objective set side by side without connecting passages. The Theognidean corpus may again at this point have exercised some influence; and there is the further possibility that Catullus 65 and the poems following it, although not necessarily originally written to be issued as a collection of elegies plus elegiac epigrams, were published in this form; and that this suggested to Gallus the idea of writing a collection of discrete elegies composed as such. The Theocritean collection which later inspired Virgil to write the *Eclogues* may have helped Gallus too. As was noted above, some non-elegiac Theocritean idylls are very close to being subjective erotic elegiac poems in everything but metre.

Tibullus and Propertius doubtless began writing in that order; but for some purposes they can better be understood if they are thought of as making independent contributions to the form as Gallus left it. Tibullus carried much further than Catullus the subordination of myth to subjective material. This implies, as was noted above, that Gallus had already made advances upon Catullus' innovation. Propertius is initially in some ways a more old-fashioned writer than Tibullus. His first book contains more mythological material than Tibullus Book 1 and the myth is less clearly subordinated to the subjective material. The prologue poem of the Monobiblos is Catullan in this respect and 1.20 is completely Greek[27] in its treatment of myth, which dominates the whole elegy. Indeed, the role of myth in the Monobiblos might suggest that, when Propertius was writing it, the primary Roman influence on him was Gallus, a view strengthened by the well-known allusions to Gallus' work in 1.8 and 1.18 and the dedication of 1.20 to Gallus himself.[28] The various poems of Tibullus Book 1 doubtless became known to Propertius at different stages in the composition of the Monobiblos, first by recitation and perhaps finally by publication. As he came to know them, Propertius seems to have been influenced by them,[29] but the Monobiblos was not able to take full account of Tibullus Book 1. As time went on Propertius developed away from Gallus, although he retained an interest in him, and came more under the influence of Tibullus, with the result that his elegies became less mythocentric. This view explains why some of the poems of the Monobiblos seem much more primitive than any in Tibullus Book 1, while others show a truly individual style, as different from Tibullus as from any Gallan model that can be hypothesised.

At several points in this book[30] a question has been raised in various forms: why did important Romans like Messalla, Maecenas and L. Volcacius Tullus patronise two of the elegiac poets, Tibullus and Propertius, whose way of life and ideals seem at first sight so different from their own? Partial answers have already been suggested. Here in conclusion an overall suggestion may be added which relates also to Tibullus' status in antiquity as the greatest of the Roman elegists. There is no doubt that patrons in late

---

[27] Cf. esp. Theocr. *Id*. 11; 13, for the technique used in Prop. 1.20 to link a myth with the addressee of the poem.

[28] The name Gallus occurs at Prop. 1.5.31; 10.5; 13.2, 4, 16; 20.1, 14, 51; 21.7; 4.1.95. The Galli of 1.21.7 and 4.1.95 are certainly not the poet C. Cornelius Gallus and the identity of the Galli of 1.5, 1.10 and 1.13 is doubtful. But it is likely that the Gallus of 1.20 is the poet. Cf. Ross, *Backgrounds* pp. 74ff.

[29] Many of the parallel passages are discussed by Jacoby, *RhM* 64 (1909) 601ff.; 65 (1910) 22ff.

[30] Above, pp. 33ff.; 86; 146.

Republican and Augustan Rome were interested in sheer literary quality. They wanted to be part of a movement which was consciously emulating and surpassing, in Latin and within two generations, the greatest achievements of five centuries of Greek literature. How far these patrons realised that the survival of classical civilisation would depend on what their contemporary Roman writers were doing is uncertain. Latin purism, of which Messalla himself was a champion, was even then a growing force. But Augustan patrons probably understood only imperfectly that Greek literature had no long-term interest in itself for the vast and now western-orientated *imperium Romanum*, and would cease to be influential unless its ideas were transmitted through a new and vigorous universal language. However, in their concern for Latin literature, these patrons sought the best writers among their own contemporaries, irrespective of social or political background.

The work of any great artist must represent, symbolise or incorporate the overall concerns of the age in which he lives. Tibullus' contribution in this area can be seen initially in relation to the form and content of his poetry. He is a Roman citizen writing elegiac love-poetry: his personality and life are therefore those of a man torn between and sometimes contriving to reconcile the twin poles of private life and public life, of leisure and active service of the state, of town and country, of duty and love, of war and farming. Propertius also understood this division and chose to set himself in his poetry firmly on one side of it.[31] But because Tibullus is a man divided in himself, his personality and imaginary life-style may well have symbolised for his contemporaries a sense of internal division which they also felt.

There were of course points at which the antithetic features of the Tibullan *persona* met, as indeed they did in the life of contemporary Rome; and there were, even in the Augustan period, changes in accepted values, including that development whereby paradoxically *otium* became linked with political loyalty.[32] Above all, it must be remembered in estimating the Tibullan *persona* that the life of the farmer in the countryside was seen throughout Roman history as the ultimate repository of the old Roman virtues; and farmers were traditionally a prime source of recruits for the legions. But nevertheless the sense of self-doubt which redoubles confidence, and the pull of self-indulgence which is the ultimate guarantee of the strength of virtue, are concepts prominent in Tibullus' poetry and in the life of his time. Much of Augustan literature deals in one way or another directly or obliquely with the sentiments which good men felt when they responded to the challenge of their generation, not naively but

[31] See *GC* pp. 4ff.; 185ff.; 197ff.; and F. Cairns, '*Propertius* on Augustus' marriage law (II, 7)', *Grazer Beiträge* (forthcoming).
[32] See A. J. Woodman, *Velleius Paterculus The Tiberian Narrative* (2.94–131) (Cambridge Classical Texts and Commentaries 19, Cambridge 1977) Indexes: I General s.v. *otiosi* and *otium*.

with all the facts to hand: they feared of course that the new age of Augustus was an illusion, that nothing had really changed since the turbulent days of the late Republic; but simultaneously they were able to hope that a new period had really begun. An important reason why Tibullus is the greatest of Roman elegists may well be that he was in the fullest sense a man of his age, who understood and in his own literary *persona* portrayed its dilemma.

GENERAL INDEX

NOTE: the references to modern scholars are to the first citation of each work only.

abbreviation, see compression
abortions, ancient 103
accumulation of detail 121, 129, 132, 134, 142, 153, 202–3.
Achilles 30, 113, 124, 160, 187
Acontiadae 120
Acontius 111, 117, 119, 190, 227
adjectives: distinguishing 105; double allusive use of 107–8; meaning limited by context 101; predicative uses of 108; proleptic uses of 109
Admetus 120, 153, 210
Aegeus (Attic king) 189
Aelia Galla 182
Aeneas 67, 68, 75f., 77f., 84, 204, 206; as founder of Rome 71–8, 84; victories won by 67, 78, 84
Aeschylus 156, 189, 201; represents older school of poetry in Aristophanes 8–9
aestheticism, see under sensory emphasis
aetiology, Hellenistic interest in 69, 118, 119, 125, 189, 222
Africanus Fabius Maximus 174
Agamemnon 30
Agathyllus 74
agnus castus 18
Agrippa 164
Ajax 160
Alba Longa 73
Alcaeus 201; moral emphasis in 113
Alcinous 45
Alcman 58–9
Alcyone 182
Alexander Aetolus 221, 223
Alexander the Great 10, 12, 50; *triumphator*, conqueror of East 43–4
Alexandria 64
Alfius (moneylender) 188
Allius 162–5, 224
allusion 112, 119, 128
Ἀλφᾶ 134
Amalthea (Sibyl name) 77
Amaryllis 26
Ambarvalia 126–34
Amburbium 130
Amor 104, 127, 131, 170, 178, 182–3, 184–6, 204, 206, 208; accompanying propemptic

traveller in propemptikon 183; as inventor 132; as rural deity 133; attributes of 133; etymologyical links 95; nudity of 37; poverty of, 37
amplification, see under expansion
Amycus 31
Anacreon 61, 190
analogia 101
anathematikon, reaction within 67
ancient literary criticism of elegy, technical terms of 4–6
André, J. 17 n.71, 90 n.13
Andromache 114–15, 116
anger, as topos of palinode 169–70
Anthesteria 134
Antichares of Eleon 73
anticipation, see under temporal dislocation 112
Antimachus of Colophon 8, 54, 219, 223, 224
antiquarianism: Hellenistic interest in 13–14, 18, 69, 79, 117, 119, 124, 129, 131, 135; in Archaic lyric 114
antistrophe 195
antithesis 195; between love and death 163; between love and war 105, 145, 183; between youth and age 141, 147–8
Antonius, M. 44, 174
antonyms 100, 101
Aphrodite 113, 161
Apollo (*see also* Phoebus) 8–9, 20, 26, 84–5, 86, 123–6, 154, 189, 206, 210–11, 221; as pastor 84, 120; in Tibullus 2.5, 65–7, 74, 75, 78, 80, 83; *ktistes* 70–1; long hair of 71, 206; lover of Admetus 112, 120; lyre of 71; νόμιος 71
Apollonia 71
Apollonius of Rhodes 69
apostrophe 135; of Muses 164
Appel, G. 129 n.35
Arabia Felix 96
arai 62
Aratus (in Theocr. *Id.* 7) 158
Arcesilas 114–15
archaic Greek elegy 216–19
archaic Greek poetry 8; debt of Hellenistic writers to 10, 63, 64; narrative techniques

231

archaic Greek poetry—*cont.*
  of influenced Hellenistic writers 112; read by Augustan poets, 62–3
archaic lyric poets, brisk summary of epic action in 113; large-scale reworking of epic action in 113–14; narrative techniques of 113–16, 120
Archias 203
Archilochus 11; deception in 187–8
Argo 24, 75, 106
Argonauts 115–16
Aristophanes, literary ideals in 8–10
Arnott, W. G. 189 n.77, 192 n.1
arrival poem 167
Arsinoe Aphrodite, new cult of 65
Artemis 117, 119, 124
Arval brothers 129, 130
Arval hymn 130
Ascanius 73
Asiatic oratory 195
Asinius Gallus 86
assonance 92
astronomy 14
asymmetry, in formal structures, 196, 202–7
asyndeton 118, 123, 124, 125, 128, 130, 135, 136, 137, 139, 140, 141, 163
Atalanta 161
Ate: in Homer 61–2; related concepts in Greek tragedy 62; silent, inexorable, 61–2
Athens 30
Augustan poetry: personal references in 67; relation of poet and patron in 146; wrongly seen as anti-imperial 86
Augustan poets: formal structures exploited by 196; indebted to Greek literature 215–16
Augustus 67, 72, 84, 85, 104, 129, 174; indirect praise of by Tibullus 104; military achievements of 33; never named by Tibullus 44; Phoebus patron of 206; public image of modelled on Alexander 44; revival of religion by 20
Aurora 97, 98
authority: appeal to learned authority in Hellenistic poetry 132; Hellenistic stress on reliability of 120; Hellenistic claim to 27–8

Bacchus 127, 128, 129, 131–2, 172, 210
Bacchylides 12, 20, 114–15; deception in 189
Badian, E. 68 n.14
Baldry, H. C. 47 n.48
Ball, F. K. 16 n.67
Ball, R. J. 204 n.18
Barber, E. A. 219
Barigazzi, A. 41 n.29
Barwick, K. 90 n.13
basilikon 172
battle of the books 7

Battus 75, 114–15
Beck, I. 194 n.4
bee, as literary symbol 5
Bellona: connected with Ma 41; uttering erotodidaxis 41
Bers, V. 101 n.25
Beyer, R. 22 n.99
Bianchi, U. 52 n.58
Bittis 220
Bompaire, J. 134 n.48
botany, Hellenistic interest in 14, 136
Bottin, L. 101 n.22
Boucher, J.-P. 215 n.5
Braswell, B. K. 57 n.66
brevity 10
bridge-passage (link between two genres) 167, 171, 183
Brink, C.O. 194 n.4
Bucaeus 159
Buchheit, U. 68 n.17
Buchholz, K. 66 n.5
bucolic fantasy 136, 170, 179
Bulloch, A. W. 6 n.26
Bundy, E. L. 7 n.28, 19 n.81
Burton, R. W. B. 189 n.76
Butler, H. E. 219

Caesar, Julius 44, 83, 86
Cahen, E. 19 n.82
Cairns, F. 5 n.20, 9 n.33, 11 n.46, 15 n.64, 17 n.75, 22 n.99, 23 n.103, 33 n.133, 55 n.62, 63 n.71, 67 n.9, 82 n.104, 85 n.118, 121 n.18, 159 n.33, 169 nn.14f., 205 n.21
Callimachus 7, 20f., 27, 30f., 34, 42, 49, 60–2, 65, 69, 130, 216, 221–3, 224, 225; deception in 189–90; defence of poetry 126; dramatic exposition in 121–6, 137, 143; imitated by Tibullus 6, 11, 43; linking devices used by 192; literary ideals of 8–9; narrative technique of 116–20; polemical language of 7; relations with Hesiod 17, 50, 221, 222–3
Callinus 216
Callirhoe 167
Canidia 170
canon of classical authors 10
canon of elegiac poets 3, 224
Cardauns, B. 76 n.69
Carians 120
Castor 31
catalogues 13, 114, 132, 133, 189, 222
Cato 68, 127
Catullus 43, 88, 164–5, 197, 227, 229; 68, first long elegiac poem in Latin 162; information conveyance in 162–5; moral interest in 163
centrepiece of poem, conceptual priority of 141, 142, 201, 203, 204, 206, 207, 211

General Index

Ceos 79, 119–20
Cephalon of Gergis 74
ceremonial poetry *see* dramatic exposition
Ceres 14, 108, 127, 128, 129
Cerri, G. 69 n.28
Ceyx 119, 182
Chalk, H. O. O. 26 n.114
Charon of Lampsacus 69
Charon the Carpenter 188
chiasmus 195
Chios, eponymos 71
Chios, foundation of 69, 71, 81–2
choric hymn, *see* hymns, choric
choric poetry: choric self-address 121; conventions of 121–2; persona of ego-figure 121, 127; self-fulfilling injunction 121, 124, 127, 128
Χύτροι 134
cicada 9
Cicero 13
Cilicia 44
Cincius Alimentus 68, 74
Civil Wars 83, 104, 205
clothing: loose clothing a sign of loose morals 104
Coleman, R. G. G. 88 n.7
Colophon 218; foundation of 69, 73
colour contrasts 141
Commager, S. 131 n.39
commands in dramatic exposition 123, 127, 128, 129, 134
compression 112, 119, 123, 225
concealment of repeated elements 137f.
conceptual jumps 138
consolation 223; in Catullus 68, 163, 165, 224f.
contaminatio 42; Roman festivals combined with Greek 134
Copley, F. O. 36 n.6, 185 nn.66f.
Coppel, B. 163 n.40
Corcyra 175; identified with Phaeacia 44–5
Cornutus 153, 155, 204
Cos 220
Costa, C. D. N. 100 n.20
countryside: being with mistress in 39, 40, 153–4, 179, 211; in Hellenistic poetry 14, 17–19, 21, 37, 135, 137; praise of 188; repository of Roman virtues 229; rural deities 14, 79–80, 127, 131–2, 133
Crete 73
culta puella 152
cults of poets 218, 220
Cumae in Italy, foundation of 74, 75
Cyclops 30
Cydippe 117, 118–20, 190
Cydnus 44
Cynthia 167

Cyrene, foundation of 73, 74–5, 80, 114–15
Cyrnus, beloved of Theognis 219

Dahlmann, H. 90 n.13
Danaids, as sinners against love 54, 55, 57
Danaus 55
Daphnis, 27, 158, 160, 190
Dawson, C. M. 36 n.7, 189 n.78
Day, A. A. 214–15, 217, 219
deception 153, 155–6, 163, Ch. 7 passim; generic deception a Tibullan invention? 191; history of 187–91; initial 163, 166, 175–6; initial, generic, in Tibullus 166–73; internal 177–87; linked to withholding of information 176, 181; trick endings 173, 175–6
delayed generic identification 158, 191
Delia 23, 38, 64, 102, 107, 108, 142, 146, 154, 167, 170, 175, 176–81, 185, 193, 212–13
Delos 154
Delphians 125
Delphic oracle 119, 125; instigator of Greek colonisation 70, 73, 75, 82
Delphis 161, 162
Demeas 191
Demeter 118, 188
Devereux, G. 168 n.13
dialectal variants 15
Diana 85, 154, 206
diatribe 15
didacticism 9, 14, 32
diegertikon 203
digression 112, 114, 118, 122, 125f.; personal 122
Diodorus 41–2
Dionysia 133
Dionysus: conqueror of East 43; identified with Osiris 41; *triumphator* 41, 43, 131
discontinuity 126
dithyramb, linked with Roman triumph 43, 171–2
dives amator, *see* rival
divine power aiding the lover 38; *see also* magic
doctrina 5, 10, 11–18; claimed by Tibullus 5; invention of erudite subject-matter 42–3; ornamental use of by Roman poets 43; Roman analogues to Greek learning 64, 86
doctus 11
Dodds, E. R. 133 n.44
Dorieus (Spartan king) 73
Dornseiff, F. 156 n.21
Dover, K. J. 8, 10, 17 n.72, 22 n.98
dramatic exposition 121–34, 144
Du Quesnay, I. M. Le M. 41 n.29, 46 n.43
Duckworth, G.E. 191 n.85
dura puella 148, 186

Eisenberger, H. 45 n.38
Eisenhut, W. 176 n.37
ekphrasis 134
Elder, J. P. 3, 3 n.13
Elea, foundation of 69
elitist claims 28
Eysium 45, 46, 51, 58; connected with Isis 47; equivalent to Isles of the Blessed 48–49; heroic martial ideal of 54; originally reserved for warriors 51; ruled by Kronos 47; scenery of 52
Elysium for lovers 51–4, 58; found in Propertius 53; perhaps invented by Tibullus 53
emotional conflict 139
emotionalism 9, 24, 121, 135–6, 137, 140–1, 181
enallage adjectivi 101
Ennius 68, 88
entry of new characters into dramatic situations 152, 154, 158–9, 160
envy (blame) 126
epibaterion, inverse 45, 167, 171
epic, rejection of 24–5
epideictic genres 37
epigrammatic tradition 190
epilepsy 118
epithalamion (wedding-song) of Helen 203
eponymos not the founder 71
epyllion 197
Ernesti, J. C. T. 92 n.15
Eros 26
erotic language (erotic senses of common words) 89, 101
erotodidactic precepts 142–3
erotodidaxis 26, 37, 147, 173
Erythrae 76
escapism, *see* bucolic fantasy
Esteve Forriol, J. 107 n.38
Eteocles 201
etymology 80–1; active reader-participation in 95, 97; ancient interest in 15, 90–2; derivation of proper names 47, 93, 97, 135; genuine philological links in ancient 96; Hellenistic interest in 69, 119–20; invention by poet of 96; Latin words derived from Greek 96–7; transformation rules of 95–6; *see also* verbal juxtapositions
eucharistikon 164
euktic hymn: elements of in 2.5, 65–6; reaction within 67
eulogy, in lyric 113, 116
euphemia (holy silence) 124, 127, 128–9
Euphorion 42; his *Hesiod* 17; imitated by Tibullus 6; influence on Tibullus 43
Euphrates 126
Euripides 8, 189, 203; formal structures in 201–2; represents new poetry in Aristophanes 8–10
Eurotas 203
Eustathius 195
Evander 79–80
Examues (friend of Mimnermus) 217–18
exclamations 120, 136
expansion (*macrologia*) 112, 119, 121, 122, 124, 135, 140, 144–5, 151, 158, 163–4, 185, 225.

Fabia Paullina 174
Fabii 174
Fabius Pictor 68
Fahz, L. 139 n.56
Faunus 79
Fedeli, P. 215 n.4
Fehling, D. 42 n.34, 92 n.15
festivals, boys and girls meet at 162
fidelity as elegiac ideal 180
figurae rationis et orationis 89
filing metaphor 10
Fisher, J. M. 204 n.18
flashback, *see under* temporal dislocation
fores, *see* komastic topoi, doorstep of mistress
formal structures ch. 8 passim; *see also* ring-structures, parallel-composition, temporal structure
Foulon, A. 157 n.25
foundation literature, *see under* ktisis
foundation oracle of Rome: dating of 71–2, 74, 80; place of delivery of 75–7
Fraenkel, E. 121 n.17. 156 n.22
Fraenkel, H. 19 n.82
Fraser, P. M. 64
frustration of reader's expectations 118
Führer, R. 156 n.21
fugitivarii, loves as 184
furtivus amor 142, 149, 224

Galatea 135–6, 158–9
Galinsky, G. K. 72 n.46
Gallus, Cornelius 6, 21, 88, 216, 224, 225–227, 227, 228; harshness of 88; imitates Euphorion 88; Quintilian's assessment of 4–6
Ganymede 56–7
Gatz, B. 52 n.58
Gaul 43
Gelzer, M. 44 n.37
genealogy 119, 222; in Pindar 115
generic complexity 190
Generic Composition: (pp. 12ff.) 187; correction of pp. 167 f. 171
generic speakers: actual 182; logical 181–2, 190; substitute 190
generic status 171

General Index

genethliakon 37, 171
Genius 131, 203
genres: bipersonal 182; non-rhetorical related to rhetorical 187; Roman analogues of Greek 171–2; tripersonal 182
Gentili, B. 42 n.33
geography: Hellenistic interest in 14, 113; in Pindar 115
Gerressen, W. 68 n.17
Giangrande, G. 12 n.50, 16 n.70, 20 n.85, 24 n.107, 117 n.9
gnome, introduced with asyndeton 124
Golden Age 37, 46, 47, 49, 50, 54, 58, 84–5, 154, 155, 192, 210–11; no travel in 106
Golden Fleece 75
Gorgianic oratory 195
Govaerts, S. 87 n.41
Grimal, P. 17 n.74
grotesquerie 22, 121, 136, 137, 141, 186
Guthrie, W. K. C. 133 n.44

Habrotonon, character in Menander 191
Hades 37, 46, 49, 54, 59
Hamaxitos, in Troad 69
Hamilton, R. 127 n.32
Hannsen, J. S. T. 91 n.13
Hanslik, R. 46 n.44, 46
Hardie, A. 133 n.45
Harrauer, H. 89 n.11
Harrington, K. P. 16 n.67
Harriott, R. 19 n.79
Hecataeus 41
Hector 114, 116, 187, 197, 201
Helen 113, 197–201, 203
Heliconian dream vision 221–2
hell, for sinners against love 51, 54–5, 57, 58–9
Hellanicus of Lesbos 69
Hellenistic epigram 146; subjective erotic 23, 216–17
Hellenistic erotic elegy 214, 215; subjective 216–17, 219–21
Hellenistic learning 119
Hellenistic manifesto, the 11–32 passim, 34
Hellenistic poetry, Greek: characteristics of 6–32; characteristics of in common with archaic poetry 8; fragmentary nature of and problems caused by 42–3, 87, 143, 165; imitation of lyric narrative technique 116; information conveyance in 157–8; interest in earlier literature 11–12; linguistic features of 87; narrative exposition in 116–17; as raw material for Roman poetry 64; imitation of archaic authors in 10–11, 48, 62–3, 64, 87–8, 214, 218
Hellenistic poetry, Roman 6–7; Greek language in 96–7
Hellenistic tendencies in Homer 112

Helm, R. 215 n.3
Hera 18, 77
Heracles 24, 77
Herescu, N. I. 134 n.48
herm, ithyphallic 189
Hermes 161–2
Hermesianax 217–18, 219–20, 223
Hermobios, enemy of Mimnermus 217
Herodas, mimes 18
Herodotus 156
Herophile, Sibyl name 77
Herter, H. 134 n.48, 137 n.52
Herzog, R. 25 n.110
Hesiod 11, 49–50, 93, 168, 201, 222–3; admired by Alexandrians 50; as figure in Hellenistic manifesto literature 17; interest in etymology 15
hetaira, excluded from countryside 146
Heumann, J. †12 n.3
Heuss, A. 44 n.37
ἰὴ ἰὴ παιῆον 124, 125
Hiero of Syracuse, patron of Theocritus 20, 160
Hill, H. 80 n.85
Hippias 15
Hippys of Rhegium 69
history, Hellenistic interest in 14, 119
Hofmann, W. and Wartenberg, G. 145 n.2
Holleman, A. W. J. 82 n.104
Hollis, A. S. 179 n.38
Holst, H. 92 n.15
Homer 11, 15, 51, 57, 61–2, 68–9, 88, 90, 93, 168, 218, 222; association of wine and tears in 39; false preparation in 187; interest in etymology 15; looking back to a distant heroic age 13; moral values in Homeric epic 29–30; narrative technique of 112–13, 116, 120; ring composition in 195, 196, 197–201, 203
Homeric exegesis 8
Homeric scholia 88
homosexual love 22, 36, 38, 56–7, 61, 173, 207, 223; moral ideal associated with 149–51
Horace 44, 50, 216; deep interest in philosophy 15; double allusive use of adjectives in 108; imitates *novem lyrici* in *Odes* 62; palinodes of 169–70; Pliny the Younger's assessment of 4
Horsfall, N. 68 n.14
Howie, J. G. 30 n.127
Hubaux, J. 25 n.110
Hubbard, M. 1 n.7
humanising of gods and heroes 8, 9, 32, 121, 137
humble characters, interest in 9, 31, 113, 137
humour 159, 190
Hylas 24

hymns 37, 126, 172; a god's past or future achievements in 66–7; choric 121–2, 123, 126, 127–8

identity of interest between speaker and addressee 205
Ilia 80, 84
Illig, L. 156 n.22
imitation: alteration of order in 54; archaic and Hellenistic predecessors alluded to together 58–63; *imitatio cum variatione* 184, 187; simultaneous imitation of two models 63
inauguration of a consul, poems on 172, 174
incest 9
inclusion 164, 171–2, 187
indirect conveyance of information (oblique exposition) 123, 129, 130
indirect encomium 131
individuality 10
innovatory spirit of Hellenistic poetry 191
Inuus 79
inventors 132–3
Ion of Chios 69, 72, 79, 81
Ionian cities, foundations of 69
Iron Age 46, 49, 84, 154, 192, 210
irony 121, 136, 142, 175, 176; dramatic 189
Isidore of Seville 91, 92
Isis 47; worshipped by Delia 47
Isis Pharia 164–5
Isles of the Blessed 45, 50, 52; *see also* Elysium
Isocrates 168
Italy, heir to Roman traditions 83
Ixion, as sinner against love 54–5, 57, 59

Jachmann, G. 163 n.41
Jacoby, F. 1 n.8, 2, 68 n.18
Jax, K. 188 n.74.
Jocasta 202
Jocelyn, H. D. 12 n.51
Julian *gens* 72, 78, 84
Juno attacked by Ixion 55
Jupiter 78, 84; as ruler of Iron Age 49, 84; as *triumphator* 67, 85, 86

Kaimio, M. 127 n.32
Kallinus 69
Karneia 121, 123, 129
Katsouris, A. G. 191 n.83
Keller, O. 90 n.13
Keyssner, K. 134 n.48
Kier, H. 145 n.1
Kleingünther, A. 133 n.43
Kleinknecht, H. 66 n.5
Kleostratus 191
kletic hymn 65, elements of in 2.5 66

kletikon 67
Klotho 188
Knecht, A. 139 n.57
Köhnken, A. 57 n.67
komastic topoi: appeal to mistress 186; attempt to abandon love 184; bucolic fantasy 170; doorstep of mistress 146, 166–7, 170, 181, 183; harshness of mistress 186; *lena* 170, 186; *rivalis* 170; slave accompanying komast 166; threat of suicide 185; wine 166–7
komos 36, 134, 158–9, 162, 166–7, 168–9, 170, 183–4, 184, 186–7, 224; commonness of 170; delayed identification of 170; processional element in 187
Kontoleon, N. M. 218 nn.14f.
Krischer, T. 46 n.43
Kroll, J. 52 n.58
Kronos: equivalent to Saturn 47; ruler in Golden Age 47; ruler of Elysium 47, 48–9
Kroton 72
ktisis 37, 68, 69–70, 74–5, 114–15, 119; divine sanction for colonisation starting point of 74; multiple foundations 72–3; of Greek cities 68–9; of Rome 68; omens in 82; prose *ktiseis* 70
ktistic elements in 2.5; address to founder in oracle 78; agricultural emphasis 78; Apollo κτίστης 70; continuity of worship 70, 71, 78; etymologies 80; foundation festival 70–1, 81–2, 83; foundation oracle 70, 72, 73–8; later history 70, 82–3; oikist (founder) 70, 71–3, 78; pre-history 70, 79–81; setting up of walls 73, 79; the gods of the city 70, 84
Kuiper, K. 19 n.82
Kurfess, A. 76 n.69

labor, see πόνος
Lamis 72
Laodamia 164, 165, 224–5
Lar 100
Lares 14, 133; of Tibullus: 20; of Troy 76, 78, 84
Latin language 229; archaic 88; compared with Greek 88, 128–9; richness of in forms of command 141; vulgar 88
Latin love elegy, *see under* Roman elegy
Latium 47
Latte 79 n.84
Lattimore, R. 107 n.38
laurel 65, 67, 71, 85, 128
Lavinium 73
learned analogical invention 126, Ch.3
learning, *see under doctrina*
Lee, Guy 16, 16 n. 67, 33 n.131
Lefkowitz, M. R. 127 n.32
legal fiction, *see* Titius

General Index

legal language 142
Legrand, P.-E. 17 n.72
Leleges 120
lena 170, 178, 180–1, 185–7, 212–13
Leonidas of Tarentum 20
λεπτότης 5, 34
Lesbos, foundation of 69
Lesky, A. 194 n.4
Leto 154; attempted rape of by Tityos 54–5
Leumann, M. 109 n.42
Levin, D. N. 19 n.82
Lewis, M. W. H. 130 n.36
lexicography 8, 12, 15
libraries (Hellenistic and Roman) 13, 29
life (the poet's) equals poetry 11
linguistic learning 15–17, 34
linguistic vulgarisms 16
linking devices; conceptual 131, 192–3; narrator in Callimachus' *Aetia* 222; verbal, *see under* verbal links
literary manifestos 8–10, 11–12, 17
local history etc., Hellenistic interest in 13, 117, 119–20
Löfstedt, E. 16 n.69
Lohmann, D. 194 n.4, 195
love: Hellenistic interest in 21–4, 120; love–war equation–opposition 105, 145, 183; temporarily dominant in Tibullus' *persona* 155; triumph of 144; timidity of youth in 105
love of goddesses, dangers of aspiring to 59
love-making: at birthdays 82; at public festivals 67; impossible after death 52
love-poet, honoured in old age 208
lover and beloved, standard distinction in antiquity 147
lover: as runaway slave 183, 184; as slave 185
low life 18, 31
Luce, J. V. 120 n.16
Lucian 52
Lucilius 88
Luck, G. 2 n.12, 3; *The Latin Love Elegy* 36, 60 n.69
Lucretius 13
Lycophron 7
Lycoris 226
lyre, attribute of Apollo 71
lyric poets, the 11–12, 120, 164, 201; influence of on Hellenistic poetry 196; narrative techniques of 112, 113–15, 116; secondary function of narrative in 116; withholding of proper names by 156

Ma (Cappadocian mother goddess) 41; served by prostitute priestesses 41
Maas, P. 87 n.2
Maass, E. 76 n.66
Macer 181–3, 184, 185, 208

Macleod C. W. 163 n.40
madness 178; as palinodic topos 282–4
Maeander 73
Maecenas 228
magic 138, 140, 162, 178; aiding the lover 38, 161
magister amoris (teacher of love) 26, 138, 139, 141, 142, 147, 150; elegiac poets as 222
Magna Graecia, foundations of cities of 80
Magnesia, foundation of 73
maids, acting as go-betweens 162
make-up: uselessness of in love 139–40, 141, 147
Manilius Vopiscus 103
Marathus 23, 140, 141–2, 147–8, 148–53, 175, 208–9
Marpesia (Sibyl name) 76–7
Marpessos, *see under* Sibyl of Erythrae
marriage, Roman, 174
Mars 84, 86, 130
Marshall, A. J. 13 n.57
materfamilias, Delia as 179–80
Matthews, V. J. 69 n.24
McCulloh, W. E. 25 n.110
McGann, M. J. 1 n.1, 15 n.64
McKay, K. J. 19 n.57
McKeown, J. C. 172 n.27
Medea, gives foundation oracle of Cyrene 73, 75
medical learning 14, 118, 169–70
Megara Hyblaea 71–2
Meincke, W. 159 n.33
Meleager 12
Menander Rhetor 65
Menander, dramatist 24, 190, 192
Menelaus 113, 200, 203
Mercury 51
meretrix 179, 180
Merkelbach, R. 85, 85 n.119
Messalinus: as future *triumphator* 65, 67, 83, 84, 86; as *XVvir* 65, 74, 76, 85, 206; in Tibullus 2.5, 65, 66, 84, 204–5
Messalla 25, 28, 33–4, 74, 130, 131, 145–6, 155, 171, 173, 174, 179, 182, 193, 228; as *Frater Arvalis* 130, 132; associated by Tibullus with Alexander 43–4; birthday of 131–2; dedicatee of Tibullus Book 1 46; Eastern campaigns 44; ex-Antonian 174; quasi-deification of by Tibullus 44, 127, 130–1; supporter of Augustus 72, 174; triumphs of 41, 130–2
metalworking metaphor 10
meteorology 14
metre: metrical innovation by Hellenistic poets 87, 88; innovation by Tibullus 89; niceties in Hellenistic poets 10; restriction in Hellenistic poets 116; *sedes* 206
Meyer, H. 129 n.35

Michel, D. 44 n.37
Milanion 161
Milctus 30–1, 202–3
Milon 159
mimetic poetry; *see* dramatic exposition
Mimnermus 2, 12, 69, 216–18, 219, 223
mineralogy 14
misinformation of reader 117, 118
Mittelstadt, M. C. 23 n.102
Molon 158
Momigliano, A. 74 n.57
morality, 9, 29–30
morbus, tristis 103
Morgan, K. 12 n.55
Moritz, L. A. 201 n.10
Moschion 191
mothers, in erotic contexts 159
Moulton, C. 194 n.4
mourning, signs of 104
Müller, R. 133 n.43
multiplication of a single deity 41
Munatius Plancus, L. 174
Murray, O. 106 n.37
Muses 17, 19, 20, 26, 221, 222
Musurillo, H. 204 n.18, 212 n.25
Myous 30–1
Myres, J. L. 194 n.4
mystery cults 118, 138; at Eleusis 118
myth, subordinated to narrative in Roman elegy 225, 226, 227–8
mythology 8, 14, 46–7, 119, 120, 136, 164; Egyptian 47; Graeco-Roman 47; Indo-European 47

Naevius 68
Naiads 164
naivety, *see* pseudo-naivety
Nanno, mistress of Mimnermus 217, 219
narrative poetry: exposition in 111–21, 122, 134, 144; formal structures in 196, 201; narrator appearing in 222; postponement of details in 156
Natalis 204
natural phenomena, Hellenistic interest in 112–13, 120
Naxos 119
Nekuia, Homeric 51
Neleus 203
Nemesis 154, 155, 184–6, 205, 209–12
New Comedy 145, 146; links with Roman elegy 9, 186, 191, 214
Newman, J. K. 3
Nicias 135, 202–3
Night (goddess) 134
Nile 43; identified with Osiris 41, 172; sources of 42
Niobe 125
Norden, E. 66 n.5, 129 n.35

novelty 9–10

Octavian *triplex triumphus* of 172; *see also* Augustus
Odysseus 30, 44–6, 136
Oltramare, A. 15 n.63
omens: in Callimachus *Hymn* 2, 123; in Tibullus (1.8) 139; (2.1) 129; prayed for at birthdays 83; relating to foundation of Rome 66, 82
Onesimos 191
ὄγκος 101
oracles of Laios 73
oral poetry, formal structures in 195
originality, applied to myths by ancient poets 57
Orpheus, Gallus as Orpheus-figure 227
Orphism 47
Ortalus 224
Osiris 41; identified (with Dionysus) 41, 131, 172; (with Nile) 41, 172
Otis, B. 112 n.3, 184, 194 n.4
otium 146, 229
Ovid 2, 3, 64, 88, 144, 191, 213, 224; acknowledges debt to Hellenistic writers 5; draws attention to own learning 12; his view of Tibullus 1, 5; modern view of 2–3; Quintilian's view of 4–5

Palatine Hill 81
Palatua diva 80
Pales 20, 79–80, 109, 164, 204
palinode 168–71
Pallanteum 80
Pan 27, 79–80, 82, 161, 204
Pan-Ionian festival 81
Panyassis 69
paradeigmata 124, 165, 167
paradeigmatic group 55
paradoxa 69
paraenesis, in elegy 216–17, 223
parallel composition 193, 202; not used by Tibullus 194
Parilia 79–82, 83, 84, 85, 134, 205
Paris 30, 113, 198, 200–1
Parmenon 191
Paros 218
Parthenius 21, 225–6; *Erotika Pathemata* 9, 21, 225
Parthian problem 86
Passennus Paulus 4
pastoral poetry 7, 37
pathos 121, 135–6, 159, 162, 178, 181, 186
patronage 13, 32, 33–4, 125, 146, 159–60, 164, 179; in Augustan age 228; patron addressed in prologue 164; semi-deification of patron 125, 127
Paullus Fabius Maximus 174

paupertas 17; in Roman Hellenistic poets 21; see also poverty
Pearce, T. E. V. 179 n.39
Pedum 1
Peleus 30
Pelops 55, 150, 188
Penates 100
Penelope 30, 218
perjury, as topos of propemptikon and renuntiatio amoris 167–8
Persius 63
personal monologue, exposition in 134–43, 144
Peter, H. 68 n.14
Pfister, F. 44 n.37
Phaeacia 44–6, 58
Phanocles 22, 56–7, 223; influence on Roman elegists 57; influence on Tibullus 43
Pharia 64
Pharos 16
Pherecles, enemy of Mimnermus 217
Philetas 2, 25, 27, 34, 43, 216, 220, 225
Philetas, in *Daphnis and Chloe* 25–7
Philicus of Corcyra 45
Philinus 158
Philodemus 13
Philostratus 39
φιλότης (friendship) 165
Phoebus 76–7, 85, 119, 164, 204–5, 206
Phoenix 30
Pholoe 142–3, 149, 153
Phrygius, king of Miletus 30–1
Pichon, R. 89 n.10
Pieria 30–1
piety 18–20, 21, 124, 125; in Italian countryside 20, 83
Pindar 11, 19–20, 48, 57, 74, 156, 196, 201; deception in 188–9; looking back to a distant heroic age 13; narrative technique of 114–15; source of Hellenistic terminology 7, 11–12, 48–9; used by Virgil 62
Pino, M. 6 n.26
Pinsent, J. 74 n.57
Plato 15, 168
Plautus 88
Pliny the Younger: criticism of Propertius and Horace 4–5; his critical vocabulary 4–5
Plutarch 219
Poena, see Ate
Pöstgens, P. 37 n.9
poet: loved for his poetry 61; old poet–lover still respected 61
poetic *persona* 19–20, 22, 29, 127, 215; Roman elegists as mythical heroes 9, 11–12, 215, 224, 227
Pollio 174
Pollux 31

Polyneices 201–2
Polyphemus 135–7, 158, 159, 171
Pompeius 44
πόνος, as Hellenistic ideal 5, 29, 198
Poseidon 150, 188
Posidonius 13
Postumus 182
poverty 18, 19, 20–1, 173; causes lack of success in love 38; of a naked divinity 37–8; see also *paupertas*
prayer: as element of kletic hymn 65; as genre 190
Prescott, H. W. 163 n.40, 215 n.3
Priam 114
Priapus 14, 108, 161–73, 175, 190, 207–8; addressed in Theocritus, *Epigram* 4, 39; nudity and poverty of 37–8, 207–8; pederasty of 37–8
primitive man 132, 133, 136
Prodicus 15
prodigia, in Tibullus 2.5 82–3, 85
programmatic poetry 221
progymnasma(ta) 172–3; assimilated into higher genres 172–3; on countryside 28
prologues (programmatic) 11, 12, 91, 164
propaganda, Augustan 85
propemptic topoi: 'You are going without me' 167; absence from loved ones 167; Amor accompanying traveller 182; command to leave 167, 168; danger at sea 182–3; danger away from home 167; excuses 167, 183; kindly deities accompanying traveller 182; land and sea 182–3; *memor sis* 167; perjury 167, 183; schetliasmos 167, 183; speaker accompanying traveller 182
propemptikon 166, 167, 171, 181–4, 187; of Gallus to Lycoris 226
Propertius 3, 4–5, 6, 12, 21, 29, 32, 44, 54, 88, 109, 111, 146, 191, 213, 219, 224, 226–7, 228; acknowledges debt to Hellenistic masters 6; ancient views of 1, 2, 4–5; double allusive use of adjectives in 108; draws attention to own learning 12, 43, 81; etymology in 81; imitates Tibullus 53; modern views of 1, 2; more old-fashioned than Tibullus 228; syntax of 107
prophecy, in Tibullus 1, 3, 66
Protesilaus 164, 165, 224
pseudo-naivety 8, 22, 136
pseudo-syndetic links, *see under* verse paragraph, triviality of links between
psogos ploutou 173, 187–8
psogos polemou, as topos of syntaktikon 173
psychology, Hellenistic interest in 23–4, 137, 147
Ptolemy 125, 127
puer delicatus 147, 148

General Index

Pythagoreanism 47
Pytho 125

Quindecemviri sacris faciundis 74, 85
Quintilian 1, 4, 89, 224; his critical vocabulary applied to Tibullus and Propertius 4–5

Rank, L. P. 15 n.65
reaction 67, 157, 159; in kletikon 67
recusatio 164; Catullus 68 (1ff.) opposite of usual type 164
Reichel, G. 172 n.27
Reinsch-Werner, H. 11 n.48
Reitzenstein, R. 2 n.9
relay transmission 62
religion 14, 18, 40, 69, 79, 117–18, 119–20, 121, 129; new cults 65; rustic 14; rustic deities, see countryside: rural deities
religious antiquarianism 14
remedies for love: other women 180; wine 180
Remus 73
renuntiatio amoris 151–2, 153, 168; infidelity and perjury of beloved in 167–8
repetition 113, 119, 122, 123, 124, 129, 132, 135, 136, 137, 138, 140–1, 206; unificatory function of 136; with additional information 113, 132, 137, 140–1
Rhadamanthus 45
rhetoric, ancient 89, 214; poetry differentiated from 196; rhetorical curriculum 92
Rhianus 60, 61
Rhodes, foundation of 69
Richardson, L. Jr 194 n.4
ring structures 162, 193; combined with parallel structure 193, 202; literary history of 193–7; minor form of 193, 195; of Tibullus (1.3) 46, 171; (1.7) 171; quantitative aspects of 196, 199, 202, 203–4, 205, 206–7; used as simply organisational 196, 202–3; used meaningfully 204–5, 206; variation in order of items in 193, 196, 209–10, 211
rival 151–3, 154, 154–5, 170, 178, 180–1, 212–13; beloved goes off with for gain 167; in Theocritean *Idylls* 158; richness of 154; *uxor* of 152–3
road-mending 132
Robertson, D. S. 19 n.81
Rohde, E. 67 n.10
Roman elegy 29, 146; changes of situation between elegies 151; conflict between public and private life in 15, 32–3; delight in imitation in 187; Hellenistic poets as primary models of 11; limited cast of characters in 177; link with Greek narrative poetry 111; literary development of 23, 214, 214–15, 216, 224–8; non-erotic themes in 216, 219; origins of 29, Ch. 9 passim; programmatic elegies 221–2; symposiastic setting of 212; unity disputed in some Roman elegies 213
Rome 14, 32, 84, 153, 163, 167, 175; continuity with Troy 71, 84; date of foundation of 74; eternity of 82, 83; foundation of 61, 68, 71, 72–4, 75–6, 204, 205–6; gods of in time of Augustus 84; lustration of 129, 130–1; more ancient than Greek cities of Sicily and Magna Graecia 80; peace of anticipated in 2.5 83; prayer for peace of in 2.5 66; pre-history of 79–82
Romulus, in foundation of Rome 71–2, 73, 82; son of Mars 84
roses 98
Ross, D. O. Jr 81 n.97, 88 n.6
Rossi, L. E. 31 n.128
Rowell, H. T. 2 n.11
Rubrum Mare 97
rural arts 119, 121

sacerdotal language 129
Saecular games 85–6, 206; of 17 BC 85
Saecular interest 86
Samos: foundation of 69; temple of Hera at 18
sandwiching technique 112–13, 122–5, 140, 141, 143
Sappho 114
Saturn 50, 84; connected with Latium 47; ruler in Golden Age 47, 49, 84; *see also* Kronos
scene-setting: absence of in non-narrative poetry 123, 128; all necessary information given at beginning in non-narrative poetry 144; in Tibullus 151, 153, 166; initial 123, 129, 135, 137; partial 138
Schadewaldt, W. 195
Schanz, M. and Hosius, C. 2 n.10
Scheid, J. 130 n.36
Schlunk, Robin 88 n.5
Schönberger, O. 26 n.114
scholarship, Hellenistic and Roman 13
Schrijvers, P. H. 212 n.25
Schröter, R. 90 n.13
Schuster, M. 2 n.11, 3
Scipio 44
sea-voyages 24
selection: of material 113; of topoi 52
self-address 118, 137; choric 121, 123
self-imitation with variation 85, 187
semantics (ancient) 99–100; related to etymology 90–1
Semonides of Amorgos 69
sensory emphasis 112, 114, 136, 140, 141
sentimentality 135, 186
Sestius 174

Sibyl: of Cumae 76–7; of Erythrae 76–7; of Tibur 77; see also Amalthea, Marpesia, Herophile
Sibyl(s) 121; as mouthpieces of Apollo 66, 73; differentiated by Tibullus 76–7; in 2.5 66, 67, 73–4, 75–7, 78, 204–5, 206
Sibylline Books 66, 74, 76, 77, 83, 204
Sicilian cities, foundations of 69, 74, 80, 81
Silvanus 79
Silver Age 196
Simaetha 161–2
Simichidas 158
simile 112–13, 120; irrational correspondences with narrative 199
Simonides 20
simplicity 18–19, 21, 34
Sisyphus 55
Skiadas, A. D. 137 n.52
Slater, W. J. 7 n.28
smallness 5, 8–9, 18–19, 21, 34
Smith, Kirby Flower 2, 36, 39, 51
smoothness 10
Smyrna 73, 218; foundation of 69
Snodgrass, A. M. 13 n.58
soldiers 17
Solmsen, F. 12 n.52
Solon 216, 219
Somnia 134
Somnus 134
Sophocles 8
soror (in Tibullan elegy) 152, 186
Sparta 69, 113
speech, direct 114, 119, 120, 142
Spies, A. 147 n.7
spinning; symbol of female domestic virtues and chastity 107, 133, 175
Spranger, P. P. 44 n.37
Steidle, Wolf 11 n.46
Steinthal, H. 90 n.13
Stesichorus 168–9
sting-in-tail technique of epigram 190; see also trick ending
Stoics, interest in language 15
streams: drying up in summer 105; flowing through rich men's houses 103
Streifinger, J. 107 n.39, 107
Stroh, W. 38 n.15
stylistic categories, ancient 111
subjectivity or objectivity in elegy 215–17, 220–1
substitute motif 46, 82–3
subtlety 10
Suetonius 1
Sullivan, J. P. 3 n.13
summons 65, 128
Svennung, J. 16 n.69
sweetness 5
symbolic *puer* of new *saeculum* 85

Syme, R. 72 n.45
symmetry 115, 202
symposium 166–7
Syndikus, H. P. 15 n.64
synkrisis bion 33, 173; warfare and agriculture 173
synonymity 100–1
syntaktikon 173
Syracuse 202–3
Syria 43
Syrinx 79, 82
Szádeczky-Kardoss, S. 217 n.8

tangential ending 125–6
Tantalus 51, 55–7
Taplin, O. 189 n.77
Tarn, W. W. 43 n.36
Tarquinius Priscus 76, 77
Taurus 43
technology, Hellenistic interest in 119
Telemachus 44
temporal dislocation 112, 129, 136, 143, 176–7, 212–13; anticipation 112–18, 120, 130, 136, 176; flashback 112, 114. 118, 120, 135, 136, 176
temporal sequence, straightforward 120, 122, 135
temporal structure 212–13
Thapsus 72
Thebes 201
thematic interweaving 118, 120, 122, 124
thematic structure, see formal structures
Theocritus: deception in 190; delayed generic identification in 191; exposition in 134–7, 143; formal structures in 202–3; *Idylls* of 17, 24, 31–2, 34, 134, 216, 228; introduces and discards bucolic characters 174; linking devices used by 192; manipulation of reader reaction by 158–9; withholding of information in 158–62, 165
Theognis 156, 216–17, 218–19, 227
theological syncretism 41, 79; see also multiplication of a single deity
Thera 75, 120
Theseus 189
Thessaly 73
Thetis 124
Theugenes of Icus 222
Theugenis 202–3
Thummer, E. 19 n.81
thunder 8
Thurii, foundation of 73
Thyrsis, in Theocritus *Idyll* 1 160–1
tibia, symbol of Roman elegy 9
Tibullus: adjectives, use of, see under adjectives; allusion to archaic Greek poetry in 12, 63; ancient views of 1–5, 6; and Greek elegy 2, 6; and Propertius 182, 184, 224,

Tibullus—cont.
228; anti-love stance adopted by 178, 183; apologetic function of internal deception in 178; arrangement of material in 2.5 83; art concealing art 2; as *magister amoris* 138, 139, 141, 142, 147, 151, 175; attitude to war 24–5, 28–9, 33–4, 103–4, 145, 146, 155; avoids open display of learning 12, 28, 43, 54, 81, 133; Callimachean characteristics not present in 27–8; characteristics in common with other Roman elegists 3–4, 88–9; compared with other Roman elegists 88, 144, 157, 184, 191; compares himself to Odysseus in 1.3 44–6; complex verbal and conceptual patterns in 101; complexity of elegies of 209; compositional methods of 2; conscious of distinctness of past 13; criticised for lack of linguistic range 2, 3, 87, 88; criticisms of 2–3, 87, 88; dates 1; debt to Hellenistic predecessors 3, 6–12; difficulty in 142; divergence from obvious order of material 70; dramatic elegies, exposition in 121, 126, 128–34; economy and precision of language 3; elegance (*cultus*) 5, 6; envisages own death 192; etymological problems posed by 96–9; etymologies in 16–17, 79, 80–1, 92–9; formal structures in 192, 193, 203–13; gentle elegiac melancholy *et sim.* 2, 3; *genus tenue* 111–12; grammatical and syntactical irregularity in 107; Hellenistic characteristics of 11, 13–14, 14–15, 15–16, 18–20, 21, 23–5; humour 121, 138–9, 154, 180; illness of at Phaeacia/Corcyra 44, 175; imitated Callimachus and Euphorion 6; indirect claim to *doctrina* in 5; information conveyance (lay-out of) 157, (narrative type used in non-narrative) 157; initial generic deception 166–73; interest (in countryside) 17, 71, 79, 83, 121, 132–3, 155, (in language 15–16, 88–110 passim, (in popular philosophy) 14; internal deception in 176–82; Lar and Penates of Tibullus, 20, 47; learning 5, 6, Ch.2 passim, 77, 86, 90, 99, 142; length of elegies 157; linking devices in 3, 43, 67, 73, 192; manipulation of reader reaction 145, 148–9, 157, 166, 175, 178–81; mentions no literary predecessor 6, 42; metrical innovations in 89; modern views of 1–3, 36; modern view of elegies as linear and unorganised 192; moralising in 32–4, 141, 146, 147, 151, 152, 154, 155, 178, 187; narrative exposition in 120–1; non-Hellenistic characteristics in 27–8, 29–30, 32–3; originality 3, 53, 57, 191; *persona* of 19–21, 23–5, 27, 28–9, 155, 175, 209, 229–30, (as *agricola*) 23, 145–6, 173, (as lover) 23, 67, 84, 145–7, (as soldier) 145–6, 183; personal monologues, exposition in 137–43; philosophic position contrasted with that of Horace 15; piety of 24, 84, 232; poverty of 19, 20–1, 24, 34, 173; pre-eminence in Roman elegy 1, 3–4, 6; problems posed by in making thematic links 204; Quintilian's critical vocabulary used of 3–4, 89, 107; rapid temporal alternation in 136; related elegies: (1.3 and 1.7) 171, (1.5 and 2.6) 185, (1.7 and 2.1) 131, (1.8 and 1.4) 148, (1.8 and 1.9) 151–3, 209, (2.3 and 2.4) 209–11; religious antiquarianism in 14, 79–80, 129, 130–1; reworking of earlier material in later elegies 155; ring-composition used by 193, 203–11, 213; self-distancing of 121; semantics, use of by 92, 99–107; structures 43–4, 66, 131, 141; syntax of 90, 107–9; temporal structure in 212; thematic structure of 1.3 46, 65, 67; Theognidean Corpus, related to 156–7; trick ending 173, 175–6; use of Hellenistic topoi 36, 140, 182; Virgil's *Eclogues*, influence of 162; *Vita Tibulli* 1; vocabulary of 87, 89, 109; withholding of information 144–9; 151–5; yearning for the past 14, 133

Timaeus 74
Titius 173–4
Titius, M. 174
Tityos, as sinner against love 54, 57, 59
Tityrus, son of Philetas in *Daphnis and Chloe* 27
topical: sophistication 170; variation 138, 139, 170, 184
topoi, combinations of 140
Townend, G. 1 n.6
Tränkle, H. 12 n.51
transitional abruptness 112, 114, 123, 129, 135, 139, 142
travel genres 37, 167, 187
travel in antiquity by sea 106
Treu, M. 218 n.14
trick ending 173, 175, 176, 190–1
Trimalchio 153
triumph 130–1
triumph, Roman 171–2; linked with dithyramb 143, 171–2
triumph-poem 171–2
triumphator: linked with Jupiter 67–8; semi-divine status of 130
Trojan War 74, 187, 199
Troy 30, 71–6, 113, 198, 200; death of Catullus' brother at 165; fall of 68, 76, 78, 84; founded by Apollo 71, 84
Tullus, L. Volcacius 183–4, 228
Tupet, A.-M. 139 n.56
Turnus 205
Tyre 43

General Index

Tyrtaeus 216

Underwood, J. T. 172 n.27
underworld, part reserved for lovers: 52; *see also* hell, Hades
untrodden path 8

Van Looy, H. 90 n.13
Van Otterloo, W. A. A. 194 n.4
variant myths 55
variatio 51–2
variation 114–15; conceptual 142, *see also* topical variation; grammatical and syntactical 107, 112, 116, 118–19, 120, 122, 124; in Bacchylides 115; in length of units 139; in Pindar 114–15; of narrative mode 113, 118, 142; verbal 88, 116–17
Varro Atacinus 225
Varro 13, 15, 80, 90, 91
Velabrum 81, 82
Velleius Paterculus 1
(F)έλος 81
Venus 45, 47, 82, 84, 163, 208; as *magister amoris* 142; as psychopomp 51; etymological links 95, 96, 104; not identified with Isis 47; offended by Danaids 55
verba rustica 104
verbal correspondences: cutting across formal structures 199, 206–7; supporting formal structures 198–9
verbal juxtapositions 93, 95
verbal links 192, 196; *see also* Tibullus, linking devices
verbal tensions 100–1
Verona 163
verse-paragraph 112, 128, 195; suppression of logical links between 118, 123, 124, 125; temporal links between 118, 122; triviality of links between 118, 140, *see also* asyndeton
Versnel, H. S. 68 n.11
Vian, F. 41 n.29
Vinalia 82, 84
Virgil 16, 20, 44, 51, 62–3, 68, 88, 127, 164, 225; double allusive use of adjectives 108; echoes of Gallus in 226–7; imitating a Hellenistic source 51; scholarly imitation of Homer in *Aeneid* 88; use of Pindar 62
Vischer, R. 145 n.1
visual interest 112, 114, 118, 119, 137, 141; in Homer 112
vivid poetic diction, in Pindar 115
vividity 114, 116, 118, 119, 121, 126, 129, 135, 137, 140
Vretska, K. 176 n.37

Wachsmuth, D. 48 n.49
Walbank, F. W. 44 n.37
war, Hellenistic attitudes to 24
wealth, attack on 154; *see also* psogos ploutou
weaving metaphor 10
Webster, T. B. L. 24 n.105
weighing metaphor 8
West, D. 100 n.20, 199 n.9
West, M. L. 15 n.65, 217 n.8, 218–19
Wheeler, A. L. 37 n.8, 121 n.17
White, H. 137 n.52
Whitman, C. H. 194 n.4
Wigodsky, M. 12 n.51
Wilhelm, F. 36 n.7, 39 n.21
Wilkinson, L. P. 21 n. 90, 215 n.3
Willcock, M. M. 57 n.66
Williams, F. J. 135 n.50
Williams, G. 3 n. 15, 3
Wimmel, W. 71 n.40, 80
wine, associated with tears 39
wine-drinking 130, 166, 180
Wiseman, T. P. 163 n.40
Wissowa 79 n.83
witch, consulted by Tibullus about love in 1.2 38
witchcraft 140, 162
withholding of information 123, 139, Ch.6 passim; in Catullus 162–5; in Theocritus 158–62; in Tibullus 144–50, 151–5, 185; literary history of 145, 156–7; proper names 142, 148–9, 154, 156, 161, 185; until end of poem 160; *see also* delayed generic identification
Wölflinn, E. 92 n.15
Woodman, A. J. 175 n.35, 194 n.4
Woodman, T. and West, D. 16 n.67
woodworking metaphor 10
word-play 10, 141, 185
Wright, J. R. G. 15 n.64
writing about something equivalent to doing it 217

Xenomedes 79, 120
Xenophanes 69, 219

Yardley, J. C. 191 n.86
Young, D. C. 7 n.28

Zancle, foundation of 69, 73, 81
Zeus 31, 55, 187, 199, 203; ruler of earth 48; of the war cry 120; xenios 55; *see also* Jupiter
Zingerle 12 n.51
zoology, Hellenistic interest in 14, 136

INDEX OF LATIN AND GREEK WORDS

ἁβρός 96–7
acer 108
addere 100
adsidere 96
adsiduus 17, 28, 100
aestivus 102–3
αἴτια 19, 69
ager 100
ἄκοιτις 198
ἄλοχος 198
amarus 103
antiquus 100
aptus 109
aqua: placida 103; praeteriens 105
Arabs 96–7
arare 93, 96
aratio 93
aratrum 93
arvum (n.) 93, 96, 100
arvus (adj.) 93
asper 100, 170, 178
aura 97, 98
aurescere 97
aureus 97
aurum 98, 100, 105

balare 80
barba 100

caeruleus 105
calidus 96
callidus 95–6
candidus 97
canere 90
canis 90
capere 94
castitas 176
catena 93–4
catenatus 94
celebrare 100
celer 100, 103
certus 100
χολή : μέλαινα, πικρά 103
classicum 108
claudere 100
coagulus 100
comis 5
componere 94
compendium 100
concordia 205
conserere 104
continere 94, 96
corona 108
coronis 189

cultus 5, 105
custos 108

δᾶερ 199
de 123
demens 170
dens 93
densum 93
dives 97
doctus 11
durus 4, 100, 102, 104

ἕζομαι 199
effusus 109
elegans 4–5
elegantia 28, 34
ensis 99
eororus 97
ἠώς 97, 98; ἠὼς ῥοδοδάκτυλος 98
Eous 97
equus, celer 103
erro 183, 184
externus 100

facere 89, 94
facilis 94, 100
farra 99
fel, triste 103
felix 89, 96–7
fera (n.s.) 99
ferre 97, 99
ferreus 99
ferrum 99
ferunt 27
ferus 99, 100, 169–70
fictilia 94, 97
figuli 94
fines 100
fingere 94
firmus 100
fixus 100
flavus 108
flebilis 109
floridus 100
fluere 92
flumen 92
fores 102
formare 94
fortiter 100
fovere 95–6
frigidus 94–5, 105
frigus (n.) 94, 96
fugere 108
fulgere 100

Index of Latin and Greek words

fulvus 105
furor 170

grandis 100

habilis 109
horridus 170
hospes 164–5
humidus 97

ibitis 167
ignotus 100
impius 100
inertia 146
inmitis 100
insidere 100
instabilis 100
invenire 104
ira 89
iucundus 5
iugerum 16

καθίζω 99

lapis 14
lascivus 4
latere 47
Latium 47
levis 100
longus 106–7, 108
luciferus 97
lustratio 127, 129
lustro 126
lutum 94

maestus 104
magnus 16
matrona 108
maturus 100
mens 94
merum 100
merx 100
metus 94
minium 68
mollis 4–5, 94, 96, 102, 108, 178
mopsopius 42
mora, tarda 109
movere 94
naufraga 109
nitens 97
novem 100
novus 100
nox 89

obrigere 100
occultus 109
opes 96
optare 96

os 100
οὗτος 198

Palatium 80–1
pallens 109
palo 81
parere 81
pastor 27, 80–1
paterfamilias 127
patrius 100
pax 33, 146
pellere 108
piger 96
pinus 106
placidus 103
plasmare 94
plenus 106–7
pomosus 108
portare 97
praeda 154
praeterire 105
proferre 99
πρόμαλος 18
promittere 89
purgare 129
purus 109

quidam 152

reddere 100
rigere 94
rigidus 94
rivus 105
ros 98
rosa 98
roscidus 98
roseus 97, 98
ruber 108
rubere 97
rusticus 104

saevire 100
saevus 100, 102
salubris 96
sanare 96
sanctus 100
securus 109
sed 130
sedulus 96, 104
senex 105, 147, 152–3
sera (n.) 100
sidus 100
sinus, maestus 104
sobrius 109
solum, cultum 105
somnus, 102
sontica causa 142
σοφία 11

σοφός 11
speca 95
sperare 95
spes 95, 185
spica 95
spiceus 14, 94
stagnare 81
stipes 14
stola 108
sulpur 109

tardus 100, 109
tener 96, 100, 104, 148
tenere 93–4, 96, 102
tepidus 108
terra 94
tersus 3, 4, 5
timor 104
toga picta 68
toga praetexta 104
tremere 105

tristis 102–4
triumpe 130
Trivia 100
tundere 96
turben 170

unda 96

vaccae 80
validus 100
vates 205
vehi 81
velum 81
venire 89, 96
vere (adv.) 99
vetus 100
vicinus 100
vincire 95
vincula 95
vinum 100

INDEX OF ANCIENT WORKS AND PASSAGES REFERRED TO IN THE TEXT

AESCHYLUS *Agamemnon* (184–205): 201
ALCAEUS
Fr. 129 (1–25 (LP)): 201
Fr. 130 (13–39 (LP)): 201
Fr. 283 (LP): 113
ALCMAN *Partheneion* (1–36): 58–9
ALEXANDER AETOLUS *Apollo*: 221
ANACREON Fr. 402 (*PMG*): 61
ANON. *ap.* Pausanias (5.22.3): 71
ANTHOLOGIA PALATINA
6 (243 (Diodorus)): 67
9 (146 (Anon.)): 185
11 (298. 6f. (Anon.)): 39
12 (229 (Straton)): 62
ANTIMACHUS *Lyde*: 219–20, 227
ARCHILOCHUS Fr. 22(D): 187, 189
ARISTOPHANES *Frogs* (785–1481): 8–10
AUGUSTUS *Res Gestae* (13): 33–4

BACCHYLIDES Dithyramb (17): 114; (18.1–30): 189

CALLIMACHUS
Aetia: 25, 221–3
Aetia 1
Fr. 1: 8–10, 19, 24, 221; (17f.): 24; (21ff.): 19; (23): 21; (37f.): 20, 26
Fr. 1f.: 11
Frr. 1ff.: 20
Fr. 2:50, 221, 222
Fr.3: 222

Fr. 7 (13f.): 221; (19ff.): 222
Fr. 41: 60–1
Aetia 2
Fr. 43 (46 ff.): 222; (58 ff.): 69
Aetia 3
Frr. 67–75: 112
Fr. 73: 227
Fr. 75: 117, 122; (1): 190; (1–9): 117–18; (10–21): 118–19; (22–37): 119; (38–49): 119; (50–77): 119–20; (53ff.): 27; (54ff.): 79
Fr. 76: 222
Fr. 79: 222
Frr. 80ff.: 30–1
Aetia 4
Fr. 86: 222
Fr. 112: 221; (5f.): 222; (7ff.): 223
Fr. 178: 222
Epigram (5): 65; (32): 20
'Foundation of Zancle': 81
Fragment (612): 27; (709): 42
Hecale: 31
Hymns: 37, 154
Hymn 2: 121–6, 127, 129, 131, 134, 135, 137; (1–31): 123–5; (8): 122; (47ff.): 112; (55ff.): 70; (97–113): 125–6
Iambi: 221
Iambus (3): 20; (9): 189
Ibis: 62
CATO
De Agricultura (141): 127
Origines: 68

Index of Ancient works and passages

CATULLUS
11(3f.): 96
61 (131–45): 174
64: 197
65: 224, 227
66: 224
67: 224
68: 162–5, 191, 197, 216, 224–5, 226; (1–4): 163; (68f.): 164; (135f.): 165
CELSUS (3.18.21): 170
CHARITON *Chaireas and Callirhoe* (13.2) 166–7
CHOERILUS Fr. 1 (Kinkel) 14
CICERO
Ad Quintum Fratrem (1.3.3): 99
Aratea (ed. Soubiran) (p. 194): 98
Pro Marcello (33): 195

DEMETRIUS *On Style*: 111
DIOMEDES p. 484 17(K): 6

ENNIUS *Annales*(1): 68; (183f.): 99
EUPHORION
Chiliades: 62
'Hesiod': 17
Collectanea Alexandrina (Powell) (pp. 28f.): 42
EURIPIDES
Hippolytus (433–85): 202
schol. on *Hippolytus* 750: 45
Phoenissae (469–96): 201–2
Fr. 979 3(N): 62

FR. TRAG. GRAEC. ADESP. (564N): 62

GALLUS
Amores: 226
propemptikon to Lycoris: 226

HERMESIANAX
Leontion: 220; (35–40): 217; (41–6): 219–20
Fr. (7.75–8): 220
HERODAS *Mimes*: 18
HERODIANUS 1.11(2): 56
HESIOD *Catalogue of Women* (*Eoiai*): 223
Theogony: 25, 221, 222–3; (22ff.): 222; (144f.): 93; (720–819): 201; (775f.): 93; (1019f.): 223; (1021f.) 223
Works and Days (167ff.): 49–50; (225ff.): 106
HOMER
Iliad: 29–30, 114, 195
3(1–37): 112–13
6(208): 30; (343–68): 197–201
9 (443): 30; (501ff.): 62; (561–4): 92–3
11 (783): 30
15 (63ff.): 187
19 (91ff.): 62
20 (schol. on 234): 56

22 (345ff.): 187
24 (767): 200
Iliad scholia: 195
Odyssey: 114
7 (schol. on 153T): 45; (216ff.): 30; (321f.): 45; (schol. on 324): 45
11 (225ff.): 51
16(284f.): 103
19 (4ff.): 103; (109ff.): 106; (122): 39; (518f.): 93
21 (293ff.): 30
Homeric Hymns: 122, 126, 222–3
HORACE
Odes books 1–3: 175
Odes 1(2): 85; (4): 174; (6): 164; (16): 169, 170; (16.3): 170; (34): 169; (37): 172
Odes 3 (11): 63, 67; (14): 67; (23): 67
Epodes 2: 187, 188, 189; (16.63f.): 50; (17): 168–9; (17.7): 170
Satires 1 (1,108): 195; (10.81ff.): 28
Carmen Saeculare: 85
PS.-HYGINUS *Fabulae* 13

ISIDORE OF SEVILLE
Etymologiae: 91
1 (29): 91–2
5 (27.9): 94; (31.13f.) 97–8
10 (24.4): 96
16 (21.1): 99
20 (4.2): 94; (13.5) 94

LONGUS
Daphnis and Chloe: 25
2: 25–7, 220; (3): 25; (5 *ad fin.*): 26; (6 *ad fin.*): 26; (7 *ad fin.*): 26; (8) 26; (15): 27; (32ff.): 27
LUCIAN
Verae Historiae: 52
2 (19): 53; (25): 52f.
LUCRETIUS
De Rerum Natura 2 (103f.): 99
3 (891f.): 94
5 (656f.): 98

MACROBIUS *Saturnalia* (3.5.7): 126
MENANDER (dramatist)
Aspis (1–69): 191; (106ff.): 191
Epitrepontes: 191
Samia (670ff.): 191; (687ff.): 191; (690): 191
MENANDER RHETOR *RG* (335.31–336.4): 65–6
MIMNERMUS: 216–18
Fr. 1(D): 217
Nanno: 217–18, 219–20

NICAENETUS Fr. 6 (Powell): 18

OROSIUS *Hist.* (1.12): 56

Index of Ancient works and passages

OVID
Amores 1(1): 12, 26, 222; (2.10): 144; (8.111f.): 39; (10.15 18): 37 8; (15.28): 5
Amores 2 (1): 222; (13): 103
Amores 3 (1): 222; (9.66): 5; (11.4): 99
Ars Amatoria 3(180): 98
Metamorphoses 11(424–7): 182
13(444): 99
Tristia 1 (6.1): 219
2: 220–1; (439f.): 225
5 (1.18) 5

PARTHENIUS OF NICAEA
Encomium of Arete: 225
Epikedion: 225
Erotika Pathemata: 9, 21–2, 225–6
PAULUS (FESTUS)
p. 8 (L): 17
p. 347 (L): 94
PETRONIUS Satyricon (75.11): 153
PHANOCLES
Ἔρωτες ἢ Καλοί: 57, 221
Fr. 4 (Powell) (p.108): 56
PHILOSTRATUS Epistle (7.44 ad init.): 38; (59.(62)): 39–40
PINDAR
Olympian 1: 150; (26–8): 188
2: 49; (58): 48; (61–9): 49; (63–8): 49; (67): 49; (68ff.): 48
7: 201
Pythian 3(27–9): 189
4: 73, 74–5, 114, 116; (1–69): 114–15
10: 196
PS.-PLACIDUS 45 (=CGL 5.7.7): 16
PLATO
Cratylus: 15
Phaedrus (232e3ff., 233e5ff., 240e8ff.): 150; (243a-b): 168
Republic: 82
Symposium (181d3ff.): 150; (203c): 38
PLAUTUS Mostellaria (157ff.): 180
PLINY THE ELDER
Natural History (7.206f.): 106; (34.8): 105; (35.72): 16
PLINY THE YOUNGER
Epistles (9.22.1f.) 4–5
PLUTARCH Romulus (2): 74
POSIDIPPUS Gow-Page H–E (3105): 16
PRISCIAN Institutiones Grammaticae (3.509.28): 97–8
PROPERTIUS
1(1): 12; (1.27f.): 169; (1,2,3,4): 151; (6): 183, 184, 187; (6.5ff.): 167; (6.33f.): 182; (8): 226, 228; (8.6ff.): 226; (9.11): 217; (12.15): 149; (14): 144; (17): 44; (18): 112, 227, 228; (18.22): 227; (20): 228
2 (1): 222; (10.23f.): 21; (13.21ff.): 21; (17):
191; (19): 39, 155, 226; (29): 184; (30 A and B): 222; (30 A and B 1ff.): 227; (34): 220
3 (1): 222; (2): 222; (3): 222; (4): 67; (12): 182; (15.3f.): 104; (23): 21
4 (7): 54; (7.59ff.): 53; (9.5f.) 81

QUINTILIAN Institutio Oratoria (10.1.93): 3–4

RHIANUS
Fr. 1 (10–16 (Powell)): 60; (17–21): 62
Fr. 10 (Powell): 112

SAPPHO Fr. (1 (LP): 65; (44 (LP)): 114, 116
SENECA De Ira (2.19): 96
STATIUS
Silvae (1.3.20ff.): 103
Thebaid (5.550): 16

THEOCRITUS
'komastic' idylls: 191
'pastoral' idylls: 17, 31
Idylls: 158
1 (64–145): 160–1; (82f.): 97f.
2: 18, 160–2, 216; (3–7): 161; (40f.): 161; (145–9) 162
3: 216
6: 158; (6f.): 158; (31–3): 158
7 (96–127): 158; (122ff.): 158
10: 31; (57f.): 159
11: 39, 134–7; (1–18): 135; (19): 159; (19–24): 135; (19–79): 159; (19ff.): 158; (25–9): 135; (30–53): 135–6; (42ff.): 170–1; (54–62): 136; (63–6): 136; (65ff.): 170–1; (67–71): 159; (67–79): 136–7; (77f.): 159
12: 216
13: 24
15: 18
16: 20, 159; (76–81): 160; (104–9): 160
17 (40ff.): 204
18: 203
20 (Ps.-Theocritus): 216
21: 31
22: 31; (54ff.) 31
23 (Ps.-Theocritus): 216
28: 202–3
29: 216; (31ff.): 150; (35–40): 150
30: 216
Epigram 4: 39, 190; (1–12): 190; (13f.): 190; (15–18): 190
THEOGNIS
Theognidean corpus: 259f., 216–17, 218–19, 227
Frr. (237–54): 219

Index of Ancient works and passages

TIBULLUS
Book 1: 227, 228
1.1: 11–34, 36, 39, 42, 133, 145–7, 153, 155; (1–2): 6, 16, 105; (1–6): 173; (3): 28, 100; (3f.): 12, 173; (4): 108; (5): 17; (6): 28; (7): 100, 173; (9–16): 94; (12): 100; (15): 28; (15–17): 108; (19f.): 17; (25f.): 145; (25–8): 105; (36): 109; (39f.): 94, 97; (45f.): 145; (46): 96; (49ff.): 25; (53): 34; (53ff.): 173; (53–6): 193; (54): 23; (55f.): 102; (75): 33; (75f.): 24
1.2: 36; (1): 100; (1–4): 166–7; (5f.): 102, 166; (6): 100; (7): 166; (13ff.): 102; (16ff.): 142; (19f.): 102; (29): 96; (46): 108; (49f.): 102; (55f.): 102; (59ff.): 38; (63ff.): 38; (70): 103; (73f.): 102; (77f.): 103; (95f.): 102
1.3: 15, 37, 44–60, 64, 84, 133, 167, 171, 175–6, 182; (thematic structure of) 46; (1): 167; (1–4): 166, 167; (3): 17; (3f.): 167; (4ff.): 46; (5–8): 104, 167; (5–20): 167; (16): 109; (23ff.): 47; (29–32): 64; (33f.): 100; (35ff.): 84; (35–8): 106; (35–50): 46; (38): 109; (39f.): 100; (43f.): 100; (47–53): 192; (48): 100; (51–6): 46, 47; (52): 100; (55f.): 46; (57): 47; (58): 47; (57–66): 51; (57–82): 46; (63f.): 53; (65): 51; (69f.): 100; (73–80): 54–7; (77f.): 108; (81f.): 51, 54; (81–4): 193; (83–6): 106; (83–8): 175; (84): 96; (89f.): 175; (91f.): 108; (93f.): 97
1.4: 36, 148, 173–5, 189, 190, 207–8; (3–6): 37; (1–8): 173; (9–14): 38; (9–72): 173; (15ff.): 38; (39ff.): 152; (41–52): 107; (61): 5; (73): 173; (74): 173; (75f.): 173; (75–80): 60, 175; (81–4): 142, 148, 149, 175
1.5: 19, 36, 39, 168–71, 176–81, 185–7, 212–13; (3f.): 178; (5f.): 169, 178; (7f.): 178; (9): 103; (9–16): 178; (11): 109; (16): 100; (17f.): 170, 178; (19–34): 136; (19ff.): 170, 179; (31ff.): 179; (37ff.): 180; (38): 39; (47f.): 170, 180; (47ff.): 180; (48ff.): 170; (67f.): 170, 181; (71): 152
1.6: 36; (5f.): 95; (5–11): 193; (9ff.): 142; (43–6): 40; (67f.): 108, 176; (75): 94
1.7: 37, 41, 43–4, 50, 121, 131–2, 171–2; (9ff.): 34; (23f.): 42; (23–48): 172; (54): 42; (60): 109
1.8: 23, 36, 137–43, 147–51, 152, 153, 209; (1–8): 138–40; (9): 109; (9–16): 138–40; (17f.): 109; (17–26): 140; (23ff.): 139; (27ff.): 147; (27–38): 140–1; (29ff.): 94; (31f.): 100; (35f.): 104; (35ff.): 142; (39–48): 140, 141; (49): 148; (49f.): 105, 148; (49–54): 140, 141–2; (51): 142; (55–66): 140, 142; (67–78): 140, 142–3; (71–6): 149; (77f.): 149
1.9: 23, 36, 151–3, 167, 208–9; (1–28): 209; (3f.): 61; (7): 109; (9f.): 167; (10): 100; (11): 167; (13–16): 167; (39f.): 151; (51): 168; (51–84): 209; (55): 152; (67f.): 93; (71): 152
1.10: 14, 15, 19, 20, 34, 36, 37, 103, 155, 173, 226; (1–6): 99; (1–10): 173; (11–13): 173; (49f.): 103
2.1: 14, 19, 37, 39, 42, 44, 121, 126–34, 135, 137; (1): 126; (1–16): 128–9; (17–26): 129–30; (20): 100; (27–36): 130–1; (31f.): 130; (37–50): 132; (46): 109; (51–6): 128; (51–66): 132; (55ff.): 133; (59f.): 133; (67–80): 132; (81–90): 134; (87f.): 128
2.2: 37, 121, 153, 204; (3f.): 96; (14): 96; (16): 97; (17–20): 95
2.3: 19, 37, 39, 112, 153–5, 209–12; (1–10): 40; (4): 104; (5f.): 100; (7f.): 93; (11ff.): 112; (11–28): 120–1; (13): 96; (14a): 40; (14b–c): 100; (49f.): 154; (50): 96; (79f.): 40
2.4: 15, 209–12; (3): 93; (3f.): 95; (10): 96, 109; (11f.): 103; (22): 109; (42): 104
2.5: 14, 19, 37, 65–86, 121, 133, 204–7; (dating of): 85–6; (15f.): 66; (19–22): 75, 78; (23f.): 79; (33–7): 81; (36): 81; (39–64): 120–1; (39ff.): 78; (61f.): 71; (67–70): 76–7; (91f.): 134; (106ff.): 132
2.6: 15, 36, 176, 181–7; (1f.): 181; (1–10): 208; (3f.): 182; (6): 184; (7f.): 183; (7–11): 183, 184; (9f.): 183; (12): 183, 184; (12–14): 184; (13f.): 184–187; (15–18): 184; (19): 184–5; (20–6): 185; 21f.): 94; (27): 185; (29–40): 186; (42): 186; (44): 186; (45f.): 109; (47–50): 186

TZETZES Schol. ad Lycophr. (355): 56

VALERIUS FLACCUS *Argonautica* (5,273): 16
VARRO ATACINUS *Leucadia*: 225
VARRO
De Lingua Latina 5–9: 91; 5 (2): 91; (6): 95; (24): 97–8; (37): 95; (39): 93; (44): 81; (61f.): 95; (92): 17; (113): 93
6(45): 94, 105
7(14): 100; (83): 97–8
10(17): 94
De Re Rustica 1 (48.2): 95
Menippean Satires (405): 99
VIRGIL
Aeneid: 51, 68, 75, 85, 88, 205

VIRGIL—cont.
  1 (1ff.): 164; 3 (589 (gloss, on)): 98; 6: 52; (442): 51; (451): 52
Culex 1ff.: 164
Eclogues: 88, 162, 227
  2 (28ff.): 171
  3 (1): 16
  4: 85, 172, 174
  5 (74f.): 126; 6: 164; 10: 226, 227
Georgics: 20, 34
  1 (338ff.): 127–8; (345f.): 126; (344–7): 128
  3 (proem of): 62; (36): 71

XENOPHON *Symposium* 8 (14): 150; (30ff.): 150